11/93

HORIZONS IN THEORY AND AMERICAN CULTURE

Bainard Cowan and Joseph G. Kronick, *Editors*

Wallace Stevens and the Question of Belief

WALLACE STEVENS AND THE QUESTION OF BELIEF

Metaphysician in the Dark

DAVID R. JARRAWAY

LOUISIANA STATE UNIVERSITY PRESS

Baton Rouge and London

02 01 00 99 98 97 96 95 94 93   5 4 3 2 1

Designer: Barbara Werden
Typeface: Linotron Galliard
Typesetter: G&S Typesetters, Inc.
Printer and binder: Thomson-Shore, Inc.

Library of Congress Cataloging-in-Publication Data
Jarraway, David R.
    Wallace Stevens and the question of belief: metaphysician in the
dark / David R. Jarraway.
        p. cm. — (Horizons in theory and American culture)
    Includes bibliographical references and index.
    ISBN 0-8071-1759-5 (alk. paper)
        1. Stevens, Wallace, 1879–1955—Philosophy.   2. Belief and doubt
in literature.   3. Metaphysics in literature.   I. Title.
    II. Series.
    PS3537.T4753Z667   1993
    811'.52—dc20   92-28610
                                                        CIP

Z
STEVENS
J

1223005

Portions of this text first appeared in the *Wallace Stevens Journal* as "Crispin's Dependent
'Airs': Psychic Crisis in Early Stevens" (XIV [Spring, 1990]), and "'Velocities of
Change': Exceeding Excess in 'Credences of Summer' and 'Auroras of Autumn'" (XV
[Spring, 1991]). The author offers grateful acknowledgment to the journal's editor for
permission to reprint this material. Excerpts from *The Collected Poems of Wallace Stevens,*
copyright 1954 by Wallace Stevens, reprinted by permission of Alfred A. Knopf, Inc.,
and by Faber and Faber Ltd. Excerpts from *Opus Posthumous,* by Wallace Stevens, copyright 1957 by Elsie Stevens and Holly Stevens, reprinted by permission of Alfred A.
Knopf, Inc.

In memory of Northrop Frye
Bene vixit qui bene latuit

The particular question—here
The particular answer to the particular
question
Is not in point—the question is in point.

If the day writhes, it is not with
revelations.
One goes on asking questions.

—Wallace Stevens,
"The Ultimate Poem Is Abstract"

CONTENTS

ACKNOWLEDGMENTS

DURING the course of writing this study, I was happy to have the assistance and support of some of the very best people writing in the fields of both criticism and theory today. So I am especially grateful to acknowledge here the judicious readings afforded my work over the past few years by Mutlu Konuk Blasing, Robert Scholes, and Walter R. Davis, all of Brown University, where the project was first conceived. In addition, I am also thankful for the encouragement provided by Lawrence Lipking at the School of Criticism and Theory at Dartmouth College. I should also like to thank the School of Criticism and Theory for its generous financial support and, in addition, Brown University and the Social Sciences and Humanities Research Council of Canada for their sponsorship of the distinguished Louis Untermeyer and Doctoral Research fellowships, respectively, which relieved considerably the financial constraints of a Canadian scholar studying abroad. My gratitude is further extended to the Research and Publications Committee of the University of Ottawa for its generous assistance on all copyrights.

Earlier portions of this work found their way into conference programs at Syracuse University, the University of Louisville, and the University of Toronto, and additionally at Brown University, which, thanks to Ellen Rooney and Neil Lazarus, invited me to read an early version of my second chapter. I am generally much in the debt of the audiences at each of these venues for helping me to sharpen and refine my arguments at a few crucial places throughout my rather extended treatment. I am also thankful to John Serio, the editor of the *Wallace Stevens Journal* at Clarkson University, for his generous aid on one early and one later section of my text in particular, both of which eventually found their place among the pages of that distinguished publication. I should also like to acknowledge the encouragement of Jacqueline Vaught Brogan at the University of Notre Dame in this work and of Joseph Kronick, co-editor of the Horizons in Theory and American Culture series at Louisiana State University Press, in which series it is proud to appear in a much more extended form. I also owe a great debt to my former colleagues at St. John's University (Collegeville), especially to Ozzie Mayers, Charles Thornbury, and Annette Atkins, all for their immeasurable support as I endeavored both to teach and to write during the tenure of an all-too-brief theory appointment. More especially, I am grateful for the seemingly endless (and today, happily ongoing) theoretical discussions with Barbara Freedman at St. John's, whose own extraordinary work on Renaissance spectatorship in her incomparable *Staging the Gaze: Postmodernism, Psychoanalysis, and Shakespearean Comedy* (Cornell, 1991), continues to hold out for me the promise of what it still might be possible to say about literature and belief in more recent times. The expert copy-editing of Christine Cowan was an additional and unexpected pleasure.

Finally, I should at last like to honor the unstinting support, throughout the entire venture of this project, of my parents, whose own belief, let it be said, for the longest time was entirely *beyond* question. Most of all, I should like to thank posthumously that prodigious scholar and unyielding friend with whom my work on Wallace Stevens first began back in Toronto several years ago and to dedicate this study to his memory—a memory that touches my words in more ways than I, at least, might possibly have imagined back then, though like most students sent away to write, I could not speak for him.

ABBREVIATIONS

BGE   Friedrich Nietzsche. *Beyond Good and Evil: Prelude to a Philosophy of the Future.* Translated by R. J. Hollingdale. Harmondsworth, Eng., 1973.

BT/GM   Friedrich Nietzsche. *The Birth of Tragedy and The Genealogy of Morals.* Translated by Francis Golffing. Garden City, N.Y., 1956.

CP   *The Collected Poems of Wallace Stevens.* New York, 1954.

CW   Friedrich Nietzsche. *The Case of Wagner.* Translated by Walter Kaufmann. New York, 1966.

GS   Friedrich Nietzsche. *The Gay Science.* Translated by Walter Kaufmann. New York, 1974.

L   Holly Stevens, ed. *Letters of Wallace Stevens.* New York, 1966.

NA   Wallace Stevens. *The Necessary Angel: Essays on Reality and the Imagination.* New York, 1951.

OP   Wallace Stevens. *Opus Posthumous.* Rev. ed. Edited by Milton J. Bates. New York, 1989.

OTL   Friedrich Nietzsche. "On Truth and Lies in a Nonmoral Sense." Translated by Daniel Brazeale. In *Philosophy and Truth: Selections from Nietzsche's Notebooks of the Early 1870's.* Atlantic Highlands, N.J., 1979.

PM   *The Palm at the End of the Mind: Selected Poems and a Play by Wallace Stevens.* Edited by Holly Stevens. New York, 1972.

PN   Friedrich Nietzsche. *The Portable Nietzsche.* Translated by Walter Kaufmann. New York, 1952.

SP   Holly Stevens. *Souvenirs and Prophecies: The Young Wallace Stevens.*
            New York, 1977.

WP   Friedrich Nietzsche. *The Will to Power.* Translated by Walter
            Kaufmann and R. J. Hollingdale. New York, 1968.

Z   Friedrich Nietzsche. *Thus Spoke Zarathustra: A Book for All and
            None.* Translated by Walter Kaufmann. New York, 1954.

Wallace Stevens and the Question of Belief

TWO OR THREE IDEAS
Modernism and the Quest for Faith

> We work in the dark—we do what we can—we give what we have. Our
> doubt is our passion and our passion is our task. The rest is the madness
> of art.
>
> —Henry James, *The Middle Years*

> The age for which the ground fails to come, hangs in the abyss. Assuming that
> a turn still remains for this destitute time at all, it can come some day only if
> the world turns about fundamentally. . . . In the age of the world's night, the
> abyss of the world must be experienced and endured. But for this it is
> necessary that there be those who reach into the abyss.
>
> —Martin Heidegger, *Poetry, Language, Thought*

> Henceforth, so that God may indeed be, as Jabès says, *an interrogation of
> God*, would we not have to transform a final affirmation into a question?
> Literature would then, perhaps, only be the dreamlike displacement of [the]
> question.
>
> —Jacques Derrida, *Writing and Difference*

BELIEF, in the theological or religious sense, has always been, and no doubt
will continue to be, a favorite crux in any complete reading of Wallace Stevens'
poetry. Yet despite the canonical disagreement surrounding this issue, we
have it on the poet's own authority that matters of faith were a perpetual
source of creative inspiration throughout his lifetime. In a late essay entitled
"The Relations Between Poetry and Painting" and published in 1951, for instance, Stevens writes "that in an age in which disbelief is so profoundly
prevalent or, if not disbelief, indifference to questions of belief, poetry and
painting, and the arts in general, are, in their measure, a compensation for
what has been lost" (*NA,* 170–71). Poetry, in particular, is an especial sort of
compensation since, according to Stevens, it is mystical and irrational to-

1

gether and prompts him to ruminate: "While it can lie in the temperament of very few of us to write poetry in order to find God, it is probably the purpose of each of us to write poetry to find the good which, in the Platonic sense, is synonymous with God" (*OP,* 228). In short, he declares in an important memorandum from 1940, "the major poetic idea in the world is and always has been the idea of God" (*L,* 378). The declaration is hardly surprising. From his early youth, and on into an adulthood that bore witness to his own marriage within the Lutheran church, the baptism of his only daughter by Episcopal rite, and a purported conversion to Roman Catholicism on his deathbed, Stevens would be drawn to and sustained by a faith whose outward and visible signs mattered less—"I hate the look of a Bible," "Impossible to be religious in a pew," for example (*L,* 102, 86)—than the inward and spiritual grace they were intended to represent: "Beautiful and full of comfort and help" (*L,* 96). In a moment of candor from his sixty-first year, therefore, Stevens could admit, "My trouble, and the trouble of a great many people, is the loss of belief in the sort of God in Whom we were all brought up to believe" (*L,* 208).

Since, as Stevens himself puts the case in one of his "Adagia," "it is the belief and not the god that counts" (*OP,* 188), one is naturally given to speculate that in the post-Romantic era a poet is most likely to recover the loss of conventional forms of belief in his own art.[1] Indeed, "Poetry is the supreme fiction, madame," a line from a fairly early poem composed in 1922 (*CP,* 59), and "We say God and the imagination are one," a line from a late text written in 1950 (*CP,* 524), when taken together, might seem to indicate that the whole notion of poetry as a substitute for religious faith was one that Stevens had suffered long and tirelessly. Several commentators on Stevens have been avid to incorporate the substitution thesis at many points in their reading of his work.[2] That kind of argument takes us back to the important memorandum from 1940 alluded to earlier, linking the major poetic idea in the world to the idea of God and correspondingly evincing one of the primary gestures of the modern imagination as, in Stevens' words, "the movement away from the idea of God" (*L,* 378). More important, the memo outlines three options, or

1. Milton J. Bates, *Wallace Stevens: A Mythology of Self* (Berkeley, 1985), 209–12.

2. See esp. Adalaide Kirby Morris, *Wallace Stevens: Imagination and Faith* (Princeton, 1974), 17–18; but also Michael Sexson, *The Quest of Self in the Collected Poems of Wallace Stevens* (Lewiston, N.Y., 1981), 2; George S. Lensing, *Wallace Stevens: A Poet's Growth* (Baton Rouge, 1986), 286–87; and Joseph Carroll, *Wallace Stevens' Supreme Fiction: A New Romanticism* (Baton Rouge, 1987), 295.

alternatives, that such a movement might take: "The poetry that created the idea of God will either adapt it to our different intelligence, or create a substitute for it, or make it unnecessary." The "either" in Stevens' notation, however, makes it fairly plain that there actually are only two alternatives worthy of serious consideration, and the fifty or so references to God and the gods throughout his work, in addition to approximately eighteen similar allusions in the "Adagia," reveal just how necessary the consideration of *both* these options was to the poet.

One of the first principles of this study of Wallace Stevens' work, therefore, is to pay close attention to the sense of alternativeness between a differing, or differentiating, intelligence, on the one hand, and an intelligence more conveniently predisposed to substituting or replacing ideas offered to it in the whole relation between imagination and faith, on the other. Stevens would have little tolerance for the work of Karl Marx in his lifetime. But the political philosopher's suggestion that the critique of religion is the premise of all critique is one that Stevens could have taken fairly rigorously to heart, turning what might seem to be a fairly simple choice between a differing, as against an identifying, mind in the matter of faith into a prolonged and enormously provocative and soul-searching question of belief, as we shall soon see.

In reopening the whole question to alternative investigation in Stevens' poetry, we might do well in this introduction to focus a bit on one of Stevens' late essays in which he appears to have devoted his longest and most searching attention to theorizing the matter in prose, as a kind of *aria da capo,* following almost three decades of revolving it scrupulously in poetic practice. One of the chief aims of a piece from 1951 entitled "Two or Three Ideas" is very quickly to unsettle the expectation that either the elimination or the substitution thesis in matters of faith is *parti pris* in any interpretive approach to his poetry, particularly in the later work. True it is that "in an age of disbelief, or, what is the same thing, in a time that is largely humanistic, in one sense or another, it is for the poet to supply the satisfactions of belief, in his measure and in his style." But Stevens desires to make it perfectly clear that in no way would such a statement necessarily imply that a philosopher, say, or a teacher or even an artist might be about to take the place of the gods. "Just so," he scruples to emphasize, "we do not say that *the poet* is to take the place of the gods" (*OP,* 260, emphasis added).

Not that Stevens himself could not imagine such an argument. In the rather Browningesque "Reply to Papini," written in 1950, one year before

"Two or Three Ideas," Stevens launches into a rather vigorous attack on institutionalized religion's exclusive authorization of spirituality, represented by Pope Celestin VI, and aims to substitute the less congealed mind of the poet in his place, on the premise that "the way through the world / Is more difficult to find than the way beyond it" (*CP*, 446). Clearly, the poet's faith is more authentic because he chooses to speak directly and, in so doing, to subject his utterance to "the confusions of intelligence" (*CP*, 446), though whether of the differing or the identifying kind, we are not really quite sure. Nor ought we to be. For as a type of the Metaphysician in the Dark, whose search for what might suffice Stevens had characterized so equivocally a decade earlier in "Of Modern Poetry" (*CP*, 239), the utterance of the man of real faith bespeaks "the formulations of midnight" (*CP*, 446). The Metaphysician in the Dark rather than Pope Celestin, then, is the better model of contemporary belief for us since, as Charles Winquist observes, "we must learn either to think *in the dark or to think darkly* if we are to discursively integrate what is already our experience . . . [which] is not so much a theory of knowledge as an experiment with the depth and density of meanings within thought and discourse."[3] His poetry is hard, accordingly, only to the extent that it challenges orthodoxy's metaphysical removes, including "the removes [taken] toward poetry" itself (*CP*, 447). Consequently, if there must be a center to the question of belief, one that is "analyzed and fixed / And final" (*CP*, 447–48), it cannot be articulated or represented at an institutional remove, as in the lip service that is paid to Celestin's absent presence by Papini, the pope's emissary. To the contrary, faith, like the poet, must increase "the aspects of experience," which, up to that very moment, consti-

---

3. Charles Winquist, *Epiphanies of Darkness: Deconstruction in Theology* (Philadelphia, 1986), 16–17. The phrase "in the dark" of my subtitle thus becomes a veritable leitmotiv throughout the Stevens canon, strategically deployed in the discourse no less than nineteen times, according to Thomas F. Walsh's *Concordance to the Poetry of Wallace Stevens* (University Park, Pa., 1963), 71. The phrase further serves to underscore the study's title, since "the structure of the question . . . comes to stand in consciousness as a presentiment of indeterminate possibility," *i.e.*, "a structure for consent to the darkness of what is unknown" (Winquist, *Epiphanies of Darkness,* 25). See also Jacques Derrida, *Of Spirit*, trans. Geoffrey Bennington and Rachel Bowlby (Chicago, 1989), 17. For the contrasting "metaphoric of light," inextricably linked to "the enormous driving-wheel of logical Socratism" by Nietzsche, "the whole of Platonic philosophy" by Heidegger, and "structuralism in the Derridean sense," all a/theological avatars of the Metaphysician in the Dark, see Allan Megill, *Prophets of Extremity: Nietzsche, Heidegger, Foucault, Derrida* (Berkeley, 1985), 214–15. *Cf.* further Geoffrey H. Hartman, *Saving the Text: Literature/Derrida/Philosophy* (Baltimore, 1981), xix, and Thomas J. J. Altizer, *The Descent into Hell: A Study of the Radical Reversal of the Christian Consciousness* (New York, 1979), 207.

tute an unformulated belief's present absence. In its heroic effort to live, then, faith must be, as Charles Altieri would suggest, "producing new configurations for experience or new ways of pressing out possibilities for spiritual life."[4] To this end there really can be no end, for

> The world is still profound and in its depths
> Man sits and studies silence and himself,
>
> Abiding the reverberations in the vaults.
>
>   (*CP*, 447)

The reverberations of Wallace Stevens' own spiritual project lie precisely in the resistance it manifests to proxied intelligence, garnering those "humane triumphals" (*CP*, 447) that Stevens himself undoubtedly accumulates through time by way of his repeated and relentless probing of what will suffice the spiritual in man. If this probing opens the way to a reading that argues the substitution of poetry for religion, we must also recognize that Stevens' project must resist even his own "still obstinate thought," as the very last line of the poet's "Reply to Papini" cautions us. No doubt his pun on "still," a favorite one in the late poetry, as the above passage also indicates, is what causes Stevens' entirely deinstitutionalized concept of faith to continue "sparkling" at the poem's close (*CP*, 448).

The caution that Stevens slips into "Reply to Papini" at its end reiterates the chief source of alarm pointed out previously in "Two or Three Ideas." As we shall see more clearly in what is to follow in this study, however, it was a realization a long time in the making. In an important letter written ten years before his essay, Stevens specifies precisely the nature of this later cause for alarm: "I ought to say that it is a habit of mind with me to be thinking of some substitute for religion. I don't necessarily mean some substitute for the church, because no one believes in the church as an institution more than I do. . . . Humanism would be the natural substitute, but the more I see of humanism the less I like it. A thing of this kind is not to be judged by ideal presentations of it, but by what it really is" (*L*, 348). Stevens' point here is that the foreclosure of spiritual experience in the matter of faith has not really altered to any significant degree if orthodoxy's transcendent theism is merely exchanged for its antinomian variation in an immanent humanism. "Objective truth collapses into subjective truth," as Carl Raschke correctly notes,

---

4. Charles Altieri, "From Expressivist Aesthetics to Expressivist Ethics," in *Literature and the Question of Philosophy,* ed. Anthony J. Cascardi (Baltimore, 1987), 148.

"since the facticity of the object re-presented reflects the certitude elicited in appealing to the very sufficiency of thought's own re-presentation." One is still in quest, though, for "the ultimate *significandum,* for the re-presentation of representation, for the supreme, intelligible ground of all thought and experience," with all of the hierarchical exclusions, institutional negations, and authoritarian repressions incident to such a pursuit left entirely intact.[5] This repetitive quest is what humanism really is, according to Stevens' letter, and it is far from "ideal." In the first chapter of the present work, therefore, I shall begin to construct a genealogy of belief in the *Collected Poems* of Wallace Stevens by examining in some detail the synchronic gestures of immanence and transcendence in Stevens' early attempts to come to terms with the contradictions inherent in a substitutive humanism. The six years of publishing silence that followed his first collection of verse are only partially offset by the equally futile diachronic extension of humanism in Stevens' *Ideas of Order* and, in particular, in the cycle of romance, which immediately ensued.

By constructing this genealogy, I do not mean to impart to the question of belief "the idea of a linear genesis," in Rodolphe Gasché's phrase. A quick look at another poem from around the time of "Two or Three Ideas" would once again make clear to Stevens, but only in retrospect, why the whole modernist conception of humanism had to be abandoned if there was to be any hope at all for the continuation of a perdurable faith. In "World Without Peculiarity," written in 1948, where Stevens continues to revolve this whole issue so late in his career, we understand how the question of belief resists what Joseph Kronick in a related context describes as "reducing history to a univocal narrative line, a *sens unique,* but [rather] keeps it open to the movement of thinking."[6] And so with belief itself.

In "World Without Peculiarity" Stevens gives us the obverse of his critique of theocentric belief, outlined previously, in the humanism that would now tend to foreground an androcentric faith of the sort privileged in the text's final line—"a single being, sure and true"—now that mankind's "father" in the opening stanza, once so great and so strong, lies discarded "in the poverty of dirt" (*CP,* 454, 453). Yet the results of the substitution are identical. Legitimizing the general tendency to totalize and absolutize the will

5. Carl A. Raschke, *The Alchemy of the Word: Language and the End of Theology* (Missoula, Mont., 1979), 69, 64.

6. Rodolphe Gasché, *The Tain of the Mirror: Derrida and the Philosophy of Reflection* (Cambridge, Mass., 1986), 157; Joseph G. Kronick, "Dr. Heidegger's Experiment," *Boundary 2,* XVII (Fall, 1990), 122.

to believe (the logocentrism of true being is a world *without* peculiarity, after all), faith's reductions, once again, make the metaphysician's active imagination the first casualty. Stevens' image here is of a female, about which a great deal more needs to be said later, but for now she can be construed as a type of generative mother figure whose love turns cold in prospect of the believer's light, but nonetheless repressive, touch. As all who have been repressed must, she thus returns as a "hating woman," a "thing" that cries on his breast so reminiscent, in Stevens' retroactive pun, of the "(s)mothering weight" burdening Samuel Taylor Coleridge's own breast in "Dejection: An Ode." Devoid of all discerning intelligence, the larger world meets with a similar reduction, coming to bear an identity only passively reflecting the singular image of humanity, wherein all "difference disappears" (*CP*, 454).

Paradoxically, however, it is the point at which a humanistic belief forecloses on the world's peculiarity—the point, that is to say, at which "it is the earth itself that is humanity" (*CP*, 454)—that turns a simple matter of faith into the question of belief, wherein lies the spirit's hope:

> What good is it that the earth is justified,
> That it is complete, that it is an end,
> That in itself it is enough?
>
> (*CP*, 453)

Yet as I already noted, this is a moment that Stevens many times could relish only with hindsight in his later work and that will have to be dealt with in turn. Until then, we are left with the valorization of identity to the exclusion of difference, of generality to the exclusion of particularity, of singularity to the exclusion of alterity in the substitutive rhetoric that is the primary register of Stevens' early discourse. Perhaps the most curious thing of all in this rhetoric sprung from the reductions of humanism is the point at which the believer becomes most unlike himself in an earth turned completely human; he is its "inhuman son" (*CP*, 454). In this further decrement, he seems even more alienated from his own self than from that which he has turned against it, "the fateful mother," whom he now appears no longer to know. Cued by this loss, Stevens' artfully collapsible discourse has only to work one final reduction, and this it achieves when father at the beginning of the poem subsumes mother at the end and the son is left in the final stanza with "the poverty of dirt" as that "thing" upon his breast (*CP*, 454). With no other spiritual options remaining, his is the stasis of the reddest of red summers, whose unitive "red ripeness" suggests the bloody extirpation of all belief.

In one of his more important "Adagia," Stevens plays with the idea of establishing aesthetics in the individual mind "as immeasurably a greater thing than religion" (*OP,* 192), the implication being that because religion is a social practice "dependent on faith," as he puts it, the faith of aesthetics might be a greater thing since it is not dependent on anything. Yet the problem with this substitution, as the preceding poem seems to make fairly clear, is, in the adage's concluding words, "the difficulty of establishing it [*i.e.,* aesthetics and, by extension, faith] *except* in the individual mind" (emphasis added) and thereby reproducing another paralyzing source of dependence. A second principle of this new study of belief in Stevens' work, therefore, and by far the major burden of the critical commentary following Chapter 1, is to follow as closely as possible the poet's efforts to get past the barriers thrown up in the way of faith as a "gradual possession" by the conventional operations of that individual mind. To this end, Stevens appears to be left with no other option, of the three outlined in the 1940 memorandum, save that of adapting the idea of God "to our different intelligence." In the genealogy of belief that this book proposes to outline beyond the spiritual impasse of his early work, we must start all over again, as Stevens obviously did. Only this time, we begin with an astonishingly precocious insight attributed to one of his early journals, the value of which the mature writer had perhaps only just begun to recognize as he was assembling material for his third book, *The Man with the Blue Guitar,* at midcareer, namely, that "the best poetry will be rhetorical criticism."[7] Translated simply in the context of belief, this observation meant that if there was to be a future in the idea of God, the intelligence might be afforded a different purchase on the whole question if it were to be examined critically from a rhetorical rather than from the usual rational, logical, or even theological perspective. The a(theo)logical and rhetorical move would shift Stevens' discourse entirely into an incalculable or unthinkable that would thus subvert the hegemonic substitution of the "individual mind" previously, something like the "intraitable dont je suis fait" of Roland Barthes, which Paul Smith translates as "the untreatable, the imponderable that constitutes me."[8]

Like a great deal of contemporary writing, and current critical theory in particular, the study of the question of belief in Stevens' work, then, is

7. Susan Sontag attributes the remark apparently to one of Stevens' journals from his Harvard years, in Roland Barthes, *A Barthes Reader,* ed. Susan Sontag (New York, 1982), vii. I have been unable to locate this entry elsewhere.

8. Paul Smith, *Discerning the Subject* (Minneapolis, 1988), 102.

largely about two ideas, and a third only when the first two would appear to have become mutually depleted or exhausted. We are thus carried once more back to Stevens' own "Two or Three Ideas" to map out in fairly general terms for now the shape a rhetorical criticism of the question might take when, as in the following passage, one order of belief has run its course and becomes taken over by another:

> To see the gods dispelled in mid-air and dissolve like clouds is one of the great human experiences. It is not as if they had gone over the horizon to disappear for a time; nor as if they had been overcome by other gods of greater power and profounder knowledge. It is simply that they came to nothing. . . . At the same time, [however,] no man ever muttered a petition in his heart for the restoration of those unreal shapes. There was always in every man the increasingly human self, which instead of remaining the observer, the non-participant, the delinquent, became constantly more and more all there was *or so it seemed;* and whether it was so *or merely seemed so* still left it for him to resolve life and the world in his own terms. (*OP,* 260, emphasis added)

God is dead, according to this further excerpt from the essay. But as Chapters 2 and 3 of this genealogy will endeavor to show, Stevens' careful reading of Friedrich Nietzsche following the writing of his first two books had taught him a great deal about the discursive, rather than the substantive, possibilities for maintaining "the satisfactions of belief" nonetheless (*OP,* 259). We might only suggest in this introduction what the final four chapters, starting with Stevens' "Notes Toward a Supreme Fiction," will attempt in some detail to make plain with respect to these possibilities in the poet's later writing. To begin, however, let us first consider the rhetorical gambit he has theoretically made above in the alterity suggested by his "seeming" self, which appears to be reopening the question of belief, and then later consider what is at stake if he were to play that gambit out in actual practice, in one of his longer and better-known poems.

In Stevens' description of a waning of faith with the dissolution of the gods, to be replaced more and more by "the increasingly human self," with life and the world viewed entirely "in [man's] own terms," we are reminded of that line of W. B. Yeats', "the soul . . . become[s] its own betrayer, its own deliverer, the one activity, the mirror turn lamp," which is used by Meyer Abrams to scaffold his massive study of the shift from classical mimesis to romantic expression, or poiesis: the mirror held up to nature on the one hand and a lamp held up to human nature on the other.[9] More recently, Michel Foucault, in an essay on the work of Friedrich Hölderlin, has described a similar shift. But when, according to Foucault, the German poet's Empedocles makes his move from thinking about "the All-in-One" and the limitless "center of things," to thinking "*he* had realized the 'Limitless,'" we become more immediately aware that poiesis, from a purely eschatological point of view, is still very much within the rhetorical ambit of mimesis. Instead of representations of nature in the classical episteme, we find the substitution of representations of the self in the romantic, or what we have come to understand more broadly as the modern, episteme, which carries through to the present century in the literature and art of the so-called high modernist mode. It is precisely this prolongation of classic representation under the guise of modern expression, what Foucault in another place calls "the double chain of Rhetoric," that brings modernism itself to an end, as it is brought to an end in Stevens' own early poetry, and that, in the later work, inaugurates what contemporary theorists are pleased to invoke as an era of postmodernism.[10] Before taking up this shift specifically in the context of the renewal of faith in Stevens, we perhaps might clarify further the rhetorical prolongation of classicism in what begins to take shape as modernism as we know it, in the early nineteenth century and onward.

In Sir Philip Sidney's classic "An Apology for Poetry," published in 1595, we find the model statement of poetry as an art of mimetic representation: "Aristotle termeth it in his word, *Mimesis*," Sidney states, "that is to say, a representing, counterfeiting, or figuring forth—to speak metaphorically, a

9. Meyer H. Abrams, *The Mirror and the Lamp: Romantic Theory and the Critical Tradition* (New York, 1953). Helen Vendler, in *On Extended Wings: Wallace Stevens' Longer Poems* (Cambridge, Mass., 1969), invites us to see this shift carried out in Stevens' own poetic practice in "An Ordinary Evening in New Haven": "The mandate to the poet is that he must re-create the world, turning Hesper into Phosphor by turning himself from a mirror to a lamp" (308). *Cf.* also Joseph N. Riddel, *The Clairvoyant Eye: The Poetry and Poetics of Wallace Stevens* (Baton Rouge, 1965): "It is by the act of mind that we make the incipient real and actual, and thus realize ourselves in a cosmos that is *self*-sufficient" (266, emphasis in original). The later reading of the poem offered here, however, will resist these generally humanistic interpretations.

10. Michel Foucault, *Language, Counter-Memory, Practice: Selected Essays and Interviews*, trans. Sherry Simon and Donald F. Bouchard, ed. Donald F. Bouchard (Ithaca, 1977), 82–83, 67. A quite similar argument for the discursive shift mapped out here is presented in the context of postmodern poetics by George Hartley in his *Textual Politics and the Language Poets* (Bloomington, 1989), in the final chapter, "Praxis and Syntaxis: Ideology and the Economy of Space," esp. 79–80.

speaking picture." Mimesis, moreover, is deductive: capitalized Nature, where the signs of God as the Supreme Author are writ large, declines through infected will to nature writ small, that is, to "the truth of a foolish world." Metaphorization, therefore, is based on a principle of analogical equivalence and moves outward and upward, attempting to bring *a*uthor back into line with *A*uthor, and ultimately *n*ature back into line with *N*ature, "the ending end of all earthly learning [and] virtuous action." When the theological paradigm shifts, in post-Cartesian times, from God to Stevens' "increasingly human self," Sidney's two natures become completely reversed. Thus, in Percy Bysshe Shelley's "A Defence of Poetry," published in 1840, poetry becomes inductive, laboring, following Aristotle again, to create actions "according to the unchangeable forms of *human* nature, as existing in the *mind* of the creator." In this model, "Poetry, and the principle of Self," Shelley states, "are the God" and "the divinity in man." Metaphorization now moves downward and inward as against the figuration in Sidney and operates synecdochically rather than analogically, which perhaps explains Shelley's own inordinate attraction in his discourse to Milton's Satan, a moral being "far superior to his God," as he states.[11]

What is most important for us in a thoroughly modern age to observe in Shelley's diametrical reversals is the persistence of the rhetoric of representation continued from the pre-Cartesian era of classical mimesis, as the images of mirroring in Shelley's apology everywhere bear out. No matter to what degree, therefore, the classical out-look of Sidney transforms itself into the modernist in-sight of Shelley, both epistemes nonetheless sustain each other within a visionary and transcendent logocentrism, as their mutually supportive discourses of self-reflection in a formulation like Friedrich von Schiller's naïve and sentimental poet would appear to bear out. Indeed, Carl Raschke, making bold his earlier suggestion, would argue, after Martin Heidegger, that theocentric faith has all along implied an egocentric "self-legitimation of the subject" and that the objective truth of God gradually collapses into the subjective truth of the poet only as the individual mind,

11. Sir Philip Sidney, "An Apology for Poetry," in *Criticism: The Major Texts,* ed. Walter Jackson Bate (New York, 1952), 86a, 91a, 87b; Dalia Judovitz, "Philosophy and Poetry: The Difference Between Them in Plato and Descartes," 46–47, and Anthony J. Cascardi, "From the Sublime to the Natural: Romantic Responses to Kant," 112, both in *Literature and the Question of Philosophy,* ed. Cascardi; Percy Bysshe Shelley, "A Defence of Poetry," in *English Romantic Writers,* ed. David Perkins (New York, 1967), 1075a (emphasis added), 1084a, 1085a, 1081b. See also Northrop Frye, *The Stubborn Structure: Essays on Criticism and Society* (Ithaca, 1970), 205, and Harold Bloom, ed., *Romanticism and Consciousness: Essays in Criticism* (New York, 1970), 15–16.

through time, gains more and more confidence in "the very sufficiency of thought's own re-presentations and the self-evidence of its categories of language and critical analysis." The implication of all of this for a poet like Wallace Stevens in the era of high modernism is that he must either approbate or at some point register his disenchantment with classic deduction posing as romantic induction, which, in the later phase of modernism, for all intents and purposes becomes a model of ontotheological reduction. There can be no doubt that in Stevens' case in particular such a reduction would be especially aggravated by his extraordinary commitment to the renewal of faith, as we have already seen. An alternative praxis would thus entail subsequent efforts to seek out new motives for metaphor "neither inscribed in the heavens, nor the brain," as Jacques Derrida succinctly puts the case, beyond, that is, the binary opposition of mimesis and poiesis, a structural opposition that Derrida in another place would describe as "the myth of a total reading . . . promoted to the status of a regulatory ideal." It should not surprise us, therefore, to find Stevens midway through his poetic career writing about the romantic in "a pejorative sense," as he phrases it, about "some phase of the romantic that has become stale" (*OP,* 183) and that he views in his letters as leading "to fatalism and then to indifferentism" (*L,* 350). [12]

It follows, then, that one of the central features in the change from modernism to postmodernism in our time—a change, that is, from an aesthetic paradigm of reduction, marked by orthodox representation, to one of production, characterized by a paradoxical repetition, "which evades every assignable destination"—that a central feature of this change is the problematizing of the essentially structural agreement of what Barthes might call "the great semiological 'versus' myth": mimesis / poiesis. [13] In the generative semi-

12. Shelley, "A Defence of Poetry," in *English Romantic Writers,* ed. Perkins, 1075a, 1078a, 1083a, and others; Raschke, *The Alchemy of the Word,* 70, 69; Jacques Derrida, *Positions,* trans. Alan Bass (Chicago, 1981), 9, and *Writing and Difference,* trans. Alan Bass (Chicago, 1978), 24; *cf.* also Jacques Derrida, *Memoires for Paul de Man,* trans. Cecile Lindsay *et al.* (New York, 1989), 239. For an account of the pejorative kind of romance Stevens wishes to move beyond, *i.e.,* the romance-quest by which "the other is amenable to being reduced to the status of the same" by the "hegemonic sway" of some heroic individual, see Wlad Godzich's "Foreword: The Further Possibility of Knowledge," in Michel de Certeau's *Heterologies: Discourse on the Other,* trans. Brian Massumi (Minneapolis, 1986), xiii, xvi. This whole issue is dealt with in more detail in Chapter 1 and will be revisited in Chapter 5.

13. Jacques Derrida, "The Purveyor of Truth," trans. Alan Bass, in *The Purloined Poe: Lacan, Derrida and Psychoanalytic Reading,* ed. John P. Muller and William J. Richardson (Baltimore, 1988), 204; Roland Barthes, *The Pleasure of the Text,* trans. Richard Miller (New York, 1975), 54. Kevin Hart's "questioning the structurality of . . . structure" in order to foreground

osis sparked by the deconstruction of the generic forms of representation of Sidney and Shelley rehearsed previously, we catch the structuralism of modernism on its way to a *third* idea, following Stevens again, that is thoroughly poststructural and thoroughly postmodern. It is this third idea, as we shall come to take it up specifically in Chapters 4 and 5, that turns the poet's objective quest for faith not into subjective art but rather into the eventful question of belief and traces a continuous pattern of spiritual rebirth spiraling through his last three collections of verse. I should point out, however, that semiosis is an invented term that can only approximate Stevens' third idea, the force of an Other he appears to descry, following Heidegger in his later work, in a space that conventional belief, in its tireless devotion to mimetic or poetic commensuration, can only leave unthought. But before turning to a model of the generative semiosis that this study purposes to argue virtually salvaged Stevens' faith, along with a writing career that threatened to become stalled in the early years of the Depression, we might pause for a moment to notice how premonitory his critical and creative discursive genealogy actually is.

In the literary criticism of Paul de Man, for instance, the representative problematic of gods and man in Stevens becomes an "organic world" equally divided between an outside "symbolic mode of analogical correspondences" and an inside "mimetic mode of representation." Thus, it is only the rhetoric of temporality—irony as opposed to metaphor, or "Metaphor as Degeneration," as in one of Stevens' late titles (*CP*, 444)—that succeeds in breaking apart the coincidence of "fiction and reality" and in sensitizing us either to "a past that is pure mystification" (Sidney) or to "a future that remains harassed forever by a relapse within the inauthentic" (Shelley), as we've just seen. J. Hillis Miller, most recently in *The Ethics of Reading*, detects a similar division in the models of literary representation in his cogent commentary on the fiction of George Eliot: "The truth of correspondence in realism is not to objective things, or only indirectly to objective things. It is rather to things as they have already made a detour into necessarily distorted subjective reflections. Eliot's obligation is, as she says, 'to give a faithful account of men and things as they have mirrored themselves in my mind.'" Eliot's conjoining

---

the "condition for the possibility of signification in general" in his recent *The Trespass of the Sign: Deconstruction, Theology and Philosophy* (New York, 1989), 197 and 38, begins to suggest perhaps what Barthes's structural "'versus' myth" aims referentially to foreclose on, as I argue in what follows. *Cf.* also in Hart, 75, 86, 94, 104, 122, 124, 134, 137, 158, 224, and 246.

of mirror and mind in this citation once again underscores a certain mimetic continuity between classical and modern times. Hence, the rhetoric of post-modernism only becomes genuinely authentic when this continuity is opened to question, as in the case of Stevens' adapting his idea of God to a differing rather than an identifying intelligence, and when the poet's idiom becomes productive rather than reductive, generative rather than generic, pro-visional rather than re-visionary. "You only escape dualisms effectively," so Gilles Deleuze and Claire Parnet write in their *Dialogues,* "by shifting them like a load, and when you find between the terms, whether they are two or more, a narrow gorge like a border or a frontier which will turn the set into a multiplicity, independently of the number of parts." For Stevens, this development, naturally enough, gets fully underway in *Parts of a World,* but only after his "Blue Guitar" has strummed a final chord for the theological openings and closings of faith in *Harmonium* and *Ideas of Order.* Not a question merely of the gods dispelled in midair or even of the other gods of profounder knowledge cited earlier, belief for the later Stevens would appear to be more a question of what Heidegger calls a "double lack and a double Not: the No-more of the gods that have fled and the Not-yet of the god that is coming." Even this quasi-teleological formulation may be too hermeneutical, however, and in many places later in this study, we shall find it necessary to invoke Derrida where Stevens would exceed even Heidegger on the question, in an effort to confront what Derrida recently has referred to as the "force of the question" itself. In Stevens' post-theological discourse, therefore, we perhaps might venture the speculation that all of the postmodern theorists above converge in his Metaphysician in the Dark, whose primary office, particularly as I discuss it in Chapter 6, is to register an enormous Jamesean doubt, as in the opening epigraph, concerning the God's-eye view of faith as an ontoepistemological institution, with its attendant spectator theories of knowledge.[14]

Wallace Stevens' "An Ordinary Evening in New Haven," one of his later works, written in 1949, can begin to suggest the process of semiosis more primordially anterior to the products of mimesis, when the rhetoric of rep-

14. Paul de Man, *Blindness and Insight: Essays in the Rhetoric of Contemporary Criticism* (Minneapolis, 1971), 222; J. Hillis Miller, *The Ethics of Reading; Kant, de Man, Eliot, Trollope, James, and Benjamin* (New York, 1987), 65; Gilles Deleuze and Claire Parnet, *Dialogues,* trans. Hugh Tomlinson and Barbara Habberjam (New York, 1987), 132–33; Kronick, "Dr. Heidegger's Experiment," 140–41; Gasché, *The Tain of the Mirror,* 149, 203–204, 292; Derrida, *Of Spirit,* 18. On the spectator theories of knowledge, see Bernd Magnus, "The End of 'The End of Philosophy,'" in *Hermeneutics and Deconstruction,* ed. Hugh J. Silverman and Don Ihde (New York, 1985), 2–10.

resentation in both of its paradigmatic forms becomes deregulated, thereby opening up a space for new belief as "an essential limit to all coinciding reflection," to borrow Gasché's phrase. In Canto V, for instance, the two ideas form the "inescapable choice / Of dreams" that appear to have "divided the world" but that more accurately, in the disillusion of romance, reflect a major division in subjectivity itself. The centuries of literary history spanning the previous two apologies for poetry Stevens remarkably sums up in a five-line genealogy of the human self:

>   One part
>   Held fast tenaciously in common earth
>   And one from central earth to central sky
>   And in moonlit extensions of them in the mind
>   Searched out such majesty as it could find.
>   (*CP,* 468–69)

Stevens' point here is in line with many of our previous theorists: neither "part," no matter how tenaciously held, represents a totally adequate discourse. "Reality as a thing seen by the mind," as the canto states, is not "that which is but that which is apprehended" (*CP,* 468), so that there is "no possibility of achieving a single authoritative language for the representation of reality."[15] In other words, if seeing is believing, it is not a matter of reference; it is a *question* of inference: "Everything as unreal as real can be, / In the in[-]exquisite eye" (*CP,* 468). With this separation between reality and fiction we noted earlier in de Man, Stevens problematizes the passive notion of self-reflection as a kind of concealment in "antic symbols" and instead foregrounds the conception of self and world as effects of a more active semiotic or rhetorical construction and, beyond that, as a question of choice among linguistic options:

>   Not merely as to depth but as to height
>
>   As well, not merely as to the commonplace
>   But, also, as to their miraculous,
>   Conceptions of new mornings of new worlds.
>   (*CP,* 470)

In classical and modern discourse, the normal tendency might be to forge a strict metaphorical identity between one whole and another (analogy)

---

15. Gasché, *The Tain of the Mirror,* 221; M. Keith Booker, "A War Between Mind and Sky: Bakhtin and Poetry, Stevens and Politics," *Wallace Stevens Journal,* XIV (Spring, 1990), 79.

or between whole and part (synecdoche) in order to declare an object of thought and, beyond that, to affirm a form of faith: "Reality IS." But more and more in the later Stevens, as Chapter 7 undertakes to argue, the tendency is to ironize the miraculous conceptions or "misted contours" of knowledge: New Haven, rather than New Heaven, in the poem's title and an Ordinary Evening, rather than an Extraordinary One. The tip-off often tends to be the insertion of the tropological *as* in place of the more expected predicative *is,* as in "Everything *as* unreal as real can be." Stevens' strategy, as we perhaps see most clearly in Canto XV, is to work against metaphysical closure, to counter "part" with "counterpoint," that is, to resist our tendency to presence univocal or mimetic truth by maintaining the forms of truth themselves in a kind of polyvocal conversation with each other. Thus, an "instinct for heaven," which finds its "counterpart" in an "instinct for earth," becomes displaced from any kind of reification within "a single world"—a world "in which [one] is, and as and is are one" (*CP,* 476)—and instead becomes re-peated all over again in the revolving "gay tournamonde" of language. As irksome as it must seem from the standpoint of mimetic representation, we are given semiotic repetition, "for its counterpart a kind of counterpoint" (*CP,* 476): "wet wallows" rather than "rainless land" and "wide delvings of wings" in place of a "ponderable source." On a more global scale, Canto XIX resists any attempt to represent the true sense of the modern age, "This pres-ent colony of a colony, / Of colonies." Accordingly, the canto privileges "the changing sense / Of things" and in place of unitive or transcendent truth leaves us "in the dark," as it states, by offering us a text instead—"A text that is an answer, although obscure" (*CP,* 479).

Suspended between the change of sense and the sense of change, the antinomian text, as Canto XXII points out, is impervious to the legitimations of either the philosopher's Reality ("an interior made exterior") or the poet's God ("the same exterior made interior") (*CP,* 481). In such a standoff be-tween interiority and exteriority, Foucault would say that literature had aban-doned its age-old "dilemma" and in passing from the poiesis of book to the semiosis of text had inscribed a "paradox" instead: "No longer the space where speech adopts a form . . . but the site where books are all recaptured and consumed: a site that is nowhere." Correspondingly, Stevens removes "the predicate of bright origin" in his own deregulation of textuality and in place of the creation of images of truth by "lone wanderers" foregrounds "re-creat[ing]" instead. Such re-creating or *re-marking* thus approximates a "space of repetition and splitting or doubling of the self"—a continuous reciting of "daily sense" according to the poem—"in which all textual traces are not only elements of referral but are also overmarked by the space of their engenderment and inscription."[16] To re-create, re-mark, or re-cite, therefore, is "to search," not to find. When the text "searches a possible for its possibleness" (*CP*, 481), it becomes an analogue of itself and in this gesture of impossible self-reflexion becomes the only means by which an act of postmodern semiosis can speak with any authority to the question of belief. Canto XXIV, consequently, is added finally by Stevens to describe just how eager we are "to refill" the emptiness of bygone authority, symbolized by the statue of Jove recently blown up by the "genius" of modernism, with the "thought of evening" and the "sound of Incomincia" to follow. But the "consolations of space," the nowhere of postmodern belief, these are "nameless things," and the hand raised later in this canto to direct faith's inscription to "a point of the sky or of the earth" can only be, as Stevens states, "an escape from repetition" (*CP*, 483), not its championing. To provide a space for the "outpouring" of the six additional cantos yet to come, Stevens must accordingly redistribute the forces of knowing and willing in play at this late stage in the poem and deflect rather than reflect its "readiness for first bells" into a new "clearing"; belief is "poised" rather than "proposed," like New Haven itself teetering "at the horizon's dip" (*CP*, 483).

There is much else this long and meandering text of Wallace Stevens will have to offer the renovation of faith, which we shall be in a better position to appreciate at the end of this study, where it will resurface as we turn "Out-words." For now, "An Ordinary Evening in New Haven" serves as a gauge of the trials and limitations of the rhetoric that the poet inherits in the wake of prior epochs of literary history and stands as a premier document that makes promise of the redeployment of that rhetoric, once its representative forms have run their course. In much broader terms, even this preliminary look at the poem shows how Stevens' two or three ideas are inaugural to an important realignment of linguistic and aesthetic priorities, as each of the next seven chapters aims to show—a realignment that allows belief to pass from a literal quest to a figural question, as the discursive paradigms shift between modernism and postmodernism in American literature. We can move forward a couple of decades, for instance, and find John Ashbery in a very much longer work like *Three Poems,* written in 1972, continuing, in Stevens' path, to be very much preoccupied with what he describes as "the

---

16. Foucault, *Language, Counter-Memory, Practice,* 67; Gasché, *The Tain of the Mirror,* 291.

enormity of the choice between two kinds of mutually exclusive universal happiness" and characterizes later as "those two static and highly artificial concepts whose fusion was nevertheless the cause of death and destruction not only for ourselves but in the world around us."

If the genealogy of belief is at all coincident, we presume that in such a world a dark abyss has swallowed up all the available spiritual options. As in another of the epigraphs, we look for a figure with an imagination like Stevens' to reach into that abyss, not so much to deliver us up, "in-words," to another meaning and another truth but, like his Metaphysician in the Dark, rhetorically to suspend the question of belief over the abyss as a question of style. "[It] becomes the question of style as the question of writing," as Derrida would say, "the question of a spurring operation, more powerful than any content, any thesis, any meaning . . . [and] *considered as a question* . . . remains, interminably." [17] In a final excerpt from his "Two or Three Ideas," Stevens explains it this way: "In an age of disbelief, when the gods have come to an end, when we think of them as the aesthetic projections of a time that has passed, men turn to a fundamental glory of their own and from that create a style of bearing themselves in reality. They create a new style of a new bearing in a new reality. This third idea, then may be . . . expressed by saying that the style of men and men themselves are one." Two ideas, then, like two poems, become three because there is something that the first two are not telling us. Or won't. [18] The really valuable insight that Stevens' interrogation of faith will ultimately be able to show is not so much

17. John Ashbery, *Three Poems* (New York, 1972), 96, 114; Jacques Derrida, *Spurs/Éperons: Nietzsche's Styles,* trans. Barbara Harlow (Chicago, 1979), 107–109, emphasis in the original essay. *Cf.* also Julia Kristeva, *Powers of Horror: An Essay on Abjection,* trans. Leon S. Roudiez (New York, 1982), 188.

18. *Cf.* Michel Foucault, *Language, Counter-Memory, Practice:* "Far from being the still incomplete and blurred image of an Idea that eternally retains our answers in some upper region . . . the Idea exists only in the form of a problem: a distinctive plurality whose obscurity is nevertheless insistent and in which the question ceaselessly stirs" (185). *Cf.* also Gerald L. Bruns, *Heidegger's Estrangements: Language, Truth, and Poetry in the Later Writings* (New Haven, 1989), 108. No doubt it is such a ceaselessly stirring question that might account for what James Longenbach has most recently termed "the aesthetic dialectic of Stevens' entire career: discovering and imposing," that is, the "tension between explicitness and reticence" over which, I am arguing (following Derrida and Foucault), Stevens' mimetic/poetic rhetoric appears to be suspended but which cannot entirely be enclosed within "the possibility of a life that may look occasionally to [the death of the active or the death of the retreating self]" that Longenbach views as "a third term complicat[ing] the dualism." See his *Wallace Stevens: The Plain Sense of Things* (New York, 1991), 35, 250–51, and 37, in addition to 54, 82, 146, 151, 202, 230, 265, and *passim.*

what can and cannot be thought once theological representation has reached its limits but rather what makes that thought and those limits possible in the first place. What follows is the history of one remarkable poet's search of "a possible for its possibleness" in the currents of postmetaphysical and post-theological thought. As a courageous theodicy in an age in which God is purported to have come to an end, it is an achievement that is not to be easily rivaled in the contemporary writing of our time.

CHAPTER I

THE GORGEOUS WHEEL
Circulating the Pleasures of Romance

I suppose that the way of all mind is from romanticism to realism, to fatalism and then to indifferentism, unless the cycle re-commences and the thing goes from indifferentism back to romanticism all over again.

—*The Letters of Wallace Stevens*

The world of art, of human culture and civilization, is a creative process informed by a vision. The focus of this vision is indicated by the polarizing in romance between the world we want and the world we don't want. The process goes on in the actual world, but the vision which informs it is clear of that world, and must be kept unspotted from it.

—Northrop Frye, *The Secular Scripture*

Must the poet's career always describe a closed circle, a faithful rounding-off of obligations, or might it stay open at every point to unexpected directions and new beginnings?

—Lawrence Lipking, *The Life of the Poet*

UNTIL Wallace Stevens begins to theorize about his poetry in a rigorously systematic way, from about the mid-1930s onward, a great deal of what can be said about belief in his first two books, *Harmonium* and *Ideas of Order,* published in 1923 and 1935, respectively, is ventured by the reader very much in the spirit of retrospection. The many critics who detect a severe animus against institutionalized religion and the conventional expressions of faith particularly in the early work are very likely working back authoritatively from Stevens' "Adagia" in the first instance.[1] What we can only infer from his first two books, that the era of Stevens' early poetry is thoroughly post-

---

1. Morris, *Imagination and Faith,* 51; Ralph J. Mills, Jr., "Wallace Stevens: The Image of the Rock," in *Wallace Stevens: A Collection of Critical Essays,* ed. Marie Borroff (Englewood Cliffs, N.J., 1963); Charles Berger, *Forms of Farewell: The Late Poetry of Wallace Stevens* (Madison, 1985), 28–29.

Romantic, marked by skepticism and "the absence of belief in God," is spelled out in no uncertain terms in the prose statements from Stevens' middle period. The shift to an "aesthetic point of view" that naturally follows on such an absence, to qualify Stevens as a writer in the high modernist mode, we have in the author's own words, as well from the later prose: "After one has abandoned a belief in god, poetry is that essence which takes its place as life's redemption," since "it is the belief and not the god that counts" (*OP*, 186, 185, 188).

Thus, the major poetic idea for any poet in any age, which is "the idea of God" according to the 1940 memorandum written to Henry Church, is one that we ought to be able to apply backward and forward in Stevens' poetry. Getting to that Archimedian point, however, was quite another matter for the poet. From 1940 onward, adapting the idea of God to what he terms a "different intelligence" comes almost like a burst of new energy or like an inhalation of fresh air. Yet much of what Stevens calls "a part of labor and a part of pain" in "Sunday Morning" (*CP*, 68), a poem written twenty-five years previously, we can too easily elide, overlooking the fact that there would first have to be efforts, also mentioned in the letter to Church, to create a substitute for the idea of God, in addition to those efforts that would attempt to eliminate Him (*L*, 378). Tracing a genealogy for the whole notion of belief in Stevens' *Collected Poems,* as this study purposes to do, can thus assume no totalizing theoretical position for his earliest work. Rather, it begins to unpack the poet's preoccupation with belief from an almost atheoretical stance, from the point of view of belief framed in the form of a question or quest.

Before arriving at the affirmation of God as poetic idea, therefore, we must first work through those earliest probing gestures of elimination and substitution. These, as Wallace Stevens could know only with hindsight, were essentially the agendas of *Harmonium* and *Ideas of Order,* respectively. The creative labors lavished upon both, divided as they are by that six-year silence roughly following the publication of Stevens' first collection, indicate perhaps much of the antipathic nature of the question of belief itself, when revolved from these two discrete perspectives. Jacques Derrida puts forward the further suggestion that the question of belief in this sense may be one of "structure," since the end or "full presence" implied by such a question entails a play of meanings about "a certain mode of being."[2] Specifically, the question can be either one of archaeology or one of eschatology, depending on

2. Derrida, *Writing and Difference,* 279.

whether the end in sight is original or terminal. Combining these insights with the agendas outlined previously, we might say, then, that *Harmonium* is an archaeological project, foregrounding the elimination of God for the purposes of originating metaphorical play, whereas *Ideas of Order* is an eschatological project, foregrounding the substitution of God as a means of ultimately terminating metaphorical play. That each book attempts to undo what the other sets out to accomplish reveals just how deeply divided Stevens' writing actually is in its conventionally theological and thoroughly structuralist phase through to the mid-1930s, a point to which we shall be recurring several times through the course of this chapter.

Beginning with *Harmonium,* our reading is first sensitized to the fairly large critique it mounts against certain aspects of transcendence, as Stevens attempts to register the incomprehensibility of the modern world in spiritually cosmic terms in the wake of "God is dead." Some of his early letters set the tone for this. In one of them he contends: "An old argument with me is that the true religious force in the world is not the church but the world itself: the mysterious callings of Nature and our responses. What incessant murmurs fill that ever-laboring, tireless church!" (*L,* 58–59). Another early letter notes what replaces religious feelings for him: "I am not in the least religious. The sun clears my spirit, if I may say that, and an occasional sight of the sea, and thinking of blue valleys, and the odor of the earth, and many things. Such things make a god of a man" (*L,* 96). In a second from the same year, 1907, he establishes a link between religious and useless: "I went through my things . . . and threw away a pile of useless stuff. How hard it is to do it! One of the things was my Bible. I hate the look of a Bible" (*L,* 102). Thus, in "Of Heaven Considered as a Tomb" from 1921, a former dispensation of spiritual meaning is described in the present as cold, remote, and vacant, an "icy Élysée" peopled by interpreters the equivalent of ghosts and comedians (*CP,* 56). Belief, by this ultra-institutional accounting, makes as unimpressionable an impact on the everyday lives of men as the narcotic rhythm of the rising and setting of the sun does:

> Or does
> That burial, pillared up each day as porte
> And spiritous passage into nothingness,
> Foretell each night the one abysmal night,
> When the host shall no more wander, nor the light
> Of the steadfast lanterns creep across the dark?
>
> (*CP,* 56)

The morbid interpreters of men in this poem, moreover, form a further link to the funereal philosophers beside whom they are placed in the poem entitled "On the Manner of Addressing Clouds," also from 1921. Existing on the same scale of transcendence as the former benighted priests, "Gloomy grammarians in golden gowns" (*CP,* 55), these new learned men, with their clouds of rhetoric, are so far beyond any kind of meaningful contact with the mundane world that their evocations constitute a rarefied intelligence that only they can magnify. To a much vaster majority, they and their work represent "mysterious seasons," a "drifting waste" that, as in the previous poem, is barely distinguishable from the tedious motions of sun and moon.

If the "abstract fanaticism" of both priest and philosopher, in George Santayana's phrase, highlights the privileged role of the poet, who theoretically and traditionally forms a more direct contact with the real world and its possible perfections, nonetheless, transcendent abstraction is an irresponsibility that the poet may sometimes be prone to as well. In "Anecdote of the Prince of Peacocks," written in 1923, which Stevens places almost immediately after the previous two poems in *Harmonium,* the prince of peacocks, as a kind of spokesman for unlicensed imagination imaged in the forms of excessive sleeping and dreaming, is suddenly brought up short by Berserk, a figure of nemesis with the blocking traps of steel he sets for the fantastically wayward (*CP,* 57–58). Their confrontation on a "bushy plain" fills the imagination with dread, and the poem concludes with the suggestion of a fall that the fanciful prince may be taking (a favored trope in *Harmonium* that we shall see a great deal more of) for indulging a feckless innocence of extravagant moonshine. The prince is therefore much like the blind creator in "Negation," composed in 1918: concentrating solely on a "harmonious whole" to the exclusion of "intermediate parts," his vague idealism leaves him prone to being overwhelmed by the bushy "afflatus," hence, an "incapable master of all force," as God must often appear in a time of war, which is the social context of the poem (*CP,* 97–98). Stevens' attack on the mythology of transcendence here and in other poems that feature the more pronounced ritualization of death for the purposes of emotional de-escalation, such as "The Worms at Heaven's Gate" in 1916, "Cortège for Rosenbloom" in 1921, and "The Jack-Rabbit" in 1923, among others, aims to eliminate the "poverty of the accustomed," in Frank Kermode's fine phrase, along with all the varieties of divine presence in which it seems most invested.[3]

3. Samuel French Morse, *Wallace Stevens: Poetry as Life* (New York, 1970), xi–xii; Frank Kermode, "Dwelling Poetically in Connecticut," in *Wallace Stevens: A Celebration,* ed. Frank Doggett and Robert Buttel (Princeton, 1980), 266.

Stevens' mounting critique against transcendence in all its forms becomes pointed against Christian rituals as specifically outworn social and institutional practices in poems such as "Ploughing on Sunday," written in 1919, in which the Sabbath interdict is transgressed needlessly if we consider how wet the fields actually are (*CP*, 20), and "Cy Est Pourtraicte, Madame Ste Ursule, et Les Unze Mille Vierges," written in 1915, where God's refusal of a sincere offering of "radishes and flowers" is so scandalous that it cannot be "writ / In any book," except, of course, in Stevens' (*CP*, 22). His condemnation of such practices is the strongest aspect of the hypothetical elimination of belief in an orthodox Christian God in *Harmonium* and has thus become one of the three or four major rallying points in the canonical reading of his work.[4] This consensus would appear to shift the center of gravity in his first collection of verse to a praise for meaning that lies within earthly immanence, in contrast to spiritual transcendence. Stevens' attention, that is, becomes trained on those "mysterious callings of Nature" he writes of in the early letter cited previously (*L*, 58) or on the "real life" mentioned in an even earlier journal entry that, in contrast to the artifice of the sonnet form, shows "where things are quick, unaccountable, responsive" (*L*, 42). Later, Stevens might even include such things as sonnets in this shift, for what is important now is the direction in which belief is nurtured rather than the specific objects of belief themselves. To return to one of the "Adagia," it is the relation of art to life, not the reverse, that is important in the face of the absence of belief in God, for "the mind turns to its own creations and examines them, not alone from the aesthetic point of view, but for what they reveal, for what they validate and invalidate, for the support they give" (*OP*, 186). To the Stevens of *Harmonium*, the mind's creations are mainly revealing of a valid metaphorical archaeology in the human, in contrast to the divine.

In this new move in his first book, Stevens' poem "Theory," composed in 1917, comes directly to the point: "I am what is around me" (*CP*, 86). The new strategy is to collapse every distant relation of space and time into a here and now, a program that Stevens adapts to his search for belief from the

---

4. *Cf.* John J. Enck, *Wallace Stevens: Images and Judgments* (Carbondale, Ill., 1964), 77; Edward Kessler, *Images of Wallace Stevens* (New York, 1972), 109; Michel Benamou, *Wallace Stevens and the Symbolist Imagination* (Princeton, 1972), 72; Riddel, *The Clairvoyant Eye*, 115; Marie Borroff, "Introduction," in *Critical Essays*, ed. Borroff, 3, 8; Northrop Frye, *Fables of Identity: Studies in Poetic Mythology* (New York, 1963), 252; J. Hillis Miller, *Poets of Reality: Six Twentieth-Century Writers* (New York, 1965), 247; Roy Harvey Pearce, *The Continuity of American Poetry* (Princeton, 1961), 377.

Imagists.[5] Thus, "one is not duchess / A hundred yards from a carriage." Presence is here. And the images of black vestibule and high bed are temporary stations of that fact, "instances" merely. Presence is now. Presence is also "in the Carolinas," in a poem of the same name, also from 1917. As one mythology fades ("The lilacs wither"), a more local, more modern, more direct one comes into being:

> Timeless mother,
> How is it that your aspic nipples
> For once vent honey?
>
> (*CP*, 5)

Rather than separate body from soul or flesh from spirit, the play in Stevens' new motive for metaphor pursues the effects of alignment and incorporation in mythology that is now a *concordia discors:* "*The pine-tree sweetens my body / The white iris beautifies me.*" In the renovation of sense experience Stevens' new metaphors promise, the archetypal biblical outcast becomes the privileged "Nomad Exquisite," about whom he writes in the eponymous poem of 1919, the wanderer who cannot seem to catch hold of enough of nature's infinite variety, its palms and vines "angering for life," its blessed mornings flinging "forms, flames, and the flakes of flames" (*CP*, 95). Now, there seem to be anecdotes of men by the thousand (*CP*, 51), and Don Joost, whose misery is recorded in a 1921 poem, is miserable only because his body, "the old animal," in its decrepitude can know nothing more of the "powerful seasons," the sights and sounds, breedings and death incited by these "genii" of nature (*CP*, 46–47).

The shift to the emphasis on immanence in *Harmonium,* therefore, would tend to feature the motion and movement within life rather than the stasis of transcendence beyond it. This featuring consequently becomes another major gathering point in critical readings of Stevens' work. As James Baird puts it, "the sense of the world is the particular subject of Stevens only when it is seen as *process.*"[6] A standard for the new impetus of belief to be

---

5. *Cf.* Robert Buttel, *Wallace Stevens: The Making of "Harmonium"* (Princeton, 1967), 125ff.

6. James Baird, *The Dome and the Rock: Structure in the Poetry of Wallace Stevens* (Baltimore, 1968), xvii, 47. *Cf.* also Borroff, "Introduction" in *Critical Essays,* ed. Borroff, 16; George Bornstein, *Transformations of Romanticism in Yeats, Eliot, and Stevens* (Chicago, 1976), 184; Samuel French Morse, "Wallace Stevens, Bergson, Pater," in *The Act of the Mind: Essays on the Poetry of Wallace Stevens,* ed. Roy Harvey Pearce and J. Hillis Miller (Baltimore, 1965), 83; Miller, *Poets of Reality,* 231.

found in process is the short 1919 poem "Life Is Motion," particularly its remythologizing, which proceeds by way of marriage:

> In Oklahoma,
> Bonnie and Josie,
> Dressed in calico,
> Danced around a stump.
> They cried,
> "Ohoyaho,
> Ohoo" . . .
> Celebrating the
>   marriage
> Of flesh and air.
>   (*CP,* 83)

The process of motion is underscored in several of the poems in *Harmonium,* those that give prominence to the movements of water and wind—movements that are almost always gauged from some fixed point of reference, usually on land, as in the case of the stump in the previous poem. A spot of red, Stevens' preferred color for reality, allows us to trace the process. In "Hibiscus on the Sleeping Shores" from 1921, the mind, like a monster moth, leaves off drowsing along a rocky shore and, negotiating "the motion of the waves" of a lazy sea, seeks out the flaming red of the hibiscus, which is compared to a red flag waving above an old café (*CP,* 22–23). Similarly, the reader's eye is drawn, like the kildeer, to "the red turban / Of the boatman" in "The Load of Sugar-Cane," also from 1921, a perpetuum mobile that provides the focus in the poem for the flowing of water, the whistling of wind, and the "going" of the glade-boat itself (*CP,* 12). If the movement of art in *Harmonium* is all in the direction of life, human speech, or "vocalissimus" (*CP,* 113), ultimately finds a model for itself there, too, in "To the Roaring Wind," composed in 1917, which Stevens puts last in the collection. So does human thought, which changes its mind irrationally as "The Wind Shifts," in a poem also written in 1917: "like a human, heavy and heavy, / Who does not care" (*CP,* 84). Therefore "Indian River," from 1917 as well, also appears near the end of the book, reinforcing in its movement the jingling of water and tradewind, which is, not unexpectedly, "the same jingle of the red-bird" breasting the trees of the fixed boskage below it (*CP,* 112).

Stevens' first volume is thus very much on the move and in ways that are not necessarily restricted to a single focused image or scene in specific poems. The point of view can sometimes be multiplex to maintain the sense of flow in the metaphorization. As its title suggests, "Metaphors of a Magnifico" from 1918 magnifies the perspectives from which the prospect of twenty men crossing a bridge into a village can be taken: from a first-person viewpoint, one bridge and one village; from a collective perspective, twenty bridges and twenty villages; or from the vantage of a completely objective third-party observer, a bridge, a village, and boots and boards and fruit-trees besides (*CP*, 19). Because meaning will not declare itself categorically in any one of these views, inference throughout is kept in a state of flux, as indicated by the poem's closing set of ellipses. This constant changing is only to be expected in an immanent world where imagination is, in Michel Benamou's words, "the active principle which transforms and extends the object by multiplying resemblances." Stevens' most notorious example of multiple perspective is "Thirteen Ways of Looking at a Blackbird," composed in 1917, a true multiplex of thirteen precisely observed and accurately etched Imagist poems that, collectively, defy the totalizing efforts of the rational mind to freeze-frame the blackbird into a single, coherent interpretation or overriding central myth. Neither a certain cause, an "indecipherable cause" in Image VI, nor a determinable effect, a peripheral "shadow" on edge in Images VI, IX, and XI (*CP*, 92–95), the blackbird is comprehensible only in terms of movement (Images I, X, XII) and multiplicity (Image II), the predominating features that we saw in the last set of poems. Defying the thin men of Haddam's conventional Yeatsian "golden birds" (Image VII), Stevens' fowl beckons to the intelligence for some kind of rationalization nonetheless: "But I know, too, / That the blackbird is involved / In what I know" (*CP*, 94). Curiously, we find ourselves at the end of this poem in the position of the mathematically minded in the concluding panel of the final of Stevens' variation forms in *Harmonium*, "Six Significant Landscapes," written in 1916:[7]

> Rationalists, wearing square hats,
> Think, in square rooms,
> Looking at the floor,
>
> . . . .
>
> If they tried rhomboids,

7. Benamou, *Symbolist Imagination*, 11; Northrop Frye, *Spiritus Mundi: Essays on Literature, Myth, and Society* (Bloomington, 1976), 275–94, for Stevens' "variation-forms."

Cones, waving lines, ellipses—
As, for example, the ellipse of the half-moon—
Rationalists would wear sombreros.

(*CP,* 75)

Obviously, some significant alteration in outlook is going to be required to overcome the conflict in vision that this new poem achieves with
its first three sections devoted to motion and its second three to stasis. Thirteen *ways* of looking at a blackbird provoke a similar crisis, and our calling
poetry a sort of inspired mathematics, as Ezra Pound once did, is only going
to take us so far.[8] "A change of style is a change of subject," Stevens will later
say (*OP,* 197). We therefore need to begin reading Stevens' new poetry of
immanence with a coherent view to the unconventional demands that such
changes would make on us. But it is just such a clear set of directions for
reading Stevens' first, innovative work that *Harmonium,* frankly, fails to provide in the larger number of poems remaining to the book.

Wallace Stevens' transition from a poetry of transcendence to a poetry of
immanence, an effort to relocate what is termed "the virtue of the commonplace" or orthodox learning under "bishops' rods" in the 1918 "Lettres d'un
Soldat" (*OP,* 30), is a highly ambiguous and never completely consistent one
in his first published work. In the shift to "introspective chaos" that it appears
to have marked, several poems in the volume, in contrast to the group we
previously dealt with, register the randomness of motion and movement in
the outside world as utterly threatening. Another of Stevens' early journal
entries provides us with a sense of the poet's ambiguous feelings about external nature:

> I thought, on the train, how utterly we have forsaken the Earth,
> in the sense of excluding it from our thoughts. There are but a
> few who consider its physical hugeness, its rough enormity. It is
> still a disparate monstrosity, full of solitudes + barrens + wilds.
> It still dwarfs + terrifies + crushes. The rivers still roar, the
> mountains still crash, the winds still shatter. Man is an affair of
> cities. His gardens + orchards + fields are mere scrapings. Some-
> how, however, he has managed to shut out the face of the giant
> from his windows. But the giant is there, nevertheless. And it is a

8. Ezra Pound, *The Spirit of Romance* (London, 1952), 14.

proper question, whether or not the Lilliputians have tied him down. There are his huge legs, Africa + South America, still, apparently, free; and the rest of him is pretty tough and unhandy. (*L,* 73)

In "The Plot Against the Giant," written in 1917, reality as some monstrous force beyond man's control, a maundering yokel "whetting his hacker" (*CP,* 6), is rendered precisely according to this description. Dwarfed by this gigantic presentiment, three little girls (the association of the second with small fish eggs suggests the contrast), in their own civilized ways, attempt the next-to-impossible when they collectively try to "check him . . . abash him . . . undo him." Perhaps it is the third's "heavenly labials [whispered] in a world of gutturals," as against the first girl's "civilest odors" or the second's "arching cloths," that holds the greatest promise of beguilement, recalling the "vocalissimus" of a previous poem that theoretically establishes the bond between man and nature. The poem, however, leaves the reader uncertain as to the confrontation's outcome.

Shutting out the face of a gigantic nature from one's windows is unfortunately what the speaker in "Domination of Black" is incapable of doing, the external threat in this poem stalking its firelit interiors in the form of descending night:

> Out of the window,
> I saw how the planets gathered
> Like the leaves themselves
> Turning in the wind.
> I saw how the night came,
> Came striding like the color of the heavy hemlocks
> I felt afraid.
> And I remembered the cry of the peacocks.
>
> (*CP,* 9)

Night is particularly daunting in this passage because of the associations its own movement has with a host of other "turnings" in the poem—turnings of leaves, flames, colors, hemlock boughs, and peacock tails, not to mention those of the earth and planets on the much larger plane. The wind, whose motions formerly constituted a source of praise in *Harmonium,* now by this poem's testimony appears to constitute a motive for panic, symbolized by "the cry of the peacocks" (*CP,* 8). This paralyzing fear, moreover, is considerably enlarged by the misery in the sound of the wind that we find in Stevens' much praised "The Snow Man" from 1921, which he places immediately following "Domination of Black": "The sound of the land / Full of the same wind / That is blowing in the same bare place" (*CP*, 10). Linked to a barren, winter landscape of pine trees shagged with ice and snow, the unrelenting sound and movement of the wind here, in contrast to earlier poems, for the first time begins to suggest how utterly bereft a world demythologized to the point of purposeless chaos actually is. Thus, "nothing" in the poem's final stanza—the "nothing that is not there"—is the downside of immanence: "The nothing that is." If located in nothing, the listener must inevitably be reduced to nothing, a confounding of the previous marriage of flesh and air, since "the world is myself" and "life is myself" (*OP*, 198). Readers of the poem who argue for Stevens' celebration of "nothing" at its conclusion, if we consider his animadversions against transcendence rehearsed earlier, would appear to lack sufficient knowledge of the context of other aspects of Stevens' early work to understand that there may at least be a minimum of ambiguity at play in his use of this resonant word.[9] The "no" buried within the "snow" of its title, thus giving us "no man," which is often pointed out by commentators, ought at least to be a clue.

Eventually, the withdrawal into some enclosed, sheltered space in several of the poems becomes a kind of strategic defense against the unpredictability lodged within an immanent world. The "dweller in the dark cabin" in the 1922 "Hymn from a Watermelon Pavilion," for instance, deliberately chooses retreat as a kind of wish-fulfillment dream.[10] From the darkness of

9. *E.g.*, Paul A. Bové, *Destructive Poetics: Heidegger and Modern Poetry* (New York, 1980), 190–92.

10. The continuous brief that Stevens mounts throughout his poetry against the solipsistic retreat into dark and enclosed domestic space might be thought to begin here, though the problematic is as old as Emerson, who writes, for instance, in his essay on Plato: "The experience of poetic creativeness . . . is not found in staying at home, nor yet in travelling, but in transitions from one to the other, which must therefore be adroitly managed to present as much transitional surface as possible" (Evan Carton, *The Rhetoric of American Romance: Dialectic and Identity in Emerson, Dickinson, Poe, and Hawthorne* [Baltimore, 1985], 20). In the context of literary modernism, and more especially in the context of belief, the problematic ideally articulates a certain "transcendental homelessness" as Marianna Torgovnick has recently argued (following Georg Lukács) in *Gone Primitive: Savage Intellects, Modern Lives* (Chicago, 1990), 188–90. But as Stevens' rhetoric shifts to the more postmodern register that we begin to notice in the next chapter, it is conceivable to link his homely critique of panicked patriarchs to a quite pronounced motive in current feminist discourse that requires, as Teresa de Lauretis notes in "Eccentric Subjects: Feminist Theory and Historical Consciousness," *Feminist Studies*, XVI, no. 1 (1990), "leaving or giving up a place that is safe, that is 'home'—physically, emotionally, linguistically, epistemologi-

that sleep, he can manage to keep obscure the by-now familiar signs of natural process (red-feathered cock, spread-tailed blackbird, sparkling sun) and thereby assure himself that in his seclusion beyond all revelries "the watermelon is *always* purple" (*CP*, 88, emphasis added). Unfortunately, the main character of "The Man Whose Pharynx Was Bad," written in 1921, cannot be quite so self-regarding. He is much too realistic to escape completely what a world in process must ultimately come to in all these poems: "The malady of the quotidian" (*CP*, 96). Ideally, summer and winter ought at last to come to rest. Some ocean obsidian or final slate ought to mark the terminal point of their endlessly repetitive natural cycle, whose routine translates into the voiceless ennui of "being pent," as the title of the poem emphasizes. At that exact point, perhaps some permanent sense, some "neater mould," might be plucked from real life; "but time will not relent":

> The wind attendant on the solstices
> Blows on the shutters of the metropoles,
> Stirring no poet in his sleep, and tolls
> The grand ideas of the villages.
>
> (*CP*, 96)

Pushed far enough, therefore, the sleeping poet and the cabin dweller willfully anesthetized to time's relentlessness are likely to become something like "The Bird with the Coppery Keen Claws" from 1921. This poem is Stevens' version of a life lived at about as maximum a distance from earthly interaction as it can possibly get without entirely annihilating itself, though the image of the parakeet as a "pip of life amid a mort of tails" comes very close (*CP*, 82). The portrait is a perfection of haughty silence and brooding stillness, reserving only the slightest glimmer of animation to a flare of feathers and a tiny drop of water that almost seems to crash from their tip. The parakeet's blindness, moreover, is the ultimate sleep that the cabin dweller only partially achieves and that the voiceless poet, so long past a natural "vocalissimus," can only long for. As his pure intellect applies its laws without the slightest hint of motion, the parakeet of parakeets, with all its "green-vented forms"

---

cally—for another place that is unknown and risky . . . from which speaking and thinking are at best tentative, uncertain, unguaranteed" (138). *Cf.* also Biddy Martin and Chandra Talpade Mohanty, "Feminist Politics: What's Home Got to Do with It?," in *Feminist Studies / Critical Studies,* ed. Teresa de Lauretis (Bloomington, 1986), 191–212, and further, Sandra M. Gilbert and Susan Gubar, *Sexchanges* (New Haven, 1989), 66, 156, 167, Vol. II of Gilbert and Gubar, *No Man's Land: The Place of the Woman Writer in the Twentieth Century,* 3 vols. projected.

(*CP,* 82), becomes that "neater mould" that all of Stevens' hermits would perhaps surrender their own lives for: a metaphysical form of forms itself, a "perfect cock" totally devoid of physical content, an emblem of the very "dry shell" he munches while invisibly exerting his will. In Stevens' pun on "par aclete," then, the coppery keen bird is a kind of secular Holy Ghost or Comforter to those in retreat from the malady of the quotidian. Except for (or maybe because of) the claws, he appears almost the very likeness of Stephen Dedalus' mysterious God of Creation, who "remains within or behind or above his handiwork, invisible, refined out of existence, indifferent, paring his fingernails."[11] If "Life Is Motion," then it must surely be the nightmare, to paraphrase Dedalus, from which all of Stevens' own tormented metaphysicians are desperately trying to awaken, as the pervasiveness of sleep imagery throughout many of these poems would seem to corroborate.[12]

A passage in Stevens' later prose significantly connected to a mention of James Joyce's *A Portrait of the Artist as a Young Man* states that "the great poems of heaven and hell have been written and the great poem of the earth remains to be written" (*NA,* 142). The assertion has licensed the view among a great many critics that Stevens' general approach to the external world is to remythologize it as a kind of earthly paradise, on the additional authority of some of the poetry in which are found lines such as "And shall the earth / Seem all of paradise that we shall know?" (*CP,* 68) and "The imperfect is our paradise" (*CP,* 194).[13] As several of the preceding poems have shown, however, the view that Stevens, like William Morris, locates renewed belief in some kind of heaven on earth is a highly problematic one, if *Harmonium* is any indication. In fact, we may begin to wonder whether Stevens finds immanent belief as tenable a proposition as a faith in transcendence was questionable. Not only are the movements of nature somewhat threatening, many of these poems tell us, but their regularization within cyclic process is a downright imposition.

The malady of the quotidian manifested as a curtailment of earthly belief in *Harmonium*'s Florida poems in this regard is exemplary. In the 1922 "O Florida, Venereal Soil," the malady is referred to as the "dreadful sundry of this world" and suffers comparison with a diseased lover, "tor-

11. James Joyce, *A Portrait of the Artist as a Young Man* (Harmondsworth, Eng., 1966), 214–15.

12. *Cf.* Frank Doggett, *Stevens' Poetry of Thought* (Baltimore, 1966), 168, 162–63.

13. See Morris, *Imagination and Faith,* 176; Doggett, *Poetry of Thought,* 30; Frye, *Fables of Identity,* 245; Kessler, *Images of Wallace Stevens,* 18; Berger, *Forms of Farewell,* 11; Benamou, *Symbolist Imagination,* 38; Enck, *Images and Judgments,* 126, 140.

menting, / Insatiable" (*CP*, 48), in addition to the usual associations with mobility ("Lasciviously as the wind") and multiplicity (Cuban, Mexican, and other sundry nationalities). "Venereal" in the title quite correctly suggests to A. Walton Litz the "infection of desire," and in the fourth stanza a kind of bizarre quarantine is invoked for Nature—a quarantine that predictably eventuates in a solitary stillness high above the moving sea.[14] From there, the dreadful sundryness will be concealed or will at least "disclose / Fewest things." But its connection to darkness and shade sustains the perennial sense of threat nonetheless. As "Fabliau of Florida," written in 1919, puts it, "There will never be an end / To this droning of the surf" (*CP*, 23). Hence, the phosphorescent barque in that poem moves outward into an alabaster heaven, where "foam and cloud are one." Alternatively, in "Floral Decoration for Bananas," composed in 1922, the affecting of a more decent, eighteenth-century style will check and abash the insolent, blunt-yellow plainness of a bunch of bananas, obviously the work of an ogre, whom we remember from "The Plot Against the Giant." In this poem he has "his eye on an outdoor gloom / And a stiff and noxious place" (*CP*, 54). There is something almost genital in the malady here ("Oozing cantankerous gum / Out of their purple maws, / Darting out of their purple craws / Their musky and tingling tongues"), and another of Stevens' clean, well-lighted places will attempt to adapt these hurricane shapes to something a good deal—"Good God!"—*less* natural. "Pettifogging" seems almost the perfect word for the decorum chosen. "Of the Surface of Things" from 1919, a rather shrewd paraphrase of "Floral Decoration" with the wordplay on "yellow air," is more to the point: the singer has pulled his cloak over his head because, in his words, "In my room, the world is beyond my understanding" (*CP*, 57). Not that it has to be. But writing hack poetry from a balcony, as described in the poem, seems a far less unsettling task than having to deal with three or four hills down below in the real world. And perhaps a cloud as well. The gesture with the cloak is repeated with a stovepipe hat and shawl in the 1921 "Doctor of Geneva," whose main character perhaps understands more the banal import of "long-rolling opulent cataracts" of a "wild and ruinous waste" (*CP*, 24) in his remove from Lake Geneva to the Pacific Ocean.

If we think, therefore, that Wallace Stevens manages to resolve the conflict in *Harmonium* between immanent and transcendent belief in "Sunday Morning," written in 1915, the most widely read and interpreted poem in the

---

14. A. Walton Litz, *Introspective Voyager: The Poetic Development of Wallace Stevens* (New York, 1972), 115.

volume, we would do well to recall the insistent refrain of "Gubbinal," written six years later in 1921, through five separate attempts to transcribe the natural sun metaphorically: "The world is ugly, / And the people are sad" (*CP*, 85).[15] Nonetheless, no other poem is quite so insistent as "Sunday Morning" on overturning the Christian ethos centered in the Passion of Jesus, the "encroachment of that old catastrophe" mentioned in the opening section (*CP*, 67). If faith is to be at all viable in the modern era, it must recognize a divinity within the lady of the poem herself, as the second section argues, that is, within the quotidian of "pungent fruit and bright, green wings" or of "any balm or beauty of the earth," but a quotidian that may also be a malady: "All pleasures and all pains, remembering / The bough of summer and the winter branch" (*CP*, 67). Substituting human passions, then, for Christological Passion, the poem's familiar statement of a secular paradise promises to mend orthodoxy's institutional rift between flesh and air reviewed earlier, respecting the later remark in Stevens' "Adagia" that "God is in me or else is not at all (does not exist)" (*OP*, 198):

> Shall our blood fail? Or shall it come to be
> The blood of paradise? And shall the earth
> Seem all of paradise that we shall know?
> The sky will be much friendlier then than now,
> A part of labor and a part of pain,
> And next in glory to enduring love,
> Not this dividing and indifferent blue.
>
> (*CP*, 68)

By the end of the first half, therefore, the poem argues itself into the rejection of all transcendent myths, the traditional haunts of sacred vision for aeons, and rests its claim for immanence in "the consummation of swallow's wings" and, rather more ominously, in an enduring "April's green" that sounds curiously like an anesthetic shade of green we encounter in the Marvellian "Banal Sojourn" (*CP*, 62) four years later.

The question that the lady puts to herself at the beginning of section five, and in fact for the remainder of the poem—the question of why she nevertheless must *still* feel the need of some imperishable bliss—might perhaps indicate that she knows something of the malady of that sojourn as we have already come to know it in several of the previous poems. Their central insight has often tended to be that death is at the very center of that sojourn.

15. *Cf.* Morse, *Poetry as Life*, 55.

So here, if "Death is the mother of beauty" (*CP,* 68), surely the imperishable bliss that belies secular contentment is pointed in the only direction in which it seems possible for beauty to hold some quarter against the physical blather of nature's dreadful sundry: the direction of the meta-physical. Gradually, then, the perspective of "Sunday Morning" begins to reverse itself in the second half, arguing now, in a not-unfamiliar way, that immanence, in the manner of death, is the mother of transcendence. It is she, in section five, who "causes boys to pile new plums and pears / On disregarded plate" (*CP,* 69), just as a venereal "Donna, donna dark" (*CP,* 48) had necessitated the pettifoggery of an "eighteenth-century dish" to refine the lascivious bananas (*CP,* 54). In section six, it is she who colors and spices the paradise wherever such paradise is mythically rationalized, since it is the "burning bosom" always attendant on the inarticulable end of human fulfillment that constitutes her motive, regardless of how the means to achieve that end are defined. Hanging boughs heavy with fruit in a perfect sky would not make sense otherwise, as the "Cold Pastoral" of John Keats's thought-teasing urn obviously invoked here substantiates. Thus, as secular an image as the orgiastic ring of naked chanting men in section seven is, their "boisterous devotion" (*CP,* 70), even though it includes lakes and trees and hills, is nonetheless intended to carry them "out of their blood," as the poem states, to some whence and whither that may manifest itself in dew but that ultimately eventuates in a transcendence, in their "returning to the sky" all the same.

The "wide water" in the final, eighth section carries us back to the lady's dreaming of Palestine at the start of the poem. It is clear, though, that the dream is one that she cannot now be so entirely complacent about. Reluctant still to attach any more spiritual significance to the tomb of Jesus than might be contained in the mundane word *grave,* she nonetheless acknowledges that however we may define our old chaos of the sun, there is a certain dependency of night on day (flesh on spirit, immanence on transcendence) making that wide water ineluctably "inescapable" (*CP,* 70). The sky, which by a former process of thinking ought to have been made friendlier, curiously ends up in a haunting "isolation" once again, and the green freedom of the cockatoo earlier is replaced by real mountain-stalking deer and real whistling quail that would appear to feel the pull of a power quite separate from the mere physical force of gravity. Even the pigeons, obviously the parodic displacements of the Johannine sacred dove, make "ambiguous undulations" as they descend on extended wings to earth's spiritual darkness below in the poem's famous final line. Yet that darkness is the most curious reversal of all. Before, it had marked the old encroachment of the Crucifixion in the opening section of the poem. Now, darkness is a kind of prevenient condition that is sought in some earnest. By closing "Sunday Morning" on this note of circular restatement, Stevens makes the earlier negation, ironically, become a kind of affirmation that would suggest anything but the dissipation of the holy hush. Like the pigeons, therefore, the question of belief for him is still left very much up in the air at the end of this long and very moving spiritual disquisition.

Having come this far, we may be tempted to the view that the program Wallace Stevens had really set for himself in *Harmonium* was one of "immanent transcendence," a synthesis of the best of both worlds, physical and metaphysical.[16] There are, however, several problems with this position. In the first place, as I argued much earlier, Stevens never really does leave the reader of his first volume with any single and consistent set of principles with which to take in the complete work. Poems tend to be arranged in nuclear clusters, some within the space of two or three pages of each other, others extended in groupings that might cover several leaves. To make the shift from one setting to another, and even these are never completely integrated thematically, requires some degree of mental dexterity in adjusting to the new metaphorical transpositions, if not a great deal of patience as well. A second problem with immanent transcendence is quite simply that several poems counter the critique lodged against transcendence we viewed earlier and rather boldly express a deep longing for it alone, regardless of the state of affairs in the natural world. Having just looked at "Sunday Morning," we can now perhaps understand why this might be so. "Explanation" from 1917, for instance, complains that there "is nothing of the ideal" in embroidering French flowers on an old black dress, that what one really wants is "romance," a total imaginative translation to some religious figuration, symbolized by an orange gown "drifting through space" (*CP,* 72–73). In the poem "Invective Against Swans," whose date of composition is unknown, the constant refrain is *beyond:* "beyond the parks," "beyond the discords of the wind" (*CP,* 4). One suspects that Yeats may not have taken transcendence far enough in "The Wild Swans at Coole," for in view of the death of the summer and the way the crows have come to dirty the parks' statues, it seems necessary to carry

16. This position is rather persuasively argued as a theme in Stevens' work as a whole by Mills, in "Wallace Stevens: The Image of the Rock," in *Critical Essays,* ed. Borroff, 99, as a possible link to the writing of Joyce and Yeats.

the soul even beyond the swans' "chilly chariots" already bequeathed to the moon, hence the source of the invective. A similar point is expressed in the need to recuperate classical mythological statements such as those of Sandro Botticelli, mangled by modernism, for example, in "The Paltry Nude Starts on a Spring Voyage" from 1919. Gone is Venus' famous shell, in its place "the first-found weed" and the quite banal "salty harbors" (*CP,* 5). Discontent with her paltry nakedness, Stevens' figure desires the royal purple of adornment and longs to touch the clouds and the "high interiors of the sea." The prediction of a more noumenous time, in place of the present meagerness, is made almost as a statement of aesthetic principle: "When the goldener nude / Of a later day / Will go, like the centre of sea-green pomp, / In an intenser calm . . . ceaselessly" (*CP,* 6).

What Stevens has in mind here we also find in the final section of "The Apostrophe to Vincentine" from the previous year, another poem figuring a nude "between / Monotonous earth and the dark blue sky" that aims to work against the namelessness of such a compromise:

> Monotonous earth I saw become
> Illimitable spheres of you,
> And that white animal, so lean,
> Turned Vincentine,
> Turned heavenly Vincentine,
> And that white animal, so lean,
> Turned heavenly, heavenly Vincentine.
>
> (*CP,* 53)

But before that time, belief must contend with the "Depression Before Spring," from the poem written in the same year. It should be clear why Stevens might want to keep his pigeons aloft at the end of "Le Monocle de Mon Oncle" (*CP,* 17) when an immanentist faith, like that exemplified in the postimpressionism and surrealism of the art world from about this period, would have, as in the parody of this poem, the inamorata's blonde hair likened to the spittle of cows! The aestheticist apocalypse heralded by the cock in the opening line has, by 1918, been a long time in the making. Stevens must have thought much of this faith misplaced when still, as at the start and finish of this text, "no queen rises" (*CP,* 63).[17]

17. Stevens notes in his "Materia Poetica": "The essential fault of surrealism is that it invents without discovering. To make a clam play an accordion is to invent not to discover. The observation of the unconscious, so far as it can be observed, should reveal things of which we

A final difficulty with the argument for an immanent transcendence in *Harmonium* is the difficulty it has in accurately registering what Harold Bloom quite correctly refers to as Wallace Stevens' "fear of his own capacity for solipsistic transport," which in its excess, unlike a Christian sensibility answerable to some external authorization, is always the unresolvable dilemma of a "poetry of earth" alone.[18] "A High-Toned Old Christian Woman," written in 1922, is usually taken to be a fairly broad satire of the doctrinaire Christian whose conscience latches on to some arbitrary "moral law" and builds a "haunted heaven" around it, tricked out with palms and windy hymns (*CP*, 59). What is often less noticed in the poem, however, is the equally biting satire it mounts against those disaffected flagellants who cling blindly to a faith in the opposing law: a supreme fiction projected beyond heaven and built around an unpurged bawdiness, garnering palms of a different sort. Yet as the poem is quite careful to note, "palm for palm," there cannot really be that much difference in the extremities indulged. The earthy devotees of the peristyle and masque can be just as self-righteously proud and vain, "well-stuffed, / Smacking their muzzy bellies in parade," as their more ascetic, wincing counterparts. Thus, "we are where we began." Sublime, fictive things may elicit a knowing wink at the uppity old Christian woman's expense, but from Stevens' point of view, there is a certain amount of winking, and wincing, that runs the other way, as well.

As the "jovial hullabaloo" of this last poem sinks in, we may start to realize that the poetry of earth licensing imaginative transport gradually begins to turn itself and the imagination over to something that has little to do with the earth at all. In Stevens' very popular "Anecdote of the Jar," composed in 1919, for instance, it takes only a second for a jar to be placed in Tennessee before it begins to force the slovenly wilderness to surround it just so, taking "dominion everywhere," as the poem states (*CP*, 76), and eventually driving the "wild" out of nature entirely, giving neither of bird nor bush. The solipsism that conspires to take hold in the poem, thanks to the portly

---

have previously been unconscious, not the familiar things of which we have been conscious plus imagination" (*OP*, 203). According to Robert Buttel, Stevens skirted surrealism "because he desired to accomplish more than presenting the unconscious . . . as a witty exercise indulged in for its superficial surprises" (*The Making of "Harmonium,"* 163 and, more generally, Chapter 6, 148ff.).

18. Harold Bloom, *Wallace Stevens: The Poems of Our Climate* (Ithaca, 1976), 52–53, 28, 47. *Cf.* also p. 109, in addition to a restatement of the problem in Marjorie Perloff's "Revolving in Crystal: The Supreme Fiction and the Impasse of Modernist Lyric," in *Wallace Stevens: The Poetics of Modernism,* ed. Albert Gelpi (New York, 1985), 55.

jar's rather gray and bare aesthetic imperialism, has nothing whatever to do with any kind of immanent transcendence, "Like nothing else in Tennessee," and, in fact, in licensing the "iconic poetics of stasis" as one of modernism's most unhappy excesses, becomes the very betrayal of that belief altogether.[19]

Where true belief arises, if it comes at all, is perhaps made clearer in "Tea at the Palaz of Hoon," which Stevens wrote in 1921, in which Hoon descends to consider the existential particularities that the previous poem appears to find so "jarring" (ointment, hymns, the sea) and *ends up* (one tends to want to stress the spatial metaphor here) in Stevens' most solipsistic and self-referential moment in the entire volume:

> Out of my mind the golden ointment rained,
> And my ears made the blowing hymns they heard.
> I was myself the compass of that sea:
>
> I was the world in which I walked, and what I saw
> Or heard or felt came not but from myself;
> And there I found myself more truly and more strange.
>
> (*CP,* 65)

By locating truth entirely in the mind, as this passage argues, Hoon reverses the perspective of "The Snow Man," written just before, and so manages to close the door on the infinite regress of a solipsistic realism. By the same token, he allows an even more untenable solipsistic idealism in through the window and acknowledges as much in the final words of the poem, "more strange." Now belief is unhinged even from any Christian sanction. It is consequently the source of much tear shedding in two further poems from roughly this period. Peering into this poisonous, dark abyss of selfhood, the character in "Another Weeping Woman," written right after "Tea at the Palaz of Hoon," discovers that imagination, the "magnificent cause of being," leaves nothing now for the human spirit to be moved by, and she feels pierced by a death (*CP,* 25). More self-critical is "The Weeping Burgher" from 1919, whose character chastises himself as a fop, a ghost, a veritable Scaramouche for the excesses that his heart and hands, "such sharp, imagined things" (*CP,* 61), have wrought. He is far more candid than Hoon could ever possibly be: "It is with a strange malice / That I distort the world." But the word *strange,* again, links the two together nonetheless.

Stevens attempted to resolve the whole question of belief definitively

---

19. William V. Spanos, *Repetitions: The Postmodern Occasion in Literature and Culture* (Baton Rouge, 1987), 35.

four years later with the writing of "The Comedian as the Letter C." For it is clear that if he was ever to clarify the relation of his art to belief in some ultimate presence, reviving the old problem of *adequatio intellectui ad rem* that reaches back, through Immanuel Kant and René Descartes, to the nominalist and realist scholastics of the medieval theologians and beyond, he would have to overcome the "crisis of representation" into which this problem issues in the so-called high modernist mode within which his initial writing was situated. This crisis of representation for modernism is formulated by Fredric Jameson, who describes it in terms of "an essentially realistic epistemology, which conceives of representation as the reproduction, for subjectivity, of an objectivity that lies outside it—projects a mirror theory of knowledge and art, whose fundamental evaluative categories are those of adequacy, accuracy, and Truth itself."[20] The crisis for Stevens is precipitated by solipsism, as we have seen; and in the later pieces in *Harmonium*, solipsism is a spurning-craving (*CP*, 88) problematic of the imagination that, for the most part, has exerted the greatest pressure on his early work to become what Gerald Bruns would call "transitive" discourse, a poetry that wants to make communicative contact with the real world rather than withdraw formally as a mere display of "intransitive" style.[21] We see Stevens greatly exercised over this problematic in the year leading up to the publication of *Harmonium*, what in "The Comedian" he refers to as a conundrum concerning man's "intelligence." We might begin to set the stage for viewing "The Comedian" by examining a few poems written around the time of its composition. In "The Ordinary Women" from 1922, for example, certain "insinuations of desire" (*CP*, 11) lead a group of females from their familiar monotony and poverty, represented by "dry catarrhs" outside a palace, into a highly stylized and severely overwrought inside, symbolized by the music of guitars, with which the catarrhs rhyme. Gradually the women are wearied by all the lacquered and diamond-pointed decorative excess, which in its own way becomes an-

20. Fredric Jameson, "Foreword," in Jean-François Lyotard, *The Postmodern Condition: A Report on Knowledge*, trans. Geoff Bennington and Brian Massumi (Minneapolis, 1984), viii.

21. Gerald L. Bruns, *Modern Poetry and the Idea of Language* (New Haven, 1974), 71–72. Bruns's useful categories are very much influenced by Roland Barthes in *Writing Degree Zero* (1970) and, in particular, by Barthes' distinction between "authoring" and "writing" (273nn74, 96), which elsewhere in Bruns become the Orphic and Hermetic modes of meaning, respectively (see esp. Part 3 and Conclusion). The distinction is a commonplace, particularly in contemporary critical discourse: for instance, between "expression" and "expressiveness" in Susanne K. Langer, *Philosophy in a New Key: A Study in the Symbolism of Reason, Rite, and Art* (Cambridge, Mass., 1957), 240; between "mimesis" and "poiesis" in Mark C. Taylor, *Erring: A Postmodern A/Theology* (Chicago, 1984), 84; and between the "descriptive" and the "literary" in Northrop Frye, *Anatomy of Criticism: Four Essays* (New York, 1957), 74–75.

other kind of "poverty" (*CP*, 12), and are seen flitting past the palace walls again at the end of the poem. Stevens' choice of highly mannered, as opposed to simpler, diction in the text conveys rather effectively the separation of his poetic style between the transitive and intransitive agendas that divide his imagination as it becomes projected in the backward and forward movement of the women: "The moonlight / Fubbed the girandoles" in the initial retreat, and "The moonlight / Rose on the beachy floors" in the later return, for example (*CP*, 11).

We sense a similar division between the imagination's intransitive "making" and its transitive "matching" in "The Emperor of Ice-Cream," composed in 1922.[22] The poem is a rambunctious wake. And just as on such occasions we sense a tension between the fiction of ceremony and the fact of death, so the poem exploits that contrariety between, for instance, the winding sheet embroidered with fantails that covers the corpse, and the face and "horny feet" of the corpse (*CP*, 64) that dumbly insist on remaining exposed. While one strain of Stevens' discourse signifies formally (emperor, *c*oncupiscent *c*urds, *d*resser of *d*eal), another strain applies pressure mimetically (wenches, last month's newspapers, ice-cream). Ultimately, the lamp of realism must affix its beam, and the referential motive of imagination wins out over the expressive, as the being of life gains the victory over the seeming of art in the delightful closure of Stevens' cadence: "Let be be finale of seem. / The only emperor is the emperor of ice-cream" (*CP*, 64).

Again from 1922, "Bantams in Pine-Woods" plays with a parallel polarization between an extremely baroque "Chieftain Iffucan of Azcan" (in caftan, no less) and a feisty Appalachian "inchling" as bristling pine spokesman (*CP*, 75–76). In the fifth of ten lines, the minimalist of the imagination would appear to give out that the confrontation with maximalist ("Fat! Fat! Fat! Fat!") is relatively evenly matched: "Your world is you," he states, not giving an inch. "I am my world." But it is clear that Stevens' deployment of internal rhymes and syncopated meters, along with clever consonance, onomatopoeia, and puns throughout the poem, have all, this time, scored the victory for the Palace of Art and that the very last word ("hoos") does give Hoon the last word. In sum, creating fictions might be the essential gift of the human mind, as Harold Bloom observes, but believing them is obviously its curse.[23] Stevens may have marked a first major creative achievement in pub-

---

22. E. H. Gombrich, *Art and Illusion: A Study in the Psychology of Pictorial Representation* (Princeton, 1961), 116.

23. This remark is offered in Susan B. Weston, *Wallace Stevens: An Introduction to the Poetry* (New York, 1977), 5. From the perspective of a chastening reality, *cf.* Georges Bataille,

lishing *Harmonium* in 1923, yet it is also true that he had written himself into a state of psychic impasse. It is "The Comedian as the Letter C" that provides us the most accurate profile of that less auspicious milestone in Wallace Stevens' early writing career, to which we now turn.

The year 1923 was an auspicious one for psychiatry as well. At that time, Sigmund Freud offered to the world *The Ego and the Id,* his formulation of the so-called second topography worked up from his earlier *Introductory Lectures on Psycho-Analysis,* written in 1916 and 1917, and *Beyond the Pleasure Principle,* authored in 1920. For the remainder of the decade, Freud's productivity would be extraordinary, as he published a number of volumes, including his study *Inhibitions* and the later *Civilization and Its Discontents,* to mention only two of his outstanding accomplishments. With Wallace Stevens, we are somewhat baffled by approximately six years of vexed silence following the trade printing of *Harmonium.* Stevens was never an avid reader of Freud. In response to a *New Verse* questionnaire on matters generally poetic, he indicates that he had read only Freud's *Interpretation of Dreams* (*OP,* 307), though it is Freud's *The Future of an Illusion* that is recorded in Stevens' library.[24] Yet it is a curious paradox that even though he wrote he would "probably not be able to stand up to Freudian analysis" (*L,* 488), nonetheless Freud's psychoanalytic theorizing helps most to fathom Stevens' several years of publishing silence. The usefulness here of Freud's "mechanics of interpretation," grounded, as

---

Inner Experience, trans. Leslie Anne Boldt (New York, 1988): "It is difficult to say to what extent belief is an obstacle to experience, to what extent the intensity of the experience overturns this obstacle" (104). These remarks would seem to suggest that Stevens was damned both ways, that imagination itself could be a kind of death wish:

> The love that will not be transported
> In an old, frizzled, flambeaued manner,
> But muses on its eccentricity,
>
> Is like a vivid apprehension
>
> . . . .
> Of bliss submerged beneath appearance,
> In an interior ocean's rocking.
>   (*CP,* 79)

24. Peter Brazeau, "Wallace Stevens at the University of Massachusetts: Check List of an Archive," *Wallace Stevens Journal,* II (Spring, 1978), 50–54. Stevens' dismissive attitude toward Freud in his letters may be further sampled in communications to Ronald Lane Latimer (January 10, 1936) and Harry Duncan (February 23, 1945), which carries over into some of the prose of *The Necessary Angel* (*NA,* 14–15, 139–40).

Jean Baudrillard notes, in "all the characteristics of objectivity and coherence," presents a quite specific analogue to the logocentric models of belief in conflict throughout *Harmonium*.[25] Such a reading is most particularly invited by the longest piece included in *Harmonium*, "The Comedian as the Letter C," composed in 1922. One thinks, in particular, of an important passage in the penultimate section that engages both the therapist's preoccupation with sleep and the poet's with silence. The setting is one of Stevens' self-enclosed rooms once again:

> So deep a sound fell down
> It was as if the solitude concealed
> And covered him and his congenial sleep.
> So deep a sound fell down it grew to be
> A long soothsaying silence down and down.
> The crickets beat their tambours in the wind,
> Marching a motionless march, custodians.
>
> (*CP*, 42)

What helpful insights, then, might a psychoanalytic view of the poem shed on the great enigma of Stevens' early career?

Paul Ricoeur's massive study of Freud points out at an important juncture a significant structural analogy between a patient's dream work and a writer's artistic work that Freud enunciates in his writings on aesthetics. Specifically, Ricoeur draws attention to the analogy Freud outlined between dreams and poetry in the life of unsatisfied man and also to the "resistances" the psychiatrist showed unhappy man had to overcome in order to interpret both of these. According to Freud, "A dream is a (disguised) fulfillment of a (suppressed or repressed) wish." Further, the so-called resistances are likely to occur where the psyche experiences the greatest amount of dissatisfaction, usually at the point of threatening contact between the aforementioned wish (or drive) and the process of rational socialization that the psyche experiences as an ego. As we know, it is ego censorship that most clearly defines this point of contact, and the labor of repression undertaken by this censorship consequently produces all those "compromise formations," dreams in the therapeutic context and poems in the artistic, that are all cleverly contrived to

25. Jean Baudrillard, "On Seduction," in *Selected Writings*, ed. Mark Poster (Stanford, 1988), 152. Freud's utility for a complete reading of Stevens' work is outlived once these models drop away, however, at which point a more "seductive version of psychoanalysis" following Lacan (Baudrillard, *Selected Writings*, 153) offers itself, as we shall see in subsequent chapters.

sneak past ego censorship. Freud's famous "repetition compulsion," which is more clearly a signal of a return to repression, shows how qualified a success these compromises actually are. Freud's theory is complicated, and we are fortunate to have a shorthand version of it in his favorite Oedipus myth, in which the illicit unconscious desire is connected to the mother, the wakeful conscious reason to the father, and the compromise formation manifested in Oedipus' unhappy sacrifice of mother love to male authority and dominance at the threat of castration, which would be the exercise, again, of repressive censorship.[26]

Taking a step back, we perhaps might see that there are two significant relations staked out by the Oedipal triangle in Freud's "family romance" above: an active one, in the psyche's instinctive pursuit of the mother; and a passive one, in its mindful capitulation to the father. When we turn from the purely theoretical statement of psychoanalysis to Stevens' "Comedian," we notice a simple structural analogy, as Ricoeur would say, in precisely the same active-passive dynamic that Stevens has constructed for his own "insatiable egotist" (*CP*, 30). In the poem, this analogy is exploited in his conception of the writer's imagination, or "intelligence" (*CP*, 27, 36).

As the discussion of the issue of solipsism previously in this chapter bears out, Stevens was of two minds concerning the imagination.[27] Of all the characters we have seen thus far, surely no other of Stevens' creation conveys this double-mindedness more than Crispin, the central figure in "The Comedian as the Letter C." Because "Poetry is the statement of a relation between a man and the world" and because "Poetry constantly requires a new relation," as two of the "Adagia" would have it, Crispin's whole journey throughout "The Comedian" is motivated by the desire to forgo a *passive* relation to the world ("Nota: man is the intelligence of his soil" [*CP*, 27]) and enact a more *active* one ("Nota: his soil is man's intelligence" [*CP*, 36]). The "snug hibernal" and the "bland complaisance" of "stale lives" (*CP*, 28–30) rather reminiscent of "Sunday Morning" must therefore be exchanged for "the droll confect" and "rebellious thought" of the Carolinas, by way of the refreshment of flourishing tropics in Yucatan (and Havana [*CP*, 40, 35]). As Stevens would write some years later to Thomas McGreevy, "One grows

26. Paul Ricoeur, *Freud and Philosophy: An Essay on Interpretation,* trans. Denis Savage (New Haven, 1970), 165–66; Sigmund Freud, *The Standard Edition of the Complete Psychological Works,* trans. James Strachey (London, 1953–74), IV, 160, XIV, 147–48, XVII, 238, and *cf.* also V, Sec. v.

27. Morse, *Poetry as Life,* 59; Vendler, *On Extended Wings,* 42.

tired of being oneself and feels the need of renewing all one's thoughts and ways of thinking . . . [for the imagination] is not likely to be satisfied with the same thing twice" (*L*, 680). And poetry, we recall from earlier, has to be a revelation of nature. Crispin's general movement in the poem, then, from land to sea, or otherwise from sun to moon, summer to winter, poetry to prose, or romance to realism, ought perhaps to be thought of not so much in terms of a shift between the vexed matrices of imagination and reality, foregrounded in *The Necessary Angel,* as the canonical reading of the poem so often invites.[28] Instead, it ought to be considered more in terms of the alternation of imagination under the impress of Freud's Oedipal differential, that is to say, between "active force" and "inactive dirge," as the poem itself insists (*CP,* 41), thus sustaining the problematic of the imagination that we spurn and crave in "To the One of Fictive Music," for example (*CP,* 88).

In its broadest sense, the saga of Crispin's voyage is a rigorous study in imaginative defamiliarization, the "word split up," as the poem puts it (*CP,* 28). What is at stake in the kind of "inverted egotism" required to make a new intelligence prevail (*CP,* 37) is given rather late, however, in the hint of an actual program in section four, "The Idea of a Colony":

> The florist asking aid from cabbages,
> The rich man going bare, the paladin
> Afraid, the blind man as astronomer,
> The appointed power unwielded from disdain.
>
> (*CP,* 37)

Such riddling paradoxes are the torment of "fastidious [*i.e.,* actively imaginative] thought" indeed, especially when placed beside the pine spokesmen of an already pine-wooded Georgia or beside the solemn señors who would insist on making their intricate Sierra scan, both later on in this section. Here, Freud enters the poem in a very useful way to explain this rather complacent belatedness. For it is Crispin's wishful dream, his "wakefulness or meditating sleep" (*CP,* 33), to seek a more active and responsible relation to his world, in contrast to the previously established idealist, perhaps even transcendentalist, cognitive predisposition. Moreover, it is in this sense that defamiliarization in the poem actually constitutes defamilialization. We notice this emphasis particularly in how Crispin must forsake the fatherland, a stale Europe

---

28. Riddel, *The Clairvoyant Eye,* 98, 96; Joseph Carroll, *A New Romanticism,* 59–61; Hi Simons, "The Genre of Wallace Stevens," in *Critical Essays,* ed. Borroff, 43–53.

of etiolated art and culture (hence the pun on Bordeaux as bored), in preference to a desire for the energetic conquest of a more exciting virgin land, rendered incestuously in terms of the mother: "gold's maternal warmth" (*CP*, 32). Harold Bloom is accurate, then, in viewing this work as "a poem 'about' the anxiety of influence."[29] Yet more needs to be said specifically about the forms this anxiety takes within the text itself and the kinds of repression that follow from it both in the life of Crispin and, risking the biographical fallacy, in Stevens' life.

On the analogy of Oedipal defamilialization ensuing from the conflict between the active-mother and the passive-father relations, it may be said that Crispin's anxiety takes three significant forms, each dealing with an important loss. The first of these is the anxiety of identity. The son who suddenly exchanges his role of passive child for the role of impulsive lover of the mother in the Oedipal triangle finds himself, like Crispin, very much "at sea," dissolved, annulled, "washed away by magnitude" (*CP*, 27, 28). The loss of identity represents a major crisis for Crispin, for what it involves is not the happy prospect of constructing a "mythology of self" while Triton and Vulcan fade but the circumstance of having one erased, "blotched out beyond unblotching" (*CP*, 28), an important qualifying phrase lost in so many readings of the poem (*L*, 788). Herein lies the key to the general ambiguity of Crispin's characterization. As a barber of old, is Crispin a surgeon or merely a cosmetician? Is he the "lutanist of fleas" or merely the "auditor of insects" (*CP*, 28, 31), is he asleep or only "halfway waking" (*CP*, 31), or, as a related poem more directly focused on defamiliarization puts it, is he "Crispin-valet" or "Crispin-saint" (*OP*, 43)?

Central to the question of Crispin's identity is his own masculinity, so that this first anxiety of loss quickly modulates into a second, an anxiety about castration. The transgression of relations in the family romance is focused on the father's threat and the child's mortal fear of castration, a situation that Freud takes up most explicitly in his essay "The Uncanny," linking the complex particularly to sleep and the loss of sight in E. T. A. Hoffmann's story about the Sandman tearing out children's eyes.[30] Yet is there not an analogy here to Crispin's own potentially transgressive imagination? The descriptions of what lies "beyond his baton's thrust" (*CP*, 28) and "across his vessel's prow" (*CP*, 35) in his uncanny voyaging are quite suggestively phallic but

29. Bloom, *Poems of Our Climate*, 72. See Morse, *Poetry as Life*, 89, for "inverted egoism."
30. Freud, "Das Unheimliche," in Freud, *The Standard Edition*, XVII, 217–56.

surely not vulgarly so. After all, the poem does end with an image of castration, the relation that is "clipped" (*CP*, 46), begin with "the Letter C," and exploit the Freudian dread several times in between: "stop short" (*CP*, 40), "sharply stopped" (*CP*, 44), "short-shanks" (*CP*, 28), and others. One of Stevens' most outrageous puns in the entire poem sums up precisely what Crispin risks if the analogy holds between the romances of defamiliarization and of defamilialization:

> Severance
> Was clear. The last distortion of romance
> Forsook the insatiable egotist. The sea
> Severs not only lands but also selves.
>
> (*CP*, 30)

Stevens' pun on the sea in this passage indicates how Crispin's third anxiety—the anxiety of repression and repetition-compulsion—is more self-reflexive than the others. It is actually Crispin, the comedian as the letter *C*, who severs, because in circumventing sedimented cultural and aesthetic practices, the "visible, circumspect presentment" (*CP*, 35), he in effect can find no way to engage an active relation to the world without incurring some loss to his very own imaginative power. This point of maximum fear, hence repression, Stevens identifies early in the poem: "His vicissitudes had much enlarged / His apprehension, made him intricate . . . and difficult and strange / In all desires" (*CP*, 31). We are reminded of Hoon and the weeping burgher in Crispin's "strange" repression of desire in this description. And Stevens deliberately makes the title of the poem, *C* for Crispin as well as for comedian, self-reflexive to underscore the point. This interpretation would also explain the image of the "sea-glass" in the poem's first section (*CP*, 28), which besides conveying the idea of the sea as a mirror in this context also suggests the idea of a telescope in which a comedian might peer and "be[hold] himself," a "C-glass" as it were. Ironically, Stevens in his letters speaks of the significance of "the Letter C" in his title only in terms of the effects he hopes it will have on the reader's ear (*L*, 294, 352, 778). But his exploiting a further pun on the word *see*, for instance in his careful deployment of eye-imagery throughout the poem—"An eye most apt," "a barber's eye" (*CP*, 27), "things within his actual eye" (*CP*, 40), and others—clearly shows that the poet has other, more thematic intentions: *e.g.*, "It made him see how much / Of what he saw he never saw at all" (*CP*, 36). Freud's castrating Sandman is never very far from the fixation on sight in these passages.

Freud's particular version of Stevens' own comedic joke here is "displacement," what Freud calls a transvaluation of physical values, which has the effect of neutralizing any threatening material in the dream work by disguising it in more palatable, that is less censorious, forms.[31] In the art work, the net effect of such displacement, at least in its more self-reflexive moments, is that even the slightest hint of the indeterminate and unknown would be emptied out, the self "concealed" and "covered," and sleep made "congenial" (*CP*, 42), in more of Stevens' own C-words. This view would tend to explain, for example, Crispin's up-and-down fluctuation between sun and moon in the third part of the poem, where a "sally into gold and crimson forms" can be nullified by retirement: "A turning back / And sinking down to the indulgences . . . [of] habitude," or, as Stevens puts it on the final page, "sequestering the fluster" (*CP*, 35, 46). If the Freudian theory of an anxiety of repression holds for Stevens' comedian, then several important implications appear to arise from it.

In the first of these, we ought to note how Crispin's project is doomed even before he begins. The exchange of "soil" for "intelligence" can establish no new relation between mind and world because the unfamiliar reality, if it is ever to see the light of day, must always be tricked out in some version of the old romance. This process is what Crispin finds so frustrating:

> These bland excursions into time to come,
> Related in romance to *backward flights*,
> However prodigal, however proud,
> Contained in their afflatus the reproach
> That first drove Crispin to his wandering.
> (*CP*, 39, emphasis added)

This passage also helps to explain all the directions in the poem, how forward is really backward, how upward previously is really down now, and how the outward bound is so insistently inward: "introspective voyager," "bore the vessel inward," "infolded to the outmost" (*CP*, 29, 36, 41), and others. It also helps clarify how repression is so thoroughly fixated on the past, more souvenirs than prophecies, one tends to think (*CP*, 37), and for that reason why it is so compulsively repetitive. In an important passage in *Beyond the Pleasure Principle*, Freud attaches the assuagement of sleep to the repetitive return of the repressed in the context of the unfamiliar, and Stevens manages to bring

31. Freud, *The Standard Edition*, V, 655.

all of these ideas together in the lines that contain the poem's most revealing wordplay: [32]

> There is a monotonous babbling in our dreams
> That makes them our dependent heirs, the heirs
> Of dreamers buried in our sleep, and not
> The oncoming fantasies of better birth.
>
> (*CP*, 39)

Once again, we are given the sense that if Crispin dreams of creating some "new reality" (*CP*, 32)—the pun on "heirs" for musical airs straddles both the poetical and the psychological dimensions of their respective romances—it can only be with a view to recycling the same enervated mythology of self, for lack of "better birth." "All dreams are vexing," the passage goes on to say. "Let them be expunged." This extirpation is perhaps so only because under such familiar / familial auspices, the fastidious thought referred to earlier grows slack (*CP*, 37). Crispin, therefore, is a profitless philosopher, "beginning with green brag. / Concluding fadedly" (*CP*, 46). On this point, we should remember the "Anecdote of Canna": "Yet thought that wakes / In sleep may never meet another thought / Or thing" (*CP*, 55).

A second implication of Crispin's repressive anxiety is rendered by his dependent heirs if, following Freud, we read them more generally as a displacement for the presentiment of artistic failure. The import of such displacement gives the sense of an even greater sequestration and passivity than the comedian might have first experienced and makes more plausible the two thoroughly domestic scenarios, "Crispin, master of a single room" (*CP*, 42), with which Stevens ends the poem, unsatisfactorily for some, Harold Bloom, for example. "Isn't the destiny of American literature," Gilles Deleuze and Félix Guattari ask in *Anti-Oedipus*, "that of crossing limits and frontiers, causing deterritorialized flows of desire to circulate, but also always making these flows transport fascisizing, moralizing, Puritan, and *familialist territorialities?*" [33] Of Crispin's moralizing in the poem before these sections, there can be little doubt: first, the paradigmatic codification, with all of its prolegomena, principles, and "premises propounding," that he attaches to his revolutionary aesthetic in compensation, one supposes, for its elusiveness; and later,

32. *Ibid.*, XVIII, 36.

33. Bloom, *Poems of Our Climate*, 82; Gilles Deleuze and Félix Guattari, *Anti-Oedipus: Capitalism and Schizophrenia*, trans. Robert Hurley, Mark Seem, and Helen R. Lane (Minneapolis, 1983), 277–78.

its puritanical consecration in "apposite ritual," "incantation," and "sacrament and celebration" (*CP*, 37–39). But it is the "familialist territorialization" that seems most central to sections five and six. For here, through the politically sanctioned practice of *c*olonization and the socially sanctioned practice of *c*opulation, Crispin can finally establish an approbated "blissful liaison, / Between himself and his environment" (*CP*, 34) and finally domesticate the driven and wayward self "that was not in him in the crusty town / From which he sailed" (*CP*, 33). And a stifling picture of utterly homogeneous and familial self-possession it is.

> Four daughters in a world too intricate
>
> . . . .
>
>   four accustomed seeds
> Hinting incredible hues, four selfsame lights
> That spread chromatics in hilarious dark,
> Four questioners and four sure answerers.
>
>   (*CP*, 45)

The uncanny, which Freud describes as "that class of the frightening which leads back to what is known of old and long familiar," in German literally translates "homeless" (*unheimlich*).[34] With Crispin's "Nice Shady Home" and "Daughters with Curls" to conclude the poem, Stevens brings his comic barber full circle, as the letter *C* might have predicted, returning him "humped" (*CP*, 43) to an even greater repression that can only eventuate in psychic, if not physical, death, since this profitless philosopher's engagement with the world ultimately has proved "nothing" (*CP*, 45–46).

One is led to speculate, finally, whether or not that profitless nothing, from the point of view of Crispin's anxiety of repression, marks a point of intersection with Stevens' own life. One need not necessarily stress here the strictly biographical alignments between poet and poem: the homebody that Stevens discovers he has become (and the family man he is about to become) working as a successful insurance company executive around 1923, while at the same time attempting to establish a respectable reputation as a writer. Neither is it necessary to rehearse the various anxieties of influence that Robert Buttel, Michel Benamou, and A. Walton Litz, among others, have so well documented. Where comedian and poet, and indeed psychoanalyst, come so inextricably together is in the experience of the individual human

---

34. Freud, *The Standard Edition*, XVII, 220.

psyche as a highly complex tangle of contradictory elements, both active and passive. For instance, while working on his "Comedian" in 1922, Wallace Stevens writes to Harriet Monroe that he elects "to regard poetry as a form of retreat" (L, 230); yet in 1936, he will say to Ronald Lane Latimer that he writes poetry in order "to relate [himself] to the world (L, 306); and to Hi Simons in 1940, he describes how isolated he feels as a writer and expresses his real desire "to get to the center," "to achieve the normal," and "to share the common life" (L, 352). In another context, to Latimer again in 1935, Stevens insists that "poetry is essentially romantic, only the romantic of poetry must be something constantly new and therefore, just the opposite of what is spoken of as the romantic" (L, 277). But four years later, to Simons, he records that "that ordinary, everyday search of the romantic mind is rewarded perhaps rather too lightly by the satisfaction that it finds in what it calls reality" (L, 346). It is this kind of contradictory aesthetic alternation that Stevens chooses to explore in detail in the life of his comic barber, a fluctuating between "sally" and "retirement," a "polyphony beyond [the] baton thrust," as we have seen. In attempting to bring it all to some kind of forced resolution or "accord" (CP, 45) at the end of the poem, Stevens expended an effort that might have cost his writing career.

Fortunately, the letters just mentioned tell a different story, as do six later books of consistently accomplished, though remarkably different, verse. This is Freud's story, too: man's perennial changefulness within what Stevens will later refer to as the "ancient cycle [of desire]" (CP, 382). In his essay on Freud in *Writing and Difference*, Derrida observes that "writing is unthinkable without repression."[35] Having taken this lesson to heart early, Sigmund Freud could continue to be endlessly productive and even be inspired by it. Wallace Stevens, though, is frankly dismayed by this conundrum, as so much of the "variable, obscure" difficulty (CP, 46) of "The Comedian as the Letter C" shows. Until he can think writing *and* repression simultaneously— "think one thing and think it long" (CP, 41)—he must continue to be silent.

Wallace Stevens' psychic division concerning the place of imagination and reality in his work, and, more generally, concerning the question of belief that each proposition threatens to prolong rather than resolve gives us an initial take on the whole problematic of writing and repression. As contemporary theory's undermining of disciplinary boundaries has shown, however, it would be a mistake to confine this problematic merely to a psychobio-

35. Jacques Derrida, *Writing and Difference*, 226.

graphical reading of Stevens' own work. There is a much larger ontological interrogation at back of Stevens' theocentric hypostatizing of reality that we encounter in "The Comedian" only in glimpses. And it would require a second book of poems by Stevens to move beyond an obvious resistance to that interrogation marked by his years of silence and to embrace it as a kind of Derridean strategy for the recirculation and reproduction of textual power. When his work did resume, therefore, *Ideas of Order* was perhaps originally intended by Stevens to answer many of the questions of belief raised in his first book—questions concerning the intensely troubled relation between immanence and transcendence, motion and stasis, and nature and art, as we have seen—and in several ways cannot be considered apart from it. Earlier, I alluded to the most important of these: how the archaeology of belief in *Harmonium* intended to eliminate the idea of God exhausts that proposition but none of its need, so that alternatives have to be sought if the wellsprings of creativity fed by faith are to continue to be rejuvenated. The idea of order that begins to evolve after Stevens' six years of silence does not technically eliminate the idea of God but functions rather as a substitute for it and shows how Stevens might reverse the psychic impasse reached in "The Comedian" without substantially changing the aesthetic contours of his early work, so strongly premised on belief in one form or another.

Reversal is the key word here. For if the tropological flow of *Harmonium* is everywhere archaeological, focused mainly in its root metaphor of falling asleep, in *Ideas of Order* we tend to sense that the flow is in the other, more eschatological direction, with a set of fixed principles of belief being less a question of departure than of arrival, as in the experience of waking up. This reversal is written into Crispin's voyage *in potentia:* the lateral progression from east to west in the first half, followed by the vertical progression from south to north in the second, pivoting, significantly enough, about Crispin's prayerful retirement into a cathedral. Because Stevens cannot unambiguously acknowledge the transcendent import of his introspective voyager's quest, however, transgressive progress quickly modulates into something plainly regressive, making of Crispin's final rest, as in the cliché, a clipped and prolonged silence.

Eighteen years later, in a letter commenting retrospectively on "The Comedian as the Letter C," Stevens is able to pinpoint precisely where the poem might have gone wrong and where *Harmonium,* too, might have been reduced to a mere thematic hodge-podge had he not formulated *Ideas of Order* as a kind of answering counterstrategy. He writes: "About the time when I, personally, began to feel round for a new romanticism, I might naturally have been expected to start on a new cycle. Instead of doing so, I began to feel that I was on the edge: that I wanted to get to the center: that I was isolated, and that I wanted to share the common life." He goes on to note that "so stated, this puts the thing out of all proportion in respect to its relation to the context of life," adding that he does not think this view necessarily implies, as some contend, "that I live in a world of my own" (*L,* 352). Sharing "the common life" undoubtedly is the intent behind many of the poems of *Harmonium,* perhaps "The Comedian" most of all. In this letter, Stevens uses the example of a "a lot of fat men and women in the woods, drinking beer and singing Hi-li Hi-lo" for what might be considered normal or central, *i.e.,* "common." Clearly, however, what makes for so much of Stevens' ambiguity concerning the quotidian, or "the common drudge" (*CP,* 84), in his first published collection, as he could have seen only with hindsight, is the lack of balance or proportion when the "commonal" (*CP,* 388) is considered from life's larger context. *Ideas of Order,* one must conclude, purposes to broaden this context by openly legitimating the question of belief revolved from the formerly repressed tropological bias of ascent, which we can now expect to find in its corresponding root metaphor of waking up, again, another reason for viewing the second volume as *Harmonium*'s intimate, rhetorical companion.

A third way that invites treatment of *Ideas of Order* in close ontological proximity to the first book has to do with Stevens' conception of romanticism. The notion is very much on his mind in the early thirties when he resumes writing, infiltrating his prose in letters to Latimer (*e.g., L,* 277), as well as critical notes on William Carlos Williams and Marianne Moore, where he also gives evidence of a close reading of A. E. Powell's *The Romantic Theory of Poetry* (*OP,* 214, 220). The configuration of a cycle in connection with romance, moreover, indicates that Stevens thinks more about the term as a structural rather than a historical or stylistic concept.[36] With this clue, it may be possible to see how the bias toward "the accepted sense of things" (*OP,* 220) in *Harmonium,* which he avers romance rejects, might be pulled round

36. Joseph Carroll takes the view that a "complete cycle" undergirds the entire of Stevens' middle and late work, "beginning with the negation of the Romantic and concluding with a visionary resurgence that prefigures the imagery of 'The Auroras of Autumn'" (*A New Romanticism,* 71; *cf.* also 74). *Cf.* further Joseph Riddel: "Beneath the particularities or contingencies of life . . . is one certainty: a roundness, a circularity, an orderly motion. Life is process; all particulars are subsumed under this first law, this 'classical sound.' Elemental, it is true! and that is exactly the point" (*The Clairvoyant Eye,* 116).

to "the living . . . the imaginative, the youthful, the delicate and a variety of [other] things" (*OP*, 220) in *Ideas of Order*, provided that Stevens remains aloof from the common center, preferring instead to give his poetry a rather uncommon edge. His *Letters* records his choice: "Without this new romantic, one gets nowhere; with it, the most casual things take on *transcendence*. . . . What one is always doing is keeping the romantic pure: eliminating from it what people [pejoratively] speak of as the romantic" (*L*, 277, emphasis added). Eleanor Cook is quite right, therefore, in viewing the whole of Stevens' second volume as "a turning from, and a turning toward, and in some ways, a returning." It is perhaps necessary only once more to emphasize the eschatological reformulation of faith at back of this returning—a reformulation that now affords a clear sense of direction for all of the "disconcerting transcendental themes" noticed in the first book and, further, for the cycle of romance to which *Ideas of Order* implicitly subscribes in order to complete those themes.[37] Far from setting the projects one against the other, Stevens apparently seems to have found a new source of creative power in attempting, through the structure of romance, to counterpose their discrete tropologies. Hence, in his "Re-statement of Romance" from 1935, we read:

> Only we two may interchange
> Each in the other what each has to give.
> Only we two are one,
>
> .   .   .   .
>
> Supremely true each to its separate self,
> In the pale light that each upon the other throws.
>
> (*CP*, 146)

The opening poem in the 1935 Alcestis Press edition of Stevens' second major publication, therefore, casts several interesting reflections on the first one from the point of view of romance, which to Stevens undoubtedly represents the premier idea of order in the volume.[38] In "Sailing After Lunch," the concept cannot be too honorific; hence, the poet offers the following "poet's prayer": "The romantic should be here. / The romantic should be there. / It ought to be everywhere" (*CP*, 120). Like Crispin, Stevens had found himself in *Harmonium* too much at sea, somewhat lost in the "blather" (*CP*, 22) of

37. Eleanor Cook, *Poetry, Word-Play, and Word-War in Wallace Stevens* (Princeton, 1988), 121; Leonora Woodman, *Stanza My Stone: Wallace Stevens and the Hermetic Tradition* (West Lafayette, Ind., 1983), 2–3, and see also Miller, *Poets of Reality*, 281.

38. J. M. Edelstein, *Wallace Stevens: A Descriptive Bibliography* (Pittsburgh, 1973), 14–15.

the commonal of everyday experience, which for him now becomes a pejorative designation, as in the last cited letter and here in the poem's opening line, "the word *pejorative* that hurts" (*CP*, 120). Compared to an idea of order, unformed sense experience is somewhat of a "crutch" for true poetic inspiration, a "heavy historical sail" that prevents his poetic agenda from really getting under way, or off the ground to mix the metaphor, and is thus "the vapidest fake" (*CP*, 120). Romanticism will change all of that. It will give a shape to the circumstantial in the form, again, of a cycle, or "gorgeous wheel," and thereby restore poetry to the condition of *feeling,* which is more in line with what the quester of belief is after anyway, rather than the condition of seeing that is usual with romanticism. It is the lunch that Stevens recognizes he perhaps should have treated himself to a decade earlier. It is still not too late, though, for a most inappropriate man to be delivered from a most unpropitious place. The key lies in cyclical transcendence:

> To expunge all people and be a pupil
> Of the gorgeous wheel and so to give
> That slight transcendence to the dirty sail,
> By light, the way one feels, sharp white,
> And then rush brightly through the summer air.
>
> (*CP*, 121)

The upshot of "Sailing After Lunch" is to make of Stevens, if not of *Ideas of Order* itself, what the neighboring "Sad Strains of a Gay Waltz," also from 1935, refers to as a "harmonious skeptic" (*CP*, 116) in consideration of the previous heterogeneous compilation of verse. This epithet is likely because *Harmonium* had simply contained too many strains, too many "forms" or "waltzes": poems exclusively imaginative, others predominantly realistic, and several degrees of solipsistic accommodation (or unaccommodation) in between. What *Harmonium* really required in order to counter the enharmonic "epic of disbelief" (*CP*, 122) so pronounced in the babel of its myriad voices was the imposition of an order *beyond* speech, some kind of totalizing form revealing in each and every particular case the mode of desire that the poems, when taken collectively, might appear to be incapable of articulating or describing on their own. Yet this is an order that could not be located in a world of contingent phenomena: "in neither sea nor sun" nor "sudden mobs of men" (*CP*, 122). It could only be discovered as an effect of transcendence appropriate to a personality like the mountain-minded Hoon, "for whom desire was never that of the waltz, / Who found all form and order in solitude, / For whom the shapes were never the figures of men" (*CP*, 121). On this last point, Stevens deliberately leaves himself open to the charge of irresponsible aestheticism in his new book—a charge that was in fact leveled at him in 1935 from the political direction by Stanley Burnshaw in the left-leaning *New Masses* and two years later from the artistic perspective by Yvor Winters in his *Primitivism and Decadence*. As early as 1922, however, Stevens had apparently been steeling himself for just such an attack. Thinking back over all the poems to be published in a first, major gathering the following year, he writes to Harriet Monroe: "The reading of these outmoded and debilitated poems does make me wish rather desperately to keep on dabbling and to be as obscure as possible until I have perfected an authentic and fluent speech for myself" (*L*, 231). In "Sad Strains," the accusation of fashionable enervation is caught in the description of the gay waltz as "so much motionless sound" and "empty of shadows." There can be no doubt, though, that in the "skeptical music" that the poem celebrates at its close, the poet has perfected a truly authentic voice in the idea of romance—a voice with which to unite, as he says, all his previous figures of men and their shapes and to impart to them a cyclical motion whose Hi-lis and Hi-los make them replete with "shadows" (*CP*, 122).

At this important point in the unfolding of a genealogy of belief, we could say that Stevens' ontological interrogation has temporarily resolved itself into a species of formalism characteristic of the structuralist poetics of the New Criticism. A little later we shall see how short-lived this formalist phase actually was, but for the moment, we might be more specific about how Stevens' new revealing mode of desire imposes its forms of unification generally in his latest work. By turning briefly to a study of the structure of romance by Northrop Frye, who also conceives of it in terms of movement through a cycle, though from a more broadly based, narrative perspective, we can see something of what Stevens was about: "Most romances end happily, with a return to the state of identity, and begin with a departure from it. Even in the most realistic stories there is usually some trace of a plunge downward at the beginning and a bounce upward at the end. This means that most romances exhibit a cyclical movement of descent into a night world and a return to the idyllic world, or to some symbol of it like a marriage." Frye maps out the departure and arrival dynamic of the romantic cycle in terms of the highly conventionalized grammars of descent and ascent in its structural movement, the declensions of which are spread between the poles of alienation and identity, a tyranny of external circumstance and a corresponding release from brute experience, respectively. This mapping implies that the romantic tendency is antirepresentational, as opposed to the realism of the novel, for instance, which historically comes to replace romance with a "greater conformity to ordinary experience." Thus, realism is to the anti-romantic what reality is to the romantic, reality being, according to Frye, "an order of existence most readily associated with the word identity."[39]

These distinctions are worth pondering a little further because they are precisely the ones that are running through Stevens' mind as he labors to write himself out of the creative impedimentia blocking any continued effort on *Harmonium* in the late twenties and to write himself into a new creative cycle in the early Depression years. The "Adagia," which he begins to set down in this period, are the most accurate record of this struggle. From their theoretical perspective, "poetry is essentially romantic," though not romantic, as Stevens never seems to tire of remarking, in any "pejorative sense," by which he means "some phase of the romantic that has become stale" (*OP,* 183). Undoubtedly, this pejorative phase of romance to Stevens comes to mean realism as Frye distinguishes it, what the "Adagia" refer to as "a corruption of reality," since "the ultimate value is reality," that is, supracircumstantial "identity" (*OP,* 192). Hence, "the more realistic life may be," part of Stevens' dust jacket blurb to the new volume's second edition reads, "the more it needs the stimulus of the imagination."[40] Moreover, since there is "an intensely pejorative aspect of the idea of the real" (*OP,* 191), the romantic is "the first phase of (a non-pejorative) lunacy" (*OP,* 197). With these two phases of romance before us, it hardly seems possible to avoid concluding that in retrospect Stevens saw very much of the first, the departure, as the realism of *Harmonium* and the second, the arrival, as the reality that lay before him in a more complete expansion of *Ideas of Order*—the reality that is "the spirit's true center" (*OP,* 201) and that is much more germane to a further probing of the question of belief. As "The Irrational Element in Poetry," possibly composed in 1937, puts it, his new work now consisted in "the transposition of an objective reality to a subjective reality," the transaction between reality and the sensibility of the poet lying precisely in that transposition (*OP,* 224). That is to say, his present agenda lay in completing the primary phase of the romance cycle by reprogramming its grammar, shifting it from alienation to identity, from descent to ascent, and, ultimately, from sleep to wakefulness, or from darkness to the return of day.

Frye also mentions the polarization in romance between an actual and

39. Northrop Frye, *The Secular Scripture: A Study of the Structure of Romance* (Cambridge, Mass., 1976), 54, 38–39, and 54.

40. Morse, *Poetry as Life,* 150.

a more desirable world, and this split between two levels gives to its structure a decidedly vertical orientation quite distinct from the horizontal continuity more favored by realism, where the interest mainly lies in getting to the end of a verbal structure rather than to the top of one.[41] Crispin as a "prickling realist" (*CP*, 40) is obviously divided between a horizontal realism and a vertical romanticism, as we noted earlier, and this division perhaps may be another way of explaining his failure. But the vertical perspective of ascent is unmistakably the metaphorical radical of *Ideas of Order*, clearly traceable to Stevens' incipient theorizing about his past and present work in the context of romance and, in particular, of the return phase of its cyclical structure. Thus in "How To Live. What To Do" from 1935, which Stevens preferred to all the other poems in the volume "because it so definitely represents [his] way of thinking" (*L*, 293), we find a man and his companion headed toward the "heroic height" of a tufted rock rising high and bare above "a world unpurged," like some massive giant with his arms among the clouds (*CP*, 125). The movement in this poem away from the muck of the land and toward a sun of fuller fire is obviously the source of its jubilant tone of optimism in the final line (*CP*, 126). The sun is "The Brave Man," in a related poem written in 1933, because he traces a similar movement: "That brave man comes up / From below and walks without meditation" (*CP*, 138). In so doing, he dissipates the "dark forms" of mundane earth; consequently, "Fears of life and fears of death / Run away." However, this is not the sun of realism, the one, for instance, in "The Sun This March" from 1930, tied in physically to the cold element of winter and a dark nature imaged in the voices of "lions coming down" (*CP*, 134). The perspective of realism reveals "A Fading of the Sun" in the poem composed in 1933—a fading connected with an old, mad world in which the tea is bad, the bread is sad, and people die (*CP*, 139). The completion of romance, to the contrary, occurs when people "awaken" (the image is a pregnant one in Stevens' current work), when they turn away from physical circumstance and "look / Within themselves" to discover a nonmaterial fulfillment to their lives. This is the point of self-recognition, to paraphrase Frye once again, at which natural creation merges with human recreation and at which the identity of romance, symbolized at the "pillars of the sun" within the dark night of man's soul, comes into its own and "[people] will not die" (*CP*, 139).[42]

41. Frye, *The Secular Scripture*, 58, 49–50; see also 53.
42. *Ibid.*, 157.

Further, "the recreation of romance brings us into a present where past and future are gathered," and the "return to Mozart" in the poem "Mozart, 1935," which unites a "lucid souvenir of the past" in the form of the divertimento and an "airy dream of the future" in that of the concerto, achieves just such a present moment: "a starry placating" by which "sorrow is released" (*CP*, 132).[43] Consequently, the body being carried down the stairs inside in the poem and the snow falling outside are reversed, "Dismissed, absolved," in a simple, spontaneous, individual creative act: "Play the present" (*CP*, 131). Stevens' own "Some Friends from Pascagoula," also from 1935, is an almost perfect illustration of this present vision at the top of romance. As a description of an eagle in sun-bronzed air, the poem's content is all descent, but its form pulls in the opposite direction, in paradoxical images such as "His slowly-falling round" and "Dropping in sovereign rings" (*CP*, 126–27). In such a complete marriage of form and content ("a sovereign sight," indeed), no one is really quite sure where the eagle's flight begins (or ends, if the fishy sea is any indication), which is surely "the [cyclical] point" (*CP*, 126) of the poem and of the lunacy of nonpejorative, nonrealistic romance in general.

The evolution of Wallace Stevens' theory of romance in this ultraformalist phase of the genealogy of belief is very much a part—but only a short-lived part—of the well-known "mythical method" of modernism, the essence of which, described by T. S. Eliot in a famous essay, is *control*, as mastered by James Joyce in *Ulysses*. In manipulating the Odyssean myth in his fiction, Joyce demonstrates to his fellow moderns "a way of controlling, of ordering, of giving a shape and a significance to the immense panorama of futility and anarchy which is contemporary history." The "messiness of experience," in Murray Krieger's phrase, which is what Eliot really has in mind by contemporary history, is the pejorative nadir reached by *Harmonium* in the "mint of dirt," so "incredible to prudes," in "The Comedian" (*CP*, 31). In *Ideas of Order*, such experience greets us again: muddy rivers under muddy skies located, predictably enough, at a far-off point where a shaft of light falls from sky to land. This time, though, the perspective is reversed. "The mind snarls" (*CP*, 148) at such a prospect, and Stevens' argument goes one better than Eliot's, positing not only a master of mud in the title of a poem, again from 1935, but a "master of the mind" as well (*CP*, 148). The mud master's labor is therefore not the old dilemma of determining the superiority of intelligence over soil or of soil over intelligence but rather the task of laying claim to "an

43. *Ibid.*, 179.

ontologically superior realm" *beyond* both, by scaling that falling shaft of light presumably, and thus entering into the "privileged modes of revelation" that transcend the temporal and historical and are the exclusive privilege of an autotelic and epiphanic order of art alone.[44]

The idea of order as achieved vision transcending both soil and self is the one that apparently visited Stevens at Key West in 1934. In the form of a disembodied female voice, this single artificer's "rage for order" transmutes the dense physicality at the beginning of the poem (grinding water, gasping wind, sunken coral, bronze shadows) into "ghostlier demarcations" by the end, so that even the speakers are perplexed by the mystified "origins" of their own identity (*CP*, 130). The one consistent theme throughout "The Idea of Order at Key West" is once again artistic control, the mastery guaranteed by a verbal order that is the "genius" beyond realism referred to in the lyric's opening line. Even nature appears to know something of this genius in its own rise from the world well found to the world well made:

> Ramon Fernandez, tell me, if you know,
> Why, when the singing ended and we turned
> Toward the town, tell why the glassy lights,
> The lights in the fishing boats at anchor there,
> As the night descended, tilting in the air,
> Mastered the night and portioned out the sea,
> Fixing emblazoned zones and fiery poles,
> Arranging, deepening, enchanting night.
>
> (*CP*, 130)

All the varieties of mastery here empowered by art, the portioning, the fixing, the emblazoning, the arranging, and so forth, hardly give the sense of a natural world in its physical presentiment. If there is a natural world, it seems "merely a place" (*CP*, 129) that exists for romance ultimately to climb around. Without doubt, life ceases to be a matter of chance under these circumstances, as Stevens himself remarks on "The Idea of Order" (*L*, 293), but with such a clamant rage for artistic Form, one really begins to wonder by the end of the poem whether real life could actually matter at all.

We might expect to find some element of that chance restored in what appears to be a random collection of aperçus on life's morbidities in the

---

44. T. S. Eliot, "*Ulysses*, Order, and Myth," in *Selected Prose of T. S. Eliot*, ed. Frank Kermode (New York, 1975), 177; Murray Krieger, *The New Apologists for Poetry* (Minneapolis, 1956), 26; Allen Thiher, *Words in Reflection: Modern Language Theory and Postmodern Fiction* (Chicago, 1984), 37.

strangely titled longer poem "Like Decorations in a Nigger Cemetery," written in 1935. Far from the anarchic demythologizing that we noticed earlier in "Thirteen Ways of Looking at a Blackbird," whose form "Like Decorations" invites comparison with, this later poem is actually very highly structured, and it is the mythic verticality of romance that oddly informs so much of what the poem calls the "morphology of regret" (*CP*, 154):

X

Between farewell and the absence of farewell,
The final mercy and the final loss,
The wind and the sudden falling of the wind.

XI

The cloud rose upward like a heavy stone
That lost its heaviness through that same will,
Which changed light green to olive then to blue.

(*CP*, 152)

The grammars of descent and ascent that complement each other in these two strophes adumbrate a fortunate "sphere" (IV) or "comic sum" (XXXV) that sets a number of "invisible currents clearly circulating" (XXXIV) through the fifty sections of the poem. The effect of the cycle is firmly to displace the dark realism centered in Stevens' title and instead to allow "the eccentric to be the base of design" (*CP*, 151), consistent with Stevens' adjuration to avoid poetic centers. Keeping another gorgeous wheel mobile in this way ("Nothing is final," and "No man shall see the end," Walt Whitman chants in the opening strophe), Stevens can pursue the search for a tranquil belief (V) in a world so relentlessly given over to physical decline and death, symbolized in the poem by perpetual autumn (IX, XII, XXVIII, XXXVII, XLIV) and the mania for time (XLVI). By completing the primary phase of the romance myth by stages—the sun about to rise at the beginning (II), the children crying on the stair halfway to bed just past the middle (XXXVI), and the building up of the city in snow at the end (L)—the poem gives us a fairly total comprehension of another idea of order into which Stevens' tranquil belief will issue. So highly structured is the progress of transcendence through this order that even the pigeons on the cemetery's entrance gate are said to appreciate symmetry (*CP*, 152), unless Stevens is entertaining a rather droll pun here (and in his odd title), and the "clanking mechanism" (*CP*, 157) of a later strophe indicates that he may very well be.

Nonetheless, it is the sense of "simple space" (*CP*, 153) beyond temporal experience that allows the poem to formulate the "union" (*CP,* 158) with which to avenge the autumn's fallen leaves at the close—a unity that Helen Vendler quite accurately perceives is simultaneously radial rather than successively linear, recalling the distinction made earlier between Stevens' realism and his more important reality.[45] In this sense, "Like Decorations" most clearly turns Stevens' second major publication into an achievement of structure, if not of modernism more generally, which the canons of contemporary taste tend to espouse as an era of formalism.[46] For Stevens, in search of substitutes for outworn faith, it is also a significant religious achievement as well. As Eliot puts it in *Four Quartets,* "Only by the form, the pattern / Can words or music reach / The stillness."[47] Or, as "Like Decorations" would have it, "Music is not yet written but is to be . . . For the time when sound shall be subtler than we ourselves" (*CP,* 158).

We come, finally, to a set of poems in *Ideas of Order* that eventually cause Stevens to become disenchanted with the excessive formalism of a romantic cycle as a new ontological site of belief and, for theoretical reasons better made plain in connection with his next major project, *The Man with the Blue Guitar,* dealt with in the following chapter, cause him to abandon the structural idea of romance altogether. One senses in the great outpouring of work from 1934 and 1935, particularly in poems such as "Meditation Celestial & Terrestrial" (Jungle = Life = Spring/Summer, on the one hand; Sky =

45. See Helen Vendler, *On Extended Wings,* 71.

46. The "structuralism" of *Ideas of Order,* which slowly begins to come undone in the second edition of the work, is nonetheless compelling enough to invite total readings of the Stevens canon from this perspective. The most exhaustive treatment of "total structure" in the poetry is that of James Baird in *The Dome and the Rock,* whose allusions to it are too numerous to cite separately. "Grand Poem" and "Grand Design," synonymic substitutions throughout his study (*e.g.,* xxxi, 5, 84, 88, 91, 324), come to be symbolized by the "dome upon the rock of being" in particular (xxvi, 10, 88, 95–96, 117, 230, 303, 307) and by Stevens' "architectural precision" more generally (xxv, 3, 6, 82, 93, 95, 117, 316). This critical approach has had adherents both early (Riddel, *The Clairvoyant Eye,* 5, 32, 49) and late (J. S. Leonard and C. E. Wharton, *The Fluent Mundo: Wallace Stevens and the Structure of Reality* [Athens, Ga., 1988], 36–37). Frank Lentricchia, in his earliest work on Stevens, *The Gaiety of Language: An Essay on the Radical Poetics of W. B. Yeats and Wallace Stevens* (Los Angeles, 1968), expresses what often becomes elided in structuralist readings of Stevens' writing, which is that the idea of order provides the poet with a release from "barren and sometimes ominous circumstances," causing him to use it as an escape from the pressure of experience, "the monotony, the pain, the horror of 'absolute fact'" (136–37), which we have already partly touched on in the previous consideration of Stevens' "mythical method."

47. T. S. Eliot, *Four Quartets* (1944; rpr. Great Britain, 1972), 19.

Reason = Winter, on the other) or, to reverse the perspective, "Botanist on Alp (No. 1)" (Claude = Art = Air, ascending; Marx = Nature = Sea, descending), or even in titles like "Nudity at the Capital" and "Nudity in the Colonies" (*CP,* 145), that the dialectic of realism and romance has become too much of a good thing for Stevens and that he gradually begins to write poems "made to order," so to speak. In the first edition of *Ideas of Order,* we get this tendency only in hints: the "symmetry" that might be "cemetery" referred to in "Like Decorations" or the "plated pairs" of the dialectic's binary oppositions that in "The American Sublime," also from 1935, are gently parodied as "mickey mockers" (*CP,* 130). Still, romance's dialectic had taught Stevens much about the dynamic relationship of the parts constituting its theocentric whole as a revealing mode of desire and principally about the "interdependence," as Frank Doggett among others observes, between world and mind written into the personal history of the several affiliations between his first and second books.[48]

In view of this interdependence, Stevens could muster the courage in the search for a perdurable faith to deal directly with the modern era's "Evening Without Angels," composed in 1934, with its darkening catalog of sad men and furious selves descending, like the sea, into the "rest and silence" of a spreading, spiritual sleep (*CP,* 137). For at the point of the barest, starkest, most abject facticity lies the potential source for some of the mind's most ingenious mediations and displays of power. Descent is always preparation for ascent, in Stevens' theory of romance; dissolution and desuetude, the occasions for a renewed energy and a more abundant growth. "The thing seen becomes the thing unseen," according to one "Adagia" (*OP,* 167), so that the motions of the mind might always find themselves "giving form / To moodiest nothings" (*CP,* 137). In fact, the idea of order only succeeds in proving that the nothing that is not there is precisely the metaphysical *raison d'être* for an imaginative something to rise up in its place:[49]

> Bare night is best. Bare earth is best. Bare, bare,
> Except for our own houses, huddled low
> Beneath the arches and their spangled air,

48. Doggett, *Poetry of Thought,* 4, and Frank Doggett, *Wallace Stevens: The Making of the Poem* (Baltimore, 1980), 98. *Cf.* also Robert Pack, *Wallace Stevens: An Approach to His Poetry and Thought* (New York, 1958), 44; Enck, *Images and Judgments,* 22; Baird, *The Dome and the Rock,* 19; Miller, *Poets of Reality,* 258; Bates, *A Mythology of Self,* 190.

49. Helen Regueiro, *The Limits of Imagination: Wordsworth, Yeats, and Stevens* (Ithaca, 1976), 10, 193, 42.

> Beneath the rhapsodies of fire and fire,
> Where the voice that is in us makes a true response,
> Where the voice that is great within us rises up,
> As we stand gazing at the rounded moon.
>
> (*CP*, 137–38)

In that *noeud vital* where a huddling low establishes an interdependence with a rising up—an interdependence that is generally lacking between reality and life (*OP*, 202)—Stevens thought he might locate the "rest and silence" of another, quite transcendent order.

In a quite other sense, however, the return marked by the later romantic discourse was becoming "academic," as "Academic Discourse at Havana" from 1923 may already have anticipated. For the 1935 Stevens, the cycle of romance becomes less a case of acting imaginatively in a situation than a case of reacting to one, which is perhaps indicated more than anything else by the moonlight on the floor in this poem and by the gazing at the rounded moon in the last. In "Anglais Mort à Florence" from 1935, we find another, similar moon whose "pale coherences" are once again linked in "particles of order" (*CP*, 149). This time, however, the ideas of order (the music of Johannes Brahms, God's help, the police) are felt to be oppressive, creating the feelings not so much of consolation as of being "naked and alien" (*CP*, 149). The several references to turning and returning in the poem remind us of the old boat going round and round on a crutch back in "Sailing After Lunch," and we wonder if the reality of order, here the "single majesty" the character has entirely given himself up to, has not itself become a second crutch as it counters the excessive realism of *Harmonium,* a liability to Stevens, not as before, in the mediation between self and world, the matrix of interdependence, but now as it becomes another center of abject dependence:

> But he remembered the time when he stood alone.
> He yielded himself to that single majesty;
>
> But he remembered the time when he stood alone
> When to be and delight to be seemed to be one,
> Before the colors deepened and grew small.
>
> (*CP*, 149)

The mention of police in this connection is instructive. Geoffrey Hartman is reminded of the image as it is used by Derrida in *Glas* in its association with a "universal passkey" that is slipped into all lacunae of signification for the purpose of semantic and thematic disclosure but that has the ultimate effect of confounding understanding, like arresting the free movement of an unknown person (Stevens' English alien fallen in Italy, say) "in the name of the law, of veracity, of the symbolic order."[50] Undeniably, there is movement abounding in *Ideas of Order:* in "Dance of the Macabre Mice," composed in 1935, "we go round and round. / What a beautiful history, beautiful surprise!" are lines intended to parody the sedentariness of the embronzed and empty "Founder of the State" (*CP,* 123), just as the turning of the birds satirizes the archbishop in "Gray Stones and Gray Pigeons," from 1934, when finally he abandons his globed and camphorous enclave for a holiday (*CP,* 140). Movement does indeed abound. Yet in "The Pleasures of Merely Circulating," also from 1934, such pleasures policed by the laws of romantic structure gradually begin to occlude identity from one verbal order to the next ("Mrs. Anderson's Swedish baby / Might well have been German or Spanish," we read in the poem [*CP,* 150]) so that the poet's infinite repetitions eventually turn sinister and, in place of a sense of renewed life coterminous with identity, actually take on the character of a "hallucinatory disease" synonymous with a mechanical uniformity.[51] Thus the "dark companion[s]" of order (*CP,* 148) of Stevens' "Anglais *Mort*" reach back to the poet's "dark, pacific words" of "Academic Discourse" (*CP,* 144) and forward to the skulls of cattle and the black hoods of drummers in "Pleasures of Merely Circulating," where the rage for circularity is perhaps more vertiginous than pleasurable:

> The garden flew round with the angel,
> The angel flew round with the clouds,
> And the clouds flew round and the clouds flew round
> And the clouds flew round with the clouds.
>
> (*CP,* 149)

Inasmuch as Stevens had hoped that *Ideas of Order* would avoid the dead center that had grounded his earliest attempts to redefine belief and would keep his work in circulation following a different agenda, he was compelled to recognize that every creative cycle has its center nonetheless and that the structure of romance is an option whose privileging of form over content has its own end clearly in sight and will therefore reach a point of diminishing return for productivity eventually as well. What Stevens wants

50. Hartman, *Saving the Text,* 103. *Cf.* also Frank Lentricchia, *Ariel and the Police: Michel Foucault, William James, Wallace Stevens* (Madison, 1988), 202.
51. Michael Beehler, *T. S. Eliot, Wallace Stevens, and the Discourses of Difference* (Baton Rouge, 1987), 59.

to resist at all cost is any suggestion of a sense of closure in his new work, in order that faith may continue to be adapted to a different intelligence beyond the containment of doctrine. "In a world without heaven to follow," he writes in "Waving Adieu, Adieu, Adieu" in 1935, "the stops / Would be endings, more poignant than partings, profounder / And that would be saying farewell, repeating farewell, / Just to be there and just to behold" (*CP*, 127). Yet the revolving of the idea of order bespeaks an even more encyclopedic containment, a contradiction that some of these poems can only intermittently acknowledge: "to be beheld, / That would be bidding farewell, be bidding farewell" (*CP*, 128). Hence, the impasse in "Botanist on Alp (No. 2)" from 1935:

> What's down below is in the past
> Like last night's crickets, far below.
>
> And what's above is in the past
> As sure as all the angels are.
>
> *(CP*, 135–36)

One has to go outside of the *Collected Poems* to get an asseveration, albeit not entirely unequivocal, that order is "the end / Of everything" ("A Room on a Garden," *OP*, 73). Nonetheless, it is another cycle ("A Fish-Scale Sunrise," "Gallant Château," and "Delightful Evening," a trio of poems from 1934) that Stevens chooses to end the first edition of *Ideas of Order* with, though the mention of "wormy metaphors" in the concluding line of the book may be just giving this final structural flourish away at last.

With the second edition of *Ideas of Order* in 1936, we are naturally curious about what adjustments Stevens might have made to his structural theory to compensate for its formalistic excesses. Frye's separation between a "sexual" and an "artificial" creation myth, for instance, in the end enables his own theorizing, via the second construct, to come quit in the final phase of his study of romance structure "at least from the facile ironies of an endlessly turning cycle."[52] All that we have from Stevens is the addition of three extra poems to his volume. By placing two of them at the very beginning of the book, however, he calls attention to a procreant revisionism that would appear to be drawing a close to the structuralist phase of his work.[53] In "Fare-

---

52. Frye, *The Secular Scripture*, 184, 112.

53. Quite contrary arguments on this very point are presented by Litz, *Introspective Voyager*, 51–52, 202, and Doggett, *The Making of the Poem*, 135.

well to Florida," for instance, a high ship makes passage from a South of excessive and luxuriant growth to a colder, sparer, less sepulchral North in the way we might expect. For with Key West sunk downward under massive clouds (*CP,* 117), there seems to be the opportunity in the boat's ascendant for a greater freedom and movement and a wider potential for change and personal transformation, suggested by the twice-mentioned image of a snake's having shed its skin upon the floor: "The past is dead." Happy to be above it all, the speaker proudly celebrates the contentment he is sure to experience sailing into the North, which is followed by an ellipsis, and then his contentment in knowing that the land is gone forever and will not follow him in thought, word, or look, which is followed by a second ellipsis. The gaps are prophetic. By the final stanza of the poem, the speaker has garnered anything but a tranquil release from the South's mundane experience. The "slime of men in crowds" and the water riven by "sullen swells" and by "shoving and slithering" all bind him even more tightly *round* than before (*CP,* 118), no matter how much he insists on protesting his freedom. His final words promising a rise, "Go on, high ship," are returned as a fall, "go on, *plunge on*" (*CP,* 118, emphasis added), that we perhaps might have anticipated in the opening with the moon riding clear at the ship's masthead, undercutting the title of the poem completely. In this exchange of one type of bondage for another, there is a kind of repressive reaction formation at work here that is curiously reminiscent of Crispin but manifests itself this time from the direction of soil ("forget the bleaching sand," "leaves half sand, half sun," and so forth) rather than from self.

In the second poem, "Ghosts as Cocoons," which immediately follows in the new edition, we are given a fairly clear acknowledgment of what the cycle cannot quite contain:

> This mangled, smutted semi-world hacked out
>
> Of dirt . . . It is not possible for the moon
> To blot this with its dove-winged blendings.
>
> She must come now.
>
> (*CP,* 119)

The "she" in this passage, the bride referred to earlier in the poem who is both natural process and the inspirational muse attendant upon it that the writing makes promise of marrying, this "love" never does arrive in the end. All the signs seem propitious for her arrival: the grass in seed, the young birds flying, and a seducing "bloodman" rampant. But a certain oversensitivity to the more indelicate presence of the fly on the rose and to the flower's fragrance falling on dung shows that there may indeed be limits to a belief in the highly structured idea of romance, even in the descent phase (hence, "semi-world") of its cycle. Consequently, a poetry of faith opened up fully to wherever the question of belief might take it must remain merely ghostly, straitjacketed by the "cocoon" of form: "Yet the house is not built, not even begun" (*CP*, 119).

Our reading of his first two books of poetry reveals, therefore, that Wallace Stevens is not quite able to center a reformulation of faith in either realism or romance, through which *Harmonium* and *Ideas of Order* are cycled, respectively. By the end of his second book, the "passkey" of symbolic order, in Derrida's phrase, which might also have unlocked the door to certain belief, has instead made his spirit grow uncertain, to recur to "Anglais Mort," once again: "Certain of its uncertainty . . . For a self returning mostly memory" (*CP*, 148). Far from concluding the quest(ion) of belief in a single, determinate point, Stevens has instead unearthed what Michel Foucault calls "a distribution of notable points," realism, reality, and romance, each a terminus ad quem that, when reached, threatens to circle viciously into a terminus a quo once again. Foucault continues: "There is no center, but always decenterings, series that register the halting passage from presence to absence, from excess to deficiency. [More important] The circle must be abandoned as a faulty principle of return; we must abandon our tendency to organize everything into a sphere. All things return on the straight and narrow, by way of a straight and labyrinthine line."[54] As early as 1918, when the firecat of "Earthy Anecdote" sends the bucks of Oklahoma clattering into swift, circular lines, "To the right," "To the left" (*CP*, 3), or 1919, when "The Paltry Nude" undertakes "the circle of her traverse of the sea" (*CP*, 5), it seems likely that Stevens had thought he might pitch his tent of faith in some artistic

---

54. Foucault, *Language, Counter-Memory, Practice*, 165–66. Having rendered the cycle of romance itself pejorative, Stevens in his later poetry can refer to it only as the "broken cartwheel on the hill" in "Continual Conversation with a Silent Man" from 1946, "the bitterest vulgar do / And die" in "The Bouquet" from 1950, and "the tired romance of imprecision" in "Adult Epigram" from 1946. Following Derrida, in *Margins of Philosophy*, trans. Alan Bass (Chicago, 1982), therefore, we look in Stevens' middle and late work for a new, poststructuralist protocol of belief, "the supplement of [or to] a code," *i.e.,* the code of romance, that "traverses its own field, [and] displaces its closure, breaks its line, opens its circle" (271). Tracing the trajectory of this "third thing" in Stevens' revolving of faith represents much of the burden of what lies ahead in this study, which the third epigraph to the present chapter can only begin to anticipate.

sphere but first needed to work through the "Preliminary Minutiae" of "The Grand Poem," the title originally proposed for *Harmonium* (*L*, 237–38) in order finally to round on that prospect. Now that he had arrived at that point almost twenty years later, it must have been baffling to him that the house of fiction was still not built, perhaps because it could not be constructed along the exceedingly geometric lines he had hoped for and, if it could be, because it was not to be lived in:

> We knew for long the mansion's look
> And what we said of it became
>
> A part of what it is . . . Children,
>
> . . . .
>
> Will say of the mansion that it seems
> As if he that lived there left behind
> A spirit storming in blank walls,
>
> A dirty house in a gutted world,
> A tatter of shadows peaked to white,
> Smeared with gold of the opulent sun.
>
> (*CP*, 159)

In this passage from the final poem added to the reissue of *Ideas of Order*, Stevens sends "A Postcard from the Volcano," for in prospect of abandoning a belief centered in the theory of romance, he stares into a blank, artistic abyss threatening ontotheological extirpation.[55] With its cries of "literate despair," the poem almost reads like a suicide note: "We left much more, left what still is / The look of things, left what we felt / At what we saw" (*CP*, 159). Unquestionably, it marks a leave-taking of the early Stevens. In the middle Stevens, which begins the following year in 1937, he enters into a

---

55. The allusion to the quick foxes in the poem's opening (*CP*, 158) would seem to indicate a continuing theological cast of mind in his second book's reissue. Cf. Ezek. 13.4: "O Israel, thy prophets are like the foxes in the deserts. Ye have not gone up into the gaps, neither made up the hedge for the house of Israel to stand in the battle in the day of the Lord" (Authorized [King James] Version). Theocentric belief falls, like the House of Israel, into the volcano; nonetheless, this does not pretermit Stevens' nostalgia for the ontological center. In a later letter to Sister M. Bernetta Quinn (April 7, 1948), for example, he writes: "Your mind is too much like my own for it to seem to be an evasion on my part to say merely that I do seek a centre and expect to go on seeking it. I don't say that I shall not find it or that I do not expect to find it. It is the great necessity even without specific identification" (*L*, 584). The "specific identification" of the idea of order by Stevens in 1935 and 1936 is perhaps another reason for him eventually to have become thoroughly disenchanted with it.

period of perpetual "homelessness" that Martin Heidegger, writing a decade later, would posit as that which "is coming to be the destiny of the world." To the title character of "The Reader," from 1935, it must look as though the question of belief has got nowhere in the twenty years spanning the two separate editions of Stevens' early work, that "everything," in the mumbling voice of this poem, "falls back to coldness" (*CP*, 147), like the dead silence in *Harmonium*'s opening "Earthy Anecdote." If Stevens was prepared to site a total faith in the idea of order, the reader, of course, would be right. One is led "to the brink of a precipitous fall," however, as Heidegger elsewhere writes, if one has only a firm commitment to order, or what he calls "enframing," which is the "supreme danger" of securing metaphysical certainty for oneself through regulation—certainty that only an ultrastructuralism can guarantee. Heidegger further explains the concept: "Enframing does not simply endanger man in his relationship to himself and to everything that is. As a destining, it banishes man into that kind of revealing which is an ordering. Where this ordering holds sway, it drives out every other possibility of revealing. Above all, Enframing conceals that revealing which, in the sense of *poiesis*, lets what presences come forth into appearance."[56]

If Stevens' three additions to the 1936 *Ideas of Order* are any indication, he strikes us as having moved his metaphysics beyond any such kind of commitment to enframement. It will be several years yet before he will be able to gaze serenely "at the violent abyss" in his later "Notes Toward a Supreme Fiction" of 1942 (*CP*, 404), which must represent the a/theological deconstruction of order, as we shall see. But as a "tatter of shadows peaked to white" by the closure of order's "shuttered mansion-house" in the unforgettable penultimate line from his parting postcard (*CP*, 159), Stevens, nonetheless, holds open the door to other possibilities of "revealing" and hence to a renewal of a literate faith.

56. Martin Heidegger, *Basic Writings, from "Being and Time" (1927) to "The Task of Thinking" (1964)*, ed. David Farrell Krell (New York, 1977), 219; Martin Heidegger, *The Question Concerning Technology and Other Essays*, trans. William Lovitt (New York, 1977), 26–27.

CHAPTER 2

ABSENCE IN REALITY

The Rhapsody of Things

The most "realistic" work will not be the one which "paints" reality, but which, using the world as content . . . will explore as profoundly as possible the *unreal* reality of language.

—Roland Barthes, *On Racine*

It is the belief and not the god that counts.

—Wallace Stevens, *Opus Posthumous*

If we affirm one single moment, we thus affirm not only ourselves but all existence. For nothing is self-sufficient, neither in us ourselves nor in things; and if our soul has trembled with happiness and sounded like a harp string just once, all eternity was needed to produce this one event.

—Friedrich Nietzsche, *The Will to Power*

ALTHOUGH T. S. Eliot was not an important influence on Stevens despite the fact that belief was also an overriding preoccupation in Eliot's middle and late career, the famous observation that mankind cannot bear "very much reality" from "Burnt Norton" would have fitted Stevens' thought precisely in the two years separating *Ideas of Order* and *The Man with the Blue Guitar*, 1935 to 1937.[1] Stanley Burnshaw's attack on these first two books in the left-leaning *New Masses* for their general lack of contact with a world on the brink of political and financial ruin was upsetting enough. Stevens' digging himself into deeper aestheticist holes with "Mr. Burnshaw and the Statue" and his much larger, and generally conceded unsuccessful, attempt at a poetry of social conscience in *Owl's Clover* in 1936 must have made reality for the long-

---

1. Eliot, *Four Quartets*, 14. "Burnt Norton" was published in the same year as Stevens' *Ideas of Order*. Fifteen years later, on the subject of his relationship to Eliot, Stevens would be given to remark, "Eliot and I are dead opposites and I have been doing about everything that he would not be likely to do" (*L*, 677).

silent poet positively oppressive.[2] It may also be true, however, that Stevens was undergoing a real crisis of a different sort. In the previous chapter, we noticed between the first two volumes a significant shift in rhetorical paradigms that Stevens resorts to in order to counter a creative impasse brought on by the need to investigate new poetical options for the decline in modern faith. Historically, Stevens follows the devolution of mimesis to poiesis in the writing of poetry, touched on in the introduction. It is also possible to describe this shift as a change in "symbolic" registers, following Northrop Frye, viewing the writing in *Harmonium* as more or less "descriptive"—writing whose direction is outward, aimed at the representation of things external to it. The writing in *Ideas of Order* then is "literary," more inwardly motivated, seeking to establish the hypothetical rather than the assertive content of poetry's autonomous verbal structure.[3] We can see perhaps that "The Comedian as the Letter C" was pivotal in this shift. The descriptive repertoire represented by the soil that is man's intelligence founders, as our analysis has shown, on the purely literary ethos of intelligence itself. Thus, Stevens' inability to overcome a certain symbolist predisposition, represented by intelligence in that poem and in other purely "harmonious" ones like it, to a certain extent validates Burnshaw's charges, particularly when this sensibility reforms itself into ideas of order in the next published collection of verse. Writing more socially correct poetry, Stevens must have secretly known, could have done nothing to resolve conflicts that were rooted at a more psychic and inspirational level.

It must have been at this point that Stevens began to give the first serious attention to the theory behind his poetry—the theory that, for better or worse, was to become the life of his poetry for the remainder of his writing career, since "the theory / Of poetry is the theory of life" (*CP*, 486). In particular, it was important for him to come to terms with the precise meaning behind "intelligence" and "soil" in that long, comedic shipwreck of a poem in his first book, or what soon transformed themselves into the terms *imagination* and *reality* in the prose essays and "Adagia" he began writing around the time of his second. After twenty-odd years of serious poetry writing, Stevens found reality to be the especially vexing issue. What is likely to have dawned on him for the first time is the impossibility of defining it and its dialectical opposite in logical or essentialist terms. Countless readings of Stevens

2. Riddel, *The Clairvoyant Eye,* 136, 147; Morse, *Poetry as Life,* 148–59. For a more positive reading, see Longenbach, *The Plain Sense of Things,* 163–73, 180–92, and *passim.*
3. Frye, *Anatomy of Criticism,* 74–75.

are stalled on this point as well.[4] The commonsensical approach is to attach reality to the descriptive motive of his work, which Stevens invites in a line such as "the real that wrenches, / Of the quick that's wry" in "The Revolutionists Stop for Orangeade" in the 1931 edition of *Harmonium* (*CP*, 103). In these terms, reality is a kind of Cartesian *res extensa,* a concrete, physical, objective manifestation of a world outside the mind that *res cogitans,* in the form of imagination's literary program, stands to correct, improve, or transform. Thus, he initiates a poetic project that opens itself up physically to a crisis in belief in the "dreadful sundry" of "O Florida, Venereal Soil" in *Harmonium* (*CP*, 47), closes itself metaphysically, once again, with "Farewell to Florida" in *Ideas of Order,* re-turning the "barer sky that does not bend" in a transitional poem such as "Anatomy of Monotony" (*CP*, 108) to the "swift circular line[s]" of "Earthy Anecdote" (*CP*, 3), with which *Harmonium* began. If the *C* signals such a crisis in Stevens' "Comedian" in 1923, moreover, by 1935 he manages to complete the partial circle that the *c* in "crisis" describes. By the same token, the vicious circle of his metaphysical logic strands Stevens within a formalist aesthetic closure that only leaves him ready for a repetition of the fall. The 1936 portrait of "The Men That Are Falling," the concluding poem of Stevens' *The Man with the Blue Guitar,* therefore, could in one sense be a carry-over of the perilous logocentrism of his previous projects, which he only now begins to disavow.

In another way, a formalist dialectic of descriptive and literary rhetoric, if inscribed, as Stevens' appears to be, within a symbolic circle, leaves no coherently logical way of clearly separating them. Just where imagination leaves off and reality begins is precisely the confusing kind of determination that makes a circle vicious, a point that lines such as "The imagination, the one reality / In this imagined world" from "Another Weeping Woman" of 1921 or "Crow is realist. But, then, / Oriole, also, may be realist" from "Like Decorations in a Nigger Cemetery" serve to illustrate (*CP*, 25, 154). This point will greet us again in the next chapter when Mrs. Uruguay approaches "the real" from the other-worldly direction of climbing a mountain (*CP*, 249). In spite of the confusion the terms generate, Stevens from this period shows no inclination to abandon them. Over twenty of the "Adagia" alone take up the subject of reality, more even than those devoted to the belief in God, and the gathering of prose published in 1951 as *The Necessary Angel* would be subtitled

---

4. *E.g.,* Suzanne Juhasz, *Metaphor and the Poetry of Williams, Pound, and Stevens* (Lewisburg, Pa., 1974), 132, 145; Riddel, *The Clairvoyant Eye,* 143.

"Essays on Reality and the Imagination." How, we might ask, could Stevens see his way clear to the publication of new verse with the critical terms of a previous dead-end formalism entirely intact?

One clue lies in a letter written to Renato Poggioli concerning the Italian translation of "The Man with the Blue Guitar" two years before Stevens' death. There, the poet explains that "the general intention of the *Blue Guitar* was to say a few things that [he] felt impelled to say 1. about reality; 2. about the imagination; 3. their inter-relations; and 4. principally, [his] attitude toward each of these things" (*L,* 788). Stevens' specification here of the *inter-relations* between imagination and reality reveals the realization that must have suddenly become apparent to him in the final formulation of the mono-logical closure of his first two books, namely, that the determination of things could not possibly be made intelligible unless there were other things to compare them to. That is to say, a poetry that ended up in an identity of self-relation, as *Ideas of Order* appeared to have, was terminal. But one that opened itself up to difference, even to poetry as different as the kind that Burnshaw's *New Masses* could approbate, was a project that could break the tautological cycle of exclusionary self-perpetuation. Writing that abandoned itself entirely to the imagination, as in the case of Stéphane Mallarmé and Paul Verlaine, was beneath contempt and always would be for Stevens (*L,* 635–36). Reality was therefore a necessary angel. Without it, there could be no way for the imagination to distinguish itself, in its presupposing "*both* distinction from *and* relation to otherness."[5] Alone, it could only suffer the fate of Jonathan Swift's spider, eventually swallowing itself up in the adhesive toils spun endlessly out of itself.

If imagination and reality declare themselves as correlative effects within an interrelation of difference, the next step would be to determine precisely how those functions might become constituted. For what will be of extreme importance for Stevens' later reformulation of conventional belief in *The Man with the Blue Guitar,* the first thing to note about reality is that it is not some objective datum of experience existing outside of imaginative sub-jectivity but is totally implicated as a factum of that subjectivity itself. Experience is much broader than reality (*OP,* 187). Hence, reality is "not that external scene [*i.e.,* that 'collection of solid, static objects extended in space'] but the life that is lived in it"; that is, "Reality is things as they are" (*NA,* 25). Thus, to the sensibility of the poet, an apparent "objective reality" is in fact a

5. Buttel, The Making of "*Harmonium*," 124; Taylor, *Erring,* 133.

"subjective reality" (*OP*, 224), an "ideology" Louis Althusser more recently would have said, foregrounding our "imaginary" or "lived" relation to the real without denying its existence.[6] By the same token, what we see in the mind can be as real to us as what we see with our eyes, for "unreal things have a reality of their own, in poetry as elsewhere" (*OP*, 188; *NA*, 4), From whichever perspective reality declares its relation to the imagination, however, the view represented evidently is one a majority of people will agree on. In Nietzschean formulations that will become clearer later in this chapter and the next, Stevens declares that reality is the object seen "in its greatest common sense," that it is the direction in which most things tend to move, and that, for this reason, it is often formed to expression in the cliché, the overt limitation of "a single effect" (*OP*, 202, 191, 204, 198).[7]

It follows, therefore, that the imagination will be doing its job not by detaching itself from reality (*OP*, 187) but by transforming reality through metaphor, thereby effecting our escape from paralyzing clichés (*OP*, 204). "The great poem," in the words of one of his more well known "Adagia," "is the disengaging of (a) reality" (*OP*, 195). In a somewhat confusing process strikingly reminiscent of Georg Wilhelm Friedrich Hegel's, Stevens proposes that the poet "abstract" himself to the degree that reality, in a corresponding abstraction, might be placed inside his imagination, presumably for the purpose of defamiliarizing its sedimented formulations (*NA*, 23). An absolute object of reality slightly turned by the imagination in this way can become a

6. Louis Althusser, *Lenin and Philosophy and Other Essays*, trans. Ben Brewster (New York, 1971), 162. Stevens' formulations on reality, however, are not too far removed from William Carlos Williams' from about the same time (1929). Williams writes in *The Embodiment of Knowledge*, ed. Ron Loewinsohn (New York, 1974): "For if words are real, not symbols, then the depiction of reality, realism, plain writing, is a denial of their actuality since the thing depicted, as in 'impressionism,' *is* the objective and the words are put back into their wornout usage as unreal. . . . But in sur-realism the distortion of the emotion, the object, the condition, makes the words (the true material of writing) real again. Out of them (real) the illusions of sur-realism (unreal) are created" (18–19).

7. This formulation for reality catches Stevens in an especially modern, some might even say postmodern, moment. *Cf.* Jean-François Lyotard: "The objects and thoughts which originate in scientific knowledge and the capitalist economy convey with them one of the rules which supports their possibility: the rule that there is no reality unless testified by a consensus between partners over a certain knowledge and certain commitments" (*The Postmodern Condition*, 77). Thus, a "text" for Stevens conceivably "liberates us from the empirical object . . . by displacing our attention to its *constitution* as an object and its *relationship* to the other objects thus constituted," according to Fredric Jameson's phrasing in *The Political Unconscious: Narrative as a Socially Symbolic Act* (Ithaca, 1981), 296–97. For a more recent restatement of this position, see Stanley Fish, *Doing What Comes Naturally: Change, Rhetoric, and the Practice of Theory in Literary and Legal Studies* (Durham, 1989), 2, 98, 193, and *passim*.

metaphor of that object, and as a result, the imagination can achieve a liberty both for the mind and for reality at one and the same time (*OP,* 204). In all of this, Stevens is utterly insistent that it is not a case of choosing one element of the relation over the other. Rather, the poet recognizes that a "universal interdependence" exists between these two subjective poles and that his artistic choices must always be guided by the acknowledgment that they are "equal and inseparable" (*NA,* 24).

For the poet, then, there is no such thing as "absolute" or "bare" fact, what the metaphysical philosopher will often erroneously refer to as the "truth" and what Stevens locates within the "normal range" of human perception (*NA,* 59–60). Since absolute fact is utterly devoid of any imaginative character, its apparently unshakable truth would be the first thing a poet would want to go to work on, opening its rigidly normative character to the alterity of a more open-ended "poetic" truth. In the essay "The Noble Rider and the Sound of Words" from 1942, Stevens includes the example of "nobility," the absolutizing of which in four separate historical eras—the eras of Plato, Andrea del Verrochio, Miguel de Cervantes, and Clark Mills—has each time required a man of imaginative vision to demystify its truthful solidity in one period and pass it on revivified to the next. The various philosophic conceptualizations of God in "A Collect of Philosophy," written in 1951, Giordano Bruno's Infinity, Gottfried Wilhelm Leibniz's Monad, and Arthur Schopenhauer's Will, are another illustration, as are Blaise Pascal's *silence,* Nietzsche's *ewiges Wiederkehr,* and Nicolas de Malebranche's *vérités éternelles* in their originally "poetic" formulations (*OP,* 272, 275). Each is an event in the history of ideas and, like any other event in the outside world, exerts a pressure on the powers of imaginative contemplation that threatens to normalize its transforming energies (*NA,* 20–21). Thus, the fundamental difficulty in any art is the problem of the normal (*OP,* 195). Poetry especially, however, is a passion and not a habit (*L,* 364) and can strike an "agreement" with reality, that is to say, with the diminished world of the philosopher's reason, only for a certain length of time (*NA,* 57–58, 54), after which it is likely the greatest pressure will be brought to bear on the imagination, in time of war especially, to define some truth categorically. At that point, the imagination rallies with a violence of its own and presses back against any kind of rational or ideological coercion by refusing to define *anything.* We must also include in this resistance Stevens' own refusal to define imagination (and reality) in anything but alogical terms: "If it is defined, it will be fixed and it must not be fixed. . . . To fix it is to put an end to it" (*NA*, 35, 34).[8] The imaginative mind can reveal a thing only through its movements and changes, that is, as an acategorical "force" in a vast network of mental forces. This is how its own ec-static freedom comes to be constituted and, in the end, how as a force itself for self-preservation it "helps us to live our lives" (*NA*, 35–36).

On this point, Stevens has in mind "the supreme fictions," that is, the metaphorical or poetic truths that the poet, "potent figure that he is," turns over to the speculative thinker for rational confirmation as philosophic truths: "[The poet] creates the world to which we turn incessantly and without knowing it." Thus, without him "we are unable to conceive of it" (*NA*, 31). Nietzsche, whom Stevens began to reread during this period, as we shall see later in the chapter, expresses similar ideas on the relation between fiction and truth, or belief, in *The Will to Power*: "Through thought the ego is posited; but hitherto one believed as ordinary people do, that in 'I think' there was something of immediate certainty, and that this 'I' was the given *cause* of thought, from which by analogy we understood all other causal relationships. However habitual and indispensable this fiction may have become by now— that in itself proves nothing against its imaginary origin: a belief can be a condition of life and nonetheless be false" (*WP*, §483, 267–68).[9]

This brief tour through Stevens' prose formulations on the codependent relativity of imagination and reality from roughly the period of *The Man with the Blue Guitar* gives a fairly clear impression of just how far behind his current projects were prepared to leave the previous formalism of the twenties and early thirties. The new poetry springing from the "fluctuations" between reality and the imagination (*L*, 364) or acknowledging that each verbal site involves an aspect of itself in every other, what Stevens now refers to as "a dithering of presences" and "a complex of differences" (*OP*, 273), such a poetry gives no sense of a closed symbolic economy rhetorically centered in a transcendant imagination. In an important letter to Hi Simons from 1940, Stevens comments closely on various sections of *Blue Guitar*: "Imagination

8. *Cf.* Roland Barthes, in *Image-Music-Text*, trans. and ed. Stephen Heath (New York, 1977): "[Writing], by refusing to assign a 'secret,' an ultimate meaning, to the text (and to the world as text), liberates what may be called an anti-theological activity, an activity that is truly revolutionary since to refuse to fix meaning is, in the end, to refuse God and his hypostases—reason, science, law" (147).

9. *Cf.* also *WP*, §487 and §493.

has no source except in reality, and ceases to have any value when it departs from reality. . . . There is nothing that exists exclusively by reason of the imagination, or that does not exist in some form in reality. Thus, reality = the imagination, and the imagination = reality" (*L,* 364). In what appears to be a rather startling poststructuralist formulation, Stevens explodes the notion of a mutually exclusive subject and object, inside and outside, or presence and absence underwriting his work. Gone as well is the autonomous self seeking imaginative mastery or spiritual dominance over the various monotonies or maladies of soil and sea. "Summed up," he states in "The Figure of the Youth as Virile Poet," "our position at the moment is that the poet must get rid of the hieratic in everything that concerns him and must move constantly in the direction of the credible . . . creat[ing] his unreal out of what is real" (*NA,* 58). Creating the unreal out of what is real makes of Stevens' reality a perpetual construction, but this is not, at the same time, to argue for a loss of belief in the external world. Rather, as Linda Hutcheon notes, it would merely imply "a loss of faith in our ability to (unproblematically) *know* that reality, and therefore be able to represent it in language."[10]

What Thomas Altizer says about the radical reversal of the Christian consciousness in modern times, therefore, could equally apply to Stevens' new understanding of the role of the imagination he aims to project in his new verse:

> Once the ground of an autonomous consciousness has been emptied or dissolved, then there can be no individual center of consciousness, or no center which is autonomous and unique. With the disappearance of the ground of individual selfhood, the unique "I" or personal ego progressively becomes a mere reflection or echo of its former self. Now the "I" takes into itself everything from which it had withdrawn itself, and therefore it ceases to stand apart. In losing its autonomy, it loses its own unique

---

10. *Cf.* once again William Carlos Williams: "To transcribe the real creates, by the same act, an unreality, something besides the real which is its transcription, since the writing is one thing, what it transcribes another, the writing a fiction, necessarily and always so. [Hence,] The only real in writing is writing itself" (*The Embodiment of Knowledge,* 13). For the reference to Linda Hutcheon, see *A Poetics of Postmodernism: History, Theory, Fiction* (New York, 1988), 119. In *The Crisis in Criticism: Theory, Literature, and Reform in English Studies* (Baltimore, 1984), William Cain makes the same point concerning the reality of the Orient in the work of Edward Said: "The Orient is always 'constituted'—the interpreter creates and produces it. Yet [Said] repeatedly insists on the presence of Oriental 'reality' or 'realities,' implying that an Orient exists that is not the work of interpreters" (212).

center or ground, and thereby it loses everything which had once appeared as an individual identity or "face." . . . Individual self-hood does not simply or literally come to an end or disappear; it appears in the other.[11]

In this passage, the "I" taking into itself everything from which it had formerly withdrawn is precisely the formulation for the relationship between imagination and reality we saw Stevens describe earlier. The exteriority it makes interior and the interiority it makes exterior thus dissolve the specter of solipsism haunting Stevens' first two books. Now, poetry is a response to the daily necessity of getting the world right, its great conquest being the conquest of reality that the imagination threatens to consume and exhaust (*OP*, 201, 194, 198). The key, once again, lies in the metaphor. As it sets about creating a new reality, the old suddenly becomes unreal, and the imagination finds itself once more with new material to work on, in a process whose repetitions promise to expand geometrically to infinity. Appearing only to disappear, and disappearing only to appear, reality is "a vacuum" (*OP*, 194), or, as we shall see more clearly in "The Man with the Blue Guitar," an "absence" (*CP*, 176) that we come more and more to confront in the poststructural theorizing, for instance, of Theodor Adorno, Jacques Lacan, and Derrida. But if reality equals imagination, then so must the presence of metaphor in its greatest conquests constitute an absence. To fix either would be the end of both: "Let me show [them] to you unfixed," as Stevens says in a related context (*NA*, 34). In the space that opens up in the infinite play of signification between these two relations, then, Stevens hoped to lodge his first entirely successful longer poem.

The dead end of logical essentialism in matters of faith, like the dead end of formalism, would appear to be the point in the opening and closing sections of "A Thought Revolved," written in 1936, the poem preceding the composition of "Blue Guitar." The mechanical optimist travestied here in the image of "indifferent curls" (*CP*, 184) in Part I, like the moralist leader in the image of his horny "great toe" (*CP*, 187) in Part IV, circumscribes the far too reductive logic of both. The complete revolution of thought in this way, from head

11. Altizer, *The Descent into Hell*, 155. *Cf. WP* §488: "No subject 'atoms.' The sphere of a subject constantly growing or decreasing, the center of the system constantly shifting . . . No 'substance,' rather something that in itself strives after greater strength, and that wants to 'preserve' itself only indirectly." See also Foucault, *Language, Counter-Memory, Practice*, 152–53.

to toe, so to speak, is instructive, particularly in view of what both optimist and moralist overlook as a potentially new way of defining the ideas of man and faith. In the poem's middling affabulations in Parts II and III, it is possible to find just that:

> An earthly leader who could stand
> Without panache, without cockade,
> Son only of man and sun of men,
> The outer captain, the inner saint,
>
> The pine, the pillar and the priest,
> The voice, the book, the hidden well,
> The faster's feast and heavy-fruited star,
> The father, the beater of the rigid drums.
>
> (*CP*, 185–86)

But logic's famous law of the excluded middle makes clear why such "romanesque" thinking is concluded to be of so little use to poet and believer alike. Seeking a dialectical structure in which to ground the presence of some central truth, theology, like eschatology, can be interested only in beginnings and concludings, the origin and the end, Alpha and Omega. And it is only interested in the second, inferior term of the binarism insofar as that term mirrors or re-presents, that is to say, brings back to itself, the superior, archaeological, or hierarchical First Term, the *causa sui*. Any uncanny ex-orbitance from some beastly middle can be only a preterit interlude—an inter-play, after the Latin *ludus*, or play—on the way to something more closed and conclusive.[12] Yet it is precisely the "exceeding music" that could possibly take the place of reason's "empty heaven" (*CP*, 167) that Stevens chooses to foreground in his longest poem to date. He, therefore, would tend to be far more interested in what Hart Crane, writing in the same year *Blue Guitar* was published, refers to as the "logic of metaphor," that is, the organic principle guiding the construction of a poem according to "metaphorical inter-relationships": associational meanings rather than categorical or logical ones.[13] The interplay of revolving thought from the middle could be the only way for him to surmount the metaphysical logic enclosing the descent to reality at the beginning and the ascent to imagination at the end of his previously

---

12. See Spanos, *Repetitions*, 182.

13. Hart Crane, *The Complete Poems and Selected Letters and Prose of Hart Crane*, ed. Brom Weber (Garden City, N.Y., 1966), 221.

stalled artistic agenda. Repositioning his project at the paralogical site of some middling beast's interlude—the "lion in the lute" (lude?) that will greet us shortly (*CP,* 175)—would be a way of revolutionizing "logic" beyond a belief in its narrow routine of fixed origins and mechanical ends. There can be nothing fortuitous about choosing a highly mannered hidalgo *at play* on a blue guitar in order to accomplish this revolution.

All Stevens' longer poems to date seem to have been undertaken for the purposes of satire, the parodies of Christological symbolism and the family romance in "Sunday Morning" and "The Comedian as the Letter C," respectively, being the most obvious examples. "The Man with the Blue Guitar" is certainly not Menippean satire by a long stretch, but the dialogism of that form's discourse is transported faithfully into Stevens' poem and for the same ironic effect. Julia Kristeva's penetrating analysis of the satirical technique of dialogism as standing against Aristotelian logic and, instead, "translating a logic of relations and analogy rather than substance and inference" might tend to explain its appearance in "Blue Guitar," in light of all the animadversions against formal logic outlined previously.[14] Stevens locates his dialogism within the wrangling between "two dreams" mentioned in the final lyric (*CP,* 183) and gives each proposition a voice for the purposes of alternative enunciation (lyrics I through IV for the first, V and VI for the second, VII through XI for the first again, and so forth), though this structured polyphony becomes progressively more difficult to identify, for reasons that will become clear as we proceed.

In the opening lyric, we are presented a precise formulation of the ideas under dispute. Whereas both a mass of men and the lone guitarist can agree that the tune the musician plays concerns a world outside the human mind, the majority insists on a portrayal of external things exactly as they are, while the guitarist finds it necessary to apologize for certain changes that such things undergo in his musical renditions. Lyric VI mounts the strongest attack by the mass on the beleaguered musician for his insistence on change:

> A tune beyond us as we are,
> Yet nothing changed by the blue guitar;
>
> Ourselves in the tune as if in space,
> Yet nothing changed, except the place

---

14. Julia Kristeva, *Desire in Language: A Semiotic Approach to Literature and Art,* trans. Leon S. Roudiez, Thomas Gora, and Alice Jardine, ed. Leon S. Roudiez (New York, 1980), 85.

> Of things as they are and only the place
> As you play them, on the blue guitar,
>
> Placed, so, beyond the compass of change,
> Perceived in a final atmosphere;
>
> For a moment final, in the way
> The thinking of art seems final when
>
> The thinking of god is smoky dew.
> The tune is space.
>
> (*CP,* 167–68)

Mass man's insistence here on a space for things beyond the reach of change sharply contrasts with the lone man's sensitivity to the process of time, imaged by the motions of the sea in lyric XI. The discord of his music from deep within his instrument's dark belly especially purposes to magnify this threatening sense of time that insistently "grows upon the rock" (*CP,* 171). Consequently, the dialogical argument Stevens constructs for his poem invites us to see a "thought" revolved once again: on the one hand, by the exclusionary synchrony of the mass and, on the other, by the more compelling diachrony of the solitary man.

By taking one further step back, we perhaps might be able to see Stevens setting into motion the symbolic rhetoric that his new thinking concerning the relationship between imagination and reality in the context of belief was beginning to leave severely open to question. For who, after all, is that scholar performing the precarious balancing act in lyric XXV if not Stevens as poetic "ephebe," previously ensconced in the mass man's literary and the lone man's descriptive tropologies fitted to a larger cyclical dialectic?

> He held the world upon his nose
> And this-a-way he gave a fling.
>
> His robes and symbols, ai-yi-yi—
> And that-a-way he twirled the thing.
>
> (*CP,* 178)

As for the specific details of the dialectic itself, lyric III offers the revolution of thought that Stevens had formerly laid out between the rhetorics of descent (the temporalization of space) and of ascent (the spatialization of time), back in his first two books.

To lay his brain upon the board
And pick the acrid colors out,

To nail his thought across the door,
Its wings spread wide to rain and snow,

To strike his living hi and ho,
To tick it, tock it, turn it true,

To bang it from a savage blue,
Jangling the metal of the strings . . .

(*CP,* 166)

That Stevens may be casting a retrospective glance at the dialectical formalism of his work in this passage is further suggested by Frank Kermode: "The clock's *tick-tock* I take to be a model of what we call a plot, an organization that humanizes time by giving it form; and the interval between *tock* and *tick* represents purely successive, disorganized time of the sort that we need to humanize. . . . *Tick* is a humble genesis, *tock* a feeble apocalypse; and *tick-tock* is in any case not much of a plot. We need much larger ones and much more complicated ones if we persist in finding 'what will suffice.'"[15]

The real question for the reader of the poem then becomes which of the two wrangling propositions, things exactly as they are or things changed, can drive the dagger to the heart of man's mystery. Or, put another way, from the point of view of Stevens himself: Which proposition holds the key to breaking the cycle of an endlessly self-referential formalism so as to "play man number one" from a wholly new perspective? That is, what must we believe?

If reality is a vacuum, as noted previously, perhaps the answer is neither. Or both. We recall that in "The Noble Rider" reality, which is "things as they are," is not a collection of solid, static objects but the life that is *lived* (*NA,* 25). In lyric IV, in a new voice that appears to be overtaking the poem, Stevens begins to suggest how woefully inadequate a blue guitar might be as a reflection in propositional terms of things as they are in comparison to the life that is lived in and through those propositions and a million others like them. "A million people on one string," this new voice asks, and all their manner (right and wrong, weak and strong) in the thing? (*CP,* 166). Thus in lyric VII, the image of the moon as a cold, remote, and detached reflection of the sun serves the purpose of foregrounding a more alive response to things as they are than

15. Frank Kermode, *The Sense of an Ending: Studies in the Theory of Fiction* (Oxford, 1968), 45.

the bloodless abstractions of creeping men as so many "mechanical beetles," reminiscences of beast and optimist in "A Thought Revolved." For them, the strings on the blue guitar must remain cold. "My imagination grows cold at the thought of such complete detachment" is part of Stevens' succinct "para phrase" of this particular section in his letters (*L*, 362).

In lyric XII, then, the reader begins to sense the frank impossibility of making any kind of strict determination for the identity of a player who is dialogically in tune with a multifarious world. Rather than a multitude dwindling to the sound of a single breath, we are given the intimation of a full orchestra filling a "high hall with shuffling men," so that the musician, like Stevens' imagination poised at the brink of reality, hardly knows where to "begin and end" (*CP*, 171). At the start of this section, he has a clear, unitive understanding of his expressive self: "The blue guitar / And I are one." After receiving those things which momentously declare themselves, however, he cannot be so sure: "Not to be I and yet / Must be." "Momentously" here registers the sense of alterity in the polyphonic voicing of the poem thus far and is obviously intended to explode any notion of a "final moment" either beyond the compass of change, in the passage quoted earlier, or exclusively within change itself, as its dialectical counterpoint. Rather than settle for the abstraction of one or the other, "pale intrusions into blue / Are corrupting pallors," Stevens' new voice will become the lover of all:

> Blue buds or pitchy blooms. Be content—
> Expansions, diffusions—content to be
>
> The unspotted imbecile revery,
> The heraldic center of the world
>
> Of blue, blue sleek with a hundred chins,
> The amorist Adjective aflame . . .
>
> (*CP*, 172)

The heraldic center, however, does not imply a fixed point of reference for the recycling of an outworn structuralism. Rather, it fulfills the function of what J. Hillis Miller describes as the deconstructive *mise en abyme:*

> *Mise en abyme* is a term in heraldry meaning a shield which has in its center (*abyme*) a smaller image of the same shield, and so, by implication, ad infinitum, with ever smaller and smaller shields receding toward the central point. . . . As in the case of a bend sinister, the implication is of a possible illegitimacy, some break

in the genetic line of filiation. . . . To name [this structure] or to give examples of it is not to create a concept, a general structure which all the examples illustrate, since it is precisely a question, in this case, of what has no concept, no literal name. Therefore it can only be "figured," each time differently, and by analogies which are not symmetrical with one another.

Stevens undertakes an asymmetrical refiguration for his guitarist in this lyric in the image of the unspotted imbecile with a hundred chins, obviously a resighting of another middling beast. Less successful might be the vocal analogy in the "amorist Adjective aflame." Undoubtedly, this phrase is Stevens' attempt to suggest a kind of "dialogized heteroglossia" for his guitarist now, to borrow the terminology of Mikhail Bakhtin; that is, he tries here to imply a multivalent discourse as a substitution for the unifying and centralizing dialectic of the previous wrangling propositions—propositions that, after this point in the poem, are no longer articulated in any coherently sequential order. For it is theoretically the "multiple play-possibilities of language" in Allen Thiher's formulation, the "expansions" and "diffusions" just cited, that immediately concern Stevens, the plurisignification of which can open up only in the "imbecile revery" of reality's present absence and imagination's absent presence.[16]

Now that things as they are, either exact or changed, have been destroyed, as announced in lyric XV, the next thought to be revolved is whether or not man has been destroyed, too, inasmuch as he perceives of himself as a thing who perceives things. Is thought, now, only a memory? Has he fragmented himself so irreparably that Pablo Picasso's own guitar player, once described by the artist himself as a "hoard of destructions," stands as a solider image of society by comparison? And is it solider than the Humpty-Dumpty figure

16. J. Hillis Miller, "Stevens' Rock and Criticism as Cure," *Georgia Review*, XXX (Spring, 1976), 11–12; M. M. Bakhtin, *The Dialogic Imagination: Four Essays,* trans. Michael Holquist and Caryl Emerson, ed. Michael Holquist (Austin, 1981), 270; and Thiher, *Words in Reflection*, 222. Ricardo Quinones, in *Mapping Literary Modernism: Time and Development* (Princeton, 1985), tags this "openness to a wide range of experiences" as "the true Modernist *disponibilité* . . . in its search for new forms, idioms, and subject matter," in its shift away from the oneness of Romantic idealism to a more contemporary "otherness" (90, 138). In "Feminism's Interrupted Genealogies," *Diacritics,* XVIII (Spring, 1988), Sharon Willis, however, in a comment more in line with what Stevens may be attempting to do with his vocal counterpoint, suggests that the "circulation of contradictory and competing discourses may constitute the very 'postmodernity' of the postmodern" (39).

Stevens' player seems destined to live out to its shattering conclusion in the fall to an oppressive, stony mother earth in lyric XVI? Or, if not a destiny quite so earth-shaking, at least a fall to some fanged desert beast attempting hopelessly to claw articulate sense out of the blue guitar, like "a worm composing on a straw" (*CP,* 174)? Since the categorical knowledge that had once underwritten belief is "no longer a dream, a thing / Of things as they are" (*CP,* 174), imagination would seem to have cast man adrift in an unknown sea, "a sea of ex," which Stevens in *Letters* glosses as "a pure irreality" (*L,* 360). All would appear as evanescent as air—good air albeit—but hardly reassuring enough to revive a former belief grounded in solider premises, reality imaged as a "lion locked in stone," for instance (*CP,* 175). No sooner does that irreality become reality, however, then in lyric XXI the imagination turns again and does provide the basis of a "substitute for all the gods" in the form of the "self." This is not the etiolated projection of some "gold self" of former times, the "shadow of Chocorua," for example, looking down from an immenser heaven and stonily etched in the mindless faith of generations. Although this new belief is solid enough to embed itself in the lives of men that live in the land, the "flesh, the bone, the dirt, the stone" (*CP,* 176), it is not so promising of rigidified institutionalization that it cannot declare itself "momentously," "without shadows, without magnificence," and pass on to something totally other, when imagination will have revolved man's thought once more.

Belief, therefore, is bipolar, just as poetry is, constantly deforming and later reforming itself within the play between imagination and reality, what Stevens refers to in lyric XXII as "issue and return":

> Poetry is the subject of the poem,
> From this the poem issues and
>
> To this returns. Between the two,
> Between issue and return, there is
>
> An absence in reality,
> Things as they are. Or so we say.
>   (*CP,* 176)

The "so we say" in this important passage reminds us, if we might still need reminding, that things as they are are not to be taken as fixed objects of knowledge. Rather, like poetry, they are their own subjects, absences perpetually in search of presences, as the lyric goes on to conclude:

> But are these separate? Is it
> An absence for the poem, which acquires
>
> Its true appearances there, sun's green,
> Cloud's red, earth feeling, sky that thinks?
>
> From these it takes. Perhaps it gives,
> In the universal intercourse.
>
> (*CP,* 177)

The utterly central implication for belief in all of this is that truth is not ontological, as it could only be in Stevens' earlier formalist rhetoric, but ontogenetic, that is to say, processual, a function of change in the universal give-and-take that is intercourse. As Stevens writes in another letter from this period, "The only possible order of life is one in which all order is incessantly changing" (*L,* 291–92). Stevens' image for the error of trying to arrest change, in the next lyric, is that of the gravedigger in the poet's well-known "duet / With the undertaker" (*CP,* 177). The undertaker's error lies in his grave attempt to halt the play of truth's dithering presences and thereby suggest "final solutions" to end the counterpoint between the dualisms of thought and truth, *Dichtung* and *Wahrheit,* the imagined and the real, and so forth: "All / Confusion solved." Yet if reality is "not what is" but "consists of the many realities which it can be made into" (*OP,* 202) and, further, if the human tendency always is that of the undertaker, "to fix the bearing of men in reality" (*OP,* 266), then it is clearly the voice of the poet and not the undertaker's song that must prevail. The "voice of ether," whose pun on "either" sustains the imagination's dialogism in the very act of punning itself, ensures the continuance of the guitar man's "playing year by year" the absence in the nature of things as they are.

The canonical view, therefore, that in "The Man with the Blue Guitar" Stevens strikes a happy balance between mind and world perhaps through some kind of Hegelian synthesis symbolized by his "universal intercourse" is simply not at all in tune with his revolutionary thinking about imagination and reality in the middle period of his writing career.[17] While composing the poem, he wrote to Ronald Lane Latimer that "the relation or balance between imagined things and real things . . . [was] a constant source of trouble to [him]" (*L,* 316). As long as things are as his reformed guitarist *thinks* they

17. Riddel, *The Clairvoyant Eye,* 147; Litz, *Introspective Voyager,* 245–47; Joseph Carroll, *A New Romanticism,* 102; Cook, *Poetry, Word-Play, and Word-War,* 135, among others.

are (*CP*, 180), the well-wrought aesthetic economy will be perpetually tipped
in favor of the initiative of imaginative force to discompose and deregulate,
to open poetic form up to the strange, as a new voice, that of a Franciscan
don, makes clear in lyric XXIX:

> "So it is to sit and to balance things
> To and to and to the point of still,
>
> To say of one mask it is like,
> To say of another it is like,
>
> To know that *the balance does not quite rest,*
> That the mask is strange, however like."
>
> (*CP*, 181, emphasis added)

Stevens' use of the mask in this passage again points up the absence in reality
that theoretically destabilizes the metaphysical ground of truth traditionally
located in some beneath or beyond and turns the transcendental signification of truth loose to the playacting of appearances merely. Similarly, as he
once observed to Hi Simons, "You do not pierce an actor's make-up: you
go to see and enjoy the make-up; you do not bother about the face beneath"
(*L*, 362). Michel Foucault makes this observation: "[Truth's] rather weak
identity, which we attempt to support and to unify under a mask, is in itself
only a parody: it is plural; countless spirits dispute its possession; numerous
systems intersect and compete."[18] Something of this intersection of competing forces and systems we find in the next section of the "Blue Guitar," in
Stevens' evolution of a new image for humanity: an "old fantoche," a mario-
nette attached to wires, with "his eye / A-cock at the cross-piece on a pole /
Supporting heavy cables, slung / Through Oxidia" (*CP*, 181–82). In place of
man centered in a circle, lyric XXX thus offers us a parody of Christian transcendence in the form of an actor hung out on a cross—"the *cross* that marks
the place where identity and difference, as well as presence and absence, repeatedly intersect."[19] Neither a complete denizen of "Oxidia, banal suburb,"
nor the "amber-ember" of some supramundane "Olympia," man is consti-

---

18. Foucault, *Language, Counter-Memory, Practice*, 161

19. Taylor, *Erring*, 138. Elsewhere in *Erring*, Taylor remarks: "The eternal recurrence of
the cross(ing) of forces marks every subject a trace. Possessing neither personal propert(y)ies nor
proper identity, the erring mark remains a wanderer, drifter, vagrant, and outlaw. Never leaving the margin and forever wandering along the border, the trace is dissolutely liminal" (158).
Stevens' characterization of Everyman in the present lyric, as an "old fantoche / Hanging his
shawl upon the wind" (*CP*, 181), would fit quite comfortably into the previous list of outsiders.

tuted at the node of a vast network of converging and diverging relations, making his authoritative, univocal identification uncertain, if not impossible: "Oxidia is Olympia" (*CP,* 182).

It is perhaps not by accident that Foucault can be brought together with Stevens in this section of the poem. One of the most important influences on Foucault's work was the German philosopher Friedrich Nietzsche, and Stevens incorporates several references to Nietzsche in this and the following lyric, XXXI.[20] Here, "Ecce, Oxidia" alludes to the title of Nietzsche's most autobiographical work, *Ecce Homo,* published posthumously in 1908, and the reference to Olympia in the context of the actor and his masks may be derived from the mention of "the whole Olympus of appearance," which Nietzsche prefers to truth in the preface to the second edition of *The Gay Science,* brought out in 1886. According to the most recent scholarship on this issue, Stevens may have begun rereading Nietzsche around 1937, the year of publication for *Blue Guitar,* and an important text such as Nietzsche's "On Truth and Lies in a Nonmoral Sense"—the text that brings his radical philosophy most closely to bear on poetical and linguistic matters—is not likely to have escaped Stevens' notice.[21] In that essay, Nietzsche proposes to argue that the fixed and canonical abstractions of the scientific rationalist or the philosophical realist are merely social agreements, "ghostly schemata" concocted by men to enable them to get on with each other in "the herd" (OTL, 90, 84). Thus, we are all "wearing a mask"; and together, "hanging in dreams on the back of a tiger," we inscribe the concepts of truth in stone to help us live our lives as masters of reality, which Nietzsche designates as "the mysterious X," to indicate that certainty must forever remain "inaccessible and undefinable for us" (OTL, 80, 83). Stevens' strange masks, wrangling dreams, "inaccessible Utopia," and "lion locked in stone" as an image for things exactly as they are could all therefore have conceivably come from Nietzsche's demystification of absolute knowledge in this text. Perhaps the genealogy of reality, from "lex" (*CP,* 27) in his early period through "ex" in "The Man with the Blue Guitar" (*CP,* 175) to the fatal "X" (*CP,* 288) in his later work might be more clearly understood with reference to Nietzsche's text as well. There certainly can be no doubt that our reading of Stevens'

20. "Foucault . . . sees himself as following in the wake of Nietzsche, whose thought he rightly interprets as existing under the Zarathustrian sign of rupture," according to Megill, *Prophets of Extremity,* 193. *Cf.* also 221, 223, 231, 245, and 254–55.

21. Milton J. Bates, "Major Man and Overman: Wallace Stevens' Use of Nietzsche," *Southern Review,* n.s., XV (October, 1979), 811–39, and also Bates, *A Mythology of Self,* 234ff.

reproach against "the lark fixed in the mind" in lyric XXXI to champion the utterly whimsical process of metaphorization as a "posture of the nerves," that this reading *improves* with the knowledge that the "thing in itself," according to Nietzsche, was only an image transferred from "a nerve stimulus" (OTL, 82). The interpretation is also bolstered by the end of the poem, where "the blue guitar surprises [us]" (*CP,* 183), since fixed concepts are supposed to protect us "against ensnaring surprise attacks" (OTL, 91).

The depth of Stevens' immersion in Nietzsche's philosophy at this time, however, can only be conjectured. Stevens would continue to read his work through the late thirties and the war years as well, if not beyond. The issue of influence, therefore, we leave for a systematic treatment in the next chapter, where the more deeply implicated poetry of his fourth volume, *Parts of a World,* published in 1942, will afford us a better, more thorough-going base on which to gauge it. Nonetheless, it is difficult to resist initial speculation that the whole process of questioning true belief in Stevens' work might not begin with the formulation of reality as an absence, which is precisely the deconstruction that Nietzsche hangs on it, particularly in *The Will to Power,* published in 1901 and then again in 1905. The mass of men in Stevens' poetry, for instance, who desire to have things exactly as they are would appear to reflect the contempt and hatred "for all that perishes, changes, varies" on the part of those, described by Nietzsche, who manifest a will to truth as "merely the desire for a world of the constant" (*WP,* §585 [A]). The more sympathetic lone guitarist, whose championing of things changed gradually modulates into that which declares itself "momentously," obviously reiterates Nietzsche's "sole fundamental fact . . . that [the motion of the world] does not aim at a final state" and that its "Becoming is of equivalent value every moment" (*WP,* §708). Stevens' whirling multitude, as we have seen, though, shows that he is not prepared to exclude any proposition from his poem's expansions and diffusions. Nietzsche frames the argument similarly: "The assumption of one single subject is perhaps unnecessary; perhaps it is just as permissible to assume a multiplicity of subjects, whose interaction and struggle is the basis of our thought and our consciousness in general" (*WP,* §490). Besides, he states in another place, "everything is so bound up with everything else, that to want to exclude something means to exclude everything" (*WP,* §293). In other words, "Oxidia is Olympia."

Eventually, all of Nietzsche's ideas converge in *The Will to Power* in the notoriously famous "nihilism," the negative side of which lies in the belief that "there simply is no *true world,*" and the positive, in the "*perspectival ap-*

pearance whose origin lies in us" (*WP,* §15). The former would be Stevens' "absence in reality," and the latter, that "things are as [we] think they are," as we have already encountered them. More important, Nietzsche's nihilism may perhaps suggest to Stevens the note (and the musical analogy is important here) on which to end "The Man with the Blue Guitar," which we find in the "rhapsody" that sounds the poem's coda, lyrics XXXII and XXXIII: "It must be this rhapsody or none, / The rhapsody of things as they are" (*CP,* 183). *Rhapsody,* in its derivation from the Greek *rhapsode,* is a double compound of the verb "to stitch," plus the substantive "song." Stevens likewise doubles his guitarist, both as a musician and as a "shearsman of sorts" (*CP,* 165), the word *sorts,* in turn, punning on its etymology from the Latin for "alteration." *Alteration,* in its turn a doubling both for castration and tailoring, invites us to see the destruction of Stevens' barber in "The Comedian as the Letter C" overtaken by the production of the dialogical patchwork in "The Man with the Blue Guitar," but only on one condition: "Nothing must stand / Between you and the shapes you take / When the crust of shape has been destroyed" (*CP,* 183). With that "crust of shape" cast aside, along with all the definitions and rotted names attached to it in lyric XXXII, the rhetoric of Stevens' formalism, what he calls "the madness of space," is double-crossed by the rhetoric of a new antiformalism, a nothing of multiple shapes and "jocular procreations," the "rhapsody of things as they are," and that surprises. If Stevens is being at all faithful to his Nietzschean sources, his rhapsody brings together the "rhapsodist" linked to the theater actor in "On Truth and Lies" (OTL, 89) and the "plurality of interpretations" that, in *The Will to Power,* displaces the aesthetic monism "depriv[ing] the world of its disturbing and enigmatic character" (*WP,* §600). Stevens thus concurs that the *sine qua non* for greatness lies in the ample and the manifold (*BGE,* §212). "The point of the poem," he writes to Hi Simons, is "not that this can be done [*i.e.,* the fabrication of dark space's 'jocular procreations'] but that, if done, it is the key to poetry, to the closed garden, if I may become *rhapsodic* about it, of the fountain of youth and life and renewal" (*L,* 364, emphasis added). On this note, Stevens and his guitarist therefore defer to the model of the *specific* rather than the absolute intellectual that Foucault extracts from Nietzsche: "No longer the rhapsodist of the eternal, but the strategist of life and death."[22]

---

22. Michel Foucault, *Power/Knowledge: Selected Writings and Other Interviews, 1972–1977,* trans. Colin Gordon *et al.,* ed. Colin Gordon (New York, 1980), 129, 133.

The promise of a paradigmatic shift in Stevens' verbal register at the end of the poem now provides him with alternative rhetorical strategies with which to pursue the question of belief. Thus, when the lights go out on his old formalist methods, the man with the blue guitar becomes the first of several figurations for the metaphysician "in the dark," as Stevens describes the state (*CP*, 183), who falls heir to this question. The final lyric provides some suggestions concerning the manner in which we can expect this question to be taken up again in *Parts of a World*. The technique of doubling and repetition is one device already touched on and is present here again in the pairings of two kinds of time, two kinds of dream, two kinds of sleep and wakefulness, and so forth. The foregrounding of imaginative play is predictably instructive as well. In the last two lines, however, Stevens' final suggestion is equally his most problematic: "The moments when we choose to play, / The imagined pine, the imagined jay" (*CP*, 184).

The allusion to a moment in time so strategically placed in the conclusion to the poem's final lyric might seem to invite a quasi-theological reading of the ending as in some sense apocalyptic or revelatory, what Meyer Abrams discovers in so many romantic writers when an instant of consciousness as an "unsustainable moment seems to arrest what is passing, and is often described as an intersection of eternity with time." Northrop Frye's models for the aesthetic or timeless moment in the *Anatomy of Criticism* are "[Arthur] Rimbaud's *illumination*, Joyce's epiphany, the *Augenblick* of modern German thought, and the kind of non-didactic revelation implied in such terms as *symbolisme* and imagism," the most famous examples in literary modernism perhaps being Stephen Dedalus' "aesthetic emotion . . . raised above desire and loathing" in prose and Ezra Pound's "intellectual and emotional complex in an instant of time" in poetry.[23] The problem with this type of an anagogic reading of Stevens' moment lies in all of the transcendental reference points used to define it: center, above, below, beginning, end, and the rest. These threaten to arrest its momentum, a pendulation that Stevens has so carefully prepared for in the distinction between "momentous" and "momentously" noted earlier, which only the absence in reality can legitimate. Again, Nietzsche seems especially influential here. "Becoming," he states, "must be explained without recourse to final intentions; becoming must appear justified *at every moment* (or incapable of being evaluated; which amounts to the same thing); the present must absolutely not be justified by reference to a future,

23. Meyer H. Abrams, *Natural Supernaturalism: Tradition and Revolution in Romantic Literature* (New York, 1973), 385; Frye, *Anatomy of Criticism*, 61.

nor the past by reference to the present" (*WP*, §708, emphasis added). With this emphasis not on the translation of identities but on the reticulation of differences, what Stevens surely must intend by making his "moments" plural, the force of these last lines emerges from their verbs, in the significant acts of choosing and playing. Overlooking these in order to fix the "Blue Guitar" in a final epiphanic revelation—"Time in its final block" (*CP*, 183)— only goes to prove that we do, in fact, sleep by night and forget by day (*CP*, 184).

By way of countering time in its final block, this chapter's opening allusion to T. S. Eliot's unbearable reality thus finds a terminal point in "The Hollow Men," whose lips, in the wasteland Oxidia of that poem, "form prayers to broken stone." [24] But the dramatic shift in Wallace Stevens' conceptualization of reality and imagination in their cooriginary double-crossings makes emphatically clear the separation he would insist on maintaining between his own work and the work of an Anglo-Catholic expatriate whom he would increasingly view, from this period to the end of his life, as "a negative rather than a positive force" (*L*, 378). The monological theism that overtakes Eliot completely after "The Hollow Men" in 1925 solidifies a closure to the question of belief that after *The Man with the Blue Guitar* Stevens himself must find anathema. In an interesting passage that brings together Eliot, Stevens, and all of the men and women falling in the poem that concludes Stevens' third major collection of verse, Martin Heidegger writes in *Being and Time* that usually in falling, "we flee *into* the 'at-home' of publicness"; that is, we flee in the face of what Heidegger refers to as *die Unheimlichkeit*, uncanniness or foreignness, mystery or strangeness. Eliot's flight to a newfound home in royalist England and his fall to the public role of something like literary elder statesman pretty well put an end to the writing of any major poetry in his career after the war. Stevens' reversal of literary priorities in the privacy of a quiet but hardly maritally settled life in New England at the age of fifty-eight presents us with something far more uncanny. For Eliot, the canonizer of still points in turning worlds, the moment would always be final in the "tune [that] is space" (*CP*, 168), as two generations of New Criticism have exhausted themselves in telling us. For Wallace Stevens, in sharp contrast, "*a moment of vision* . . . is at the same time a *disavowal* of that which in the 'today,' is working itself out as the 'past.'" [25] In both Eliot's and Stevens'

24. T. S. Eliot, *The Complete Poems and Plays: 1909–1950* (New York, 1971), 58.

25. Martin Heidegger, *Being and Time*, trans. John Macquarrie and Edward Robinson (New York, 1962), 234, 438. Wallace Stevens' life-long association with William Carlos Williams, in contrast to Eliot, no doubt intensified with Williams' own clear separation from Eliot's poetics

contemporary though distinct literary careers, therefore, is pitched the wrangling of two of modernism's most celebrated dreams. By 1937, time was in its final block for Eliot. With Stevens' achievement of his new antiformalist voice(s) in *The Man with the Blue Guitar,* time, and the hope for new belief, was yet to come.

---

as well, as Joseph N. Riddel thoroughly documents in *The Inverted Bell: Modernism and the Counterpoetics of William Carlos Williams* (Baton Rouge, 1974), xx, 104n8, 141, 166, 209, 241, 266–69, 270–74, and *passim.* For a parallel alignment along Nietzschean lines in the modernism of Ezra Pound, see Kathryne V. Lindberg, *Reading Pound Reading: Modernism After Nietzsche* (New York, 1987), Chap. 3, esp. 114–15.

CHAPTER 3

SEASONS OF BELIEF
The Destruction of Being

I think that everything that takes place in a consciousness at a certain moment
is necessarily bound, even conceived, by the presence or even the absence,
at that moment, of the existence of the other.
                    —Jean-Paul Sartre, *La Critique de la raison dialectique*

It is one of the peculiarities of the imagination that it is always at the end of an
era . . . that it is always attaching itself to a new reality, and adhering to it.
                    —Wallace Stevens, *The Necessary Angel*

Language is seen as the scene of the whole, the way to infinity: he who
knows not language serves idols, he who would see his language would see
his god.
                    —Philippe Sollers, *Logiques*

FOR Wallace Stevens, the idea of God continues to be "the ultimate poetic
idea" (*OP,* 274) through the 1930s. The archaeological fall to realism in *Harmonium* and the teleological rise to romance in *Ideas of Order,* to which his
first two volumes roughly correspond, both make his intentions for writing
within a larger ontological framework plain through to 1935 and 1936. But
The Man with the Blue Guitar in 1936 put all of this into serious doubt, as we
have seen. So with *Parts of a World,* published in 1942, there is the sense that
Stevens is beginning to question the very notion of belief based on logocentric premises. The new direction of his thinking, thus, forms a striking similarity to the ideas of Martin Heidegger. We "do not seek that force [of earlier
thinking] in what has already been thought," writes Heidegger. "We seek it
in something that has not been thought, and from which what has been
thought receives its essential space."[1] As the title of the new book suggests,

---

1. Martin Heidegger, *Identity and Difference,* trans. Joan Stambaugh (New York,
1969), 48.

Parts of a World is both a continuation of and a de*part*ure from previous projects. Establishing the relationship between discrete parts and worldly wholes would continue to flesh out more of the "Whole of Harmonium," a further totalizing of the idea of order that subsequent publications could endeavor to supplement. However, it is clearly the "parts" on which Stevens intends the emphasis to fall throughout the new collection. For every "great disorder" that might be transformed into "an order," there is equally a "violent order" threatening "disorder" (*CP,* 215). In relation to what has gone before and to what it might anticipate, *Parts of a World* is therefore a collection whose opening up new "essential space" for belief can hardly be underestimated in the dramatic genealogy of Stevens' thinking in the pre- and early war years.[2]

"Of Bright & Blue Birds & the Gala Sun," written in 1940, begins to suggest just how problematic the renewal of belief along aestheticist or formalist lines, as a substitute for the "empty heaven and its hymns" mentioned in *Blue Guitar,* can be. "Some things," we learn from the poem, can be "a part" of larger, ontological constructs; "the exactest element" is synonymous with the "gaiety that is being" (*CP,* 248). To this extent, the "will to be" a part sustains the being "total in belief." That the achievement of such a being is only momentary and thus "imperfect," that it is the occasion less of assurance than "surprise," and that it provokes a kind of Nietzschean "laughter" all supply a second meaning for "a part"—the meaning of disaffection and alienation that *doubles* orderly and harmonious integration in the line "And we feel in a way apart . . . [of] a bright *scienza.*" The Zarathustrian laughter here is almost certainly provoked by the equating of the "gaiety that is being" with "a bright *scienza,*" an absolutist formulation that Nietzsche's *Gay Science* could only hold with the utmost contempt, particularly in Book 5.[3]

What begins to take shape in a poem like "Of Bright & Blue Birds" and

2. Michael Sexson catalogs the generally dismissive attitude that has inexplicably permeated the reading of *Parts of a World,* with citations from such notable commentators as Joseph Riddel ("loss of power"), Michel Benamou ("cluttered with paraphernalia"), and Helen Vendler ("laboratory experiments") among others, only to add an impatient fillip of his own: "In the museum of 'Parts of a World,' impermanence is accorded a negative status" (*The Quest of Self,* 85–86).

3. *Cf.* especially *GS,* §353, §354. Additionally, see Stevens' "Yellow Afternoon," written earlier the same year: "One loves that / Of which one is a part as in a unity / A unity that is the life one loves." Assuredly these lines best explain the "celestial ennui" of apart-ments in the 1942 "Notes Toward a Supreme Fiction" (*CP,* 381). For an exhaustive treatment of Stevens' punning "apartments," see Cook, *Poetry, Word-Play, and Word-War,* 220–21.

in so many other "parts" of Stevens' new collection, then, is a deliberate interrogation of a belief founded on the notion of Being considered pure, absolute, stable, and totally self-contained. By continually revolving this notion, Stevens further attempts, in Nietzschean fashion, to trace the genealogy of its provenance and, in the question of belief, his own a/theological refusal. Stevens' "will to be and to be total in belief" in this regard, if it were not framed with such irony, might win for him a place in modern metaphysics, which, according to Heidegger, is a "metaphysics of subjectness [that] thinks the Being of that which is in the sense of will."[4] Consequently, Stevens' impatience with the mediation of "merely knowing" in this poem forms the basis of a much larger effort in the collection to articulate precisely the permissions of the will to absolute Being and total Self-Presence on which belief might be founded.

A central text in the early investigation of this issue is "A Rabbit as King of the Ghosts" from 1937, in which the rabbit "humped high, humped up" represents the omnivorous desire for pure Being and a "fat cat" its corresponding cerebral obstructions (the "difficulty to think at the end of the day"):

> And to feel that the light is a rabbit-light,
> In which everything is meant for you
> And nothing need be explained;
>
> Then there is nothing to think of. It comes of itself;
> And east rushes west and west rushes down,
> No matter. The grass is full
>
> And full of yourself. The trees around are for you,
> The whole of the wideness of night is for you,
> A self that touches all edges,
>
> You become a self that fills the four corners of night.
>
> (*CP*, 209)

Once again, the procession from alien part to ontological whole—the "whole of the wideness of night"—is a deeply felt need, as in all forms of belief.[5]

---

4. Heidegger, *The Question Concerning Technology,* 88.

5. Thus W. H. Auden, who comes at the question of belief so much like T. S. Eliot, after a rare mystical conversion to Christianity in 1933, can write in "The Poet & The City" in *The Dyer's Hand, and Other Essays* (New York, 1968): "A society which was really like a good poem embodying the aesthetic virtues of beauty, order, economy and subordination of detail to the whole, would be a nightmare of horror. . . . Vice versa, a poem which was really like a political

That access to pure Being can never be entirely unmediated, however, also reveals certain fundamental strategies of negation characteristic of these forms of belief as well. The "monument of cat" reveals two in particular: the active gesture of exclusion to which it is subjected in its reduction to "a bug in the grass" by the rabbit at the end of the poem; and the more passive operation of repression that it imparts to the rabbit's totalizing mind, suggested in the passage by "No matter," an important phrase to which we must later return. Either way, the poem's double negative reveals once more how the desire for a-part-ness signals both a gain and a loss when the rabbit merely supplants one form of monument for another in his stony transformation to "a carving in space." Because "spacing" is an opening of presence to absence and absence to presence, "the enigmatic relationship of the living to its other and of an inside to an outside," the poem finally reveals precisely what is at stake in conventional belief traced by its *via negativa* of exclusion and negation.[6]

Two further poems that appear to mirror each other in the hazardous dedication to an ontologically certain faith are "Mrs. Alfred Uruguay" and "Oak Leaves Are Hands," composed in 1940 and 1942, respectively. In the former, Mrs. Uruguay is a figure of pure negation. She says "no / To everything, in order to get at [herself]" (*CP*, 249). Because "for her / To be" can never be more than "to be," that is, she can never be by the inclusion of that which is other than self, "Her no and no [make] yes impossible." It is by such "degenerate forms" that she feels assured she approaches "the real" atop her mountain, despite the bell with which the donkey she rides might falsify her. In the second poem, Lady Lowzen takes a completely opposite tack. For her, "what is [is] other things," and so she "skims the real for its unreal" (*CP*, 272). Her position is only the inversion of Mrs. Uruguay's, though, not its subversion. The principle of exclusion is equally maintained, as is its extension in a more personal set of "degenerate forms": twelve legs, many arms, "metamorphorid" gender, and so forth. We might therefore be tempted to look to the "figure of capable imagination" back in "Mrs. Uruguay" as a way out of this impasse of negation and as a more appropriate model of belief. Stevens, however, turns the youth's "capability" into a question in at least

---

democracy—examples, unfortunately, exist—would be formless, windy, banal and utterly boring" (85).

    6. Jacques Derrida, *Of Grammatology,* trans. Gayatri Chakravorty Spivak (Baltimore, 1974), 70.

two places, so that we wonder if his own blindness and arrogance and impatience "of the bells and midnight forms" do not make of him an "equally outrageous" character, as Harold Bloom suggests. Moreover, this parodic knight's ("chevalere") creation of an imagined land "out of" the bones of martyrs puts us once again in mind of Flora Lowzen, herself a "bachelor" (from the French *bas chevalier,* a young, vassalless knight who therefore must follow the banner of another), who also creates "out of" a sense of deprivation, "out of the movement of few words" (*CP,* 272). It would therefore seem that their unreal opposition to the "real" of Mrs. Uruguay's mountain vision earlier stakes out the other limit that, together, might point to a new "space where the divine," according to Foucault, could conceivably function.[7] The rabbit's carving in space has itself been born "out of" a parallel sense of exclusionary self-possession and problematic limits. Stevens' use here of the phrase *out of* can thus be profitably linked to what Derrida refers to as an "anasemic operation [that] does not result in a growing explicitness" or "virtual significance."[8]

So far, Stevens' argument seems to be that an absolute sense of the truth of Being as the foundation for total belief is possible only to the extent that an individual is able to experience such truth in the fullness of an uninterrupted sense of self. It is fairly evident, however, that pure self-possession is an impossible contradiction, that "no thing can be itself by itself," and that specific definitions and determinations of Being "presuppose *both* distinction from *and* relation to otherness." In this light, the exclusions and repressions that we have seen are incorrigibly paradoxical. From the subject's point of view, the negation they represent is necessary for the stable mastery of self-knowledge, but knowledge of self would not be possible without their constant and mediative irruption from a side other than self. Julia Kristeva puts this point succinctly in *Powers of Horror* when she remarks that "the advent of one's proper identity demands a law that mutilates." Stevens' version of such a law is the 1938 poem "A Weak Mind in the Mountains," a violent anticipation of the equally weak-minded Mrs. Uruguay in the person of a butcher whose "thoughts" appear to be in a life-and-death struggle with superhuman

7. Bloom, *Poems of Our Climate,* 162; Foucault, *Language, Counter-Memory, Practice,* 117.

8. Derrida writes, in "'Fors,'" trans. Barbara Johnson, *Georgia Review,* XXXI (Spring, 1977): "It is 'from out of' [*depuis*] the possibility of this 'loss' or of the 'death' of the subject (these words to be read anasemically), from out of the possibility of a sepulcher, in one form or another, that the entire theoretical space is redistributed. The anasemic account thus has an essential relation to a sepulcher" (96–97). For a contrasting use of the phrase, see Northrop Frye, *The Great Code: The Bible as Narrative* (Toronto, 1982), 193.

forces from outside (*CP*, 212). His response is a bravado exercise of his own power, squeezing some "thing" from nature until "blood / Spurt[s] from between the fingers" and it falls to the floor. Stevens is deliberately vague about what dies in the poem, and such deliberate vagueness makes for considerable irony in the poem's final line, in which the butcher standing "sharply in the sky" is belied by the "blood of the mind" that falls to the floor, the price presumably for the assertion of total self-identity.[9]

Some "thing" in "A Weak Mind in the Mountains" is the means by which the self attempts to establish full presence, what Heidegger in his essay on "The Thing" refers to as "nearness." Although the nearness of things "presences nearness," it nonetheless perpetually "conceals its own self," and this absence (Nothing, Death) points to a mystery at the heart of Being itself.[10] The presence that simultaneously doubles as absence helps to explain the irony in Stevens' poem and also the poem's preoccupation with death. This presence also helps to explain the lengths, bordering almost on obsession, to which the mind is carried in many of Stevens' other poems in order to ground itself in some fixed center of unalterable belief. "It can never be satisfied, the mind, never," concludes the title character of "The Well Dressed Man with a Beard," composed in 1941:

> One only, one thing that was firm, even
> No greater than a cricket's horn, no more
> Than a thought to be rehearsed all day, a speech
> Of the self that must sustain itself on speech,
> One thing remaining, infallible, would be
> Enough, Ah! douce campagna of that thing!
>
>   (*CP*, 247)

Speech, "the infinite vocation of full presence," is naturally privileged in the mind's search for ultimate satisfaction, for "out of a thing believed," it will declare "a thing affirmed" (*CP*, 247).[11] Even if Phosphor in "Phosphor Read-

---

9. Taylor, *Erring*, 112–13; Kristeva, *Powers of Horror*, 54. For a sense of negation contrasting to that described previously, see also Julia Kristeva, *Revolution in Poetic Language*, trans. Margaret Waller (New York, 1984), esp. Part II, "Negativity: Rejection."

10. Martin Heidegger, *Poetry, Language, Thought*, trans. Albert Hofstadter (New York, 1975), 178–79.

11. Jacques Derrida, *Speech and Phenomena, and Other Essays on Husserl's Theory of Signs*, trans. David B. Allison (Evanston, 1973), 102. In "The Beast of Lascaux," published in 1956, Maurice Blanchot writes, apropos Stevens' "thing": "There could be nothing more striking than this shock, this uneasiness which the silence of art inspires in the lover of the spoken word, the faithful upholder of the honor of living speech; which is nothing but a semblance, a thing which speaks truth and yet with nothing but a void behind it, no possibility of discussion, so that in it

ing by His Own Light" from 1942 is not given to expect what he may be reading, it is "speech" nevertheless that will make him think "that that is what [he] expect[s]," for he is his own "realist" (from the Latin *realis,* from *res,* or thing) and proceeds by the oneness of self-illumination (*CP,* 267).

It is precisely the self-contradictory sense of an other, therefore, that fills "The Man on the Dump," written in 1938, with such ambiguity. If nearness is the necessary condition for the presencing of self, as Heidegger suggests, and for the centering of belief, one beats and beats (tin cans, lard pails), "for that which one believes," because "that's what one wants to get near" (*CP,* 202). So many of the images in this poem thus tend to be holders of things (paper bags, corsets, boxes, chests) because belief is impossible without a total self-containment, an idea that is developed more generally in many of the titles included in *Parts of a World:* "The Glass of Water," "A Dish of Peaches in Russia," "Man and Bottle," and so on. Self-containment, however, is an impossible project for the genuinely creative poet or artist. One advances one's art only by creating wholly new work, by remaining open to "the purifying change" and by "reject[ing] / The trash." Advancement under these rules requires a certain originality. It is not enough merely to *copy* the novel, for instance, the "freshness of night," "the dew in the green," or "the time of spring," as some kind of academic exercise. That gives the view of the public dump as seen from the ivory tower—a view for which Stevens had little patience, for example, in the writing of William Carlos Williams (*OP,* 214). And, as the poem makes clear, it is a view that one can easily grow to hate "*except* on the dump" (emphasis added). That is to say, it promotes the work of a second-rate imagination, the passive or reactive imagination we encountered in Crispin's artistic repressions back in Chapter 1, the creative sensibility that works under the reflective impress of "the moon" and the "empty sky" that inevitably goes along with it.[12] Yet if the poet is equally to achieve any kind of immediate transcendence amid change, there does not

---

the truth has nothing with which to confirm itself, appears without support, is only a scandalous semblance of truth, an image, and by its imagery and seeming draws away truth into depths where there is neither truth nor meaning, not even error" (Megill, *Prophets of Extremity,* 287). *Cf.* further Jacques Derrida, *Dissemination,* trans. Barbara Johnson (Chicago, 1981), 211.

12. David M. La Guardia, in *Advance on Chaos: The Sanctifying Imagination of Wallace Stevens* (Hanover, N.H., 1983), also rescinds the canonical view of this symbol. He notes: "The moon is not Stevens' familiar figure for the imagination. Because it was 'a supremacy always / Above him' and 'was always free from him' (*CP* 314), the moon becomes a figure for the consolation man provides for himself by inventing spiritual and poetic systems of belief" (102). This is a view, however, that Stevens developed much before the later *Transport to Summer,* where La Guardia situates it.

seem to be any way around the "philosopher's honeymoon" (*CP,* 203). If there is to be any peace, phenomenological truth must be derived from things outworn and discarded even though, from the artistic standpoint, these constitute the very things that stand to alienate the imager from his self. That the absolutism of this position is, once again, fissured with questions, reveals that such a totalizing belief puts the man on the dump completely beside himself:

> Is it to sit among mattresses of the dead,
> Bottles, pots, shoes and grass and murmur *aptest eve:*
> Is it to hear the blatter of grackles and say
> *Invisible priest;* is it to eject, to pull
> The day to pieces and cry *stanza my stone?*
>
> (*CP,* 203)

"Is there an economy of the eve?" asks Jacques Derrida in his conclusion to "The Ends of Man." He answers: "Perhaps we are between these two eves [*i.e.,* the truth of Being and that which lies 'beyond' metaphysics], which are also two ends of man. But who, we?"[13] Stevens is equally dubious about a univocal belief in humanism located "between the things / That are on the dump," which he expresses in the final line of his poem: "Where was it one first heard of the truth? The the." With that final question, written in 1938, and its unspeakable answer, a whole new verbal register in Stevens' poetry begins to open up.

We can begin to map some of the new imagery that partly accounts for the notable discursive shift in Stevens' new collection by observing, first of all, that until the question of belief is broached in terms that point to something more radical and ex-centric than the full plenitude of univocal Truth, the self perpetually struggles to make Being pure and transparent to itself. In "Country Words" from 1937, for instance, transparent selfhood is centered in a "diamond pivot" (*CP,* 207), and if it were possible for Belshazzar, the last of the Chaldean kings, to read the "luminous pages . . . / Of being" from that fulcrum, there would be no need for prophets like Daniel to sing an "old rebellious song" of salvation or to inscribe portentous messages of doom on the walls of caves.[14] The cloud "that hangs / Upon the heart and round the mind"

---

13. Derrida, *Margins of Philosophy,* 136.

14. The diamond as a symbol of transparent self-affirmation has some analogy to the crystal used in several similar contexts in Derrida's *Grammatology, e.g.,* the "model of a small community with a 'crystalline' structure, completely self-present, assembled in its own neighborhood, [which] is undoubtedly Rousseauistic" (137) and others. *Cf.* 262, 267, 314, 348*n,* and also Derrida, "'Fors,'" 108.

would already be cleared, like the ruby-red sun hanging in the height that functions as another image for self-certain knowledge, already encountered in poems like "Of Bright & Blue Birds," "Mrs. Alfred Uruguay," and "The Well Dressed Man with a Beard." With such clairvoyance, there may not be any need at all for Belshazzar's "reading right" or for the song of Daniel, which in any event "never clears."

A parallel shift in Stevens' imagery throughout *Parts of a World* can, second, be noted in his handling of female figures, which in several of the poems become interchangeable with the red sun and the diamond day in the tropology of metaphysical presence. However, since in the previous poems identity tends more and more to be "established and maintained by relation to difference . . . from terms other than itself" (rabbit and cat, Mrs. Uruguay and the youth, Belshazzar and Daniel) and presence tends to remain outside the grasp of the totalizing and homogenizing consciousness, the females in this poetry are therefore ultimately made elusive and exceedingly hard to pin down.[15] Thus, in the 1939 "Bouquet of Belle Scavoir," it is a female that the poem's protagonist desires "to look at directly, / Someone before him to see and to know." Absolute knowledge (the "s[c]avoir" of the title, which forms a significant link to the "SA" in Derrida's *Glas*), though, remains frustratingly evasive:

III

How often had he walked
Beneath summer and the sky
To receive her shadow into his mind . . .
Miserable that it was not she.

. . . .

V

The reflection of her here, and then there,
Is another shadow, another evasion,
Another denial. If she is everywhere,
She is nowhere, to him.

(*CP*, 231)

The "everywhere" that is "nowhere" again raises the issue of how unstable presence and an exclusionary belief in presence are when their very interiority seems to have been made possible only through the infarction of exteriority. That their being has been *made* by some "other," there can be no doubt: "If

15. Mark C. Taylor, *Altarity* (Chicago, 1987), 197; and further, Derrida, *Spurs,* 55.

it is / Another image, it is one she has made" (*CP*, 232). The speaker in the poem consequently can only conclude that "it is she alone that matters."

Earlier I mentioned that the rejection of the "fat cat" in "A Rabbit as King of the Ghosts" as of "no matter," repeated with the "cat in the paper-bag" in "The Man on the Dump" (*CP*, 201), was a repressive gesture to which we would return. Now, it is possible to see that the "mother" buried in "matter" (from the Latin *mater*, or mother) surreptitiously underscores a female principle that, because it resists apprehension in ontological terms, because it indeed refuses the very logocentrism of such a metaphysics, "forbids our speak-ing." [16] In "Yellow Afternoon," written in 1940, the man described is so unsettled that a woman is constitutive of his own being ("she caught his breath") that he molds "the bottom of things" into the completing sculpture of a "patriarch," a conceptual unity that he loves as a part belonging to a greater whole: "There he touches his being" (*CP*, 236–37). But the collapse of the very difference through which his identity has been constructed, into a "fatal unity," only fills him with an even greater sense of mystery. Lying on his bed in the dark at the end of the poem, "close to a face / Without eyes or mouth," he is made to feel, as we have seen before, only that much more a/part. In the following "Martial Cadenza," also from 1940, Stevens reverses the perspective on the scandalous a-part-ness of presence, wedging its cadence (from the Latin *cadere*, or to fall) between the movements of the military in the poem's first and final parts, much as in the first and final movements of the classical concerto (*CP*, 237–38). What an "evening star," symbolizing the "present close, the present realized," and a silent "world without time" can possibly have to do with war-torn Europe in 1940 seems odd at first, until the speaker realizes that the process of symbolization, as the signification of that which is other, has already made rupture originary to Being's expression. In a paradoxical way, the apartness of the "vivid thing in the air" joins a parallel sense of the soldier's feelings of separation on earth, and only with that realization can he dare to breathe and move again, as can the star flash again, in acknowledgment of a renewed sense of changefulness.

A third and final pattern that figures significantly in Stevens' reformulation of the premises of belief is a certain hand-eye coordination that finds its thematic locus in the image of the human head in several of these poems. Self-presence as an effect of reason in ego consciousness naturally privileges

16. Jacques Lacan, *Feminine Sexuality: Jacques Lacan and the École Freudienne*, trans. J. Rose, ed. J. Mitchell and J. Rose (New York, 1982), 144; *Cf.* also Luce Irigaray, *Speculum of the Other Woman*, trans. Gillian C. Gill (Ithaca, 1985), 165–66, 176, 183, 210, 212, and *passim*.

rationalization and conceptualization as ways of clarifying Being to itself, as the whole history of modern philosophy in the West since Descartes and Kant can show. The image of the evening star in "Martial Cadenza" and the blood-red sun elsewhere strengthen the desire for philosophy's rational enlightenment. The reasoning mind is also the seat of reflection, however, and reflection on self-knowledge can only represent certain truth, not inhabit it. Consequently, there is the sense in which self-conscious thought is a double-dealer, that it unifies only as it alienates, that it destroys in the very act of creation. "Bouquet of Belle Scavoir" comes close to this idea with its view of "reflection" as "evasion," but "Cuisine Bourgeoise," composed in 1939, adds the element of cannibalistic self-destruction and is more deadly accurate:

> We feast on human heads, brought in on leaves,
> Crowned with the first cold buds.
>
> . . . .
>
>   This bitter meat
> Sustains us . . . Who, then, are they, seated here?
> Is the table a mirror in which they sit and look?
> Are they men eating reflections of themselves?
>   (*CP*, 228)

Later in "Extracts from Addresses to the Academy of Fine Ideas," in a similar context, Stevens will attack the severe limitations of egocentric thought in the image of "starvation's head" and "the single man" (*CP*, 254), as "science" is made synonymous with "this present" in "Cuisine Bourgeoise" (*CP*, 228). All of this has surely been anticipated in the "head like a carving in space" in "A Rabbit as King of the Ghosts" (*CP*, 210), whose link to the savage attack on knowledge in "Bouquet of Belle Scavoir" comes with the image of "the stone bouquet" in the final line of "Of Hartford in a Purple Light" (*CP*, 227).

From the fantasy of total consciousness symbolized by a stone head, Stevens' imagery modulates to the image of a gigantic hand, in "Poem with Rhythms" from 1941, made large by a candle on a wall, reminiscent of the famous cave in Plato's *Republic* since the hand parallels how the mind becomes enlarged "between this light or that and space" (*CP*, 245–46). Lady Lowzen "putting hand to brow" had established a similar connection between the hand and the mind. Here, the hand's will to grow larger and sturdier than the wall, like the mind's "wish and will" to compose or presence itself cleanly in a powerful mirror, corresponds to what Heidegger would describe as "the making secure of the constant reserve." By such means, "man makes secure for himself material, bodily, psychic, and spiritual resources, and this for the sake of his own security, which wills dominion over whatever is . . . in order to correspond to the Being of whatever is, to the will to power." As we have seen several times already, however, a re-serving or a re-presenting faults the project of egocentrism at its inception, as Stevens appears to indicate in the poem either in the familar figure of the female who receives into her heart the lover that mysteriously never comes or, more generally, in the exercise of a bodily part that a much larger mental whole seems ill-suited for. Stevens' choice of the hand in this exercise, or quest for ultimate truth, is perhaps something that our language has arranged idiomatically. As William Spanos observes, "the degree to which metaphysical man, whether Platonic, Cartesian, Hegelian, or technocratic, attempts to take hold of, to seize, to comprehend, to manipulate, the temporality of being . . . is precisely the degree to which the inscrutable mystery of being eludes and recedes from his grasp, indeed, is alienated and transformed into a retaliatory force."[17] This observation would also help to explain Stevens' baffling title. A poem with "rhythms" would, on principle, want to maintain a broad sense of temporality and resist metaphysical reduction to a single, present, epiphanic moment so contrary to thought in its metonymic extensions. Predictably, Stevens' thought is Heideggerian, once again: "For Heidegger, Being is neither substance nor form. It is rhythm . . . an ordered and recurrent alternation . . . [that] implies determination of 'form' as imprint, seal, and character . . . [but] withholds itself in what springs forth from it."[18] In a second way, as Kristeva notes, "rhythm that multiplies language . . . withdraws from its transcendental position," and Stevens' highly irregular shaping of the poem, more in terms of thought units than a regular stanzaic pattern, seems deliberately calculated to baffle the orderly logic that a transcendental position would naturally assume. Besides, "a poem need not have a meaning, and like most things in nature often does not have" (*OP*, 201). Rhythm thus "severs the 'self,' the body and each organ."[19] In a curious way, then, the hand in this poem, like the one in "A Weak Mind in the Mountains," reverses rather than re-serves its own semantic import, despite the hyperconscious effort to

17. Heidegger, *The Question Concerning Technology*, 107; Spanos, *Repetitions*, 135.

18. Rodolphe Gasché, "Joining the Text: From Heidegger to Derrida," in *The Yale Critics: Deconstruction in America*, ed. Jonathan Arac, Wlad Godzich, and Wallace Martin (Minneapolis, 1983), 162–63; *cf.* also Derrida, *Grammatology*, 8.

19. Kristeva, *Desire in Language*, 184.

maintain (from the French *main,* or hand, and *tenir,* or to hold) its own "apprehension."

The hand's project of mental manumission in Stevens' texts ideally points to a universal life recollected in unity and wholeness. Provided that the will is strong enough, even Lady Lowzen, re-membering the centuries as "the acorn broods on former oaks," can turn "oak leaves" into "hands." In the hand's metonymic aspect of dismemberment and departure, though, there is no return save for that marked by a wholly other, that is, death. "In the sum of the parts, / There are only the parts" (*CP,* 204), which also seems to be the point of a wonderful passage in Lacan where Reason, trying to trap the feminine mystery of Being in a Platonic enclosure, is left only with the "nonsense" traced by "the profile of Cleopatra's nose." A dungeon or a cave, however, need not be the only setting for the deadly displacement of self-secure belief. In an important passage in *Letters,* Stevens outlines another that he will later use in "Notes," namely, the base of a tree: "There is a double meaning: a. on reflection (a man stretched out at his ease, underneath a tree, thinking;) b. a great tree is a symbol of fixity, permanence, completion, the opposite of a 'moving contour'" (*L,* 444). In "The Hand as a Being," a poem written in 1942, a year after "Poem with Rhythms," and inserted in the *Collected Poems* just before "Oak Leaves," Stevens once again brings the figures of tree, hand, and "naked, nameless dame" together for yet another treatment of death inhabiting a mind "too conscious of too many things at once" (*CP,* 271). A more likely alternative he provides in "The Sense of the Sleight-of-hand Man" from 1939. For this is a man who does not secure for himself recognition at the expense of others, including himself, but one who re*mains* "alone," an "ignorant man" in an "empty house" (*CP,* 168). His ignorance shows that the best sense, if it is to be manhandled, may just be no sense at all—nonsense—and that life, that "sensual, pearly spouse" once again, is not one "fixed in a profound defeat" as in "Martial Cadenza" (*CP,* 238). Rather, it is "the life / That is fluent," in other words, the life that is open to time, to the rhythms of bluejay and dove and geese. Things "occur as they occur." As Giles Gunn recently observes, "the inevitable passage of experience, its disappearance and loss, necessarily condemns as illusory and fictitious any efforts to forestall its dissolutions . . . and hence may only represent, curiously enough, the form of our despair." Without such openness to time and experience, there does not appear to be any chance for the ignorant man to "mate his life with life," a conclusion that forms a very strong connection to Heidegger's *Die Gelassenheit zu den Dingen,* that is, to the "releasement toward things and openness to the mystery [that] belong together" and to "the possibility of dwelling in the world in a totally *different* way." The invitation in *Parts of a World* is therefore "Piece the world together, boys, but not with your hands" (*CP,* 192).[20]

After the thorough debasement of the head and hand in Stevens' thematization of belief rooted in egocentrism, there remains only the image of the eye in the ravaging dismemberment of *Parts.* The eye is the eye of Reason in the Western metaphysical tradition, overlooking the safety and security of stable self-presence, the first-person "I," on which it plays and with which it equivocates. Of the five senses, sight rules supreme, if the others matter at all, since in the commonsense view of human affairs seeing is believing. "A man must be very poor / With a single sense," yet in "Arcades of Philadelphia the Past," written in 1939, the image of the eyes held in the palm of the hand makes it absolutely clear that super-vision is the privileged power in the mental economy:

> Do they touch the thing they see,
> Feel the wind of it, smell the dust of it?
> They do not touch it. Sounds never rise
> Out of what they see. They polish their eyes
> In their hands.
>
>   .   .   .   .   .
>
> The tongue, the fingers, and the nose
> Are comic trash, the ears are dirt,
> But the eyes are men in the palm of the hand.
>   (*CP,* 225)

Linked to the power of sight is the heavy mood of nostalgia throughout the poem, suggested by the archaeology of the title and also by the effort in the opening lines to "remember the past," to domesticate absence by shaping it to the present in an act of retention, as the imagery of hands once again underscores. That "the town and the fragrance [of lilacs] were never [really] one" or that their red-blue and red-purple were "never quite red" seems not to matter. Eyes operating in concert with rather than exclusive of the other

20. Jacques Lacan, *Écrits: A Selection,* trans. Alan Sheridan (New York, 1977), 122; Martin Heidegger, *Discourse on Thinking,* trans. John M. Anderson and E. Hans Freund (New York, 1966), 55, emphasis added; Giles Gunn, *Thinking Across the American Grain: Ideology, Intellect, and the New Pragmatism* (Chicago, 1992), 184.

senses could tell another story, but that would constitute a genuine *dérègle-ment du sens*. "The search for the ground of a lost harmony is a counterrevolutionary act," however, and in the last few words of the poem a clear fake.[21]

Curiously, therefore, sight as a kind of exclusive common sense handed around by men ultimately becomes the source of its opposite, the most intolerable blindness, and of what follows, the most impossible doubt. In the "Cartesian formula" of doubt, Foucault tells us, "Descartes closes his eyes and plugs up his ears the better to see the true brightness of essential daylight [and thus] . . . is secured against the dazzlement of the madman." This is precisely Cotton Mather's position in "The Blue Buildings in the Summer Air" from 1938. His antinomian inner light, "the honey-comb of the seeing man," must doubt the existence of heaven every place but where he "think[s] it is"; and deep within the arches of his dungeonlike church, reading "all night and all the nights," he is intermittently startled by what he rejects:

> The shore, the sea, the sun,
> Their brilliance through the lattices, crippled
> The chandeliers, their morning glazes spread
> In opal blobs along the walls and floor.
>
> (*CP*, 217)

In this poem, the madman is played by a tiny mouse, the projection of Mather's riddling "doubt," nibbling away inside the church walls. So thunderous is it in its undermining of faith's sure foundations ("arches" from the Greek *archē*, or beginning, origin), that it compels Mather to preach all the louder, in his longing "for a church / In which his voice would . . . quiet that mouse in the wall" (*CP*, 216). The tiny mouse here is obviously connected to "the little green cat" in "A Rabbit as King of the Ghosts" and to the "little owl" both in "On the Adequacy of Landscape" and in "Woman Looking at a Vase of Flowers" in a way suggested by Mark Taylor, who paraphrases Emmanuel Levinas in the following: "The enigmatic trace drives the philosopher mad by 'throw[ing] "a grain of folly" [*grain de folie*] into the universal ego.' . . . This excessive grain is the 'infinitesimal difference' (*différence infinitésimale*) that renders the aspirations of philosophy laughable."[22]

The irony that a monological belief centered in an indifferent self ("You are one") should at the same time create such division in the world, whence

21. Altizer, *The Descent into Hell*, 41–42.

22. Michel Foucault, *Madness and Civilization: A History of Insanity in the Age of Reason*, trans. Richard Howard (New York, 1973), 108; Taylor, *Altarity*, 195.

"Lenin in his tomb," is one we are by now quite familiar with. The "not-numberable mice," like the myriad cells of the honeycomb that summer is cut up to find, only go to prove, in lines from the 1942 "Dezembrum," that "over and over again . . . This great world divides itself" and that in the face of it "The reason can give nothing at all / Like the response to desire" (*CP*, 218). So we turn next to the very group of poems in *Parts of a World* that cause Reason's cavernous repose to "burst into flames," as "Girl in a Nightgown," composed in 1942, puts it (*CP*, 214).

The phase of Stevens' writing that this next set of poems develops carries to completion a radical process of thinking I could only begin to suggest in the last chapter, when we saw Stevens begin to rethink the whole conceptual foundation of "reality" in its relation to the notions of both imagination and belief while he was writing *The Man with the Blue Guitar*. Two poems written in 1939, a couple of years after the publication of *Blue Guitar*, indicate that the new book of verse submitted for publication in 1942 would be of an entirely different character than the previous three volumes.[23] In "Forces, the Will & the Weather," Stevens is emphatic that the fundamental "shift / Of realities" (*CP*, 229) that would manifest itself plainly in his new writing would involve a condemnation of ideas. His attack, however, would not be directed at the *contents* of ideas themselves, for, like "nougats" and "dog-woods," "white ones and pink ones . . . handfuls thrown up / To spread colors," there would always be plenty of those: "anti-ideas," "counter-ideas," and so forth. Instead, his attention would be focused on the *addiction* to ideas and, in particular, on singular addictions like that, for instance, embodied in communism in the reference to Lenin in "The Bagatelles the Madrigals," composed in 1942, and to Moscow in the present poem. The big idea in "Of Hartford in a Purple Light," written in 1939, the same year as "Forces," is like "Master Soleil," a harsh, invariant, masculine light that the aunts of Pasadena abhor because it works with "big hands" (naturally), imposing "heroic attitudes" on their town, and leaving entirely out of account more particular, more precise, more regional "intonings": "Hartford seen in a *purple* light,"

23. The view taken here is thus not the canonical one of *Parts of a World* or the view of Stevens' oeuvre in general, if Alan Perlis may be said to represent a wider consensus: "The few writers who mark significant changes in the poems from *Harmonium* (1923) to *The Rock* (1955) insist that these changes concern emphasis and impact rather than a radical shift of ideas." See Perlis, *Wallace Stevens: A World of Transforming Shapes* (Lewisburg, Pa., 1976), 21. One of the reasons Stevens himself considered *Parts* his "best book," according to Peter Brazeau in *Parts of a World: Wallace Stevens Remembered, an Oral Biography* (New York, 1983), 201, is perhaps because it represented such a departure from anything he had accomplished up until its 1942 publication.

for instance (*CP*, 226, emphasis added). The link to "Forces," comes by way of the Hartford museum's large plaster horses contraposed to "lights feminine" in the image of a poodle splattering thousands of "petty tricolor" drops, since in "Forces," we are made to feel that the pink girl walking her fluffy dog would find similar "large white horses" equally oppressive (*CP*, 229). Of parallel importance in the Hartford poem is the shift to the leaves of the trees and to their blooms and nuts rather than to the trees themselves, as if Lady Lowzen's acorns were a more appropriate subject for brooding than "former oaks." The poems we should therefore next want to take up would help to show why "a land without ideas"—a land with "nothing," nugatory, to follow the pun on the nuts—held such attraction for Stevens.

The two central texts among these, perhaps the two most important in the whole book, categorically dismiss the effort, in what we have thus far seen, to make the idea of Being present to itself. They simply assert that "there is no such thing as the truth" (*CP*, 203). The entire metaphysical project of centering absolute knowledge within the rational self, and belief on the consequence of prophylactic self-reflection, is suddenly no more when these words are first spoken in "On the Road Home" from 1938. As soon as it is admitted that there are "many truths" (the anti- and counter-ideas back in "Forces") but that these are not "parts" of "*a* truth" (or "*an* idea"), only then is there a shift of realities. Only then is the cat out of the bag, or in this poem the fox "out of his hole," and only then does "the tree, at night, [begin] to change" (*CP*, 203).[24] Since there is no absolute relation between a transcendent sum and its demotic parts, the new attitude taken toward the eye/I is that it must now begin carefully to measure its world, rather than blindly impose or assume shapes fitted to its self-serving occasions. The implication is that surrounded by such multifariousness, it is helpless by itself, like the "weak mind" standing all alone "in the mountains." For the first time, eye/I is compelled to open wide and affirm a correlative role in sense experience, thereby determining "the noncenter otherwise than as the loss of center" and the nontruth as coincident with an "active interpretation."[25]

---

24. The image of the wily fox being roused from its home occurs in a very similar context in a letter Stevens wrote to Henry Church in 1942. In it, he expresses some doubt about the definitiveness with which Lionello Venturi philosophizes about "The Idea of the Renaissance" in a recent volume of the *Gazette des Beaux Arts:* "This gets the Renaissance into focus momentarily . . . and yet, when you think it over afterwards . . . you think it is just one more proof that the right always comes to nothing. . . . Venturi is to me what a very smelly fox is to a young dog: I don't need any horn to follow him" (*L*, 432).

25. Derrida, *Writing and Difference*, 292.

It was at that time, that the silence was largest
And longest, the night was roundest,
The fragrance of the autumn warmest,
Closest and strongest.

(*CP,* 204)

Stevens' carefully chosen title therefore helps *us* to see that it is not "home" itself that is being rejected outright in the poem, just as centers of truth are not to be entirely dismissed. What is opened to question is a certain nostalgia connected with both (from the Greek *nostos,* or return home, and *algos,* or pain) in the impossible certainty of singular self-reflection. By foregrounding reflective process, Stevens hopes to displace its dreamy products permanently.

In a second, even more radical text written the same year, 1938, it is precisely this displacement that constitutes liberation for the title character of "The Latest Freed Man." The products of truth requiring dispersal are "the old descriptions of the world" and, in particular, "the importance of the trees outdoors," as in "On the Road Home": "The freshness of the oak-leaves, not so much / That they were oak-leaves, as the way they looked" (*CP,* 205). Over and over again in this poem, the emphasis falls not on what causes the man's elation, his having escaped from the truth (the "doctrine" to a landscape), but instead on how "his freedom came" and how he sheds the gift of its light: in a word, the "overtaking" of doctrine (*CP,* 204). Consequently, what is more important than the stasis of description is the exstasis of transformation, "the ant of the self changed to an ox," for instance, or "a doctor into an ox." These can be as utterly bizarre as Stevens intends, since their point, as with the oak leaves, is not to mean, in the tag from Archibald MacLeish, but rather to be: "It was everything being more real . . . bulging and blazing and big in itself." Stevens' placement of the latest freed man on the edge of his bed at the beginning of the poem achieves precisely this dislodgment of logocentric overdetermination. Geoffrey Hartman notes in a related context:

> What the edge means is impossible to define in terms of inside and outside or balance and imbalance. The equilibrium of page or book is like the illusory concept of Greek repose; that balance, as in Hegel's dialectic, is continually thrown off balance, the limit-boundary is crossed or sublated. . . . The form of the book is a Kantian limit that both justifies and disables metaphysical (onto-theological) questions concerning the relation of knowledge to truth, names to things, and writing to reality . . . [so] what mat-

ters is the antithetical *éc* in *écriture*, which writes something in (or out) without naming it.[26]

The full weight of the poem, therefore, would appear to fall on its moments: "the moment's rain and sea" at one time, the "moment's sun" at another, and so forth. This is the "moment," as we saw in the last chapter, in which Stevens brings *The Man with the Blue Guitar* to an important thematic conclusion. But from the perspective of *Parts of a World,* and of "The Latest Freed Man" in particular, he perhaps might now see that such moments in the position of closure argue too much for "recognition" as "returns of the same" rather than as "unsettling acknowledgements of the other," which in the present poem constitute truth at the edge, from *wherever* one might possibly happen to be.[27]

Earlier, I mentioned the radical process of thinking that Stevens brings to full development in these texts, and there can be no doubt that his model for this radical thought continues to be the writings of Friedrich Nietzsche, noted briefly in our examination of *Blue Guitar.* Now, five years after that volume, the evidence of the German philosopher's influence would appear to be so substantial that we can no longer postpone dealing with its subject as we did in the last chapter. This is an especially tricky issue in the study of Stevens, since we have the explicit denial of "Nietzschean shadows" in at least two published letters from 1942 (*L,* 409, 485). As the recent work on his personal life appears to indicate, however, Stevens was notoriously secretive about his reading and writing and sometimes even downright mendacious, so it is perhaps without exaggeration that in the case of Nietzsche, as Milton J. Bates has recently concluded, "nowhere else in Stevens does one have an intellectual influence whose sources and extent can be specified with as much certainty."[28]

26. Hartman, *Saving the Text,* 85. Some difficulty, therefore, may be provoked by the later description of the man "being more real, himself / At the centre of reality, seeing it" (*CP,* 205). Kristeva cites Philippe Sollers in a related passage that sheds some light: "This is not mysticism saying 'I am the truth.' The polylogue says, 'i truth i have a right to lie in the manner that suits me' [p. 35]. For this polylogical 'I' speaks *before:* before logic, before language, before being" (*Desire in Language,* 188).

27. David Tracy, *Plurality and Ambiguity: Hermeneutics, Religion, Hope* (San Francisco, 1987), 83.

28. Bates, *A Mythology of Self,* 248. *Cf.* also Riddel, *The Clairvoyant Eye,* 211, Leonard and Wharton, *The Fluent Mundo,* 182, B. J. Leggett, "Apollonian and Dionysian in 'Peter Quince at the Clavier,'" *Wallace Stevens Journal,* XIV (Spring, 1990), 59. See Brazeau, *Parts of a World,* 139, 142, 149, for Stevens' notorious secrecy. The final form of B. J. Leggett's extended project, *Early*

In the poems previously discussed, for instance, the citations in "On the Road Home" that "there is no such thing as the truth," that "there are many truths," and that there exists no one single "truth" are all direct transcriptions from *The Will to Power*, where Nietzsche states that "there are many kinds . . . of 'truths,' and consequently there is no truth" and that "whatever is real, whatever is true, is neither one nor even reducible as one" (*WP*, §540, §536). Similarly, when "the strong" man achieves his moment in the sun in "The Latest Freed Man" by escaping "from the truth" and "overtaking the doctrine," his genesis is in *Thus Spoke Zarathustra*, where "good men never speak the truth" but, like Zarathustra, "annihilate in victory" with the sun of their "inexorable solar will" (*Z*, 200, 215) and where we also read chapters "On Self-Overcoming" and "The Return Home." Further, that "*the* way [to truth] . . . does not exist," for "thus spoke Zarathustra" (*Z*, 195), accords precisely with Stevens' emphasis in his text on "the *way* [the oak-leaves] looked," which too often gets lost in the names for things themselves. Names make things "familiar" to us, "and what we are used to is most difficult to 'know'—that is, to see . . . as strange, as distant, as 'outside us'" (*GS*, 301). Besides, the "'thing-in-itself' is nonsensical"; it is "a dogmatic idea with which one must break absolutely," since truth is "not something there, that might be found or discovered—but something that must be created and that gives a name to a process, or rather to a will to overcome that has in itself no end—introducing truth, as a *processus in infinitum*, an active determining" (*WP*, §557, §559, §552). If there is anything that might be deemed absolute, therefore, Stevens and Nietzsche would both agree that it is skepticism, "an absolute skepticism toward all inherited concepts (of the kind that one philosopher

---

Stevens: The Nietzschean Intertext (Durham, 1992), acknowledging also the work of Rajeev S. Patke (*The Long Poems of Wallace Stevens: An Interpretative Study* [Cambridge, Eng., 1985]) and Robert Rehder (*The Poetry of Wallace Stevens* [London, 1988]) in corroborating Stevens' Nietzschean intertextuality, prefers not to view the philosopher as a direct source of influence on the poet as I do here, but via the interpretive theories of Michael Riffaterre and Pierre Macherey, to perceive Nietzsche as "an infinitely deferred tension in the cross-reading of texts" since "in arguments of this sort there always must seem an unbridgeable abyss between obvious parallels in texts and the implicit claim for an experience in a world outside the texts where one work became the source of the other" (81, 16; see also 19, 252, 258n4). The position, elegant and eloquent as it is, nonetheless seems peculiarly at odds with Leggett's insistent use of the superseded Oscar Levy editions of Nietzsche (1909, 1911), along with reference to contemporary interpretations by H. L. Mencken (1908) and Anthony M. Ludovici (1911). Leggett's work on the "intertext" is important and, in places, astonishing in the parallels it turns up (*e.g.* 107, 165, 191, 195, 210–11, 226, 229–30, 231, 241, 245, 256–57n3, 258n4 and *passim*). Unfortunately, it arrives too late for me to make any further use for what follows in my own argument.

perhaps possessed—Plato, of course—for he taught the reverse)" (*WP*, §409).

Once the influence of Nietzsche is acknowledged here, many of the other poems in *Parts of a World* begin to take on an extra dimension that bears directly on Nietzsche's own massive attempt to formulate a departure from the Western philosophical tradition in practically every one of his writings. The criticism of Plato just cited, for instance, explains several of Stevens' own settings in Platonic enclosures for the purpose of exposing the fallacy of egocentric knowledge, as in "Poem with Rhythms" and "The Blue Buildings in the Summer Air." "A thing believed, a thing affirmed" from "The Well Dressed Man with a Beard" carries forward Nietzsche's critique of the thing-in-itself, as does "The Man on the Dump" his disparagement of certain truth in the concluding "The the." When Nietzsche writes in *Beyond Good and Evil* that "truth has so much to stifle her yawns here when answers are demanded of her" and that because she is "after all, a woman: one ought not to violate her," Wallace Stevens, too, supposes the mystery of Being "to be a woman" and perhaps follows the philosopher's suggestion in turning her into a "beautiful cat 'woman'" (*BGE*, §220, "Preface," §239). Zarathustra's carrying "the blessings of [his] Yes into all abysses" in several places (*Z*, 165, 27, 323) echoes the important affirmations and denials featured in "The Well Dressed Man with a Beard" and "Mrs. Alfred Uruguay." It is even possible to trace Stevens' praise for "the ignorant man" in "The Sense of the Sleight-of-hand Man" to Nietzsche's own caution that "without this kind of ignorance life itself would be impossible" (*WP*, §609), as opposed to the grasping butcher in "Thunder by the Musician" limned by "the great *passion* of the seeker after knowledge who lives and must live continually in the thundercloud of the highest problems and the heaviest responsibilities," in Nietzsche's *Gay Science* (*GS*, §351).

Martin Heidegger has remarked that in the history of Western philosophy, "thought up to now is metaphysics, and Nietzsche's thinking presumably brings it to an end." In particular, Nietzsche attacks the prejudice of metaphysicians of all ages, their unshakable and solemn faith in the knowledge of the truth hidden in the thing-in-itself. His prediction for philosophers of the future is that "they will not be dogmatists," that their pride will be offended "if their truth is supposed to be a truth for everyman" (*BGE*, 16, 53). Echoing Nietzsche's philosophical pessimism (*WP*, §708), Wallace Stevens, too, thinks the aim of the philosopher a cause for despair and warns that "we do not want to be metaphysicians" (*NA*, 43, 59). Although both the poet and the philosopher might probe for truthful "integrations," the poet intends his to be "fortuitous" and "effective," whereas the philosopher intends his to be "deliberate" and "fateful" (*OP*, 276). Further, because, according to Nietzsche, the "total value of the world cannot be evaluated," the thinker ideally "seeks a picture of the world in that philosophy in which [he] feel[s] freest; *i.e.*, in which [his] most powerful drives feel free to function" (*WP*, §708, §418). That this is so infrequently the case urged Stevens, on one occasion, to make it clear that he did not think of himself as a philosopher and therefore did not want to be thought one by others. It is doubly amusing to note how frustrated practicing philosophers would become at his talks on philosophical subjects when he would offer them "flashes of insight" rather than "solutions." Even if, as one report has it, "his ultimate passion was to try to get to the clean clear ultimate reality, which required a thrust through everything," Stevens would never make it clear to his audience what he saw when he got there. Is it not therefore the case that both in his prose and in his poetry something comes to the fore in Stevens' thought, as Heidegger saw so well in Nietzsche—something that thinking finds unthinkable, something impenetrable that might account for or in some way produce metaphysical thinking itself?[29]

For Stevens' questioning of belief, two further ideas become significant in his reading of Nietzsche. If the metaphysician's will to logical truth constitutes "a fundamental *falsification* of all events," a preference for "a handful of 'certainty,'" or "a sure nothing," as opposed to "a whole cartful of beautiful possibilities," or "an uncertain something" (*WP*, §512, *BGE*, §10), then it follows, first of all, that there can be no such things as "facts": there can only be "interpretations" (*WP*, §481). Second, if factual truth is thoroughly interpretive, then knowledge is a question not of meaning but of "perspective." It could only be relative to a particular point of view imposed on experience and to the value system integral to the construction of such a view. Hence, "the essence of a thing is only an *opinion* about the 'thing'": if we take away all opinions of the thing, *i.e.*, the network of perspectives constituting the facts so-called, the thing itself would disappear (*WP*, §556, §558, §560). Alexander Nehamas' instructive reading of Nietzsche summarizes these important implications:

> All the effects of what we construe as a single thing are essentially interconnected and derive their character from their interconnec-

29. Brazeau, *Parts of a World*, 202, 212–13; Martin Heidegger, "Who Is Nietzsche's Zarathustra?," in *The New Nietzsche: Contemporary Styles of Interpretation*, ed. David B. Allison (Cambridge, Mass., 1985), 76, 76–79.

tions. What something is or does is not independent of anything else that it does or is. And whatever a thing is or does is itself not given: it is constantly in motion, being changed, revised, recon-strued, and reinterpreted in the light of new events. . . . The char-acter and nature of every event is inseparable from the character and nature of every other occurrence with which it is associated. This relationship is holistic and hermeneutical.[30]

Having worked through Nietzsche's thinking on the perspective "truth" of factual knowledge, Stevens confirmed his hunch that it is futile to attempt to strike a balance—"that balance [that] does not quite rest"—between the two competing views of "things as they are" in *Blue Guitar*. It was perhaps at this time that he penned two of his most important "Adagia": "Nothing is itself taken alone" since "things are because of interrelations or interactions," and therefore "Poetry is the statement of a relation between a man and the world" (*OP*, 189, 197). He could have gone back to revise his earlier, more metaphysi-cal assertions on all these matters, but "poetry constantly requires a new re-lation" (*OP*, 202). He therefore continued to write several more of his most radical poems to date.

We miss much of the daring of "Connoisseur of Chaos," composed in 1938, by focusing on its "connoisseurship" (from the Latin *con*, or together, and *gnoscere*, or to know), that is, its elegant dialectical formulation of absolute knowledge: the "violent order [that] is disorder" recuperated in the "great disorder [that] is an order," and vice-versa (*CP*, 215). Stevens' real in-terest in the poem is the *chaos*, which is not at all to be confused with disorder but from a Nietzschean purview is "the multiplicity of impulses, the entire horizon of forces" that calls forth thinking from differing perspectives.[31] The disorder would necessarily be what any act of interpretation must jettison *in order* to will itself into being as truth, *i.e.*, knowledge. Yet even the extra-ordinary can be "an order," as Lady Lowzen proves; hence, "These / Two things are one. (Pages of illustrations.)" Stevens' argument really gets going when it helps us past the "law of inherent opposites" and its "essential unity," what Nietzsche so disparagingly refers to as "the fundamental faith of the metaphysicians [in] antithetical values" (*BGE*, §2), and allows us to see order itself as an effect of relation (*CP*, 215). In this context, we see not rigid anti-

30. Alexander Nehamas, *Nietzsche: Life as Literature* (Cambridge, Mass., 1985), 87–88.
31. Michael Haar, "Nietzsche and Metaphysical Language," in *The New Nietzsche*, ed. Allison, 11.

thetical values but instead competing centers of force, "chaos," that is, each asserting its claim for the "world of the constant" (*WP,* §585 [A]), or what the poem refers to as the "most fixed" (*CP,* 216). This would be truth seen from the side of "squirming facts," interpretations in *other* words, and not from the side of "the squamous [that is, scale-covered] mind." Once relation is admitted, and we notice how Stevens has it appear, like the latest freed man, from the edge, as "a shape on the side of a hill" and later as a figure "chalked / On the sidewalk," once relation reveals order to be *one* truth "in the immense disorder of truths," then metaphysical theory as the self-reflection of knowledge implodes, negating the possibility of going back to pristine resolutions of the world, caught handily in the image of the "bishops' books."

In the same way, "Connoisseur of Chaos" makes it impossible for Stevens to return to his earlier projects (*e.g., Ideas of Order*), revealing once again the radical departure he had undertaken in *Parts of a World.* Now that "thinking well . . . *is* an action" (*WP,* §458), "life no longer resides in the whole." Additionally, "the word becomes sovereign . . . and obscures the meaning of the page, and the page comes to life at the expense of the whole—the whole is no longer a whole" (*CW,* §7). The eagle that floats over "the intricate Alps" at the end of the poem, therefore, tropes precisely this absence of a whole in the image of the "single nest." Doubling as an allusion both to the mastery of absolute knowledge in the philosophy of Hegel (like *aigle,* taking Derrida's favorite pun) and also to one of the favorite animals of Zarathustra (*Z,* Prologue, 9), its uncertain meaning shatters the wish fulfillment of the "pensive man," who remains divided between it and the indecipherable traces chalked on the sidewalk. In the ellipsis that separates them plays an irony that Stevens opens up to ensure that ideas, like propositions A and B, are "never fixed but always in transition; thus . . . irrepressibly transitory."[32] This transitoriness would appear to be the significance of the "statuary" in the Louvre, which, like the doctrine overtaken in "The Latest Freed Man," is gradually dissolved by the expansion of "shade." From this point onward, shade (and its intensification in darkness) will mark in Stevens' poetry the metaphor for a new belief, one based on what Nietzsche would call "perspectival appearance," given that belief as "a considering-something-true" is necessarily false, there being "no *true world*" (*WP,* §15). "Poetry," after all, "is often a revelation of the elements of appearance" (*OP,* 201); and a shady metaphysics could only be part—but only a part—of poetry's effort to complicate experience, "to perceive the intricacy of appearance" (*OP,* 201), signified by "the intricate

32. Taylor, *Erring,* 13.

Alps." If the abstraction of shadow, connected interestingly to absence and doubling in *Letters* (*L,* 348) sounds very much like nihilism, that would be all right, too, since "nihilism, as the denial of a truthful world, of being, might be," according to Nietzsche, "*a divine way of thinking*" (*WP,* §15).[33]

Before taking up the two longest texts of *Parts of a World,* in which Stevens pursued with the greatest care the radicalization of belief in the shadow of Nietzsche's influence, a further ground must yet be cleared with respect to his reading. It is unlikely that we will ever be certain precisely the extent to which Stevens cultivated an active interest in the philosopher's work, because of the disarray of Stevens' library after his death.[34] However, in the face of the close intertextuality between poet-philosopher and philosopher-poet advanced thus far, it seems fairly certain that a text of Nietzsche's in which Stevens must have taken an inordinate interest would be one in which the philosopher brought the representative character of his thought most to bear on the use of language and, in particular, on the writing of poetry itself. In the last chapter, I argued that Nietzsche's "On Truth and Lies in a Nonmoral Sense" might have helped Stevens rethink the issue of the writer's relationship to the world that the completion of *Ideas of Order* appears to have brought to a crisis and that the writing of *Owl's Clover* had only succeeded in intensifying. With *The Man with the Blue Guitar* behind him, Stevens entered a period of creativity that he had not known since the decade prior to the publication of *Harmonium* in 1923, composing roughly twice as many poems as he did for *Ideas of Order* and in half the time. Obviously, several creative obstacles had been cleared in the relatively short interval between his third and fourth publications. When we find him taking up the genre of the apo-

---

33. Martin Heidegger, too, is considerably attracted to the notion of a "shady metaphysics." In "The Age of the World Picture," he writes: "Everyday opinion sees in the shadow only the lack of light, if not light's complete denial. In truth, however, the shadow is a manifest, though impenetrable, testimony to the concealed emitting of light. In keeping with this concept of shadow, we experience the incalculable as that which, withdrawn from representation, is nevertheless manifest in whatever is, pointing to Being, which remains concealed" (*The Question Concerning Technology,* 154).

34. Part of Stevens' library was sold in two lots after his death: two hundred to three hundred volumes in 1958, of which no record of titles was kept, and an additional number in 1959. The largest portion of over five hundred titles was left to Holly Stevens at her mother's death in 1963 and is presently housed at the Huntington Library in San Marino, California. In this last collection, only a 1910 volume of Nietzsche's *Thoughts out of Season: Part I,* trans. Anthony M. Ludovici, has thus far been cataloged. See Milton J. Bates, "Stevens' Books at the Huntington: An Annotated Checklist," *Wallace Stevens Journal,* II (Fall, 1978), 45–61, and its conclusion in vol. III (Spring, 1979), 15–33.

thegm in the "Adagia" of this period and also beginning to write "philo-sophical" arguments in a similarly aphoristic style that would almost seem to defy philosophy's traditional logic, in addition to developing an interest in the work of contemporary thinkers connected with *Les Entretiens de Pontigny* abroad, we could certainly be led to conclude that he had set up the German philosopher almost as a kind of model for his own thought, and perhaps the "poetics" encapsulated in "On Truth and Lies" as a signature *moyen de par-venir*.[35] Indeed, several shorter poems in *Parts of a World* reveal that the contents of this essay could supply the creative artist with *materia poetica* as well.

One of the key images in Nietzsche's "On Truth and Lies" is the leaf, and it recurs in almost identical contexts in Stevens' present work, some of which we have seen. Nietzsche uses the image to explain the difference be-tween metaphor and concept mediated by words in our encounter with the world of experience outside ourselves. There can never be any absolute or certain contact with real or actual experience, Nietzsche argues, since each individual registers such experience differently according to his own primary engagement in sense perceptions. At this level, sense perception forms itself to expression in metaphors: in images, first of all, then later, in the form of sounds. The word makes the transition from the level of percept to the level of concept when people feel the need to communicate with each other. At such times, the individual differences involved in perception must be evened out so that communication might proceed along channels that all can agree on. The word *leaf,* therefore, though it is "never totally the same as another," becomes the concept "leaf" at the same time that we arbitrarily force it "to fit countless more or less similar cases" by discarding or forgetting its distin-guishing traits (OTL, 82–83).

There is thus a positive and a negative side to the concept. In addition to the expedient of consistency in communication, the positive side of con-cepts affords us a certain security and repose, a "momentary stay against confusion," as Robert Frost would say, in the face of an uncertain and inde-terminate world, the "frightful powers" of which no one individual can con-front, much less fathom (OTL, 85, 88). On the negative side—and this side happens far more frequently to be the case—concepts can harden and con-geal, as we noted earlier, into things-in-themselves, into rigid abstractions or "schemata," gradually becoming rooted in the mind as unalterable, short-form habits of thought to which we attach the universal cognomen: Truth

35. Brazeau, *Parts of a World*, 164n, 201, 211.

(OTL, 87, 85). Hence, Nietzsche lays bare the nature of truth in a famous statement that in some minds has become a kind of manifesto for contemporary deconstructive criticism: "What then is truth? A movable host of metaphors, metonymies, and anthropomorphisms: in short, a sum of relations which have been poetically and rhetorically intensified, transferred, and embellished, and which, after long usage, seem to a people to be fixed, canonical, and binding. Truths are illusions which we have forgotten are illusions; they are metaphors that have become worn out and have been drained of sensuous force, coins which have lost their embossing and are now considered as metal and no longer as coins" (OTL, 84).[36] Nietzsche's conclusion seems simple enough: truth and falsehood are not core ethical determinations but rather epistemological or linguistic ones. The truth teller, on the one hand, is simply a person who desires its "pleasant, life-preserving consequences"; the liar, on the other, is one who uses words "in order to make something which is unreal appear to be real" (OTL, 81). The liar, in other words, is in transit, from metaphor to concept. In Stevens' version of Nietzsche's theory, Lady Lowzen is a liar precisely in this sense: she "skims the real for its unreal" and comes up with the unusual metaphor "Oak Leaves Are Hands." Why "hands" and not some other body part is suggested by Nietzsche in his essay when he notes that were there such a thing as an original "model leaf" in nature, all the individual versions of it would appear to have been fabricated by "incompetent hands" (OTL, 83). Lady Lowzen's "many arms" and "glittering seven-colored changes" suggest that she is at least faithful to Nietzsche's premises up to the point at which a single, determinate truth ought to remain outside her reach. There is also the sense that she is a person of "few words," implying that there may be a point beyond which even she is not prepared to allow her comparisons to go. If truth is to have its entitlements, if oak leaves *are* hands, then she, too, is a "son of death" ("Mac Mort" [*CP*, 272]) and, like Mrs. Uruguay, must be rejected.

Stevens' argument is not that Lady Lowzen should be rejected for her deceptive appearances. In his new world, there is nothing *but* appearances. It is simply that in affecting an interest in "other things," she nevertheless maintains a firm hand on the center and, in so doing, is being less than honest with herself and others. This is precisely Nietzsche's point in "On Truth and Lies" when he notes that "the intellect is free" only when the master of de-

---

36. *E.g.*, Joseph N. Riddel, "'Neo-Nietzschean Clatter'—Speculation and the Modernist Poetic Image," in *Why Nietzsche Now?*, ed. Daniel O'Hara (Bloomington, 1985), 209–39.

ception "is able to deceive without *injuring*" (OTL, 89–90). With that deliberate intent to mislead, lying then does become an ethical issue, and Nietzsche takes it up as such in *The Genealogy of Morals* in Chapter 14 under the
heading of "bad conscience."[37] Stevens' latest freed man maintains his freedom by concerning himself more with the appearance of the oak leaves than
with naming them and gets around the problem that way. But the scientist
and the mathematician, both in Stevens and in Nietzsche, can never be quite
so honorable. They are dedicated to the very life of logic, which trafficks in
nothing but concepts, so that their lives are entirely controlled by abstractions
and can therefore know nothing but a "regulative and imperative world"
(OTL, 84). Nietzsche's two chief images for such conceptual thinking are the
rigid stone and the spider web (OTL, 90, 85, 87), and we find these repeated
over and over in Stevens' work. In "The Common Life" written in 1939, for
instance, "a page of Euclid" is connected to "a morbid light," and its figures
and alphabetical notations are likened to "webs / Of wire," crowding out the
whiteness of the paper on which they are printed (*CP*, 221). The geometrical
volumes so described are "like marble ruins," emblems of fixed thought already encountered in the stone stanzas, heads, horses, bouquets, and Louvre
statuary of previous poems, which is what makes the "common sense," in
"The Common Life" and elsewhere, so common. In such a purely mathe-
matical glare, human life appears truncated, the matter of mere "result" and
"demonstration," so that "the women have only one side." Not unexpectedly,
shadows are conspicuously absent in Euclidean geometry.

From reading Nietzsche, therefore, Stevens aims his project to shift the
reader's attention from "things," to "words," to privilege the direction set in
the 1938 "Prelude to Objects," to emphasize the prelude rather than the objects themselves. His nonsense verse ("Damariscotta da da doo," "halloo,
halloo, halloo," and "Pipperoo, pippera, pipperum" [*CP*, 235, 191, 230]) is a
necessary part of this strategy. The model of this kind of "desemanticization"
in *Parts of a World* is perhaps "Metamorphosis," composed in 1942, with its
transformations of seasons into a type of tactile signification halfway between
signifiers and signifieds, in examples like "Oto - otu - bre" and "Niz - nil -
imbo" (*CP*, 266). "For writing to be writing," as Walter Benn Michaels observes, "it can neither transcend the marks it is made of nor be reduced to
those marks. Writing is, in this sense, intrinsically different from itself, neither material nor ideal." Hence, "language [is] the material of poetry not its
mere medium or instrument" (*OP*, 196), and "above everything else, poetry

37. See Nehamas, *Life as Literature*, 67, 105, 126.

is words [which] . . . are, in poetry, sounds" (*NA,* 32). In still more radical terms, if the impossible is ever to be made readable, as Mark Taylor insists, "the writer makes reading impossible."[38] The poet, "patting more nonsense . . . in common forms," conceives "the diviner health," according to "Prelude to Objects" (*CP,* 194–95); "being nothing otherwise," he no longer has to visit the statuary of "the Louvre to behold himself." To do so would be another exercise of the fatal unity of war back in "Yellow Afternoon," which now makes perfect (non)sense in the context of "the final sculpture," to which it, too, is equated (*CP,* 236). Now it is useless to husband one's eye/I in the arcades of Philadelphia, the city of Ptolemy, for the spiders have eaten it (*CP,* 225). The "stars that move together as one," Nietzsche teaches Stevens, are now disbanded: "Pipperoo, pippera, pipperum" (*CP,* 230). "The rest"—sound free from motion, etched in stone, or caught in web—"The rest is rot."

There is one final thing that needs to be said about Stevens' reading of Nietzsche, and Nietzsche's metaphor of the actor and his mask carries us to the heart of it. Much earlier, in our first approach to Stevens' interrogation of belief, we had occasion to notice the gestures of exclusion and repression that seemed to be at the center of its metaphysical formulation. Self-presence, absolute knowledge, certain truth, immediate Being, all install themselves as the foundation of belief at the expense of an Other, of that which threatens to undermine from some outside, exterior to the locus of belief itself. The logical concept operates in much the same way. Sarah Kofman discusses the repressions involved with it: "The concept plays the role . . . of the force that maintains repression. Along with primary 'forgetting,' it brings about a secondary repression . . . a system of secondary and subsequent rationalizations, rationalizations that efface the founding character of metaphorical activity— namely, of what is found at the origin of all knowledge and activity."[39] Metaphor's response to this repression of force by meaning must always be a redoubling of force, in an effort to disperse the concept's initial act of neutralization. As Nietzsche describes it, "[the drive toward the formation of metaphors] continually confuses the conceptual categories . . . continually manifests an ardent desire to refashion the world which presents itself to waking man, so that it will be as colorful, irregular, lacking in results and coherence, charming, and eternally new as the world of dreams . . . when this web of concepts is torn away" (OTL, 89). In other words, metaphor per-

---

38. Walter Benn Michaels, *The Gold Standard and the Logic of Naturalism* (Berkeley, 1987), 21; Taylor, *Altarity,* 251.

39. Sarah Kofman, "Metaphor, Symbol, Metamorphosis," in *The New Nietzsche,* ed. Allison, 213n.

forms a feat of duplication, repeating in "scene" what the concept has achieved in "act."[40] As that last sentence shows, there does not seem to be any way around the theater images to convey this new direction from which belief will arise. And Stevens' attempt at this reformulation in the 1940 "Of Modern Poetry," with his distinction between the poem "of the mind" at its opening and "of the act of the mind" at its closing, does its best to transcribe Nietzsche's totally original insights (*CP,* 239–40).

In the first place, Stevens' theater metaphor opens out poetry, as it does belief, to what Nietzsche would call "a cartful of possibilities." Stevens' "acting," on this point, is thus a highly qualified metaphor: it is "not just any acting," as Rodolphe Gasché views the trope also operating in Heidegger, but "an acting at the limit of acting in that it affirms the play without consequences of the merely potential, the 'sheer superabundance without purpose or end' of the event itself."[41] If ontological conceptualization, meaning in the conventional sense, is "the fatal unity of war," then poetry taken in a wholly modern way cannot exclude that tendency. It, too, "has to think about war" as one of the many options available as it thinks about thinking. "Man and Bottle," in likening poetry to the mind, puts it this way:

> It has to content the reason concerning war,
> It has to persuade that war is part of itself,
> A manner of thinking, a mode
> Of destroying, as the mind destroys.
>
> (*CP,* 239)

Second, the theater metaphor is now able to suggest a supplementation of understanding by way of the ear, that "delicatest ear of the mind," for so long repressed by the eye of reason when the mind, in the former ontological

40. Charles Winquist, "Body, Text, Imagination," in *Deconstruction and Theology,* ed. Thomas J. J. Altizer *et al.* (New York, 1982), 45. Jacques Derrida also notes this shift from "act-ive" to "perform-ative" meaning at the point when a text withdraws from the representation of Nature and makes a "scene" (*théâtre*), through a "dangerous supplement," in doing so (*Grammatology,* 151). The important difference is that in the latter, the *mise en scène* is upstaged by the force of its own spectacle (*Writing and Difference,* 238). Megill's distinction between meaning as representation and as signification is also helpful here (*Prophets of Extremity,* 209–10), as is the act of reflection as opposed to the act of reflexion in Mark C. Taylor's "Foiling Reflection," *Diacritics,* XVIII (Spring, 1988), 57–58.

41. Rodolphe Gasché, "'Like the Rose–Without Why': Postmodern Transcendentalism and Practical Philosophy," *Diacritics,* XIX (Fall/Winter, 1989), 112. For a further expansion of Nietzsche's "cartful of possibilities" in the context of American pragmatism, within which both Nietzsche and Stevens intersect under the influence of Emerson, see Gunn, *Thinking Across the American Grain,* 54, 74, 102, 108, 115, and 136.

dispensation, looked to draw near to itself in some transcendent "below" or "beyond," in some "old affair with the sun," to quote "Man and Bottle" again, or in some "impossible aberration with the moon." This is not to argue the repression of outlook or insight, the "in-words" of my introduction, in their turn; but it does suggest that the modern believer is a "metaphysician in the dark" and that though every resource must be brought to bear in the "act of finding / What will suffice," it would be entirely fallacious to make any kind of prejudgment about just where that satisfaction might ultimately lie. Stevens' frequent puns on "apart" and "aversion" from this period (*CP*, 236, 239, 248) are consequently intended to signal that rejection can never be final, indeed that exclusion always already presupposes its opposite, the originary "source" of Being itself.

Martin Heidegger writes that "all Being is for Nietzsche a Becoming," and this, finally, is what Stevens' theater of trope can only impart to a mind in search of an active faith. The man skating, the women dancing and combing in the last lines of "Of Modern Poetry" all help to flesh out the new direction for thinking and writing, as their "script" shifts to "something else" and they begin to learn "to face the men of the time and to meet / The women of the time" (*CP*, 240). The "anti-master-man" in "Landscape with Boat," written in 1940, only begins to have intimations of this new direction in thinking once he forgoes "the colossal illusion of heaven" and the single-colored "neutral centre" in his impossible wanting to see and even more impossible desiring to know (*CP*, 241):

> He never supposed
> That he might be truth, himself, or part of it,
> That the things that he rejected might be part
> And the irregular turquoise, part, the perceptible blue,
> Grown denser, part, the eye so touched, so played
> Upon by clouds, the ear so magnified
> By thunder, parts, and all these things together,
> Parts, and more things, parts. He never supposed divine
> Things might not look divine, nor that if nothing
> Was divine then all things were, the world itself,
> And that if nothing was the truth, then all
> Things were the truth, the world itself was the truth.
>
> (*CP*, 242)

This is the hint of a belief turned inside out—belief *in other words:* the interior is made exterior, and the other made party to the same. It comes to this "nabob of bones," once again, "in the dark," as stony forms of heavenly Being dissolve into the Mediterranean's more fluent "emerald / *Becoming* emeralds" (*CP,* 243, emphasis added). There is nothing in *Parts of a World* that moves beyond the development of thought of this passage in Stevens' attempt to evolve alternative ways of articulating the principles of a new faith for the modern era. Its irony, that arrival is made possible only through denial ("To be projected by one void into / Another"), is one Stevens himself knew only too well. There could not possibly have been a *Parts of a World* without there having been a *Harmonium* and an *Ideas of Order* first. "A new world or future," as Thomas Altizer notes, "can become real only by way of a total negation and reversal of the world of the past." To determine just how much of the past Stevens is prepared to rewrite, we must now turn to his two longest poems, positioned in the last part of the volume.[42]

By the onset of the 1940s, Stevens was perhaps anxious to take up his new ideas in the social arena, at the intersection of contexts where his work would have a significant effect and where it was at the same time being itself significantly affected. These were the areas of academia and war. His study of Nietzsche would have told him that these were entirely *related* contexts, the acrimony of scholarly interpretation conducive to a fatal unity in one equating itself to the militaristic evacuation of political differences in the other. The "gregarization" of leaves in "On Truth and Lies" thus finds an exact counterpart in the leaves of the scholars' books in the 1940 "Extracts from Addresses to the Academy of Fine Ideas," on the one hand, and in speculation about soldiers on leave from active combat in the 1942 "Examination of the Hero in a Time of War," on the other.[43] The join is in the final two lines of "Extracts," where academics, rather curiously described as "in helmets borne on steel," are depicted as "going to defeat" (*CP,* 259). If the scholar-soldier was a fairly current poetic commonplace in bygone eras, precisely how does Stevens make this leap in the quest for belief in the twentieth century?

42. Martin Heidegger, *The Will to Power as Art,* trans. David Farrell Krell (San Francisco, 1979), 7, Vol. I of Heidegger, *Nietzsche,* 4 vols.; Altizer, *The Descent into Hell,* 53.

43. The term *gregarization* is taken from Michael Haar: "Far from attaining to the 'truth,' a concept, like language in general, functions as an instrument of 'gregarization': *viz.,* it is an identification for the greatest number" ("Nietzsche and Metaphysical Language," in *The New Nietzsche,* ed. Allison, 6). The most notorious instances of gregarization would therefore be the self and the individual: "[They are] fictions concealing a complexity, a plurality of forces in conflict . . . hid[ing] the original and fundamental plurality constituting the Will to Power in bodily form. 'We are a plurality that has imagined itself a unity' [*WP,* §333]" (18).

The clue, once again, lies in the insight into the concept's repression of metaphor in the communal expression of ideas. "A rose is a rose is a rose" only outside a community, as Gertrude Stein knew only too well. Inside, as, for instance, within the academic community, the rose assumes quite deliberate conceptual forms, depending on the interest group. Two that intrigue Stevens in particular in "Extracts" are the idealist version of the rose, the crinkled, wrinkled "paper ones," and the realist version, "the blood-rose living in its smell" (*CP,* 252), but he might just as easily have chosen modernist, expressionist, or minimalist versions of the rose, which also have their ardent champions. What "states the point" for Stevens is exactly how the different versions of a "thing" are taken up within a closed community and not the specific versions themselves, though this conceivably might have an effect on how they do become taken up. Originally, that is, "the law of chaos is the law of ideas," and as we noted earlier, there can be as many metaphorical versions of roses as there are individuals interacting with them in the protean world of experience beyond the self. As we learn in Part V of "Extracts," however, "Chaos is not / The mass of meaning" (*CP,* 255). It is not the "three or four / Ideas or, say, five men or, possibly, six." Rather, at the level of gregarized communication, the forces of expression are reduced to a lowest common denominator, what Stevens refers to as "the mass of meaning," or what Nietzsche would call "a fixed convention" that inevitably must "lie with the herd [*i.e.,* mass] and in a manner binding upon everyone" (OTL, 84). To reach this point, though, as even absent-minded professors are sometimes aware, many exacerbating academic skirmishes must be waged, so that the community might finally come to its dispassionate (con)senses:

> In the end, these philosophic assassins pull
> Revolvers and shoot each other. One remains.
>
> The mass of meaning becomes composed again.
> He that remains plays on an instrument.
>
> A good agreement between himself and night,
> A chord between the mass of men and himself,
>
> Far, far beyond the putative canzones
> Of love and summer.
>
> (*CP,* 256)

Thus, the "singular romance" with which a community consoles itself en masse is remarkable only for its exclusions, the Alpine "single nest" of the connoisseur of chaos once again, and not for its naïve, intellectual esprit de corps. In the interpretive community, "nothing is or ever was innocent, integral, undivided."[44] The scholarly assassin's "inability to find a sound / That clings to the mind like that right sound" only goes to show just how fake mountains can be, particularly when they arise from academic molehills.

In Part VI of the poem, then, we meet up with another "cavern of thinking" that Stevens attaches to "systematic thinking" and beyond that to death, for both of which mental "indifference" clears the way (*CP,* 256–57). Here in this "single place," where thinking is being, the academy completely reverses the conclusion of "The Well Dressed Man with a Beard" with its contention that the mind *has* an end ("redeeming thought") and that it *can* "be satisfied." Moreover, the enormous emphasis on singularity shows precisely how the academy, in its total dedication to unified self-reference, would define goodness. Anything different from or other than fatal unity, from the point of view of fixed category and congealed convention, is the "evil" of "catastrophe" and must be handled by another spokesman for statutory repression, "the Secretary for Porcelain," in Part II:

> Let the Secretary for Porcelain observe
> That evil made magic, as in catastrophe,
> If neatly glazed, becomes the same as the fruit
> Of an emperor
>
> . . . .
>
>   [and] equates ten thousand deaths
> With a single well-tempered apricot, or, say,
> An egg-plant of good air.
>
>   (*CP,* 253)

Behind the secretary's homogenizing gesture, we are perhaps made to feel the presence of Plato's noumenal ideas of order. We are also, however, intended to hear most audibly the secretary's suppressions greeted with subversive laughter—the "laughter of evil" (*CP,* 253)—intended to "kill the spirit of [Platonic] gravity" that we also hear from Zarathustra (*Z,* 41) but, more tellingly, from Dionysus, whose laughter is intended to carry mankind beyond the academic reductionism of both good *and* evil (*BGE,* §295).[45] Therefore,

---

44. John D. Caputo, *Radical Hermeneutics: Repetition, Deconstruction, and the Hermeneutic Project* (Bloomington, 1987), 130. Cf. also Fish, *Doing What Comes Naturally,* 78, 80–81.

45. Derrida's own massive onslaught on the semantic closures of the academy ("SARL") confronts the very same equation between evil and the multiplication of perspectives that "Lim-

depending on the scholarly lobby, evil is a rose by any other name. The realist a/version only happens to win out in Part V because there are more gray-beards around today who happen to find the idealist proposition less service-able (*WP,* §1025), but that perspective can just as easily change. Today's concepts will be tomorrow's discarded metaphors, as "The Man on the Dump" can also show.

Once again, in Part III, Stevens' cats become exemplary. At one time, they seem transparently to fit the de-signed spiritual edifice of the "per-noble master," basking in the sunlight of its excessively rational proportions. At another, however, their leanness causes them to disappear, to dissolve into a "little beyond," incorporating an absence in the midst of presence: "the exquisite errors of time" (*CP,* 254). The cats, thus, take us back to "catastrophe" and the evil magic that is all a matter of perspective or point of view. Through time, idealist and realist conceptions, like the cats, appear alternatively erroneous. From the perspective of the law of chaos, however, they only come to matter as "improvisations," that is, as "seasons of belief" (*CP,* 255). And only in the context of the alterity of chaos can it be said that "the false and true are one" (*CP,* 253). Similarly, next door in "Montrachet-le-Jardin," composed in 1942, Stevens aims to affirm as his chief good "life's thousand senses" rather than life's usual normative or categorical deprivations ("yesterday's devotions") in both the academic and religious senses (*CP,* 264). Even in saying this, however, he risks conceptual recuperation. Hence, yet another cat, troping the truth of nontruth and the identity of difference, leaps quickly from the fireside of linguistic territorialization "and is gone" (*CP,* 264).

If the lean cats of the arches in "Extracts" are saying anything at all, it is perhaps only that in Stevens' quest for a "new world" belief, "all men are priests" (*CP,* 254). His title is enormously suggestive in this regard. When Captain Ahab in *Moby-Dick* exclaims, "The path to my fixed purpose is laid with iron rails, whereon my soul is grooved to run," he assumes a categorical attitude typical of an ironclad academy that only "ex-tracks" from a number of addresses, not from a single address itself, can derail. The holding action,

---

ited Inc. abc." finds so threatening. See *Glyph,* II (1977), 222–23; *cf.* also Derrida, *Dissemination,* 133. Hence, evil for Stevens (as for Nietzsche) is valuative in a quite "nonmoral sense": it is "the 'fault' of deviation from the 'simplicity' and perfection of a timeless nature—defin[ing] the 'never-resting mind,' the 'evilly compounded vital I,'" according to Mutlu Konuk Blasing in *American Poetry: The Rhetoric of Its Forms* (New Haven, 1987), 96. *Cf.* also Bloom, *Poems of Our Climate,* 156–57, 158. "For any monistic philosophy," in the words of Roland Barthes, "plural is the Evil" (*Image-Music-Text,* 160).

consequently, with which Stevens ends the poem is a bitter indictment against the blind scholar who would rather die than forgo the war on difference, the absence of which already inhabits him as the "chants of final peace"—peace being merely the *absence* of war:

> Thence come the final chants, the chants
> Of the brooder seeking the acutest end
> Of speech: to pierce the heart's residuum
> And there to find music for a single line,
> Equal to memory, one line in which
> The vital music formulates the words.
>
> (*CP,* 259)

The "heart's residuum" here answers to Nietzsche's definition of the concept in "On Truth and Lies," which is "the *residue of a metaphor*" (OTL, 85). Re-membering the concept in Stevens' conclusion is thus the poem's greatest irony, an act, in effect, of reconstituting metaphor, which can only send a singular academy "borne on steel" to its ultimate defeat (*CP,* 259).

Now that Stevens had completely exercised a new manner of thinking through the question of belief on the scholarly side, he would always feel somewhat uneasy about the eclecticism of his efforts were he not able to bring them to bear on political issues affecting the larger world. The letters from this period of his writing reveal that he was enormously influenced by the day-to-day occurrences in wartime Europe, to the extent of feeling not a little irresponsible in continuing to write poetry. In one letter, for example, sent off near the end of the war, Stevens had occasion to remark that the theater of conflict was shifting from Europe to Asia and that it was "hard to understand" why anyone should even care to write about writing (*L,* 501). There was, however, one important area in which the writing of poetry could perform a useful function at such a time of crisis. This was in the area of thinking "factually" about the reality of war.

Stevens' "Prose Statement on the Poetry of War" from 1942 is a central document for understanding the very last and longest poem he included in *Parts of a World.* In "Prose Statement," he makes three observations that provide great insight into how he attempts to shape the argument of his "Examination of the Hero in a Time of War," and it is interesting to note how each of these reflects the radical turn his own thinking had taken in the four or five years leading up to America's entry into battle and the publication of his fourth volume. The first observation is that in the presence of a "violent reality" such as war, "consciousness"—that is, "a consciousness of fact"—will take the place of the imagination in human affairs. Second, he notes that at a time when we are conscious of the victories and defeats of nations, "everything moves . . . in the direction of fact," with the important qualification that "fact" is "fact as we want it to be." Finally, it is poetry, "the work of the imagination," that wages a "fundamental and endless struggle with fact," the consciousness of which everyone is at least satisfied "to have it be" (*PM,* 206). It is fairly clear that "fact" as it is used in these statements, particularly fact in the grip of a consciousness that has usurped the power of poetry, is not the fact that Stevens had learned about from Nietzsche but is fact in the community sense of the word, fact as a fixed or conventional datum of experience. This is not fact as an effect of interpretation but fact as "truth," what, especially in a time of war, we are not happy to have until we can see it clearly in our midst. What in the interpretive sense might otherwise have been imagination's metaphorical ally is now the conscript of the dread concept. With the substitution of conscious for imaginative mind in this repression, we are once again in the presence of a fatal unity, which Stevens had defined earlier as a fairly ubiquitous prospect whether or not there was a global confrontation.

If the academy, as we suggested earlier, is a microcosm of mental stratification integral to belief in the macrocosmic social order, then heroism in a time of world war raises the question of belief writ large. "Unless we believe in the hero," Stevens writes in Canto VI of "Examination of the Hero," "what is there / To believe?" (*CP,* 275). Thus, the heroism that is "leafed out in adjectives" (*CP,* 277) in this longest of poems grows out of the approach toward belief taken in the previous one. That is to say, it evolves diacritically, opening up differentially in the space between binary propositions like idealism and realism, metaphor and concept, and, in view of the "Prose Statement," imaginative fact and conscious fact, or the intuitive and the rational. In Canto VII, then, Stevens is quite specific about two very different types of hero in play when the question of belief is revolved. The *Gazette Guerrière* offers the paradigm of "the classic hero," on the one hand, and *L'Observateur de la Paix,* the model of the "bourgeois," on the other. There are certainly others, but as in "Extracts," Stevens is once again interested in the playful interaction between ideas rather than in the pure content itself of the ideas. If things are because of "interrelations," there seems to be little doubt in his mind by the end of *Parts of a World* that the pure content of the thing-in-itself is thoroughly tautological. Heroism, therefore, like belief, is of overriding importance to Stevens for what it might say about its adherents. In a time of great crisis, especially, such understanding is crucial.

In Cantos VIII through X, Stevens takes up the description of the classical paradigm of the hero. The model here would appear to be the type of thing that would have greatest appeal to Nietzsche's "rational man" as opposed to "intuitive" man (OTL, 90). Its expression in the forms of the "still-life" and in "marbles" betokening a "white abstraction," along with the sublimation of its apparent "force" in a more self-contained barbarous "image," gives it the air of total regularity and predictability (*CP*, 276–77). "Xenophon" is its archetype, not the Xenophon that might actually have lived but one the X of whose name puts us in mind of "X, the per-noble master" referred to back in "Extracts" (*CP*, 254) and echoed in the "x malisons" of "Montrachet-le-Jardin" (*CP*, 261): that is, the Xenophon of a hugely inflated ego that is self-manufactured for myth and legend in a historical record like the *Anabasis*. Such a hero is a wishful fantasy, less a person than a human emblem, a prodigy of "thoughts begotten at clear sources" (*CP*, 277). So magnified a phenomenon is he that his heroism becomes practically oppressive in its conceptualization, an almost "too voluminous / Air-earth" (*CP*, 278); and he really begins to raise the question of whether or not the "dry descriptions" he evokes can sustain belief in such a model at all.

The type of the "bourgeois" or "common hero," by contrast, is rendered in Cantos IV through VI. The model here is of a more "familiar companion," one whose power seems to spring from "living and being about us" and the "mud, / For every day" (*CP*, 275–76). His provenance seems to be intuitive, less the determination of a winter-logic than a summer-imagination, a kind of "golden rescue" (*CP*, 275) from a previous starvation's head, one could say. He might, like Xenophon, appear on a horse. He is also as much at home playing Chopin on the piano as he is performing drills on a submarine "beyond the oyster-beds" (*CP*, 274). Herein lies his difficulty, for the intuitive model of heroic belief, like the "cat," the "kneeling woman," and the "nothing" with which it is associated in Canto V, cannot be pinned down exactly. All of the images that in previous poems Stevens associates with that which resists formulaic conceptualization are thus brought to bear on this second, "eccentric" figure: his thinking in "darkness," his sense of temporal "improvisation," his manifest repetition between two "less neatly measured common-places," and so forth (*CP*, 275). Like that great "Roman columbarium" of solid logic in Nietzsche (OTL, 85), "the sea-tower, shaken, / Sways slightly" in the presence of this indeterminate other-hero, but he is nonetheless real, the "bread and wine of the mind," for all that (*CP*, 274, 275).

With these two paradigms fleshed out, Stevens invites us to see that there are "more heroes than marbles of them," indeed, that the marble version seems somewhat inadequate for this reason, more a "pinching of an idea," as he notes in Canto VII, than the idea itself of the classic hero. For not all heroes are the "things" of public gardens. Some have something of the secret and the passionate about them. Hence, in Canto XI, thought, imaged in the form of a skeleton, can make do with the desiccated model when it likes, but it can just as easily throw that "crust" away and feast on the more profane, more everyday pastry-and-vegetable version in the privates-on-parade episode.

> The skeleton throwing
> His crust away eats of this meat, drinks
> Of this tabernacle, this communion,
> Sleeps in the sun no thing recalling.
>
> (*CP,* 278)

That skeleton thought forgets from one paradigm to the next once more reiterates the error that all logic since Aristotle is prone to, for Aristotle, too, is a skeleton (*OP,* 194). This is the error of confusing truth with illusion, truths originarily being metaphors that we forget are metaphors. Thus, the skeleton here sleeps the sleep of reason once more.

At this point in "Examination of the Hero," we are in the position of the 1940 "Asides on the Oboe": "The prologues are over. It is a question, now, / Of final belief." Stevens seems to be saying, "It is time to choose" (*CP,* 250). Our choice is spread out between two "fictions," that is, two illusions of the hero, or two metaphorical versions. Which one do we select? If an Aristotelian process of thought fails to help us make the right choice, then perhaps it is the model of the "impossible possible philosophers' man" in "Asides" that we should be following. Then, however, we realize the approach of this "central man" in "Asides" is not toward choosing at all. His response is always additive, like the super-man as opposed to the root-man in "Montrachet-le-Jardin" (*CP,* 262). The possible philosopher is never one to seize the "diamond pivot" for knowledge absolute. His tack is always plural, multiple, plurisignificant, making of himself a "human globe" and "sum[ming] us up" with "a million diamonds" (*CP,* 250).

A refusal to make an absolute choice seems also to be the point in Canto XII of "Examination of the Hero." It is not logic that arbitrates in the matter of declaring for a hero but rather "emotion," the feeling that gets us to see objects in certain ways and puts that very experience before us in the first place. As one of the "Adagia" states, "The more intensely one feels something that one likes the more one is willing for it to be what it is" (*OP,* 200). Thus, in "Poem Written at Morning" from 1942, Stevens says: "The truth must be / That you do not see, you experience, you feel, / That the buxom eye brings merely its element / To the total thing" (*CP,* 219). This sense of a personally constructed or projected truth goes back to the very Blakean notion, mentioned in "Extracts," of seeing not with the eye, as the logician might, but "through the eye" (*CP,* 253), as in the case of the mystic. Since feelings will vary from person to person, an examination of the hero comes back, once again, to knowledge that is perspective. In these terms, any notion of a "concept" for the hero becomes meaningless:

> The hero is a feeling, a man seen
> As if the eye was an emotion,
> As if in seeing we saw our feeling
> In the object seen and saved that mystic
> Against the sight, the penetrating,
> Pure eye. Instead of allegory,
> We have and are the man, capable
> Of his brave quickenings, the human
> Accelerations that seem inhuman.
>
> (*CP,* 278–79)

In a curious way, moreover, by recognizing a perspective knowledge in heroism, we seem to be incorporating in our own lives certain facets of the common model of the hero who does not appear to want to sit still for the kind of normative promulgation at work in his more rational, more "allegorical" version. The "brave quickenings," the "human accelerations," and, in Canto XIII, the "many references" are the central man's million diamonds that we only begin to acknowledge once we go beyond "the tranquil familiarity . . . of the order of truth" and begin "to hear the otherness within our own discourse . . . possibilities we have never dared to dream."[46] In a sense, it might even be said that heroism chooses us and in this way makes us "heroic." Yet as Canto XIII goes on to relate, it is more likely that the hero acting out his role in the world "adds nothing / To what he does" (*CP,* 279). In a time of war, even though it is not part of his conception to be conceived, the hero nonetheless is made to conform to some fatal unity like "nationality" or "reality" and, in being "made one," destroys all references save for that of his

---

46. Derrida, *Speech and Phenomena,* 134; Tracy, *Plurality and Ambiguity,* 79.

categorical anonymity. "Heroism" thus becomes the very first fatality of war: fact not "as it was" under a former imaginative dispensation but fact that a community under siege is "at least satisfied to have it be."

"The crisis in Europe . . . involve[s] us all," Wallace Stevens writes in a letter from 1940, "at least in the sense of occupying our thoughts *to the exclusion* of anything except the actual and the necessary" (*L,* 365, emphasis added). Hence, with the hero as a bourgeois fiction in Canto XIV, "we had always been partly one." Now that we have come to "see him"—to see, that is, his classic fiction—we are "wholly one" (*CP,* 251), and this identification is what is so terribly wrong. For with the classical paradigm of the hero in a time of war, we are given a vision of man in full possession of his ego and of all the fears, repressions, anxieties, and negations of a defensive self-presence that go along with it, corresponding to the vision that began this chapter:

> The highest man with nothing higher
> Than himself, his self, the self that embraces
> The self of the hero, the solar single,
> Man-sun, man-moon, man-earth, man-ocean,
>
> . . . .
>
> The man-sun being hero rejects that
> False empire . . . These are the works and pastimes
> Of the highest self.
>
> . . . .
>
>   With nothing lost, he
> Arrives at the man-man as he wanted.
> This is his night and meditation.
>
>   (*CP,* 280)

In the final canto, XVI, we are given to understand just how false a thing the reduction of "familiar man" to "the hero artificial" actually is. For while in "Extracts" we were at least given the sense of a freer potentiality for man beyond the mass of meaning in the improvisations of "seasons of belief," now it seems we are left with only one season: "How did we come to think that autumn / Was the veritable season, that familiar / Man was the veritable [*i.e.,* artificial] man?" Julia Kristeva remarks that "you become someone who wonders if the communal euphoria is not a lie, a lie involving not only harvest time enthusiasm, but something no one talks about: devious words."[47] These

47. Kristeva, *Desire in Language,* 162.

are the words with which Stevens ends the poem: "savagest diamonds" and "azure-doubled crimsons" (*CP,* 281). However, it is impossible to speak fully of them there, for consciousness has taken the place of imagination in the time of war, and man's travail must be to bear the counterpart to imagination's demise, truth as the "solar single," and fact as we want fact to be, as "the large, the solitary figure" in the poem's final line.

One question thus remains to be answered from Canto XVI: "But was the summer false?" (*CP,* 280). According to Stevens' opening of the poem, the answer is no. The "lot" of the hero in the poem's very first word is "force" (*CP,* 273), and force, according to Mark Taylor, "is absolute passage or passage as absolute [and] . . . is never simple or merely one but always inherently complex and intrinsically (at least) double."[48] The implication right from the beginning is that though heroic force may encounter opposition from various quarters, Roma, Avignon, Leyden, it is not itself identifiable with any one of them. In this regard it is like metaphor, risking conceptualization at every turn, a "movable host" as Nietzsche would say (OTL, 84), and always "bearing the brightness of arms" in opposition to "cold fate" in its cavern of consciousness (*CP,* 273), just as the hero appears to be doing here in his winter element of wind and snow. In the same way, the "conception" of God in Canto II, as a force of ten times ten the "dynamite" of the hero, as one who can deliver us from the hands of our enemies, is utter nonsense. Were God a "thing" possessed in this way ("Got"), a kind of "still magic . . . moving yet motionless" and at one with us (*CP,* 273), what might this "prester" do for our foes, whose belief compels them to invoke the same "convulsive / Angel" as "the savage weapon" against us? This is logic's lowest common denominator at work again, returning itself, as is noted in Canto III, to the same tired old romance, the same comforting "old revolving dance" and too familiar music, in a "museum [from the Latin *musa,* or remember] of euphonies":

> How strange the hero
> To this accurate, exacting eye. Sight
> Hangs heaven with flash drapery. Sight
> Is a museum of things seen.
>
> (*CP,* 274)

It is at this point in *Parts of a World* that Wallace Stevens would have anything resembling a heroic being destroyed and would take his stand

---

48. Taylor, *Erring,* III.

within the *seasons* of belief. His whole "Examination of the Hero in a Time of War" is thus a searching attempt to affirm that the wellsprings of faith, like the prophet and the hero himself, must continue to remain "unaccountable," as in Canto II, in spite of the "sudden sublimations" of what the consciousness of man in the *sight* of God might dictate. Anything less is the sacrifice of the imagination to truth's "solar single," the forfeit of a "noble centre" to the fury of war (*CP,* 274), in the heart of self-certain peace itself.

CHAPTER 4

THE VIOLENT ABYSS
Reasoning with a Later Reason

It is precisely a *discourse, not* embodied in God that assures us of a living God among us . . . [as] protection against the madness of direct contact with the Sacred without the mediation of reason. . . . The spiritual does not present itself as a tenable substance but, rather, through its absence.
—Emmanuel Levinas, "To Love the Torah More than God"

The abstract does not exist, but it is certainly as immanent: that is to say, the fictive abstract is as immanent in the mind of the poet, as the idea of God is immanent in the mind of the theologian.
—*Letters of Wallace Stevens*

You cannot solder an Abyss
With air.

—Emily Dickinson, No. 546

WALLACE Stevens' next major collection of verse, his fifth, was published five years after *Parts of a World,* in a trade edition of 1947 entitled *Transport to Summer.* The project, however, to which he turned immediately after completing *Parts of a World* in 1942 was his longest composition to date and is perhaps his best known, "Notes Toward a Supreme Fiction," published in the same year and reissued by the Cummington Press in a second edition a year later. "Notes" would appear for the third time as the final item in *Transport to Summer.* But the attention lavished on it in the years preceding that republication would suggest that volume five of the *Collected Poems* is more accurately to be taken as the programmatic culmination of "Notes Toward a Supreme Fiction," rather than the reverse—a culmination that the longer poem's title itself authenticates, as we shall see in the next chapter.

In this chapter, we shall examine Stevens' "Notes" in a somewhat parallel relation to "The Man with the Blue Guitar," which we discussed back in

Chapter 2. Like "Blue Guitar," this even longer poem stands as a kind of exploratory gesture, a breathing space as it were, in the great and oftentimes sinuous trajectory of the question of belief, wedged in between one outpouring of verse not quite completed the year previous and a later outpouring that, for the poet, as shown also with his next two volumes, would require a gestation cycle of roughly four to five years. "Notes" stands apart from all previous work in one enormously significant respect. Not once in any of its three main divisions and thirty-odd cantos is there a moment's ambivalent hesitation about the displacement of belief away from any kind of ontotheological idea of order.[1] With the destruction of Being behind him, the Metaphysician in the Dark no longer sends postcards from the volcano in moments when he chooses to play that imagined tune. In "Notes," the decreative Metaphysician *is* that volcano. And he chooses not a "violent order" either, as some perverse connoisseur of chaos would do, but what "Notes" in its final section, as we shall see in greater detail later, calls "the violent abyss" in response to the question "What am I to believe?" (*CP*, 404). Indeed, the frame of the question, and not some kind of overriding "answer," one is tempted to assert, is the very trajectory of "Notes" itself, for in the postmodern ambience within which *Parts of a World* destines to lodge Stevens' supreme fiction, first coined as far back as 1922 (*CP*, 59), "we must," Michel Foucault cautions, "think problematically rather than question and answer dialectically." For Foucault, who like Stevens also finds "thought is again possible" once Being is destroyed, the question of belief thus requires "the interrogation of the limit," the idea of order, say, in place of "the search for totality."[2]

As with *Blue Guitar* earlier, "Notes" represents, then, yet another significant intersection with a Foucauldian discourse since the work, which draws the middle corpus of Stevens' poetry to an end, or alternatively opens his poetry onto a new beginning in the later writing starting in 1947, so relentlessly problematizes the absoluteness of the links between belief, truth,

---

1. The a/theology that thus supersedes the ontotheology of Stevens' "Notes" authenticates, more generally, a movement in recent years away from purely formalist theorizings about his work (*e.g.*, Litz, Vendler, Pearce, Peterson) to ones more postformalist (*e.g.*, later Riddel and Miller, Beehler, Parker). Rather than offer a theoretical reading for theory's sake, it is the aim of the present study to show how Stevens' own question of belief provides a possibly more compelling reason for this shift in critical procedure.

2. Foucault, *Language, Counter-Memory, Practice*, 186, 196, 50. For a further link between the destruction of Being and the volcano image, which is also tied to "the 'material' expression of Force," as we shall understand later, see Kristeva, *Revolution in Poetic Language*, 115.

and God. "God is nothing if not the surpassing of God in every sense of vulgar being," we read in Foucault's "Preface to Transgression." From Stevens' "Notes" comes "The death of one god is the death of all" (*CP,* 381). Undeniably, it is the influence of Friedrich Nietzsche that is strongly felt behind both of these statements, yet it would be entirely erroneous to conclude on the basis of "God Is Dead" that either Stevens or Foucault could ever abandon the question of belief. Nietzsche certainly never did.[3] Consequently, when Foucault maps the genealogy of truth throughout the work of the German romantic poet Hölderlin in the last century, he curiously traces the evolution of an American romantic, volcano and all, in the early part of this one:

> [Hölderlin's *Empedocles*] sets out in search of the profound center of things, this central "Limitless" where all determinations are invalidated. To disappear into the fire of the volcano is to rejoin, at the point of its inaccessible and open hearth, the All-in-One—simultaneously, the subterranean vitality of stones and the bright flame of truth. But as Hölderlin reworked this theme, he modified the basic spatial relationships: the burning proximity of the divine . . . is transformed into the distant radiance of the unfaithful gods; Empedocles destroyed the lovely alliance by assuming the status of a mediator with divine powers. Thinking he had realised the "Limitless," he had, in fact merely succeeded in driving the Limits further away in a transgression that stood for his entire existence and that was the product of his "handiwork."[4]

Surely this, too, is Wallace Stevens in his own modification of the basic spatial relationship between belief and truth in the "Adagia," as "the priest of the invisible" from around the time of the second edition of *Ideas of Order* in 1936, in which he notes that "God is a postulate of the ego" and further that "God is in me or else is not at all (does not exist)" (*OP,* 195, 197, 198). Where could these modifications possibly lead when, after *Blue Guitar* and *Parts of a World,* even truth itself must be denied?

---

3. *Cf. WP,* §161: "The Kingdom of Heaven is a condition of the heart (—it is said of children 'for theirs is the Kingdom of Heaven'): Not something 'above the earth.' The Kingdom of God does not 'come' chronologically-historically, on a certain day in the calendar, something that might be here one day but not the day before: it is an 'inward change in the individual,' something that comes at every moment and at every moment has not yet arrived" (98–99).

4. Foucault, *Language, Counter-Memory, Practice,* 33, 82–83.

Nietzsche, again, seems to provide the best clue and, for both Stevens and Foucault, a most provocative image: "Is it to avoid chance that we take refuge in life? In its brilliance, its *falseness,* its *superficiality,* its shimmering falsehood? If we seem joyous, is it because we are profoundly sad? We are grave, we know the abyss." Thus, "falseness," "superficiality," "falsehood," in a word, Absence, or the hole truth and *nothing but* the truth, as a pun in Derrida might suggest, would form the new contour of Wallace Stevens' interrogation of belief for the remainder of his writing life.[5] It would become the fiction (or the abstract) that one approached asymptotically, so to speak, the "Limitless" for which the more one compiled one's "notes," the more one sensed its retreat further away into the abyss of distance. As an important letter written to Henry Church, the poem's dedicatee, shortly after the initial publication explained the case, fiction was "something that one knew was not true" but, despite all reasonable protest, something one believed in nonetheless as a possible construction in reality's absence. With Stevens' particular meaning of the word *reality* in mind from Chapter 2, the commentary in this letter on the word *Fiction* deserves fairly lengthy citation:

> I thought that we had reached a point at which we could no longer really believe in anything unless we recognized that it was a fiction. [To which a student interlocutor replied] that there was no such thing as believing in something that one knew was not true. It is obvious, however, that we are doing that all the time. There are things with respect to which we willingly suspend disbelief; if there is instinctive in us a will to believe, or if there is a will to believe, whether or not it is instinctive, it seems to me that we can suspend disbelief with reference to a fiction as easily as we can suspend it with reference to anything else. There are fictions that are extensions of reality. There are plenty of people who believe in Heaven as definitely as your New England ancestors and my Dutch ancestors believed in it. But Heaven is an extension of reality. (*L,* 430)

The implication here for Stevens' longest work to date, therefore, might be to observe how what is given by its notes must be taken away almost in the very same moment by the word *fiction,* along a continuum of infinite

5. Jean Granier, "Perspectivism and Interpretation," in *The New Nietzsche,* ed. Allison, 139; Derrida, *Writing and Difference,* 297–98.

regress, what Foucault would call "an exponential series of endless epi-
sodes."[6] Stevens himself refers to this continuum as "breadth" in a concluding comment on the matter in a letter to Hi Simons from early 1943: "The
next thing for me to do will be to try to be a little more precise about this
enigma [*i.e.,* supreme fiction]. I hold off from even attempting that because,
as soon as I start to rationalize, I lose the poetry of the idea. . . . In trying to
create something as valid as the idea of God has been, and for that matter
remains, the first necessity seems to be breadth. It is true that the thing would
never amount to much . . . [if] it has all come to a point" (*L,* 435). It is always
necessary to propose an enigma to the (re)solution-filled mind (*OP,* 194), and
Nietzsche's paraphrase of this passage would simply be that we have the
enigma of a supreme fiction or abstract lest we perish of the truth (*WP,* §822).
In other words, poetry is, in a phrase taken from the same letter to Simons,
"a struggle with the inaccessibility of the abstract" (*L,* 434), which is the real
"point" mentioned in the above passage and which rather uncannily recalls
"the point of [the volcano's] *inaccessible* and *open* hearth" in Foucault's description of Hölderlin cited earlier (emphasis added). "Notes Toward a Supreme Fiction," in simplest terms, then, is a discourse directed toward metaphysical absence. As such, it succeeded in delivering Wallace Stevens
permanently from the impasse of order that threatened to paralyze him halfway through his successful achievement as a published poet. Eight years later,
as I noted in Chapter 1, he was to record that "one grows tired of being
oneself and feels the need of renewing all one's thoughts and ways of thinking . . . [since poetry] is not likely to be satisfied with the same thing twice"
(*L,* 680). Stevens' "Notes," in turning the question of belief into an infinitely
renewable problematic, gave him the artistic and the spiritual assurance that
fiction and faith, now that he was beginning to write about both in much the
same terms, were themselves infinitely renewable.[7] To the largely indifferent
reviews that *Parts of a World* and "Notes" were garnering, Stevens himself
could remain indifferent (*L,* 436, 442); for with the travail of a new way of
thinking in the questioning of certain Being behind him, in the words of
Ecclesiastes, "of making many books there [could be] no end."

6. Foucault, *Language, Counter-Memory, Practice,* 65; *cf.* also Derrida, "Limited Inc.," 243.

7. On the quite specific use of the word *problematic* here, see Louis Althusser and
Étienne Balibar, *Reading Capital,* trans. Ben Brewster (London, 1977), 24–25. See also Henry A.
Giroux, *Theory and Resistance in Education: A Pedagogy for the Opposition* (South Hadley, Mass.,
1983), 172–73.

In beginning the very first line of the prologue of "Notes Toward a Supreme Fiction" in the form of a question ("And for what, except for you, do I feel love?" [*CP*, 380]) and by leaving the referent for the pronoun *you* deliberately vague, Stevens' strategy right from the start is calculated to vex the reader's hankering for "single, certain truth," which is equated to "the central of our being," with indeterminacy and doubt, imaged by "uncertain light." The Metaphysician is truly in the Dark with such an introduction and is offered only the certitude, the "vivid transparence," of a poetry's willful changefulness, but only for a moment, to provide him with any kind of peace. Theodor Adorno, perhaps a type of "the wisest man" in this opening prologue, would attach such a moment to modernism's dialectic of enlightenment—the moment of anti-art, when art goes beyond its own concept, beyond some enduring abstract essence of "the long demystified illusion of duration," and in order to be faithful to itself incorporates instead a "sympathy with the ephemeral, which is life."[8] Stevens' own attachment to improvisation throughout the poem—a poem that allows its materials to evolve musically, "for internal reasons and not with reference to an external program" (*L*, 483)—would certainly be in keeping with such a dialectic. We have this note sounded in the quite unusual use of the coordinating conjunction *and* as the poem's first word. The introduction therefore makes it quite plain that Stevens' "Notes" are to be taken musically as well as thematically. However, all of this can only be made "implicit" in the title, as Stevens states once again in the letter to Church. "I have no idea of the form that a supreme fiction would take," he remarks, for "the essence of poetry is change" and the essence of change is not that it provides stable truths, rather "that it gives pleasure" (*L*, 430). Hence, the second and third of the poem's major divisions, "It Must Change" and "It Must Give Pleasure," respectively, are very much anticipated in these opening eight lines.

"The inconceivable idea of the sun" in Canto I of the first major division of the poem, "It Must Be Abstract," fits perfectly Stevens' plea of ignorance concerning the supreme fiction's form. Ignorance for the "ephebe," or apprentice poet, is not a mental condition to be eschewed but a disposition to be cultivated—the ignorance that Stevens identifies in his "Adagia" as the poet's "chief asset" and "one of the sources of poetry" (*OP*, 202, 198): "You

---

8. T[heodor] W. Adorno, *Aesthetic Theory*, trans. C. Lenhardt, ed. Gretel Adorno and Rolf Tiedelmann (London, 1982), 42–43.

must become an ignorant man again / And see the sun again with an ignorant eye / And see it clearly in the idea of it" (*CP,* 380). The idea, the First Idea as it turns out, which is itself unnameable but which the ephebe must neverthe-less attempt repeatedly to name, can consequently be linked to the limitless Absence integral to Stevens' belief in the abstractness of fiction, with which we dealt earlier. As such, it is rather like Jean-François Lyotard's view of the idea in Kant's philosophy: "An Idea, in Kant's sense, is different from a con-cept in that it does not correspond to any object and thus cannot be proved to exist; yet, it nevertheless can be (in fact, must be) presumed as a regulating principle. It has an 'as-if' rather than an actual existence; thus, analogy could be said to be its principal mode of indirect 'presentation.'"[9] As a result, by our conceiving of it in terms of the *je ne sais quoi* of a paraesthetic "sublime" (the sun in Stevens' own analogy cannot be looked at directly yet is a genuine experience nonetheless), the idea is able to postpone indefinitely any kind of conceptual or doctrinal closure imposed on it from the outside, having built within itself "a kind of critical safeguard against the dogmatism of the theo-retical in general."[10]

"The project for the sun" that Stevens announces in his first canto, then, is one that will take twenty-nine additional cantos to carry out. Even then, it is not likely ever to be completed, not even perhaps in Stevens' own lifetime. Like Phoebus slumbering in the death of autumn umber, the project is ter-minal, but only in the sense of its interminableness, and this "inconceivable" aspect of the sun is what must be seen cleanly in its idea. As Derrida rightly

9. David Carroll, *Paraesthetics: Foucault, Lyotard, Derrida* (New York, 1987), 174. B. J. Leggett has a note on other possible philosophical sources for Stevens' notion of a First Idea, including Paul Valéry, Alfred North Whitehead, F. H. Bradley, Charles Sanders Peirce, and the composer Charles Ives, in *Wallace Stevens and Poetic Theory: Conceiving the Supreme Fiction* (Chapel Hill, 1987), 207n35. For a parallel sense of "analogy" as it is used here, see also Jacques Derrida, *The Truth in Painting,* trans. Geoff Bennington and Ian McLeod (Chicago, 1987), 36, 75–76. For another likely source, in Gustave Flaubert, see Eugenio Donato, "The Ruins of Memory: Archeological Fragments and Textual Artifacts," *MLN,* XCIII (1978), 593, and Bruns, *Modern Poetry,* 194, 198, and *passim.*

10. David Carroll, *Paraesthetics,* 182. Leggett's study of the sources of influence on Stevens' "Notes" (I. A. Richards, Giambattista Vico, Charles Mauron, Henri Focillon, *et al.*) suggests that perhaps Immanuel Kant's idea comes highly mediated to Stevens, through Stevens' reading of Richards' reading of Samuel Taylor Coleridge's reading of Kant. Thus, in a passage from *The Statesman's Manual* cited by Richards in *Coleridge on Imagination,* Stevens may have read of "an educt of the imagination actuated by the pure reason" that "neither refers to outward facts, nor yet is abstracted from the forms of perception contained in the understanding" and "to which there neither is nor can be an adequate correspondent in the world of the senses": "This and this alone is—an Idea" (Leggett, *Poetic Theory,* 33).

notes, "the sun is never properly present in discourse . . . but each time that there is sun, metaphor has begun." It is "this abyss of metaphor . . . simultaneously widening and consolidating itself," about which the ephebe can be expected to rejoice. The only danger to which the apprentice might be prone lies in his imparting to the First Idea some attribution of metaphysical presence and, by further implication, some theological commitment to belief located either ontologically as source *outside* the inventing mind, as in the classic rhetorical paradigm of mimesis (the "voluminous master folded in his fire" [*CP*, 381]), or epistemologically *within* the human mind, as in the romantic rhetorical paradigm of poiesis—within the "gold flourisher" of the ephebe himself. Both paradigms are latent in what B. J. Leggett refers to as "the dilemma of the mind-world duality," that is, "the imagination-reality" conflict in Stevens, and both have consistently stalled the critical appreciation of his work within an impossible formalist or structuralist modernism, as I described back in the Introduction, which it has been a major purpose of this study of belief in Stevens to attempt to obviate. We only begin to move into a new critical appraisal of Wallace Stevens when, like the ephebe, we cease trying to find a correspondent truth for Stevens' images—cease, that is to say, living in the "essentially theological" age of the sign—and accept the fact of a heaven, as the poem puts it, "that has expelled us and our images" (*CP*, 381).[11] To achieve this position, we must accept the poet's reality as a factitious "concept," an imaginative construction either in the Nietzschean sense taken up in the last two chapters or in the Kantean sense just outlined but, no matter which, as the figuration of something that will *never* properly be named. Merely because one name or image dies is no reason to abandon altogether the endless process of naming. The notions of absolutes and of definitions are relative, after all; we never "arrive" intellectually (*OP*, 185, 198).

The project for the sun, therefore, continues to exist, for the "impossible possible philosophers' man" (*CP*, 250), as well as for us, as long as reality is held open to the imagination. By moving out from under the finite paradigms of presence structured by both the classic mimesis and romantic poiesis of bygone eras and into the infinite model of Absence remarked by the thoroughly modern rhetoric of a limitless semiosis, imagination can keep reality open, using the very language by which its "forms of thought" are constructed to point it *toward* the Supreme Absence that alone makes its exis-

---

11. Derrida, *Margins of Philosophy*, 251, 253; Leggett, *Poetic Theory*, 34, 40; Derrida, *Grammatology*, 13–14.

tence possible.[12] In such a tendentiously complex and inscrutable opening canto, Stevens becomes the postmodern spokesman for "the difficulty of what it is to be" and, more important, of what it is to believe, in the contemporary world of diminished faith. "I ought to say that I have not defined a supreme fiction," he candidly admits about his poem. He then further confesses, "I don't want to say that I don't mean poetry; I don't know what I mean" (*L,* 435). Yet such opacity, measured in terms of the ultimate aesthetic and spiritual rewards he hoped his long work would generate, seemed worth the risk in any case: "It Must Be Abstract."

Canto II of "It Must Be Abstract," consequently, is a veritable celebration of Supreme Absence, the First Idea that, never to be fully disclosed within the poet's metaphors, becomes the hermit insistently haunting his work, an absent presence "who comes and goes and comes and goes all day" (*CP,* 381). Moreover, because truth stands to draw the process of metaphorization to a definite close at some point, compared to the quick invention of the ephebe who must be sent repeatedly back to the First Idea, truth's ravishments must seem "poisonous," even fatal perhaps to the notion of truth itself. In its place, the artist must be made to suffer the longeurs of Desire, that is, the condition of perpetual lack or longing for an impossible transcendental completion, in order to guarantee a process of creativity "perpetually in construction" and "perpetually open to change."[13] Desire for the poet, therefore, becomes the "celestial ennui" of apart-ments, to return to an overworked pun in *Parts of a World*—the ennui of "not to have" that, in its "ancient cycle," will cause the artist to cast aside even that which he has ("As morning throws off stale moonlight and shabby sleep" [*CP,* 382]) in order to perpetuate the motions of the cycle indefinitely. Stevens offers a fairly accurate description of the cycle of desire *in moto* in Canto III:

> The poem refreshes life so that we share,
> For a moment, the first idea . . . It satisfies
> Belief in an immaculate beginning

12. See Michel Foucault, *The Order of Things: An Archaeology of the Human Sciences* (New York, 1970), 294–300.

13. Catherine Belsey, *Critical Practice* (New York, 1980), 132. John Irwin brings the condition of "a never-to-be-satisfied desire" back to the idea of the abyss, once again, when he notes in *American Hieroglyphics: The Symbol of the Egyptian Hieroglyphics in the American Renaissance* (New Haven, 1980), in the context of the "open road" in Walt Whitman's poetry, that "the image of limitless possibility, of an infinite 'second chance' or new beginning" will never quite be understood "unless we see it as one pole of an opposition whose other pole is the voyage to the abyss" (112).

> And sends us, winged by an unconscious will,
> To an immaculate end. We move between these points:
> From that ever-early candor to its late plural
>
> And the candor of them is the strong exhilaration
> Of what we feel from what we think, of thought
> Beating in the heart, as if blood newly came,
>
> An elixir, an excitation, a pure power.
>
> (*CP,* 382)

By shuttling between the initial intimation of the First Idea ("ever-early candor") and the final interpretations or concepts constructed to contain it ("late plural"), which can never be quite good enough, belief is forced to be continually on the move. It is the perpetuum mobile between these two points, so reminiscent of Heidegger's "ontological difference," that imparts to poetry its moments of greatest refreshment and to life the opportunities for strongest exhilaration.[14] For truth cannot be said to reside in either point.

The infinite rotation of desire is picked up in the next canto in the endless sequence of repetitions, as old as Adam, by which man has endeavored to represent truth to himself. Recurring to the paradigms of representation rehearsed previously, we see this process meant, in classical rhetorical terms, placing oneself in an analogical relationship to the image of godhead, finding oneself in heaven "as in a glass," as a "second earth" mimics an original Eden; later, in postclassical or modern rhetorical terms, the process elevates the human image to godhead and places everything in metaphorical equivalence to the self, as Eve, after the Fall to the green earth and in an anticipation of Descartes' cogito, makes her sons and daughters and even the air itself (with a pun perhaps on "heir") "the mirror of herself" (*CP,* 383). Hence, the "myth before the myth" in this canto suggests the complementary relation between these two well-known metaphysical models of representation, as dreams "for indubitable truth."[15] In spite of these "blazoned days," however, Stevens' "Notes" is attempting to evolve a quite other myth before the myth, the originary (as opposed to original) myth of a/theological Ab-

14. See esp. Robert P. Scharlemann, "The Being of God When God Is Not Being God: Deconstructing the History of Theism," in *Deconstruction and Theology,* ed. Thomas J. J. Altizer *et al.* (New York, 1982), 38, 95.

15. Tracy, *Plurality and Ambiguity,* 25. The double myth of "correspondence to reality" (Richard Rorty, *Philosophy and the Mirror of Nature* [Princeton, 1979], 333) highly distilled in Stevens' first two stanzas is also nicely unpacked by J. Hillis Miller: "When everything exists only as reflected in the ego . . . everything else turns into . . . an object of thought like any other. . . . In this way man is the murderer of God" (*Poets of Reality,* 3).

sence that always already constitutes the metaphysical representations of
mythic Presence, that is, the utterly formless First Idea, once again, which
cannot "shape the clouds / In imitation" because it is that "huge abstraction,"
as Stevens writes in his letters, "venerable and articulate and complete, that
has no reference to us" (*L,* 444). Consequently, there can never be any ultimately clear locus of imminent transfiguration (God as "pathetic fallacy" in
Letters or clouds as "pedagogues" in the poem) but instead only "a muddy
centre," a "bright-dark, tragic chiaroscuro" abyss, to which we can add
"sweeping meanings" with the pipping sounds of "abysmal instruments" yet
which we cannot even remotely hope to plumb. In place of any kind of unitive self-knowledge, Stevens privileges the sense of Being's "confused or
clouded intelligibility" and, consequently, man's sense of abject alienation:

> From this the poem springs: that we live in a place
> That is not our own and, much more, not ourselves
> And hard it is in spite of blazoned days.

> (*CP,* 383)[16]

Stevens extends this ennui of apart-ment even further, in the following canto,
in the images of the roaring lion, the blaring elephant, and the snarling bear,
the first two of which will appear to the same effect seven years later in "Puella
Parvula" (*CP,* 456). All this red-colored and shattering faraway noise arouses
in the ephebe, in his human center high atop the urban jungle of attic windows and mansard roofs, a fear and loathing for the dumb violence of an
abysmal otherness, to which these exotic animals are obviously connected.
His instinctive reaction to it all, to strike out "against the first idea—to lash
the lion, / Caparison elephants, teach bears to juggle" (*CP,* 385)—merely
shows how hopelessly entangled he is himself in the toils of the outworn,
egocentric myths of theological self-representation.

In the next two cantos of "It Must Be Abstract," we watch Stevens'
poetry give birth to an image that will recur constantly in the late poetry for
the a/theological Absence that holds out the only hope for keeping the question of belief alive in all his thinking and writing to the end. This is the image

---

16. Being's "confused or clouded intelligibility" in place of "a translucent *logos,*" on which
Jean Granier says Nietzsche insists, may have suggested to Stevens the image of the "muddy
centre" in this canto ("Perspectivism and Interpretation," in *The New Nietzsche,* ed. Allison, 192).
Thus, the image of the "muddy centre" is one of many significant aspects of "Notes" that puts
Stevens' discourse outside the Western metaphysical tradition, "the very centre of the human
being," as Lacan argues, that "was no longer to be found at the place assigned to it by a whole
humanist tradition," that is, "the mirage that renders modern man so sure of being himself even
in his uncertainties about himself" (*Écrits,* 114, 165).

of the giant, which will greet us over and over in such important later texts as "Chocorua to Its Neighbor," "The Owl in the Sarcophagus," "A Primitive like an Orb," and "An Ordinary Evening in New Haven," written in 1943, 1947, 1948, and 1949, respectively. It is a particularly perilous moment in Stevens' discourse and one that he will repeatedly attempt to write his way around since it presents him with the somewhat contradictory predicament of attempting to represent what should by all a/theological expectations be considered arepresentational, the problem, as David Carroll describes it in a purely philosophical context, of trying "to exceed language while using language." If the giant is "an imagined thing" (*CP,* 387), would it not be retrograde to allow it to evolve into a type of American Everyman as the "Notes" allow, the MacCullough in Canto VIII that Harold Bloom views along these lines as a kind of cross between Whitman and Nietzsche, "an American Over-Man" and "a grand trope or noble synecdoche of Power"? The formula, one tends to feel, is entirely too pat. If Stevens is entertaining such an expedient, the densely logocentric descriptors with which he renders such an identification ("Logos and logic, crystal hypothesis, / Incipit and a form," and so forth) suggest that he may be doing so only for purposes of irony, in order to explode the hypothesis entirely: "But the MacCullough is MacCullough. / It does not follow that major man is man" (*CP,* 387). There is always a danger in strictly analogical thinking of this type, as in the paradigms of theocentric representation described earlier, that comes in revolving the First Idea as metaphor—"Metaphor as Degeneration" (*CP,* 444), as we shall have occasion to take it up in Chapter 5. There is the ever-present danger that we, like MacCullough lounging by the sea, can "take habit" in our thought and can too easily become lulled by the self-referentiality of its "deepened speech" into replacing the difficulty of being of Canto I with a "leaner being" here, only because it has the access of "greater aptitude and apprehension" or the ease of language in suddenly saying things that had formerly been "laboriously spoken." Michel Foucault remarks it is "the over-familiar that constantly eludes one; those familiar transparencies, which, although they conceal nothing in their density, are nevertheless not entirely clear."[17] Perhaps for this reason, and for this reason alone, the too easy identification of major man with MacCullough as American Every- or Over- or Super-man has immediately to be abandoned: "Give him / No names. Dismiss him from your images" (*CP,* 388). As the possible/impossible Supreme Absence, Stevens'

17. David Carroll, *Paraesthetics,* 34; Bloom, *Poems of Our Climate,* 189; Michel Foucault, *The Archaeology of Knowledge,* trans. A. M. Sheridan Smith (London, 1972), III.

giant must destroy every foil, must evade every thought, must repel every look into his colored eyes, yet at the same time must *continue* to invite, "in the manner of his hand," all manner of "accurate songs" and all method of "studious" approach: "But oh! he is, he is." Thinking itself is likely our greatest shortcoming, therefore, in attempting to deal with major man; and it may just be that in bringing us up short on this point, Stevens would have us *feel* our way to MacCullough's "*summarium in excelsis*" (*CP,* 456), allowing us to fall back, as "the good of April falls tenderly, / Falls down," into the ancient cycle of Desire once again, where the hot of him is purest: "in the heart" (*CP,* 388).

In Stevens' summing up the "major abstraction" in the last canto of the poem's first section, of which the giant or "major man" has been ventured as the abstraction's fictional "exponent," the poet's final strategy for placing it beyond the closure of rational comprehension is to link the abstract to the happy fecundity of a "flor-abundant force" (*CP,* 388). Force, for Stevens, will gradually become something of an obsession in his work, as we shall see more clearly in the next chapter. But we can be certain, if the "Adagia" are any indication, that generally he intends to subvert both physical and metaphysical apprehensions of the notion: "The mind is the most terrible force in the world"—a world that is itself a textual construction, and imagination one of its leading forces, yet a world that is unquestionably "not a presence" (*OP,* 199, 196, 198). In Canto X, the whole refusal of force to be framed categorically is suggested by its generative as opposed to its generic character, its polyvalent, heterogeneity ("commonal" rather than "singular" or "particle") made more emphatic with the word *more* as intensifier: "More fecund as principle," "more than an exception," and so forth. Jacques Derrida's conception (one hesitates to use the word) of force as "a power of pure equivocality" and "dislocation," a disappearing possibility that is "in excess of everything, the essential nothing on whose basis everything can appear and be produced," would seem to apply to a notion that Stevens can as yet only awkwardly enunciate, with images such as "the inantimate, difficult visage."[18] It should be clear by the end of "It Must Be Abstract," however, that the visage is made difficult not in its unitive deployment but in its extension in so many

18. Derrida, *Writing and Difference,* 9, 20, 8. On a possible connection between Stevens' "inanimate, difficult visage" and his preoccupation with the Supreme Fiction's "abyss," we might turn to "the face of the other" in Emmanuel Levinas, by which, according to John Caputo, we are "dis-comforted, dis-concerted, de-centered, dis-placed," by which "stable structures shake loose, the whole trembles, the abyss opens up," and "we are brought tripping before the mystery" (*Radical Hermeneutics,* 276).

versions of the Supreme Fiction thus far: giant, major man, MacCullough, and now, in Canto X, rabbi, chieftain, and a Chaplinesque figure in an old coat and slouching pantaloons who would appear to be a synopsis of them all:

> What rabbi, grown furious with human wish,
> What chieftain, walking by himself
>
> . . . .
>
> Does not see these separate figures one by one,
> And yet see only one
>
> . . . .
>
> It is he. The man
> In that old coat, those sagging pantaloons,
>
> It is of him, ephebe, to make, to confect
> The final elegance, not to console
> Nor sanctify, but plainly to propound.
>
> (*CP*, 389)

If Stevens' Abstraction is preeminently a force of multitudinous difference, a creative "concentration of power" that Susan Handelman, in her thorough study of the Hebraic traditions of textuality, associates with the rabbinic tendency toward "differentiation, metaphorical multiplicity, [and] multiple meaning," then it is perhaps possible to view the Supreme Fiction as an accommodation within the "one," as the above passage suggests, but a one that can only be a "presence-as-separation," in Handelman's phrase. Ultimately, the Supreme Fiction is an acceptance of one-as-Other, which the language of Stevens' text has repeatedly struggled to engage. Thus, the furious rabbi marshaling his figures "one by one" seems just the right climax for the opening movement of "Notes." Handelman writes: "Rabbinic interpretation never dispenses with the particular form in which the idea is clothed. The text, for the Rabbis, is a continuous generator of meaning, which arises from the innate logic of the divine language, the letter itself, and is not sought in a nonlinguistic realm external to the text. Language and the text are, to use a contemporary term, the space of *differences,* and truth as conceived by the Rabbis was not an instantaneous unveiling of the One, but a continuous sequential process of interpretation."[19] To console and to sanctify, accord-

---

19. Susan A. Handelman, *The Slayers of Moses: The Emergence of Rabbinic Interpretation in Modern Literary Theory* (Albany, 1982), 32–33, 173, 88–89. Stevens' attraction to the rabbinic model of interpretation was first pointed out by Daniel Fuchs in *The Comic Spirit of Wallace Stevens* (Durham, 1963), citing a comment by the poet in *Mattino Domenicale:* "Frankly, the figure

ingly, are the functions of fiction directed toward the limited satisfactions of self-regarding knowledge, the "final elegance" that we recall in Mrs. Uruguay's struggle to "get at [herself]" (*CP,* 248–49). To propound a final elegance for a beggar, though, is a project limited only by the time it takes language to make plain the limitlessness of its own fictional resources and, if it were possible, to carry the Supreme Fiction even beyond the infinity of Absence itself.

The metaphysics of Presence, so much under attack in the first division of Stevens' poem, in the second part, "It Must Change," is radically altered in the opening canto by an elaborate wordplay on the word *bee.* Bee-ing now comes "booming" in Stevens' "Notes," for it is the accretive processes of Being, under the impetus of linguistic change, that the first ten cantos of the text have delivered us into. "The seraph / Is satyr in Saturn" (*CP,* 390), like the well-known rain in Spain midplain, is a pure instance of language in the very act of transforming thought from word to word where the only rule seems to be the abandonment of all rules, in deference to a constant inconstancy:

> We say,
> This changes and that changes. Thus the constant
>
> Violets, doves, girls, bees and hyacinths
> Are inconstant objects of inconstant cause
> In a universe of inconstancy. This means
>
> . . . .
>
> the distaste we feel for this withered scene
>
> Is that it has not changed enough.
>
> (*CP,* 389–90)

In this limitless dissemination of language, what the canto foregrounds as "repetition," *is* becomes *as*—the bees come booming "as if"—so that the emphasis lands now not so much on the signifieds of textuality as on the relations among its signifiers. One cannot linger too long over what any particular relationship means: "The blooming is blunt, not broken in subtleties."

---

of the rabbi has always been an exceedingly attractive one to me because it is the figure of a man devoted in the extreme to scholarship and at the same time making some use of it for human purposes" (132). *Cf.* further in Handelman, 146 , 172–73, 195, 222.

Of course, the highly erratic motions of bee-ing contribute to the subversion of logical thought as well. "The unexpectedness of logically progressive or zigzag development," Bertolt Brecht once remarked, coupled with "the instability of every circumstance [and] the joke of contradiction . . . heighten both our capacity for life and our pleasure in it"—the very pleasure upon which change will later devolve in the third division of Stevens' text.[20]

In the next two cantos, we are presented with types of the enemy of change, an important principle that had already begun to evolve for Stevens in the seasons of belief. The President, in Canto II, is a figure of absolute transcendental authority, right from the disposition of "barefoot servants" around his august personage (one thinks of the ring of naked men chanting "boisterous devotion" to their sunlike lord back in "Sunday Morning" [*CP*, 70]) through to the veiling of his presence with curtains adjusted "to a metaphysical t" (*CP*, 390). Naturally, his agenda is the immortalizing of "an inexhaustible being." No doubt, he is extremely discomfited by the booming of bee-ing started up in Canto I and continued here in the droning of "the green phrases" of spring's juvenal, through which the question of belief in terms of theological self-reference, tied in with the sleep and death of reason formerly, is resumed once again:

> When, then, when in golden fury
>
> Spring vanishes the scraps of winter, why
> Should there be a question of returning or
> Of death in memory's dream? Is spring a sleep?
> (*CP*, 390–91)

Change, therefore, rather than the President, ordains life a beginning of repetition ("Booming and booming of the new-come bee") and not a resuming of representation in what John Ashbery, perhaps following Stevens here, will call "The Double Dream of Spring" but that to the lovers at the end of the canto is more like an abyssal or "bottomless trophy." Hence, the President modulates into the egregious statue of General Du Puy in Canto III, a reprise of Stevens' mockery of monumental ideas of order reviewed back in Chapter 1.

Thus far, "It Must Change" has been intensely critical of belief arrived at through extreme, and ultimately repressive, postures of self-transcendence

---

20. Bertolt Brecht, *Brecht on Theatre: The Development of an Aesthetic*, trans. John Willett (London, 1986), 277.

that set the limits, both mental and spiritual, to human knowledge and self-consciousness. What the gestures of exclusion and repression, sustained by a metaphysics of Presence and rehearsed repeatedly in the last chapter, tend to elide more than anything else is the textual relationality mentioned in the first canto. This textual disposition is the "continuous network of differential oppositions," as John Irwin describes it, that "establishes man in an essentially mediate, relational condition between the poles of primal dualities," which in "his quest for self-definition" become fused in his effort "to transcend the mediate and reach . . . that totality of undifferentiated Being that, because it is without differentiation, can only be experienced as a kind of nothingness—a sublime that is an abyss." Stevens had worked through the diacritical coimplication of propositionality in poems such as "Extracts" and "Examination of a Hero" earlier, so that now he is able to offer the argument for difference from his last volume as an even *more* compelling argument as and for change in the present text. In the opening stanzas of Canto IV, therefore, the mutually constitutive force of differential oppositions becomes linked to change as follows:

> Two things of opposite natures seem to depend
> On one another, as a man depends
> On a woman, day on night, the imagined
>
> On the real. This is the origin of change.
> Winter and spring, cold copulars, embrace
> And forth the particulars of rapture come.
>
> (*CP*, 392)[21]

And the host of examples whose identities are reducible to no truth save a changing interrelative oppositionality (music and silence, morning and afternoon, sun and rain, sailor and sea, etc.) is once again a presentiment that escapes the logic of the metaphysician. It is a presentiment that is perhaps

21. Irwin, *American Hieroglyphics*, 51. Irwin brings out to a much greater degree the aspect of change in his description of the differential matrix of "cold copulars" announced here when he notes: "In imagining the structure of a bipolar opposition, we should think of it not as static but dynamic: as an equilibrium or equivalence of opposing forces on the model of electrical polarity . . . oscillation in the sense of a flickering in or hovering about of one opposite in the other" (102). *Cf.* also Joseph G. Kronick in *American Poetics of History: From Emerson to the Moderns* (Baton Rouge, 1984) on a remarkably similar passage in William Carlos Williams' *Pictures from Brueghel and Other Poems:* "Man and woman do not join together and dissolve all differences between them; they remain two in the figure. In the dance, 'there are always two, / yourself and the other' . . . and self and other exist only in the difference measured by the dance" (223).

more readily taken in by what we feel than what we see: "Reason, / Lighted at midnight" earlier in "It Must Be Abstract" (*CP*, 388), or here "a passion that we feel, not understand" (*CP*, 392).

Without language, of course, animals do not enter into the network of relations that a human and desiring consciousness establishes and with which it works itself into a vast texture of political, social, and cultural beliefs.[22] This disparity seems to be the point, in Canto VI, of the birds' "idiot minstrelsy," the granite monotony whose "single text" can only be the benighted product of the "eye without lid, [and] mind without any dream":

> Bethou me, said sparrow, to the crackled blade,
> And you, and you, bethou me as you blow,
> When in my coppice you behold me be.
>
> . . . .
>
> These are of minstrels lacking minstrelsy,
> Of an earth in which the first leaf is the tale
> Of leaves, in which the sparrow is a bird
>
> Of stone, that never changes.
>
> (*CP*, 393–94)

Once again, Stevens recurs to Nietzsche's argument of the gregarizing concept through the well-worn illustration of the leaf reviewed in the last chapter. Again, his purpose is to indict the fatal unities to which experience is prone when self-reference sets the standard for single, certain truth—the fragile standard, in a related image, of the destiny of the glassblower, whose bubbles Stevens parallels in *Letters* with the reduction of myriad faces to a single face, rather than oak-leaf and hand (*L*, 435), perhaps thinking of the "inanimate, difficult visage" scanned earlier. However, like the romantic paradigm of self-referential rhetoric, with the bow to Shelley's "Ode to the West Wind" ("Be thou, Spirit fierce, / My spirit! Be thou me"), the logocentrism will end; and in changing its tune, the minstrelsy of a later day will have displaced "Ah, ké!" and "Ké-ké!" into the more flor-abundant spaces multiplied by language.

The circuit around the world described by Nanzia Nunzio in the following Canto VIII is nothing (hence, her name) like Stevens' spiraling or abyssal desire but is more like the negative theology contained by the cycle

22. The argument that "the animal does not enter into 'relations'" on the model of "language" as "practical consciousness" may be found in Karl Marx and Friedrich Engels, *Marx and Engels: Basic Writings on Politics and Philosophy*, ed. Lewis S. Feuer (New York, 1959), 157–58.

of romance dealt with back in Chapter 1. Here the negative theology is called the "inflexible / Order" before which Nanzia abases herself, as the fallen Ozymandias' "contemplated spouse" (*CP,* 395–96). Stevens thus continues his parody of Shelleyean rhetoric, extending it in another Mrs. Uruguay-type figure, maniacally attempting to fabricate some metaphysical identity in order to "get at" herself. She does this by divesting her person of all worldly trappings, golden necklace, stone-studded belt, precious ornament, in exchange for an ultimate translation to a supramundane world far beyond the scholar's, a transcendental apotheosis symbolized by the spirit's "final filament" and "diamond coronal" and hidden in another absurd statue's perfecting word. Nanzia's unitive confounding of the representative and semantic functions of language ("As I am, I am") and the further collapsing into the larger hegemony of Ozymandias' patriarchal authority and cultural tradition constitute perhaps an act of what Paul de Man would call "ontological bad faith." She pays for it dearly in the perverse twist that Stevens imparts to the ruin's response to her: "The bride / Is never naked. A fictive covering / Weaves always glistening from the heart and mind" (*CP,* 396). In the myriad fictions spun from the interior of humankind, Stevens thus reverses the point of view of the single text's "granite monotony," which was earlier strictly for the birds. As far as man is concerned, the perfecting word is a force for the liberation of all totalizing forms of absolute thought and not one for the exclusionary reduction of the different and diverse to the homologous above and beyond. Anyone who cannot see the evidence for the fatal consequences of the latter so plainly before her is obviously doomed to go the way of the lone and level Ozymandias.[23]

The displacement of Nanzia's closed circle onto something more resembling an endless textual covering or web allows Stevens to bring the second division of his poem back, once again in its finale, to movement and change, particularly the movement among its constituent and correlative elements. In Canto IX, the interanimation between the gibberish of the poet and the gibberish of the vulgate, or between the "imagination's Latin" and the "lingua franca et jocundissima" (*CP,* 397), provides an access to both that a semantically absolutist approach to either would quite likely repel. The proof lies in the sorts of categorical questions being directed toward the poetic text through the canto's early stanzas, the momentum of which issues in a searching meditation on a text's evasion of categorical questions in general and the

---

23. De Man, *Blindness and Insight,* 211. *Cf.* Linda Hutcheon, "The Postmodern Problematizing of History," *English Studies in Canada,* XIV (December, 1988), 376.

privileging instead of "a thing not apprehended" or, at any rate, "not apprehended well." But since the very *raison d'être* of change is movement, we expect the questions to continue nonetheless, particularly those concerning the poet and his relation to the Supreme Fiction ("senseless element") and beyond that, as he is "the spokesman at our bluntest barriers," his relation to the question of belief. That there may be a connection between the two is perhaps suggested by gibberish of the vulgate with which, once he is past the President, Du Puy, and Nanzia, the enquiring poet may now set about to probe the "peculiar potency of the general" (*CP*, 397). In the final canto of "It Must Change," the moment for revolving the ultimate question arrives for the Metaphysician in the Dark on a bench of catalepsy, "a place of trance" according to the letters (*L*, 435); and Herbert Blau's suggestion that the theater is a paradigm for escaping consciousness probably suggests the right connection between the cataleptic bench and the "Theatre / Of Trope" that Stevens uses to qualify it (*CP*, 397).[24]

The final canto's Theater of Trope becomes the medium for what Stevens describes as "a will to change" and what he specifically equates with a necessitous "presentation" (*CP*, 398) through metaphor. The suggestion is a particularly trying one, especially in its connection later with "a glass in which we peer," calling up as it does the outworn rhetoric of arbitrary and privileged representations in the thoroughly self-referential "Mirror of Nature" in romantic epistemology, which we have already watched Stevens several times attempt to explode. We are perhaps invited to take an alternative approach to these passages if the "vagabond in metaphor" who catches Stevens' eye in the affirmation of a preconscious tropology is identified as Walt Whitman and the "page of music" to which Stevens sets his "presentation" is the very presentation found in Whitman's "Song of the Rolling Earth":

> I swear I begin to see little or nothing in audible words,
> All merges toward the presentation of the unspoken meanings
> of the earth,
> Toward him who sings the songs of the body and of the truths
> of the earth,
> Toward him who makes the dictionaries of words that print
> cannot touch.

Stevens' hypothetical borrowing from Whitman for his own "presentation" ("The freshness of transformation is / The freshness of a world. It is our

---

24. Herbert Blau, *The Eye of Prey: Subversions of the Postmodern* (Bloomington, 1987), xxxii.

own, / It is ourselves, the freshness of ourselves" [*CP,* 397–98]) helps us to
see that no self-reference is intended at all. Rather, Stevens' unspoken meanings of the earth are still those to be constituted in a "present way" by the
Supreme Absence; they mean to tell us that the glass in which we peer *is* that
absence, in the inscription of yet another ever-early candor of White Mythology, the "blank" (from the French *blanc,* or white) on which we make
"iris frettings" with the will to change, hence the more important "rubbings"
on that glass, which become in the final lines of Canto X our new "beginnings" and more "suitable amours." Moreover, if Stevens' rubbings become
the words "that print cannot touch," as in Whitman, then his presentation of
"changing essences" and "artificial things" in the Theater of Trope is perhaps
more correctly the catalepsy of the *unpresentable,* the force of fiction and the
fiction of force, in parodic association with the music of Shelley's west wind
(*CP,* 397), which Lyotard would tend to characterize as thoroughly postmodern: "The postmodern would be that which, in the modern, puts forward the
unpresentable in presentation itself; that which denies itself the solace of
good forms, the consensus of a taste which would make it possible to share
collectively the nostalgia for the unattainable; that which searches for new
presentations, not in order to enjoy them but in order to impart a stronger
sense of the unpresentable."[25] In making his unpresentable presentation the
will to change, therefore, Stevens continues to drive his notes toward an ex-
orbitant and inaccessible emptiness—an emptiness too volatile a warrant for
the solace of nostalgic conventional faith yet, in the words of this most elusive
of cantos, "too constant to be denied" all the same (*CP,* 397).

In the opening canto of "It Must Give Pleasure," the third and final division
of "Notes Toward a Supreme Fiction," Stevens' persistence in revolving the
question of belief when answers are possible only in their impossibility and
presentable only in their unpresentableness becomes the project of "the difficultest rigor" (*CP,* 398) and the focus for the remainder of the poem. To
this (non)end, the first thing to go in erecting a faith in fiction must be
fiction's access by way of the customary and sensible, the sounding out the
heart that is "common" (as in common sense), which is but a "facile exercise."
Stevens' countermodel in this project is Jerome, whose redactions of the
Bible, in their curious "tubas" rather than harps (*L,* 435), must have struck
his Christian interpreters as the bleakest (*i.e.,* "difficultest") of translitera-

---

25. Walt Whitman, *Complete Poetry and Collected Prose,* ed. Justin Kaplan (New York,
1982), 367; Lyotard, *The Postmodern Condition,* 81.

tions: "Golden fingers picking dark-blue air" and in "more than sensual mode." Jerome captures that irrational moment in the interpretation of his fictions, particularly that "unreasoning" so problematic to the seeing that is believing from the previous chapter, if Stevens' own collocation of rising sun, clearing sea, and hanging moon as a conglomerate image for "heaven-haven" is any indication (*CP*, 398–99). This is the unreasoning that Stevens has been foregrounding so much up to now in his own "Notes," that which works not according to the more accustomed and exact logic of Western ontology but follows instead "an underlying principle of juxtaposition" that in the Hebraic hermeneutic, for instance, defamiliarizes ontological sameness and cause-and-effect and leads alternatively to "the mysterious unknown, beyond reason, explanation, and understanding," what Canto I finally describes as reasoning "with a later reason" (*CP*, 399). Moreover, the reason that defamiliarizes reason itself provides an important qualification for the transformations outlined in the last canto of "It Must Change." For it is not the "things" themselves that become transformed but *we* who are shaken by them *as if* they were. In the context of faith, we should now want to begin thinking less about seeing and believing and more about seeing and interpreting, a crucial issue to which we shall return in the final chapter, with reference to shorter pieces such as "What We See Is What We Think" (*CP*, 459). [26]

The textual juxtapositions that eventuate in mystery, Stevens' earlier "nonsense [that] pierces us with strange relation" from Canto III of "It Must Be Abstract," are a part of Susan Handelman's much larger analysis of an unseen yet "all-pervasive unity of the text" coterminous with the *kal ve-chomer* ("how much more") tradition of rabbinic interpretation (Stevens' music "in *more* than sensual mode" already cited [*CP*, 398]) that tends to privilege "a simultaneous coexistence of various related and constantly proliferating meanings . . . especially [in] the use of plays on words and numbers." This pervasive sense of mystery therefore would represent Stevens' most irrational moment in the present canto's treatment of the otherwise Christo-Hellenic Jerome, whom Frank Kermode views generally as "offering *hebraic veritas*" to the more conventional "Greek truth." Pushed a bit further, Stevens' rhetorical strategy in "It Must Give Pleasure" might lead to Foucault's "thought-event," defined with "a later reason" in his own Theater of Trope, "Theatrum Philosophicum," as requiring something more than the conventional ternary logic, traditionally centered on the referent, necessitating rather "a more complex

26. See Edward Said, *Beginnings: Intention and Method* (New York, 1985), 305. The previous quotations are from Handelman, cited below.

logic" based on "interrelationship," *i.e.,* the "thought-phantasm [that] does not search for truth, but repeats thought" instead.[27] Hence, Stevens emphasizes repetition in the booming of bee-ing in the opening canto of "It Must Change" and later in the present division of the poem, as we shall see shortly.

For now, our being shaken by the transformations of "later reason" continues Stevens' increasing preoccupation with the dynamics of an *active* faith, which we saw coming into such prominence in *Parts of a World* in poems such as "Of Modern Poetry" and "Landscape with Boat" and continued in the present text in his severe treatment of nostalgic forms of belief that must be countered, as in the last canto, with the timely presentation of repeated rubbings and fresh beginnings, irrational moments, if you will. The dynamics of an active faith place tremendous responsibility on the individual, and the next two cantos in "It Must Give Pleasure" reveal that not everyone may be up to the task. In Canto II, the blue woman remains locked up in a total self-regard ("linked and lacquered") simply because she has no desire or, at any rate, no desire for anything *more*. There is the possibility that silver might become cold silver, frothy clouds, foamy waves, summer heat, nocturnal fragrance, and so forth. The woman is quite content, though, to indulge past memories of the way things were and to continue them in the present as "abortive dreams" (*CP,* 399). In a slightly altered context, however, Stevens tells us in his letters that "we do not live in memory," that life "is always new," and, most important, that "fiction is part of this beginning" (*L,* 434). Yet nothing could be further from the blue woman's presencing state of mind than fiction: "The frothy clouds / Are nothing but frothy clouds . . . It was enough for her that she remembered." Except for the presentiment of her eye/I, another old pun from *Parts,* "being real" for her is a life lived utterly without intrusion. In Canto III, therefore, we are invited to view Stevens' apostrophe to the "face of stone," a "lasting visage in a lasting bush" (*CP,* 400), as perhaps the outward and visible sign that the blue woman's predictably conventional religious experience might take, that is, a total rejection of the absent difficult visage earlier to favor what Stevens has disparagingly referred to as "the elementary idea of God,"or "Adoration [as] a form of face to face" (*L,* 438). The earlier satire of General Du Puy and Ozymandias plays insistently behind the deity frozen in time now and made more repulsive for its sneering defiance of the pleasures of change that threaten to strangulate:

27. Handelman, *The Slayers of Moses,* 149–50; Frank Kermode, "The Plain Sense of Things," in *Midrash and Literature,* ed. Geoffrey H. Hartman and Sanford Budick (New Haven, 1986), 183, 185; Foucault, *Language, Counter-Memory, Practice,* 173–79.

> The vines around the throat, the shapeless lips,
> The frown like serpents basking on the brow,
> The spent feeling leaving nothing of itself,
>
> Red-in-red repetitions never going
> Away, a little rusty, a little rouged,
> A little roughened and ruder, a crown
>
> The eye could not escape.
>
> (*CP,* 400)

"We struggle with the face," Stevens further remarks in *Letters,* and when "the compulsion to adoration grows less, or merely changes, unless the change is complete, the face changes" merely. Presumably, in feeling the effects of the force of fiction, "in the case of a face at which one has looked for a long time" and "in the depths of concentration, the whole thing *disappears*" (*L,* 438, emphasis added). This is a startlingly postmodern insight, at least as Alice Jardine views it in her problematizing of the genderization of the visage in contemporary feminist discourse, citing Deleuze and Guattari: "Yes, the *visage* has a great future, provided it is destroyed, undone. En route toward the asignificant, toward the asubjective. But we still have explained nothing about what we feel."[28] In the a/theological context of contemporary belief, the shift from the presencing of the visage to its effacement requires nothing less than a radical alteration in the rhetorical register of fiction's Theater of Trope from the signification of the face-to-face metaphoric apostrophe to the asignification of metonymic prosopopoeia, wherein, according to Paul de Man, "to give a face . . . implies that the original can be missing or nonexistent," *i.e.,* the difficultest rigor of Stevens' "inanimate, difficult visage" connected to the First Idea in "It Must Be Abstract."[29] As the passage from Canto III above shows, however, for someone so ineradicably locked into the presencing of former memories, the eye/I is not likely to escape the face of slate, no matter how much its effulgence has faded or the degree to which it has become "too venerably used" (*CP,* 400). As the canto notes at the end, Orpheus turned his face from the gods, and though he suffered irreparable

---

28. Alice Jardine, *Gynesis: Configurations of Woman and Modernity* (Ithaca, 1985), 100. Jardine follows Derrida's commentary on Levinas' *Beyond the Face* (in *Writing and Difference,* 100) for her own feminist recontextualizations (*Gynesis,* 78–79). On this point, see also Derrida, *Margins of Philosophy,* 268, Kristeva, *Powers of Horror,* 143, and more recently J. Hillis Miller, *The Ethics of Reading,* 21, and his *Versions of Pygmalion* (Cambridge, Mass., 1990), 182.

29. Kronick, *American Poetics of History,* 107.

loss for it, he brought "tremendous chords from hell" and taught sheep to carouse, despite his loss. Surely generations of institutionalized shepherds and sheep, which we shall meet again in "The Old Lutheran Bells at Home" (*CP,* 461), might do no less: nothing less, indeed, than the rejection of ontological sameness and the prefacing of a/theological difference, as in the concluding image of children scattering flowers, "no two alike" (*CP,* 400).

Reasoning with a later reason, and perhaps, in the wider purview of Stevens' discourse, believing with a later belief, has thus very much to do with a rhetorical sophistication in language. Stevens would not have had to be steeped in contemporary Saussurean linguistics to realize how subjectivity is functionally inscribed (and inscribing) in language as a system of differences. He was already there on his own, writing for instance at the opening of Canto IV of "It Must Give Pleasure" that reasoning about things with a sensitivity to the mind's powers of rhetorical construction allows us the insight that oftentimes "what we see clearly" we ourselves "make of what we see" and that, far from being dependent on realities external to us, language itself offers us a "series of positions" through which we ourselves might choose to fabricate "relations with the real."[30] So, in the words of the canto, we make "a place dependent on ourselves" (*CP,* 401). Thought, in other words, is to Stevens a problematic of the *relation* between sign and referent, no less in the sphere of knowledge than in the sphere of belief. Reasoning with a later reason, or turning belief itself into a question, would largely depend on whether one chose to remain within the conventional and doctrinal structures of that essentially grammatical relation or chose instead to depart from it. "I am afraid that we are not rid of God," Nietzsche writes, "because we still have faith in grammar" (*PN,* 483)—a grammar that, for Stevens, too often made conventional faith dependent on a "lasting" visage rather than a "difficult" one. We thus can finally begin to understand the "mystic marriage" of the great captain and the maiden Bawda in the present canto, in Stevens' probing of the question of belief, by viewing it as a refusal of the sign's erasure *in the face of* the normative, transcendent structures of hegemonic or meaning-full union, when "love's characters come face to face" (*CP,* 401). We can then see the marriage as a differential relationship (hence mystic) attuned to the integrity of the sign and to the very materiality of its provenance, approbated to such a degree in "It Must Change":

30. Belsey, *Critical Practice,* 61. *Cf.* also Kristeva's "realm of *positions*" in *Revolution in Poetic Language,* 42, from which we ought to derive a "constructionist" argument for subjectivity, as in Stevens here, rather than an "essentialist" one as David Bergman tends to misread the case (*Gaiety Transfigured. Gay Self-Representation in American Literature* [Madison, 1991], 17).

This was their ceremonial hymn: Anon
We loved but would no marriage make. Anon
The one refused the other one to take,

Foreswore the sipping of the marriage wine.
Each must the other take not for his high,
His puissant front nor for her subtle sound,

The shoo-shoo-shoo of secret cymbals round.
Each must the other take *as sign, short sign*
To stop the whirlwind, balk the elements.
(*CP,* 401, emphasis added)

Though it is not a whirlwind marriage, Stevens insists that the captain's and the maiden Bawda's is a marriage nonetheless, a relationship freed up from the repressions and dependencies of subjectivity instituted by a belief in overriding ideological and metaphysical determinations, as in the previous divisions of the poem. "Neither heaven nor hell," it is a marriage respectful of its "earthy birth" earlier: the maiden as "ever-hill Catawba," the captain as "the sun," and love itself as "marriage-*place,*" as "Esthétique du Mal" will later put it, "as and where we live" (*CP,* 326, emphasis added).

We are given to wonder, therefore, whether the single-parenthood portrayed for the sister of Canon Aspirin, in Canto V, despite "her widow's gayety" (*CP,* 402), is not the unfortunate result of some self-promoting marital arrangement whose fate the previous couple has managed successfully to elude. Or going even further back, we wonder if it might be the result of recapitulating the "rigid statement" of Crispin's family romance, with which the domestic repressions of the canon's sister bear comparison, as we note in the tyrannical uprearing of her two daughters: "She hid them under simple names. She held / Them closelier to her by rejecting dreams. / The words they spoke were voices that she heard" (*CP,* 402). Her "rejecting dreams" and earlier "sensible ecstasy" thus bring forward Stevens' criticisms of the blue woman and of Jerome's antagonists formerly, made even plainer in *Letters,* where we learn that the sister "has never explored anything at all and shrinks from doing so" (*L,* 445). In place of such repressive regulation, Stevens offers Aspirin's fugal canon in Canto VI: "The whole, / The complicate, the amassing harmony" (*CP,* 403). The musical image at this point transforms the rejection of dreams previously into a kind of moral introjection, when we learn (as we already had in the "cold copulars" passage back in Canto II of "It Must Change") that an act of choice is never one of excluding things but is rather one of inclusion: "It was not a choice / Between, but of" (*CP,* 403).

Stevens' presentation of choice as an affirmation of difference is punishingly tangled here. In our passing on to the next canto, it is perhaps necessary only that we note the point of naked "nothingness" leading up to choice, beyond which neither fact nor thought proceeds in and of itself. Stevens' no-thing-ness bears obvious resemblance to fiction, First Idea, force, and change in the way the "huge pathetic force" that is in play between the limitations it appears to constitute for everything (*L,* 445) establishes the conjunctive disjunction and the disjunctive conjunction to which each, as near as the children's bed or as far as the utmost crown of night, is subject. Recapitulating an earlier insight from "It Must Be Abstract," Canon Aspirin's bizarre ascents downward and descents upward would merely serve to prove, once again, that the death of one god is the death of all or, reaching even further back to *Parts of a World,* that things are because of interactions or interrelations (*OP,* 189).

In reasoning, later or otherwise, about that no-thing-ness in Canto VII, which is the climax of "It Must Give Pleasure" and perhaps the *refacimento* (*L,* 431) toward which Stevens' "Notes" has all the while been building, Stevens' greatest insight from the point of view of belief is that his supreme fiction is not to be reasoned about at all. Determinations of meaning can be only impositions, never discoveries, and as Robert Duncan observes, "the order man may contrive to impose upon the things about him or upon his own language is trivial beside the divine order or natural order he may discover in them."[31] To impose, therefore, is not to discover:

> To discover an order as of
> A season, to discover summer and know it,
>
> To discover winter and know it well, to find,
> Not to impose, not to have reasoned at all,
> Out of nothing to have come on major weather,
>
> It is possible, possible, possible. It must
> Be possible.
>
> (*CP,* 403–404)

---

31. Michael Davidson, "Archaeologist of Morning: Charles Olson, Edward Dorn and Historical Method," *ELH,* XLVII (1980), 160. For readings valorizing "imposition" in the following excerpt from "Notes," see Morris, *Imagination and Faith,* 106; Mills, "Wallace Stevens: The Image of the Rock," 104, and Louis L. Martz, "Wallace Stevens: The World as Meditation," 149, both in *Critical Essays,* ed. Borroff; Doggett, *Poetry of Thought,* 21; Lentricchia, *The Gaiety of Language,* 140; Baird, *The Dome and the Rock,* 81; and Leggett, *Poetic Theory,* 39. For "discovery," see Frye, *Fables of Identity,* 239–40; Borroff, "Introduction," in *Critical Essays,* ed. Borroff,

This is the kind of passage one finds now and again in a poet's work that stands to sum up an entire career. One might almost speculate that Wallace Stevens was doing just that here: reviewing the "brave affair" of his first volume and revolving the various immanent and transcendent orders of seasonal belief as he had once thought each of them up; next, turning to his second volume and imagining it to be the great capitol of order, with its lesser corridors of statues and waxwork reticulations on which he had established a kind of "sonorous fame"; but in his third and fourth books and now in the *aria da capo* of his fifth, gradually working himself, part by part, out of the artistic and spiritual closure of his overdetermined, formalist projects and, like Aspirin, making felt beneath the surface of his eye and making audible in the mountain of his ear something like a faith in dis-closure and a belief in dis-covery, not a credence in the being-present of order itself. But the dis-articulation of a belief and a faith in "nothing"? And why not? "What makes the presentation of being-present possible," as Derrida argues, is precisely "neither a word nor a concept," precisely something inarticulable that never presences itself as such: "It is never given in the present or to anyone. Holding back and not exposing itself, it goes beyond *the order of truth* on this specific point and in this determined way, yet is not itself concealed, as if it were something, a mysterious being, in the occult zone of a nonknowing." It is possible, possible, possible: it must be! The risk, therefore, that Stevens ventures in allowing "nothing" to appear as the absolute fiction of an angel in a luminous cloud, attentive only to the "luminous melody of proper sound" (*CP*, 404), seems worth taking if we should understand it only as one version of the many "crude compoundings" of the real that may possibly be constituted ("a beast disgorged, unlike, / Warmed by a desperate milk") yet at the same time be bent on an instantaneous act of disappearance, so that it might reappear in yet another form, and still another form, and so on to infinity.[32]

Once he has made his appearance in only the most tentative and momentary way, it seems only appropriate that Stevens' Angel of Absence should then, in Canto VIII, immediately demystify his "evening's revela-

---

14; Enck, *Images and Judgments*, 17; Kessler, *Images of Wallace Stevens*, 77; and finally, Bornstein, *Transformations of Romanticism*, 225.

32. Derrida, *Speech and Phenomena*, 134, 135, emphasis added. In relation to Stevens' "risk," see also Derrida's *Speech and Phenomena*, 134–35, *Grammatology*, 29, *Positions*, 14, and other works.

tions," that is to say, disperse even the slightest suggestion of his presence as a "gold centre" or the "golden destiny" of "need's golden hand" and leap downward into a "violent abyss" (*CP,* 404–405).[33] It is equally important for Stevens to suspend, over that abyss, belief in the form of a question: "What am I to believe?" For if belief, like writing, to which Stevens has endeavored to link it inextricably in both writing's graphical and fictional senses—if belief is to avoid absolutely the self-presencing of knowledge in its search for origins, the "solacing majesty" once again of the execrable "mirror of the self," it must undertake, as John Irwin sees everywhere in Edgar Allan Poe, "the self-dissolving voyage to the abyss." In many of his other works, but especially in *The Narrative of Arthur Gordon Pym of Nantucket,* Poe displaces "the dangers of the abyss from the act of exploring to the act of writing," and it is "that 'fiction of its own presence' [that] is just what . . . *Pym* refuses to provide," since "the abyss represents the dissolution of mediation in the absolute," that is, "the ontological undoing of narrator and narrative" and "the dissolution of the logical status of discourse."[34]

Belief, therefore, becomes an absolute question simply as a violence perpetrated against absolute Truth that Stevens imagines might only be possible in the "nothing," imaged here as "deep space" (*CP,* 404). Again, it is almost impossible not to think of such a space for the description of belief in terms of Derrida's "general space" of writing, where "spacing as writing" works against all determinate representations of truth, in the "becoming-absent and the becoming-unconscious of the subject." Hence, for the former, we find Stevens' equation between the "reflections" we use to fill these X-ternal "regions" of space and "death," and for the latter, the reversal of Nan-

33. Compare Heidegger's "ontological difference" to Stevens' leap here, as that which brings thought into Being: "Such thought of the leap into presence is also, and necessarily, the most empty thought, empty of content . . . Yet [nonetheless] . . . an unheard-of response to the traditional philosophical wonder of why there is something rather than nothing" (Gasché, "'Like the Rose—Without Why,'" III). A similar leap is described by Foucault in the "Preface to Transgression" (*Language, Counter-Memory, Practice,* 35). Jardine's elaboration is more generally a descent (*Gynesis,* 77).

34. Irwin, *American Hieroglyphics,* 91, 68–69; *cf.* also 73, 79, 112, 162, 187, 194, and 228 for further references to Poe. In "Three Transgressions: Nietzsche, Heidegger, and Derrida," *Research in Phenomenology,* XV (1985), John D. Caputo distinguishes between two kinds of abyss: *Abgrund* in Heidegger, "a concealed, dark abyss," and *Abîme* in Derrida, "the endless mirror-play of reflections of reflections of reflections" (76). In view of Stevens' disparagement of the single mirror in this canto and of his suggestion of an infinite dissemination of versions for the real in the previous one, it would seem that Derrida's version of the abyss would best fit Stevens' own. For an extended commentary on this issue, see also Caputo, *The Mystical Element in Heidegger's Thought* (New York, 1986), 29, 40; and for commentary on Derrida, see "Abysses of Truth" in Jardine, *Gynesis,* 197–98.

zia's earlier asseveration of selfhood near the end of the canto, which we might unpack as "I have *not* . . . 'I am' and 'as I am,' [but have only] [not-] I am," that is, the not-I of a self thoroughly infected by desire, "less satisfied" by the motionless motion of the angel earlier (*CP*, 405). This radical reversal of subjectivity is made entirely more forceful in the concluding equation between death and the dream narrative of Cinderella "fulfilling herself beneath the roof," the spurious temptation of literature, as de Man reminds us (and, Stevens would argue, of belief by implication), "to fulfill itself in a single moment."[35]

The last two cantos of "It Must Give Pleasure" constitute a kind of meditation on the single word *repetition*, which allows Stevens to look back on his text, and also on his previous work, so as to locate precisely the source of pleasure that "Notes Toward a Supreme Fiction" has, in its rather circuitous and improvisational way, endeavored over and over to provide as a basis for renewed faith. Both cantos, in the first place, appear to want to make good the insight of Canon Aspirin earlier and proceed not by excluding things in the moments of creative choice but rather by gathering them up in a profoundly co(i)mplicated sense of massive harmony, since each can only be thought as diacritically included in the other in any case. It should not surprise us, therefore, to find Stevens' birds putting in a return appearance in Canto IX. We notice, however, a significant refiguration of the fowl as images of absence now rather than of maniacal presence: the whistling wren permanently separated from its mate and the bugling robin stopped short, ironically, in its preludes, "mere repetitions," as the canto puts it. Stevens seems, moreover, to be rather insistent on a parable with these birds; each is a thing "final in itself and, therefore, good" (*CP*, 405). It would be a mistake, however, to think that anything teleological was meant here. Actually, the way the text would appear to be turning back on itself gives it the cast of something rather tautological. Surely, this is the point. If the fictional abyss is approached, as suggested in the last canto, through a constant stripping away of different versions of the real, in an infinite circulation about a central absence (in *Letters*, Stevens uses the example of removing layers of varnish and dirt accumulated over generations on the surface of a painting in order to get at the First Idea [*L*, 426–27]), then surely it is the *process* of repeated contextualization that constitutes the believer's art rather than some ultimately representable *product*, which theoretically cannot nor should exist.[36] The "vast

35. Derrida, *Writing and Difference*, 217, and *Grammatology*, 69, 203; de Man, *Blindness and Insight*, 152.
36. See Derrida, *Speech and Phenomena*, 52.

repetitions" Stevens envisions for the text have a final good only in this sense: "The going round / And round and round, the merely going round, / Until merely going round is a final good" (*CP*, 405).

But repetition, rounding textuality back onto itself as it spins "its eccentric measure," gathers up into the "man-hero" that Stevens imagines to be a new kind of artist, "he that of repetition is most master" (*CP*, 406), a much longer view that seems destined, in a second way, for inclusion in the question of belief. The men enjoying the way Stevens' favorite leaf "spins its constant spin" above the table in the wood take enormous pleasure thereby as men, the canto scruples, and not as exceptional monsters, because the pleasures of merely circulating, after two initial volumes structured within its aesthetic and religious circumscriptions, traced back in Chapter 1, are not exactly foreign. What is new, however, is the withdrawal of any kind of eschatological predetermination underwriting the circulatings (one hesitates to speak in the singular) of the Supreme Fiction. Pleasure now is a function of the openness, the errancy, the a-mazing circuitry rather than the fixed circularity of the text's proclivities and declivities. It is as if Stevens' poetry, almost at the brink of casting itself into the center of some sweeping and revelatory apocalyptic, something very close to a perfected theory of romance (around the time of "A Postcard from the Volcano", say) had pulled back for its very life and suddenly found itself open to a whole new repertoire of strategies for dealing with humankind's contingent and utterly intractable existential encumbrances, where we live and everywhere we live. Perhaps Irwin, again, captures the pleasures of Stevens' new mode of circulating best when he describes in so many instances with writers of the American Renaissance experience, to which Stevens falls directly heir, that sense of "language's recoil from [the] ultimate limit—but a recoil that has, through its proximity to the abyss, absorbed the circularizing influence of the vortex."[37] One does tend to feel that all of that going round and round and round in the penultimate canto of "It Must Give Pleasure" is precisely the fallout from Stevens' own recoil from an earlier textual centralization that would have entirely removed his need to write and, what is more, his belief in the need to write.

A third and final pleasure afforded by the text repeatedly rounding on itself is offered in the final canto of "Notes," in which Stevens decides to return to the character of woman for a final time. Except for the maiden Bawda, females generally have not come off very well throughout "Notes

37. Irwin, *American Hieroglyphics*, 196.

Toward a Supreme Fiction." It seems rather a happy stroke of inspiration, therefore, that Stevens, fired by the force of an amassing and inclusionary agenda, should cram all of his differing females into a final acceptance of woman herself in the persona of the "fat girl, terrestrial" and allow the flor-abundance of her changeful, aberrant, and evasive character to embody a difference with which, as "a moving contour" and a "more than natural figure," she can exceed all words and all names. Paradoxically, his final reading of the difference of woman is to understand her ultimately as the provocation of the otherness of fiction itself:

> You
> Become the soft-footed phantom, the irrational
>
> Distortion, however fragrant, however dear.
> That's it: the more than rational distortion,
> The fiction that results from feeling. Yes, that.
>
> (*CP,* 406)

Because Stevens' female other will resist every kind of rational appropriation, because her green and "fluent mundo" will continue to revolve for him in a crystalline refusal the questions of literature, art, and religion that the twilight lectures of the Sorbonne savants, themselves Metaphysicians in the Dark, would hope to stop but can never resolve, so must she open even wider the violent space of textuality to the repeated pleasures of its discursive continuances. With this difference, the "fat girl" becomes for Stevens the muse of every repetition of the absent fiction in the past and of every impossible attempt to force its completion in times to come. Alice Jardine explains:

> The space "outside of" the conscious subject has always connoted the feminine in the history of Western thought—and any movement into alterity is a movement into that female space; any attempt to give a place to that alterity within discourse involves a putting into discourse of "woman." If an autonomous "I" or "he" can no longer exist, then only an anonymous "she" can be seen to. . . . That which forces him to desire, that is, to write . . . [and, citing Michel Leiris,] "to fill a void or at least to situate, with respect to the most lucid part of ourselves, the place where gapes this incommensurable abyss" . . . that place, the emptiness of that abyss in his self, is female.[38]

38. Jardine, *Gynesis,* 114–15.

The last observation thus helps finally to identify Stevens' baffling pronoun references. In this canto, the "you" in "I think of you as strong or tired, /
Bent over work, anxious, content, alone" becomes the identification of the
female abyss in his own creative non- or female-self, a suggestion thrown out
at the beginning of this chapter. Also much earlier, the "you" in the opening
words of the prologue ("And for what, except for you"), for whom the poet
expresses an abiding love, becomes understandable now, only because he
holds "you" to yourself, *i.e.,* himself in the present canto of the poem, allowing him finally to say, "You are familiar yet an aberration" (*CP,* 406). One
wants to avoid at all cost, however, throwing too much light on these identifications. We are left in the dark of a summer night at the last, after all, and
the illuminations we receive from any other absolutely rational source *except*
those of revolving crystal "will have stopped," returning us, once again, to a
kind of volcanic or abyssal flickering, rather like "a gildered street" flicked by
feeling (*CP,* 407) or perhaps, in Roland Barthes' words, like "a network of
jewels in which each jewel reflects all the others and so on, to infinity, without
there ever being a center to grasp, a primary core of irradiation."[39]

The withholding of a graspable center repeats, in a final way, Stevens' affirmation of the willing suspension of disbelief I referred to at the top of this
chapter as a clue to the supreme fiction's constitution of renewable faith. For
all the parallels between the fictive hero and the real hero mentioned in the
concluding epilogue of "Notes Toward a Supreme Fiction," this is perhaps
the one point in which there can be no intersection of soldier and nonsoldier
in an otherwise continuous shadowing of conflicted human endeavor, one in
the other. For the soldier's war must ultimately end; he simply has to believe
in and work toward that end in order to be the soldier he is. The poet, however, "is always in the sun" (*CP,* 407) and, if anything like the irresolute
Hamlet, perhaps too much so. Although an "inconceivable" idea like the sun
and an "ignorant" man like the poet are the "proper words" to a fictive hero,
to the soldier they are absolutely deadly unless he, too, can find within them
the sustenance of "faithful speech" rather than the "petty syllabi" of sounds
that stick "in the blood" (*CP,* 407–408). Contrary to most readings of Ste-

39. Roland Barthes, *Empire of Signs,* trans. Richard Howard (New York, 1982), 78; *cf.* also
Foucault, *Language, Counter-Memory, Practice,* 61, and Derrida, *Dissemination,* 208. For the
counterargument to this paragraph's conclusion, see Thomas J. Hines, *The Later Poetry of Wallace
Stevens: Phenomenological Parallels with Husserl and Heidegger* (Lewisburg, Pa., 1976), 154, along
with Leggett, *Poetic Theory,* 37, and Bloom, *Poems of Our Climate,* 168.

vens' closing, this one sees the war between mind and sky, "between thought and day and night" (*CP,* 407) as less likely the old Cartesian standoff between the fictive thinker and the real doer (the text had worked itself much beyond that in the first division, as we had seen) than the more important standoff between how each attempts to answer the most important question of "Notes": "What am I to believe?"

The two easiest answers that the passive imagination has contrived for centuries, and that the real hero has always been content to run away with, are the "up down" formulae patched together from moonshine and tricked out in "Virgilian cadences," as Stevens refers to them disparagingly. T. S. Eliot proudly described both as far back as 1923 in his essay "The Function of Criticism" when he wrote, "Those of us who find ourselves supporting . . . Classicism believe that men cannot get on without giving allegiance to something outside themselves." As for the other side, the down side, the essay continues, "There is, nevertheless, an alternative . . . a sense that in the last resort [men] must depend upon the inner voice." Further, his "belief is that those who possess this inner voice are ready enough to hearken to it, and will hear no other." A belief that is centered in the metaphysics of either an outside or an inside and that *will hear no other* shows no willingness to suspend disbelief should the need arise. Here is the source of the soldier's war. And even though it may end, his return home with the booty of battle, "six meats and twelves wines," only makes inevitable some future outbreak in "another room." It is precisely against the endemic closure of one or the other kind of faith nurtured and sustained in these frightful rooms that Wallace Stevens wrote his longest, and arguably his greatest, poem. "We are confronted by a choice of ideas, the idea of God and the idea of man," he writes in an unpublished letter. "The purpose of the *Notes* is to suggest the possibility of *a third idea:* the idea of a fictive being, or state, or thing as the object of belief by way of making up for that element in humanism which is its chief defect."[40] Abstraction, force, change, nothing, difference, woman, all of these are notes *toward* that "third idea"—an idea that dares to reason with a later reason, to make belief an open question, and even to suggest that a soldier may be *poor* "without the poet's lines" (*CP,* 407). Thus, the defective humanism that manufactures the real hero's dependence on war at the same time creates the opportunity for the fictive hero's subsequent intervention and subsequent

40. Eliot, *Selected Prose,* 70–71; Cook, *Poetry, Word-Play, and Word-War,* 214, emphasis added.

proliferation of an even more urgent set of notes. To Stevens in 1942, World War II must have seemed self-defeating in just this way. In the next chapter, we shall see even more clearly how one dependence at such a time feeds the Other. For unless Stevens' current "Notes" can refigure the space between fiction and faith, it is a war in whatever past or future form, in the words of the epilogue, "that never ends" (*CP*, 407).

CHAPTER 5

MOMENTS OF ENLARGEMENT
De-Scribing the World of Words

The more purely the work is itself transported into the openness of beings—
an openness opened by itself—the more simply does it transport us into
this openness and thus at the same time transport us out of the realm of
the ordinary. To submit to this displacement means: to transform our
accustomed ties to world and to earth and henceforth to restrain all usual
doing and prizing, knowing and looking, in order to stay within the truth that
is happening in the work.

—Martin Heidegger, *Poetry, Language, Thought*

Thinking about the nature of our relation to what one sees out of the
window . . . without any effort to see to the bottom of things, may some day
disclose a force capable of destroying nihilism.

—*Letters of Wallace Stevens*

The truth is that the particular poetic production is simply a moment.

—Søren Kierkegaard, *The Concept of Irony*

THE title of Wallace Stevens' sixth volume of poetry, *Transport to Summer*,
published in 1947 and arguably the most popular in the *Collected Poems*, has a
rather transcendent air about it. It may even touch us with a certain note of
nostalgia, a longing perhaps for the lush verdures and homey pastorals once
again of the earlier *Ideas of Order*. Is such retrenchment ultimately where the
last chapter's "Violent Abyss" catapults the question of belief? Had "Notes
Toward a Supreme Fiction" so completely transformed the world into "a relic
of farewells," to paraphrase a letter from 1940, that "the imagination with its
typical nostalgia for reality tried to go back to recover the world," to approbate the feeling, in the words of a letter a decade later, "for the necessity of a
final accord with reality" (*L*, 364, 719)? If "reality was the summer" merely
(*L*, 719), what then might become of modern reality as "a reality of decrea-

173

tion, in which our revelations are not the revelations of [conventional] belief"
(*NA*, 175)? Or what, indeed, might become of modern man's "willingness to
believe beyond belief" (*OP*, 280)—a belief in which "art and religion . . .
have to mediate for us a reality not ourselves"?[1] Clearly, Stevens' 1947 "transport" carries us to an enormous paradox at the center of his later work.

Perhaps not. At least, it is perhaps not so enormously problematic a
paradox once we begin, using the insights of the 1942 "Notes," to read the
later Stevens in a not just perfunctorily but rather *programmatically* new way.
The passing of belief beyond the watershed marked by the previous chapter,
from a literal quest to a rhetorical quest(ion), teaches us at least three things
about such a new protocol. First, we totally abandon now any sense of a
sequential or narrative progression in Stevens' thematization of the renewal
of faith. Instead, we come more and more to expect in the later poems a
discontinuous series of attempts or random wagers at moments more or less
fraught with spiritual insight, in summer's transport in the present volume
or, equally, in "winter's nick" (*CP*, 421) of *The Auroras of Autumn* to follow
in 1950, without the expectation of some kind of apodictic payoff lying in
store at the close of a seamless, epiphanic theodicy or of any other such conventionally homogeneous master narrative. "One no longer needs to wait
solemnly for [the unsaid's] advent in the fullness of time," as Carl Raschke
puts it on the final page of *The Alchemy of the Word*, "for the fullness of time
is now."[2] In this way, the genealogy of Stevens' belief in his later work may
be compared to the genealogy of the "history of Being" in the later writing of Martin Heidegger: belief as emergent dis-closure in the sense of an
a/theological unfolding of phenomenological experience within a temporal
horizon rather than a theological dawning of revelation at the end of one.
Heidegger's "essence of Being," according to Robert Bernasconi, is "ambiguous in the sense of having a multiplicity of meanings," and its "lack of a
sweeping transformation is in keeping with the history of Being as a history
of errancy . . . a concealed destiny not subject to human ordering." Bernasconi further elaborates a Heidegger I and a Heidegger II, the former abandoning a continuing elucidation of the essence of Being in its traditional
sense in *Being and Time*, published in 1927, and the latter taking up the ex-

1. The second citation, which Stevens cared enough about to copy out by hand, is attributable to H. D. Lewis, in Thomas B. Byers, *What I Cannot Say: Self, Word, and World in
Whitman, Stevens, and Merwin* (Urbana, 1989), 73. Perhaps it was true, as Stevens elsewhere
recorded in his Commonplace Book (II, 10 WAS, 70–73, Huntington Library), that "la nostalgie
de l'éternel est au fond de toutes les oeuvres des philosophes, des romanciers et des poètes"
(Cook, *Poetry, Word-Play, and Word-War*, 206).
2. Raschke, *The Alchemy of the Word*, 91.

foliation of Being's essence in its "verbal sense," starting with *The Origin of the Work of Art,* first made public in 1935 after he spent a relatively quiet period of intense reading in Nietzschean and Kantean aesthetics. Such a bifocal history corresponds remarkably to Stevens' own long period of silence and radical alteration of philosophical outlook, which we can nail down almost to exactly the same year and to exactly the same sources of influence.[3] This parallel is surely not surprising given Stevens' great interest in one of the most seminal French interpreters of Heidegger in the postwar years, Jean Wahl, whose work Stevens had come to know fairly intimately in his final years.[4]

The genealogy of belief in Stevens' late work, in a second way, therefore, instead of solidifying completely new theological parameters, continuously acclimates us to a refurbishment through reengagement with the old. If *Transport to Summer* sounds too much like a former transcendence, it is quite likely because we are not reasoning about this transport with a later reason and are thus missing much of Stevens' intended irony.[5] The point that deserves considerable pondering here is an important one. Simply put, it requires us to understand that there can never be a moving beyond theological transcendence without at the same time a moving through that very same tradition. Once again, Stevens strikes a very resonant chord in Heidegger's

3. Robert Bernasconi, *The Question of Language in Heidegger's History of Being* (Atlantic Highlands, N.J., 1985), 9, 93–94, 69–70, 31–32, and *passim;* see also 40, 44. For a further description of the significant shift in Heidegger's thinking, so applicable to Stevens, see William Richardson, *Heidegger: From Phenomenology to Thought* (The Hague, 1963), where it was perhaps first elaborated, and also John Sallis' "Into the Clearing," in *Heidegger: The Man and the Thinker,* ed. Thomas Sheehan (Chicago, 1981), 107–15.

4. *Cf. L,* 601, 721–22, 812, and others. James Baird was the first to make the link between Stevens and Heidegger via Jean Wahl (*The Dome and the Rock,* 268–69). Although he is scrupulous to document the relationship between Stevens and Wahl from as far back as 1938, Baird is reluctant to impute "very much importance" to what Stevens was actually able to read of the French philosopher, namely, *Les Philosophes de l'Existence,* published in 1954, since it came to hand so late in the poet's career. Specifically what Stevens was reading of Wahl, and by extension Martin Heidegger, through the war years and beyond, for example in French journals such as *La Nouvelle Nouvelle Revue Française* (*L,* 781, 797, 799, 817, 877, 879, and 890), will perhaps never be determined for certain. Nonetheless, the influence of Heidegger ought not be gainsaid entirely, as both Benamou (*Symbolist Imagination,* 138) and Kermode ("Dwelling Poetically in Connecticut," in *Stevens: A Celebration,* ed. Doggett and Buttel, 267) have continued to argue.

5. Helen Vendler detects none of this in the Stevens from this period and is happy merely to register the "sleek ensolacings" of "a memorable poet of nostalgia" (*On Extended Wings,* 207, 210). Joseph N. Riddel, following Charles Feidelson's *Symbolism and American Literature,* is somewhat more circumspect, offering for *Transport to Summer* the reading of "an aesthetic which, short of brief moments of ecstasy or apocalypse, cannot deliver what it promises—transcendence" (*The Clairvoyant Eye,* 188). The question this chapter would pose right at the outset is whether Wallace Stevens' new book of poetry was promising transcendence *tout court* in the first place.

thought. "Whatever and however we may try to think, we think within the sphere of tradition," writes the philosopher. "Only when we turn thought-fully toward what has already been thought, will we be turned to use for what must still be thought."[6] The "turning," which we can commence specu-lation about in Stevens' new title, therefore, marks the point at which his discourse becomes, in the parlance of postmodernism, thoroughly reflexive (not self-reflective), that is, the stage in which his new thinking not so much becomes a dismissal or departure from old but, as it rounds on former atti-tudes and postures of belief, becomes instead their nonrecuperative solicita-tion and deconstructive transformation.

A third aspect, then, of an alternative programmatic reading of the later Stevens takes us back to his "violent abyss," which we may begin to see yawn-ing in the space most clearly opened up between his first four books (if we count "Notes Toward a Supreme Fiction") and his second four, ending with the *Collected Poems,* published one year before his death in 1955. The abyss, as an image of present absence and absent presence in the previous chapter, establishes itself as a kind of limit, margin, or threshold against which writ-ing renews itself in the intersection between past and future, tradition and change, form and force, representation and repetition. For Stevens, thinking about the abyss in relation to his entire work becomes as it does for Heideg-ger, according to Joseph Riddel, "the thinking of 'nothing' as a productive principle."[7] Paradoxically, the process *turns* an apparently regressive trans-port back in time into a progressive movement forward and, like spiritual dearth, the Death of God, even Absence itself, becomes an ever-fecund source for a continuing hope and a renewable faith. From the other side of the abyss, Stevens' rethinking and reworking of old themes may not be entirely the anachronistic and empty endeavor in the question of belief that they first

6. Heidegger, *Identity and Difference,* 41; *cf.* also Heidegger, *Being and Time,* 262. For the separation between Heidegger and Derrida on this point, see Kevin Hart, *Trespass of the Sign,* 88, 107, 116, 137, 157–58, 173, and *passim.*

7. Joseph N. Riddel, "From Heidegger to Derrida to Chance: Doubling and (Poetic) Language," in *Martin Heidegger and the Question of Literature: Toward a Postmodern Literary Hermeneutics,* ed. William V. Spanos (Bloomington, 1979), 240. In this passage, Riddel also notes how Heidegger's "thinking of the abyss" is responsible for the philosophical "turn" (*Kehre*) in his later meditations "from language as the structure of *Dasein* to language as the 'house of Being,'" an image that becomes crucial to all of the writing of Wallace Stevens in his late period. On the abyssal limit as a fecundating principle in a related context, see also Foucault, "The Discourse on Language," in *Archaeology of Knowledge,* 224, and further, my own *"My Life Through the 80's: The Exemplary L-A-N-G-U-A-G-E of Lyn Hejinian," Contemporary Litera-ture,* XXXIII (Summer, 1992).

appear to be. Absence is never void, after all, as part of the commentary in the last chapter endeavored to show. Heidegger's words, which Stevens may never have read but would certainly have approved, define Absence this way: "[Absence] is not nothing; rather it is precisely the presence, which must first be appropriated, or the hidden fullness and wealth of what has been and what, thus gathered, is presencing, of the divine in the world of the Greeks, in prophetic Judaism, in the preaching of Jesus. This no-longer is in itself a not-yet of the veiled arrival of its inexhaustible nature."[8] Precisely the degree to which the "no-longer" measures the extent of the "not-yet" consequently becomes fairly much the agenda of Wallace Stevens' sixth book of verse.

We begin *Transport to Summer,* then, with an especially significant group of poems that establishes the limit case of belief constituted by Stevens' abyss, the no-longer of a necessity, against whose backdrop the not-yet of chance forces the issue as a question from the other side. Later, we must take up the question from that other side of the "endless calculus," but for now we concentrate on what Michael Beehler usefully describes as the "forestructuring" or "constraining dynamics" of the boundary, or horizon, whose law "first produces the figure of the other or unknown."[9] One important aspect of this law is the apparently fundamental human need for the authorization of approximations or representations of foundational truth it seeks to satisfy. In "A Woman Sings a Song for a Soldier Come Home" from 1946, she sings, theoretically, because the soldier's narrative logically mirrors some metaphysical archē, theological *revelatum,* or metaphysical a priori and quite naturally brings it to completion "Under the white clouds piled and piled / Like gathered-up forgetfulness, / In sleeping air" (*CP,* 360). Anything that falls outside the law of such a transcendental imperative simply has no meaning. A wound that did not bleed, like a man who did not eventually fall, could imply only that "nothing survives," not even the law of transcendence itself. Hence, the wounded soldier who addresses only the clouds or the odd person who might stumble his way "by chance" (the phrase is significant) constitutes a considerable threat to the traditional ways such songs get sung, especially in that the soldier does survive by the end of the poem, completely outside

8. Heidegger, *Poetry, Language, Thought,* 184. Along similar lines, Paul de Man writes: "Consciousness does not result from the absence of something, but consists of the presence of a nothingness. Poetic language names this void with ever-renewed understanding and . . . it never tires of naming it again. This persistent naming is what we call literature" (*Blindness and Insight,* 18).

9. Derrida, *Speech and Phenomena,* 135; Michael Beehler, "Stevens' Boundaries," *Wallace Stevens Journal,* VII (Fall, 1983), 103.

the pull of its "narrative" conventions: "Just out of the village, at its edge, /
In the quiet there" (*CP,* 361).

In the less ironic "Pediment of Appearance" from the same year, the
transcendental need to underwrite lawful representations of truth undergoes
a reversal of perspective. Rather than an operative exerting control on human
destiny from the outside, the men in the poem search after the truth of "savage transparence" (*CP,* 361) as a kind of ontological keystone or "algorithm"
to the universe that they ultimately hope to find within themselves.[10] "They
go crying / The world is myself, life is myself" (*CP,* 361) and, in experiencing
this radical shift in the presencing of truth's "essential ornament," are somewhat dismayed to discover when the pediment of appearance bares a "heavy
scowl" before them in the poem's concluding line that they have merely exchanged the authority of one metaphysical oppression for another. A similar
obsessively metaphysical model for "Human Arrangement" is represented in
the poem by that name, again from 1946. Its transcendental *relève* is purely
Platonic and in this way perhaps a parody of George Herbert's "Jordan (I)":

> In the sky, an imagined, wooden chair
> Is the clear-point of an edifice,
>
> Forced up from nothing, evening's chair,
> Blue-strutted curule, true—unreal,
>
> The centre of transformations that
> Transform for transformation's self,
>
> In a glitter that is a life, a gold
> That is a being, a will, a fate.
>
> (*CP,* 363)

Yet in the willful obliteration of change symbolized by the place-bound and
time-bound sound of the "evening rain" in the first part of the poem, we are
perhaps reminded of both the parallel critique of Platonic abasement in Heidegger, disparaging for the exaltation of Being as *idea,* and the corresponding
displacement of Being as *physis.*[11]

In a related poem in Stevens' ironic sequence, the Platonic abasement

---

10. Rorty, *Philosophy and the Mirror of Nature,* 341.

11. Martin Heidegger, *An Introduction to Metaphysics,* trans. Ralph Manheim (Garden
City, N.Y., 1959), 54–74, esp. 60–61. For the text of Herbert's poem, see *The English Poems of
George Herbert,* ed. C. A. Patrides (London, 1974), 75. On the idea of change more generally as
a global thematic in the corpus of Stevens' writing, see Longenbach, *The Plain Sense of Things,*
150–51, 154, 159, 167, 174, 206, 240, 256, 262, and 301–302.

is given a specifically theocentric cast in "The Good Man Has No Shape" from 1946. The odd title would appear to imply that, from the previous arguments for transcendent form or structure, there ought to be some moral equivalent for the overall design of human history teleologically directed toward God's "elegance" and away from human poverty and misery. The law invoked here is one governing the myth of progress ("generation by generation [we grow] / Stronger and freer, a little better off"), and if human life is at all bad along the way, it is only because the "good life [will] be possible" in the end (*CP*, 364). However, the mock handed down to humankind by Lazarus from the bosom of Abraham (Luke 16:19–31), alluded to in the second half of the poem, emphasizes once again how much of the existential texture of real life is repressed by the "good sleep" of transcendent longing, by now a recurrent image, the subtle, counternarrative tendencies of which are to be found in sour wine, empty books, and the very title of the poem itself, repeated in the final line. Nonetheless, the narrative of transcendence holds more firmly because the key to the will to power not just in Western thought but "with *all* thought," as Barbara Herrnstein Smith suggests, is the metaphysics of presence.[12] "The Dove in the Belly," also written in 1946, is Stevens' most explicit symbol of this more ingrained aspect of the ontology of law, whose deep dove ("oh, brave salut!") must constantly be placated "in [its] hiddenness," since "the whole of appearance is a toy" (*CP*, 367, 366).

The critique of transcendent formalism that gradually emerges in the above sequence Stevens had already, however, clarified for himself in two previous poems. In "The Bed of Old John Zeller," composed in 1944, we read that the "structure of ideas" can result only in disaster (*CP*, 326). What is perhaps even more difficult to evade than such ghostly sequences of the mind is accepting "the structure / Of things as the structure of ideas," the old argument of immanence that, along with transcendence, continues to haunt the question of belief from Stevens' earliest work. A casual poet—a poet, say, of *Parts of a World*—might add his own disorder to the general disaster, but that would succeed only in sparking "the habit of wishing" for other structures of ideas and for more ghostly sequences. What is required is a complete deconstruction of the narcotic of hegemonic and lawful order, symbolized by Old Zeller's bed and its somnolent line of patrilinear descent. The starting place for the Metaphysician in the Dark in that "old peak of night" is not human consciousness but rather the habit of wishing itself, that is to say, the

12. Barbara Herrnstein Smith, *Contingencies of Value: Alternative Perspectives for Critical Theory* (Cambridge, Mass., 1988), 119.

"ting-tang tossing" (*CP*, 327) of desire, in which art and belief and consciousness itself may all be said to have their true origin. Even having admitted this
much, though, the metaphysics of presence continues to die a hard death, in
"The House Was Quiet and the World Was Calm" a year later in 1945. A home
in which a reader actually becomes "the conscious being of [his] book" is a
typical enough nighttime venue of the linguistic house of Being in the later
Heidegger, particularly in its noticeable "quiet" and "calm" (*CP*, 358). Still,
there is the tendency for the reader, leaning above his work, to make his
book, his house, and, beyond that, his entire world exclusionary encounters
with truth, each in its way a "perfection of thought" in part and the whole
an "access of perfection to the page," whose meaning can then be gathered
up in the reader's own mind. If the truth in a calm world allows for no other
meaning but this, then the reader's desire is a false one and its termination in
the logocentrism of kerygmatic consciousness, as in all of the previous
poems, must be strenuously resisted. The deconstruction of otherness will be
the price of staying home, Clifford Geertz warns, ironically at the limit of the
last instauration of home truths.[13]

A quartet of poems placed together in *Transport to Summer* commences
to break open the unity of the preceding sequence and begins, appropriately
enough, with "The Lack of Repose," written in 1943. With the ironizing of
truth previously, belief, inasmuch as it is pendant on truth, can be only partially affirmed in this poem, if at all, like the few sounds of meaning making
up its "momentary end": "Is good, is a good" (*CP*, 303). Before that point is
reached, however, a whole series of issues that a reader quite like the one in
"The House Was Quiet" takes for granted, questions of meaning, of interpretation, of authorship, are made problematic as well, as a young man at the
opening attempts to decipher "the secretions of the words" from a book
that some indeterminate "you"—the "you" encountered in the prologue
to "Notes" (*CP*, 380)—apparently has never written. Still, the young man
imposes on his author determinations in any case (as we do interpreting
Stevens' text), turning his ghostly presence into a likable grandfather and his
disembodied voice into a source of "intense disclosures." Although the book
remains a "cloud," indecipherable in any definitive sense, the reader swears
by it nonetheless: "What a thing it is to believe that / One understands" (*CP*,
303). One suspects, however, that it is the doubleness of textuality, known/

13. Heidegger, *Existence and Being* (Chicago, 1949), 337; Clifford Geertz, "Anti Anti-
Relativism," in *Relativism: Interpretation and Confrontation,* ed. Michael Krausz (Notre Dame,
1989), 30, 32. See also Chap. 1, n.10 above.

unknown, written/unwritten, disclosed/undisclosed, that is, the "complication" connected to that "good" in the final line of the poem, that has everything to do with keeping the reader's belief alive.

Comprehension, therefore, is like the "thin bird" in the next poem, the 1943 "Somnambulisma," which rounds back on "The Dove in the Belly." In describing the bird's vain attempts to settle on a nest precariously located by a turbulent seashore, the text once again underscores life's lack of repose. In the face of the most impossible odds, the creature persists, wings spreading and claws scratching, for without this futile effort, and the efforts of all the generations that have come before and will come after, the chaos of ocean would be overwhelmingly fatal, "a geography of the dead" (*CP*, 304). The bird thus becomes a type of the ideal scholar, who, too, has not retreated to a separate dwelling inland but has affirmed the pervasiveness of being's *lack* at the margin or boundary between sea and land. So he has been able to withstand, indeed to thrive in, existential indeterminacy by imagining life's "falling and falling" as the locus of a profusion of "personalia" that all along were his. Similarly in "Crude Foyer," written in 1947, "thought" (fixed truth, belief), once considered another kind of repose—a repose of pure presence—turns out to be lacking as well: "Thought is false happiness" (*CP*, 305). Humanity's assumption perennially has been that through thought, "merely by thinking," mankind might, nay could, penetrate to the heart, the veritable "end" of the human condition:

> That there lies at the end of thought
> A foyer of the spirit in a landscape
> Of the mind, in which we sit
> And wear humanity's bleak crown;
>
> In which we read the critique of paradise
> And say it is the work
> Of a comedian, this critique;
> In which we sit and breathe
>
> An innocence of an absolute.
>
> (*CP*, 305)

Humanity's "bleak crown" in this passage turns back on "the pediment of appearance" once again, as the several references to *Harmonium* (the land-locked room, the comedian, the blood of paradise) recollect a great deal of Stevens' earlier work. The access to perfection that the crown so bleakly represents in much of that work is achieved only at the cost of what it every-where seeks to exclude, as Stevens has so carefully worked that issue out in *Parts of a World*. Here, a landscape accessible "only [to] the eye" (*CP,* 305) thus repeats an old argument and an old pun, the false happiness of the ex-clusionary "eye [I] as faculty." What must be new to Stevens, however, is how important the no-longer of past effort will be in helping him to chart the not-yet of future belief, or, in the words of the final stanza of "Crude Foyer," how the *there* of ignorant man's "least, minor, vital metaphor"— surely the ignorant man of the opening of "Notes," learning to see the sun again (*CP,* 380)—turns out to be *here,* not in a disparaging but in a usable way. Hence, whereas we see separation from and repression of the past mark-ing a consistent theme through Stevens' books before the "Notes," we shall more and more begin to find petition and invocation of the past threading their way through the books that follow. Nietzsche would describe the point here as an instance of the Eternal Recurrence of the Same. It seems quite likely with reference to the here-there collocation in the present poem's con-clusion that the well-known tag from *Zarathustra* is yet another of Stevens' many debts to Nietzsche in pursuing the question of belief in his later work and a debt to a more and more usable past in general: "Round every Here rolls the sphere There. The center is everywhere. Bent is the path of eternity" (*Z,* 218).[14] The citation is taken from "The Convalescent" in the third part, and the preceding lines perhaps reveal a couple of other borrowings of Stevens as well: "Everything breaks, everything is joined anew; eternally the same house of being is built. Everything parts, everything greets every other thing again; eternally the ring of being remains faithful to itself" (*Z,* 217). As with tradi-tion and change, necessity and chance, the no-longer and the not-yet, past thought might even be the very thing that makes future belief possible, an insight shared by the most important group of poems by far in Stevens' fifth volume of verse.

It is perhaps not too much of a simplification, by this late stage in our study of Wallace Stevens, to suggest that when belief ceases to be either a subject or an object of thought and becomes instead the *question* of thought (or presence or certainty or truth) itself, then what constitutes meaning for the

14. The argument presented here for Stevens' relation to a usable past casts a somewhat ironic reflection on the more general view taken toward the literary canon presented recently in Russell Reising's *The Unusable Past: Theory and the Study of American Literature* (New York, 1986).

poet begins to take on a far greater significance than the actual meanings of his poems. In the later poetry, therefore, we find belief, in Emmanuel Levinas' searching words, "not answering *only* to the question of knowing 'What is?' but to the question 'How *is* what is?' [or] 'What does it mean that it is?'" This articulation tends to explain Stevens' reputation, particularly in his last years, as a highly philosophical poet, a self-reflexive poet, the quintessential poet's poet. *Transport to Summer* has more than its share of texts that continue to sustain this profile. The question of belief, however, provides one of the more incisive entry points into their thematic provenance. Previously, we have been concerned with the limit case of that thematization in Stevens' new work from the point of view of the no-longer. Now, we turn to a rather extensive group of texts that tend to urge the question from the other direction, from the other of a not-yet. We could describe this movement in Stevens' discourse as a shift from form to force. Yet the many paradoxes of the violent abyss, opened up by the consideration of a supreme form or fiction as a model for belief in the last chapter, appear to indicate that we never really quite come clear of the forms, limits, or laws of expression. We come to realize, then, that freedom is a function of constraint inasmuch as constraint is a condition of freedom. Thus, Julia Kristeva's now infamous *cri de coeur* in "Stabat Mater" ("I yearn for the Law [since] only the law sets anything down") is every bit as relevant to the question of an *écriture féminine* today as it is to Stevens' interrogation of faith a generation ago. For, to paraphrase Ernesto Laclau in a related context, one wants not so much to set the limits of an answer in either case as to re-create the original meaning of the question that prompted their discourse in the first place.[15]

The shift in emphasis, nonetheless, from the exclusionary limits of form to a more expansionary discourse that might account for the otherness constituting those very limits was enough to keep the issue of faith alive in Stevens for the remainder of his writing career. In "The Motive for Metaphor" from 1943, Stevens addresses his text self-reflexively to that originary being or motive, the mysterious "you" of the opening line (*CP*, 288), like that anonymous "you" previously in "The Lack of Repose," which might account

15. Emmanuel Levinas, *Ethics and Infinity: Conversations with Phillippe Nemo,* trans. Richard A. Cohen (Pittsburgh, 1985), 31; Julia Kristeva, *The Kristeva Reader,* ed. Toril Moi (New York, 1986), 175a; Ernesto Laclau, "Politics and the Limits of Modernity," in *Universal Abandon? The Politics of Postmodernism,* ed. Andrew Ross (Minneapolis, 1988), 77. "Perception is always mediated (and therefore objects are never available directly), and . . . perception is always conventional (and therefore readers are never free)" is Stanley Fish's admirably succinct summation in *Doing What Comes Naturally,* 83–84, but see also 12–13, 26, 32, 89, 128, 152, and 179.

for the very "A B C" of its printed form on the page. In a sense, the project is a rather futile one, since it attempts to name that which ceases to exist at the very point of being named; hence, "steel against intimation" appears in the final quatrain, along with several other vague references in the text to something *like* the intimation of a nameless force: "half colors," "quarter-things," and things "never . . . quite expressed." The motive's "shrinking" from the weight of Stevens' intense examination may perhaps put us in mind of Derrida's description of "The 'Retrait' of Metaphor," the "trait" or "trace" in discourse "that brings together and separates at once the veiling and the unveiling, the withdrawal and the withdrawal of the withdrawal."[16] With Stevens' final invocation of "the sharp flash, / The vital, arrogant, fatal, dominant X" (*CP*, 288), though, one is tempted to think he comes closer to Heidegger in *On the Way to Language* and to the more violent notion of "appropriation": "What if Appropriation—no one knows when or how—were to become an insight whose illuminating lightening [*sic*] flash enters into what is and what is taken to be? What if Appropriation, by its entry, were to remove everything that is in present being from its subjection to a commandeering order and bring it back into its own?"[17] If the motive of Stevens' metaphors, the desire for "the exhilarations of changes" rather than the changes themselves, manifests itself in the wresting of existence from a too controlling and sedimented order in the way that Heidegger describes, then, again, we recognize the importance of a limiting form to the ongoing production of force. We would do well also to view its fatal X not as the mark of an annihilating destruction, though it is certainly that in part, but rather as a re-mark on the crossing and recrossing (X-hilarations, X-changes) of the expansionary limits of belief by identity and difference at once.[18]

16. Derrida, "The 'Retrait' of Metaphor," *Enclitic*, II (1978), 31. We should note, however, an even more precise parallel between Stevens' assemblage of "steel against intimation" and Derrida's version of it in *Memoires for Paul de Man*, namely, an "'intimation' whose artifice could signal, at once, the intimacy of an interiority and the open order or injunction [*i.e.*, 'A B C of being']; [thus,] in French, we intimate an order: we give it: *il faut*, one *must*" (35).

17. Martin Heidegger, *On the Way to Language*, trans. Peter D. Hertz (New York, 1971), 133. *Cf.* also Heidegger, *The Question Concerning Technology:* "Do we see the lightning flash of Being in the essence of technology? The flash that comes out of silence, as silence itself? Silence stills" (49).

18. See Taylor, *Erring*, 138, 142, 158, 172–73. Both Patricia A. Parker, in "The Motive for Metaphor: Stevens and Derrida," *Wallace Stevens Journal*, VII (Fall, 1983), 87, and Joseph N. Riddel, in "The Climate of Our Poems," *Wallace Stevens Journal*, VII (Fall, 1983), 69, 73, have ventured similar readings of the poem's chiasmatic crossings. Stevens' "dominant X," of course, has many parallels in contemporary philosophical/critical discourse, most notably in the (non)concepts of Jacques Derrida's *écriture* ("'Fors,'" 94) and *différance* (*Grammatology*, 60). *Cf.* also "the form of the chiasmus, the X . . . a figure of the double gesture," in Derrida, *The Truth in*

What makes all the difference for belief, then, in the largest sense of the motive for metaphor, is the process of language itself, whose chiasmatic modus vivendi is more accessible to the ear as temporal absence than to the faculty of eye/I as spatial presence: Heidegger's interpretation of Logos as *legein* rather than as *ratio*.[19] Hence, "if the poetry of *X* was music" (*CP,* 310), as Stevens points out in "The Creation of Sound" from 1944, it is the mystery of sound to which the poet owes his creativity and not to its meaning, institutionalized in the conventions of authorial intention and identity. Sound comes to the poet "without understanding," a matter about which he does not appear to have any choice. In this sense, he functions as a conduit or medium for verbal music, and his freedom lies precisely in the degree to which he agrees to serve as a kind of lightning rod, or perhaps even a sounding board, for the "obstruction" of X. Without attributing any kind of determinate identity to this role, he therefore becomes one with the "being of sound"; he is "a different poet," "an artificial man," "a secondary expositor," who is "intelligent / Beyond intelligence" (*CP,* 311). Because it is absence constituting presence both for creator and created, speech is a case not of clarifying silence but of making silence dirtier, making the visible harder to see. It powerfully "eke[s] out the mind" on the horns of its mimetic or representational dilemma and refers everything to the co(i)mplication of "the spontaneous particulars of sound" for its (ir)resolution: the "speech we do not speak," as the groundless "floor" raised up to an infinite signification (*CP,* 311).

Throughout this text, and in several related to it, one becomes especially sensitized to a certain ferocity at work in the transport of Stevens' language, whose voice, in J. Hillis Miller's words, is now "something unpredictable, savage, violent, without cause or explanation, irrational—as [Stevens] always knew genuine poetry must be . . . a principle of discontinuity."[20] Desire, as the (e)motive radical of metaphor glanced at previously, is an im-

---

Painting, 166. Nietzsche undoubtedly is the anxiety of influence at back of all of this, as suggested earlier in Chapter 3. J. Hillis Miller supplies a further contextualization in this direction in *The Linguistic Moment: From Wordsworth to Stevens* (Princeton, 1985), 50–52. Jacques Lacan also establishes a link between Stevens' "dominant X" and "sharp flash" when he writes that "it is between the signifier in the form of the proper name of a man, and the signifier which metaphorically abolishes him that the *poetic spark* is produced" (*Écrits,* 158, emphasis added). *Cf.* also Foucault: "Transgression is an action which involves the limit, that narrow zone of a line where it displays the flash of its passage, but perhaps also its entire trajectory" (*Language, Counter-Memory, Practice,* 33–34).

19. See Spanos, *Repetitions,* 116.

20. J. Hillis Miller, "Theoretical and Atheoretical in Stevens," in *Stevens: A Celebration,* ed. Doggett and Buttel, 283.

portant factor in this shift. The 1945 "Two Tales of Liadoff" is a poem about the perpetual prolongation of desire. On the one hand, it fuels "the need of soaring, the need / Of air" (*CP,* 347) past the "fantastic fortune of fantastic blood" weighing humanity down, as for instance, in Part I, where a community seeks transcendent fulfillment in the explosion of a gigantic Roman rocket, whose profusion of "resplendent forms" (men wearing pantaloons of fire, children like golden wicks, and so forth) symbolizes the citizenry's desire to emulate at least one tale told by Liadoff, now long dead, who practices epiphanic arpeggios on Cloud Nine. Liadoff, however, has an alternative tale to the "narration / Of incredible colors ex, ex and ex and out" (*CP,* 347), a tale of the downside of desire, about what makes his scales so "haunted" and "tragical," which the people discover only as their fantasy explodes and they fall back to reality in the "whole return / From thought." His other tale bespeaks the absence built into the structure of desire, that is, the "violent pulse" in the lack of repose that not only piques desire but also becomes the point of articulation for poetry as well: the "instant of the change that was the poem" (*CP,* 347). Poetry, therefore, is both the "beau caboose," at the level of both rocket and cloud, and the smothering body, because all are "inferior" in the sense of being captive to originary "want."

It seems almost inevitable, however, that one tale or another is eventually going to win its way into the head of mankind as essential truth and into the heart as foundational belief as well. Such irreducible certainty is referred to in "Man Carrying Thing" from 1946 as our "most necessitous sense" (*CP,* 350)—perhaps the very "Thing" in the title itself—and it is for the poem as its first responsibility to resist such necessary intelligence "almost successfully," if that were possible. Richard Rorty describes precisely what is at stake in the text's objurgation:

> If we could convert knowledge from something discursive, something attained by continual adjustments of ideas or words, into something as ineluctable as being shoved about, or being transfixed by a sight which leaves us speechless, then we should no longer have the responsibility for choice among competing ideas and words, theories and vocabularies. This attempt to slough off responsibility is what Sartre describes as the attempt to turn oneself into a thing—into an *être-en-soi*. In the visions of the epistemologist, this incoherent notion takes the form of seeing the attainment of truth as a matter of *necessity,* either the "logical"

necessity of the transcendentalist or the "physical" necessity of the evolutionary "naturalizing" epistemologist. From Sartre's point of view, the urge to find such necessities is the urge to be rid of one's freedom to erect yet another alternative theory or vocabulary.[21]

In Stevens' poem, therefore, rather than capitulate to the epistemological necessities of either the transcendentalist or the realist, or the projections of "B" and "A" as we also find them in "So-and-So Reclining on Her Couch" from 1943, the responsible believer, perhaps the poem's "brune figure" resisting identity in the winter evening (as a type of our Metaphysician in the Dark), is urged to lay by "the primary free from doubt" and accept "a storm of secondary things" for what they are and can only continue to remain being, "uncertain particles" (*CP,* 350–51). As parts not quite perceived of some ontologically "obvious whole" or "certain solid," their very indeterminacy ironically becomes the "bright obvious" that stands motionless in the dark night of the soul's unmooring and makes continual and open adjustment to it possible, as Rorty would say, and endurable, according to Stevens. Besides, "most of the dark nights of the soul consist of self-pity," anyway (*L,* 863).

With this reading of the conclusion to "Man Carrying Thing" before us, we might be tempted to view that dead-winter Thing in transport to summer in the poem somewhat along the lines of what Heidegger, in his essay "The Thing," describes as "something altogether different, to which no thought whatever has hitherto been given" and "which in every respect is never something that merely exists, but which nevertheless presences, even as the mystery of Being itself."[22] If we are tempted to that view, then what resists the intelligence almost successfully is once again likely to be some intimation of the motive for metaphor, some exuberance of force like the wind in the 1946 poem entitled, appropriately enough, "Pieces." In this text, a very strong tension is set up in the opening two stanzas between the mul-

21. Rorty, *Philosophy and the Mirror of Nature,* 375–76.

22. Heidegger, *Poetry, Language, Thought,* 176, 178. Cary Nelson, in *Repression and Recovery: Modern American Poetry and the Politics of Cultural Memory, 1910–1945* (Madison, 1989), also notes: "If the 'thing itself' were available to us, it would have no meaning whatsoever. There is no perceptible, unmediated, unconstructed zero degree of literary materiality that serves as a consensual basis for interpretation. Even what is to count as a poem has to be decided before the words in white space will have any meaning" (10). *Cf.* also Jacques Derrida's description of "the story of language and writing as the inscription of the thing itself as other, of the spongetowel, the paradigm of the thing itself as other thing, the other inaccessible thing, the impossible subject . . . the allure of an inappropriable event (*Ereignis* in abyss)," in *Signéponge/Signsponge,* trans. Richard Rand (New York, 1984), 102.

tiple and variegated, the "millefiori bluely magnified" (*CP,* 351), and a kind of necessitous sense to bring more of these uncertain part-icles into some form of totalizing elucidation. Hence, the double cry of "Come home, wind," on the one hand, is countered by the "things" that are said to be beside man's reason, on the other. Rather than helping to clarify things, however, the wind instead reveals in the sounds of things a sense "beyond their meaning" (*CP,* 352), as the text states, the "fidgets of all-related fire," for example. Although it comes close to creating an identity for itself in so doing—an identity as family member, ethereal cousin, or familiar milleman—in the end, the wind itself reverts to a mysterious motion that lives in space and runs away like a dog or like a horse (*CP,* 352). So strong is the desire, then, for the exhilaration in the mystery of change, by this point, that Stevens' discourse seems almost on the verge of what Sartre had previously referred to as an alternative theory of vocabulary. It settles, instead, for "A Completely New Set of Objects" as the 1946 poem of that name indicates, a set that is rigorous enough in any case, unhinged as it is from any kind of definable epistemological context:

> From a Schuylkill in mid-earth there came emerging
> Flotillas, willed and wanted, bearing in them
>
> Shadows of friends, of those he knew, each bringing
> From the water in which he believed and out of desire
>
> Things made by mid-terrestrial, mid-human
> Makers without knowing, or intending, uses.
>
> (*CP,* 352)

The very determined effort to contextualize the existential quality of the passage of metaphor's motive "mid-earth," "mid-terrestrial," "mid-human," along with its plurisignative aspect in the later mention of the "thousand thousand, / Carrying . . . shapes" and "the exactest shaping / Of a vast people," would appear to be consistent in the discourse. But the demands on the reader's comprehension, if *comprehension* is the right word (what could it possibly mean to believe in "things" like water "out of desire," for instance?) are like nothing else in Stevens' writing up to this point. One really does sense a new order of make-believe emergent here, particularly in view of the fact that the fathers of these "makers without knowing" have been left far behind, to "lie and weather" so much in the shadow of the lesser mountains at the poem's close.

Several poems win their place in *Transport to Summer* purely on the basis of Stevens' insistence on continuing to probe to the last nuance the specific relation between metaphor and desire, sounding out as many implications for the question of belief as might be possible. The question of belief, in fact, *becomes* the question of desire, the force of desire itself manifesting yet another aspect of the violent abyss, or vortex, the "being of language," as Foucault would say, into which the "being of representation" is discreetly but continuously rushing. A less Heideggerian discourse would prefer to talk about desire as a "field," specifically "a field of infinite substitutions only because . . . there is something missing from it: a center which arrests and grounds the play of substitutions," thus inaugurating "a linked chain of determinations of . . . different forms or names." First Idea, fiction, and female were some of the substitutions discovered in the last chapter. Now thing, being, and language figure into the desire for that recoverable Origin, at whose "center," in Joseph Riddel's words, "Stevens seems to sense a presence" but whose "every penetration to that presence only reveals that the place is a fiction, an interpretation, and thus not an ultimate or supreme or central poem but only another lesser poem." [23] "From the Packet of Anacharsis," written in 1946, is one of several texts in Stevens' new writing to attempt a synoptic genealogy of the tense relationship between expression and desire, the one constituting itself while in full pursuit of the Other. In this text, a return to the ever-early candor, or White Mythology, of "Notes" is the point of departure for the desire of expression and the expression of desire, as it is for both Puvis and Bloom, characters who have their own separate ideas concerning the interpretation of the white farm evoked in some lines by Anacharsis as a model of perfect clarity in the Western tradition of aesthetic representation. Their differing versions ("gray-rose" as opposed to something more "floridest" [*CP*, 366]), which circle the coincidental "bright vista" or field in the poem, problematize for them the "punctual centre of all circles white," perhaps in the way that Stevens' own intertextuality is made more complicated by its allusions to Ralph Waldo Emerson ("*around every circle another can be drawn*," from the essay "Circles") and to Herman Melville (the "colorless all-color of atheism from which we shrink," from "The Whiteness of the Whale" in *Moby-Dick*). The poem thus displaces the representation of meaning away from the center and locates it in the production or repetition of meaning as meaning recedes in a quickening of rings cut, as Derrida

23. Foucault, *The Order of Things*, 118–19; Derrida, *Writing and Difference*, 289, 279; Joseph N. Riddel, "Interpreting Stevens: An Essay on Poetry and Thinking," *Boundary 2*, I (Fall, 1972), 85.

would say, from "an *unwiederholbar* singularity," or "deportation as the ring's condition" from the beyond of knowledge or, as Stevens' own text describes them, "impinged / By difference and then by definition" (*CP*, 366).[24] Through the temporal dislocation created by the dynamic of form and force, the poem thus disseminates a life for itself, as its "crystal colors come," in Stevens' pun. Its "vast accumulation" promises a continuation even beyond its own textual margins, as Bloom stands at the last of these, yet again, and "repeats the primitive lines" (*CP*, 366).

In the present arrangement of texts with which we are dealing, therefore, we reverse the perspective from the previous sequence. By revolving the whole issue of desire, we now start to think in pertinaciously nontranscendental terms and, in particular, about how things want to resist singularity, unity, totality and about how they wish instead to remain diffuse, multiple, variable. In "Thinking of a Relation Between Images of Metaphors" from 1945, for instance, the fisherman may be all "ear" to the wood-doves; but to the bass, he is all "eye" (*CP*, 356). In that one eye, of course, all might proceed to unity ("one dove, one bass, one fisherman") quite as easily as the wood-doves might be made to sing "a single song" in one ear. Yet as we learn in an earlier text such as "Certain Phenomena of Sound" from 1942, life is made out of variable sound, and it is sound that makes life variable. Here, it is the "coo [that] becomes rou-coo, rou-coo" (*CP*, 356). Now it may happen that the wood-doves strike the perfect note for man or even spring into perfect sight and so become complete in their disclosure. The dove in this way growing "still" in mankind's breast is likely now, however, to be the condition of absence sufficiently lacking in its repose to throw him continually into a renewed search for renewable "relations" among his metaphoric images, best shown perhaps in the way the poem itself has been put together. "Jouga," written in 1945, makes the same point but from the perspective of the animal. "Two beasts but two of a kind" are not only "not beasts" (*CP*, 337). Without

---

24. Jacques Derrida, "Shibboleth," in *Midrash and Literature,* ed. Geoffrey H. Hartman and Sanford Budick (New Haven, 1986), 328–29. One might also fruitfully consider Stevens' text in terms of the despotic-authoritarian "assemblage" that Deleuze and Parnet describe as the "circular segmentarity of simultaneity" and define as "a regime where the 'sign' keeps on referring back to the sign, in each circle and from one circle to the next, the totality of signs in turn referring back to a mobile signifier or to a centre of signifiance; and where interpretation, attribution of a signified, keeps on giving us back the signifier, as if to recharge the regime and overcome its entropy" (*Dialogues*, 105–106, 113). See also the Wilhelm von Humboldt epigraph to Sam Weber's introduction, "Translating the Untranslatable," in Theodor W. Adorno, *Prisms,* trans. Samuel Weber and Shierry Weber (Cambridge, Mass., 1986), 9.

the impingement of difference, they do not even exist. The exclusionary logic of transcendence endemic to desire creates such impediments to a knowledge redolent with the subtlest nuances of meaning that it is quite possible "there are many . . . beasts that one never sees" (*CP*, 337). Or if they are seen, the sheer force of their relational identity is so foreshortened as to become negligible, the great running jaguar making "a little sound," for instance. In this text, Stevens perhaps wishes to revive the earlier argument for "Poetry [As] a Destructive Force" (*CP*, 192).

The double dynamic of desire, as a mutual relation of things no-longer and things not-yet that we have seen in the last three texts, is resistant to the belief in transcendence in one important respect above all. Put simply, it adamantly refuses the repression of time in the stabilization of axiological faith— a repression that would be death to the discourse of difference, whose very motive for metaphor is the rhetoric of temporality. Conventional belief is foundationally the eternization of the unific and timeless moment that we find Stevens time after time calling into question, particularly in his first two volumes. Postaxiological belief, though, privileges the timely moment, since the impingement or play of differences through which it seeks expression in the fulfillment of desire "supposes, in effect, syntheses and referrals which forbid at any moment, or in any sense, that a simple element be *present* in and of itself, referring only to itself."[25]

We pause over this whole issue in a new sequence of texts in *Transport to Summer* because, for literary critics, it has always been a highly contentious issue in Stevens' work, both for those who use it for or against Stevens in the furthering of their own theoretical projects, like Frank Lentricchia, or those who simply use it to diminish the achievement of Stevens himself, like Marjorie Perloff.[26] To begin with, "Prejudice Against the Past," written in 1946, is a devastating portrait of a retreat from temporal experience that we find Stevens himself wanting so much to foreground, both in the spacing of his present discourse in relation to the discourse of the past reviewed earlier and also in the timing of the motive for metaphor of the current discourse itself. This timing is utterly antithetical to the "aquiline pedants" here, whose

25. Derrida, *Positions*, 26; *cf.* also Beehler, *Discourses of Difference*, 55.
26. Frank Lentricchia, *After the New Criticism* (Chicago, 1980), 156–210; Marjorie Perloff, "Revolving in Crystal: The Supreme Fiction and the Impasse of Modernist Lyric," in *Stevens: The Poetics of Modernism*, ed. Gelpi, 41–64. The critical debates surrounding this issue are explored in some detail in Melita Schaum, *Wallace Stevens and the Critical Schools* (Tuscaloosa, 1988), 129–82.

addiction to im-mediate vision and to the recuperation of worldly exteriority
to the interiority of presence in the final stanza (the "philosopher's hat" as
"part of the mind," the "Swedish cart" as "part of the heart" [*CP,* 369]) forces
them to become strictly confined by what they are able only to see. The
children of the poem establish an ironic contrast. In their intellectual innocence, they make up for lost time by allowing it to enter into their lives in the
way that Paul de Man would call a "generative power," establishing for them
a historically differential relation to the object world and, consequently, a
temporally authentic sense of identity as beings *in that world:*

> Of day, then, children make
> What aquiline pedants take
> For souvenirs of time, lost time,
>
> Adieux, shapes, images—
> No, not of day, but of themselves,
> Not of perpetual time.
>   (*CP,* 368–69)

"Perpetual time" is a fruitful aporia in this passage, suggesting the coimplication of the timeless with the timely and vice-versa and underscoring
with the strongest irony in the poem the rank futility of the exclusionary
transcendental gesture, that is, the prejudice against time, which exists only
at the cost of effacing itself as well. Translated to the literary (or even the
theological) context, "the desire to break out of literature toward the reality
of the moment . . . engenders the repetition and the continuation of literature."[27] So in the 1946 "Extraordinary References," a mother's historical
reminiscences to her child of a great-grandfather who was an Indian fighter
and a father who was the victim of war become the creative source of "an
equilibrium" in the final stanza. These historical relations or "extraordinary
references," moreover, achieve their peace in the same way that the "cool
sun's" timely relation to the barbarous Tulpehocken River composes its own
kind of "peace" (*CP,* 369). Temporality is textuality, Stevens seems to be saying, just as textuality is temporality, the codependent relation between which
we find in both the slow, textual weave the mother makes of her child's rib-
bons and plaited hair and the "second-hand" (of a watch) supervening the
hair styling, like "a fragile breath." Clearly, the final mention of "the inherited
garden," to which humankind may commit its belief, is that garden that is

27. De Man, *Blindness and Insight,* 150, 162.

broached, hence breached, by time and not the garden conventionally re-deemed *by* time, in being perpetually removed *from* time, a thought to which Stevens will return in a much grander sense in "Credences of Summer."[28]

Desire, then, in its strictest sense is an infection of time, and its force lies precisely in its inability to bring itself to any kind of culminating comple-tion. Put the other way, desire's prolongation amounts to its ability to inhabit disconnection and fragmentation, to bear within itself "the destiny of its non-satisfaction."[29] In "God Is Good. It Is a Beautiful Night," written in 1942, with a wonderfully disconnected title if ever there was one, Stevens presents an image of the poet as severely fragmented: a head and zither here, a book and shoe there, and a rotted rose someplace else. We then witness some sort of attempt to integrate the whole, as when the head reading the book and speaking "becomes the scholar again, seeking celestial / Rendezvous" (*CP*, 285). But still the zither remains rusty, and the poet's music thin, since the truly venerable song—"The song of the great space of [the] age"—must refuse precise formulation and exact containment. On the whole, the text implies that the mind is better served not by squeezing the last "reddest fra-grance from the stump / Of summer" (*CP*, 285) but instead by accommo-dating itself to the elusiveness of time, rather like the suddenness of the moon rising to fly in the first line or like the surprise of the bird song piercing the fresh night in the last. When the subject of that elusiveness does turn out to be God, as in "Less and Less Human, O Savage Spirit" two years later, God *is* good as a postulate of faith only because such a postulate resists all the atem-poral, conventional, logocentric approaches to its proof as dogma. "[God] must be incapable of speaking," therefore, and is "closed," like Plato's ghost or Aristotle's skeleton, only in the sense that his existence in language is never conceptually determinate but always infinitely interpretable, that is, onto-logically undecidable, as Lyotard suggests the addresser in any language game must be. "He must dwell quietly," consequently (*CP*, 327). What is accessible, however, is *movement*, "God" as a kind of Foucauldian thought-event, pass-ing as the sunlight on the floor or hanging his stars out along the wall but

28. On "breaching" and "broaching," and the "iterability inscrib[ing] alteration irreduc-ibly in repetition" between them, see Derrida, "Limited Inc.," 199–200. "Accordingly," observes Mark Taylor, "'exile' is 'original' and is not subsequent to an antecedent 'time' that was unstained by the agony of 'loss' and untainted by the tension of 'estrangement.'" He continues, "Instead of an ideal state that once was enjoyed and now has been lost, the harmonious origin appears to be 'an illusion' created to explain and repress the tensions that forever inhere in everything that is actual" (*Erring*, 154–55).

29. Derrida, *Grammatology*, 143; *cf.* also Deleuze and Parnet, *Dialogues*, 89.

remaining utterly opaque to transitive thought. Above all, God resists an anthropomorphizing faith, resists, in specific terms, "the human that demands his speech." Thus, the liturgical invocation "O, Lord, hear our prayer" can only be answered by "one / That will not hear us when we speak," since "it is the human that is . . . alien"—alien, that is, to a "vermilioned nothingness" (*CP*, 328). Is that final image that so invites problematical a-part-ness perhaps a scarlet letter: *A* for Absence? If so, then we may perhaps find a Heideggerian discourse helpful once again here and, in particular, the "concept" of *Ereignis,* or experience, whose impenetrable mystery Bernasconi reads this way:

> It can happen that in the absence of someone we experience the depth of our love for them and thus enter into a relation not bound by presence. Mystics have found God in the dark night of the soul and it is now almost commonplace among theologians to recognize the experience of the loss of God in a secular society as an experience of God. Such experiences do not reestablish presence in the midst of absence. They break with the dichotomy of presence and absence, establishing absence as present precisely in its absence.[30]

This "absence as present" that unfolds in the infectious temporality of being's desire becomes the "nothingness of human after-death" in "Flyer's Fall," composed in 1945, whose provocation in "the deepnesses of space," solemnized by a pilot's noble death, becomes the very generative matrix of belief. But it is a belief "without belief," without any single, total, imperative truth; hence, it is a belief "*beyond belief,*" a belief in "darkness," outside the dirty fates of convention (*CP*, 336, emphasis added).

As with Stevens' violent abyss in the last chapter, there is no promise here of comfort or consolation, "No Possum, No Sop, No Taters," as in the 1943 poem, either in the new rhetoric of temporality or in the new forms of belief it opens to question. Not any consolation in any customary sense, at any rate. In this final text of the sequence we have been examining, there is no test of faith like the casualties of war in the last. There is, however, something perhaps even more universal: the dismemberment incident with a brutal January winter (broken stalks without hands, trunks without legs or

---

30. Jean-François Lyotard and Jean-Loup Thébaud, *Just Gaming,* trans. Wlad Godzich (Minneapolis, 1985), 51–52; Bernasconi, *The Question of Language,* 84.

heads, and so forth) and something even worse than the presentiment of bleakness and waste of "The Snow Man" so strongly recollected by this poem: the old sun "as absent as if we were asleep" (*CP*, 293). Because seeing has fallen brightly away as a result, "bad is final in this light," even more so since where there is sight, as for instance in the starting of a rusty crow, the eye is filled with malice. Still, the ellipsis in the penultimate stanza of the text does give the reader sufficient opportunity to take notice that in spite of this savagest of solitudes, a poem has been called forth: "A syllable, / Out of these gawky flitterings, / Intones" (*CP*, 294). Again, the experience repeats itself, as out of anterior absence a presence moves forward—the presence of the Word. Here, one vaguely senses, is perhaps the counter to life's malice, one moreover that has not evolved apart from the images of winter and crow but that has been generated in relation to them, albeit "at a distance, in another tree." Apparently, the recurrent insight back in "Certain Phenomena of Sound," that "there is no life except in the word of it" (*CP*, 287) has succeeded in turning the mood of the poem around 180 degrees, for "It is here, in this bad, that we reach / The last purity of the knowledge of good" (*CP*, 294). Until that alteration in mood is reached, though, we can be legitimately pre-occupied only with "time's haggard mongrels," from the 1945 "Analysis of a Theme" (*CP*, 348). We are in transport between the no-longer and the not-yet, having surrendered any transcendent wish "of returning 'strategically,' ideally, to an origin or to a 'priority' held to be simple, intact, normal, pure, standard, self-identical," either in the context of the work of art itself or, as most of these texts have stressed, in the equally significant context of belief that the motive for metaphor desires continually to question.[31]

Before taking up the question of belief as it becomes further elaborated in some of the longer texts of *Transport to Summer* and now that we know a little more about the relation of desire to faith and the direction in which the relation is headed in the new verse, we might come back for a moment to the problematic of war left hanging at the end of the previous chapter. The violence of global conflict that Stevens wrote through, ultimately to publish his fifth book of poetry in 1947, undoubtedly had provided him endless opportunities to consider the issue of violence in his own work. Poetry must resist the intelligence almost successfully, obviously, in the way meretricious political and social ideologies must be resisted and in the same manner: "A violence

31. Derrida, "Limited Inc.," 236.

from within that protects us from a violence without . . . the imagination pressing back against the pressure of reality . . . hav[ing] something to do with our self-preservation" (*NA*, 36), in a famous statement from 1942, which I made much of back in Chapter 2. When wars end and beliefs are either realigned or reconfirmed in one form of treaty or another, it would have been clear to Stevens (who was to witness the outbreak of a second major conflict between America and a far region of the world), that violence never entirely disappears in times of peace but instead enters into the lives of men and women on new and perhaps far more repressive and repressed subterranean levels.

Where might this realization take the reader of Stevens' later writing? J. Hillis Miller has made the suggestion that "to identify [a] disrupting element in Stevens' poetry . . . would require a full reading of his work" and, further, that "it may be that the identification would be a discovery of what cannot be named or identified in so many words, even figurative ones." In the present reading of the thematization of faith in the canon, it is true that many words, such as *thing, intimation, desire, difference, word,* to cite only a few from this chapter alone, continue to problematize a disrupting element in Stevens' discourse. For what remains to be said about this thematization, however, it might be better to begin thinking about that "vital, arrogant, fatal, dominant X" less as an element than as an *event* and, further, to entertain the speculation that specifically in terms of the writing of poetry, it is on the level of event that Stevens imagined war or violence continuing to be manifested in his work. For it could be not on the level of thought but *only* on the level of event—that is, on the level of the interaction and interchange of co-implicated, co-operative forces, the dynamic double-crossing of desire—that violence could possibly receive legitimation in what Riddel has aptly described as "the 'war' of [Stevens'] incessant, revolutionary writing." [32] "Resistance to the pressures of ominous and destructive circumstance," then, as we learn in "The Irrational Element in Poetry," "consists of its *conversion,* so far as possible, into a different, an explicable, an amenable circumstance" (*OP,* 230, emphasis added). We thus might choose to mark such a conversion in the maturation of the poet's discourse, from belief-as-thought to belief-

---

32. Miller, "Theoretical and Atheoretical in Stevens," 284, and Joseph N. Riddel, "Metaphoric Staging: Stevens' Beginning Again of the 'End of the Book,'" 316, both in *Stevens: A Celebration,* ed. Doggett and Buttel. On the legitimation of violence in the context of a discursive "event," see also Foucault, *Power/Knowledge,* 114, 142, and further, Michel Foucault, *Politics, Philosophy, Culture: Interviews and Other Writings, 1977–1984* (New York, 1988), 203–204, 208.

as-event, which Stevens himself encapsulates in a poetic aphorism entitled "Adult Epigram," written in 1946. Specifically, he describes a shift from "the tired romance of imprecision" to "the romance of the precise" through the exact mediation, significantly, of a female figure apostrophized as "Again," that is, as the force of repetition:

> The romance of the precise is not the elision
> Of the tired romance of imprecision.
> It is the ever-never-changing same,
> An appearance of Again, the diva-dame.
>
> (*CP*, 353)

Having finally fathomed the full implications of the perpetual war between mind and sky, or between thought and day and night, in his epilogue to "Notes," Stevens can now turn his attention to some of the more salutary aspects of the ever-never absent presence of changeful violence in the question of faith's reappearance in his work: the romance of the precise.

One of the most important of these aspects is, paradoxically, the constructive nature of the abyssal force at work in the romance of the precise, romance as a kind of belief event. From the point of view of the reason beyond reason and the intelligence beyond intelligence, the transcendent formalism, for example, of a figure like John Zeller can never really be destroyed. As we had earlier observed in relation to Stevens' former writing, which a figure like Old Zeller might be taken to represent, one moves beyond the past only by moving through it, according to the productive nature of absent force. It seems only inevitable, therefore, that Old John Zeller should come round, once again, in a text entitled "Two Versions of the Same Poem," written a year later, in 1946, with the important subtitle "That Which Cannot Be Fixed." In this piece, Stevens intends to present two versions of the generic notion of text rather than to deal with any one specific poem per se, so that what appears in Part I is the idea of the text more as a multiplier of meaning than as iconic formalizer and fixer, as in Part II. Thus, in the first part, the force of textuality, the "strength that tumbles everywhere" (*CP*, 354), is identifiable neither as land ("insolid rock") nor sea ("sailor's metier") but can be linked only to temporal process: "A body, turbulent / With time" and "a puissant heart / To toll its pulses" (*CP*, 354). Because this "water-carcass nevernamed" is productive of so many difficult images impossible to fix, it becomes, in a phrase much indebted to Stevens' previous "Notes," "reason's constant ruin," by whose perverse logic more and more becomes less and less in a space that is infinitely divisible. John Zeller, as humanity's eponymous hegemonic patriarch, subsequently appears in Part II to demand a resolution to the conflicting energies of this "perverse marine." Standing on a hill over-looking its rising and falling, he is perplexed by the lack of repose, a "golden solvent" with which to reconcile the elements. In the end, however, he re-ceives no ontological reaffirmation through the restitution of "an undivided whole." A formalist too completely out of his element ("old mould"), he looks for answers where there are no longer any to be found and must be content with the poem's final ellipsis, a fissure that appears to mock him with the division of even more hybrid images, of sea and earth and sky and water and fire and air, and that makes no promise of surcease or predetermined reconciliation, discomposed as the images are out of "ignorance." Because there is no "uptopping top and tip of things," there cannot even be the self-delusion that the jostling of competing forms will eventually escape the "ca-daverous undulations" of force and thereby silence the text with a present close. That pat, logocentric faith has had its day, and Old Zeller would ap-pear, like the ghost of Hamlet's father, to have had his, too: "Sleep deep, good eel. . . . Rest, old mould" (*CP*, 354–55).

In "Continual Conversation with a Silent Man" a year later, the struc-tural whole in which the man of order thought he might be contained (John Zeller's "bed" previously and here a "broken cartwheel on the hill" [*CP*, 359]) we find replaced by a vast, reticulated network of "never-ending things," tem-pest linked to farm, turquoise hen chained to sky, in a "never-ending storm of will." By attending to things in never-ending relation to other things (Ste-vens' iteration of the romance of the precise) rather than as objects of thought in themselves, this poem contrives to come up with a totally unconventional approach to understanding the world and with a totally unconventional view of the individual to fit it to; hence, the sound of things and their motion are privileged in the conversation with the "other man" as a turquoise monster moving about at the end of the poem. This other man seems to come very close to Richard Rorty's notion of the "edifying" (as opposed to the "episte-mological") philosopher as a "conversational partner": "One way of thinking of wisdom . . . is to think of it as the practical wisdom necessary to participate in a conversation. One way to see edifying philosophy *as* the love of wisdom is to see it as the attempt to prevent conversation from degenerating into . . . the self-deception of thinking that we possess a deep, hidden, metaphysically significant nature which makes us 'irreducibly' different."[33] Stevens' Nietz-

33. Rorty, *Philosophy and the Mirror of Nature*, 372–73.

schean image of his favorite wind, and its rustling "of many meanings in the leaves" of this text, perhaps suggests that an alternative rather than irreducible difference might be possible for his listening man.

The formal transformation of the poem from static construct or fixture to something more like a moving network or conversation, that is, from less precise text-object to more precise text-event, answers very much to Heidegger's assessment of the estranging or defamiliarizing "poetic nature" of genuine art—art that "in the midst of what is . . . breaks open an open place, in whose openness everything is other than usual . . . everything ordinary and hitherto existing becomes an unbeing . . . a change, happening from out of the work, of the unconcealedness of what is."[34] Gerald Bruns points out with regard to Heidegger's defamiliarization that the intention is not, in the long run, to break down convention, overturn tradition, and completely do away with "the forms and habits of mind, perception, or experience in which we encounter anything." Once again, we encounter the idea of moving beyond traditions by moving through them and a certain coincidence of necessity and desire, discussed earlier.[35] The questioning of belief, therefore, requires an opening and a changing exactly of this sort, an estranging of the tendency for people to inhere in what is most familiar in their lives and, in a poem such as the 1945 "Wild Ducks, People and Distances," of the tendency for people to distance themselves from disruption and change from the outside that so much threatens their identity inside. The irony, however, is that such a prophylactic sense of selfhood does not, nor could it ever, properly exist and that "the final, fatal distances" held off at the end of the poem are perhaps the very means by which their identity is held on, revealing another characteristically Heideggerian thematic of Stevens' discourse. Herman Rapaport describes this thematic fairly accurately: "The 'event' or *Ereignis* is not a moment present to itself but that of a correspondence of thoughts which in their arrival together are divided or dis-tanced." This explanation perhaps lends an added significance to Stevens' title.[36]

---

34. Heidegger, *Poetry, Language, Thought,* 72.

35. Bruns, *Heidegger's Estrangements,* 45; *cf.* also 43, 49–50, 72, 118, 130, and 184. For further expansions of the notion of defamiliarization or estrangement in Wallace Stevens' work, see Kermode, "Dwelling Poetically in Connecticut," in *Stevens: A Celebration,* ed. Doggett and Buttel, 267; Borroff, "Introduction," in *Critical Essays,* ed. Borroff, 18; Kessler, *Images of Wallace Stevens,* 226; Leggett, *Poetic Theory,* 91; Michael Davidson, "Notes Beyond the *Notes:* Wallace Stevens and Contemporary Poetics," in *Stevens: The Poetics of Modernism,* ed. Gelpi, 153, 146; Lentricchia, *Ariel and the Police,* 204–205; and Bates, *A Mythology of Self,* 270–71.

36. Herman Rapaport, *Heidegger and Derrida: Reflections on Time and Language* (Lincoln, 1989), 145. Edward Said comments on a parallel significance in Foucault's indebtedness to

The pursuit of the question of belief in the direction of the defamiliar-ized and the estranged was perhaps inevitable for Stevens. For, as Giles Gunn points out, "the problem of imagining and responding to that which is ex-perienced as 'other' is at once an ethical and a religious problem—ethical insofar as it involves a question of the 'right relation' to that which is experi-enced as 'other,' religious insofar as it also involves a question about the na-ture of reality so experienced." Gunn continues:

> Man becomes fully human, or at least comes fully into possession of such opportunities as are afforded him to be human, only to the degree that he is willing to acknowledge the "other" and then respond to it. . . . It can shock us out of the boredom and com-placency of the daily round, out of the grim banalities of every-dayness, and thus retrieve for us some comprehension of what Alfred North Whitehead meant by the word *importance,* that root notion by which we distinguish between crude matter-of-fact and its significance.[37]

Thus, "to give a sense of the freshness or vividness of life," Stevens writes in the "Adagia," "is a valid purpose for poetry" (*OP,* 184; *cf.* also *L,* 590). But a man sometimes can become even too familiar with his own poetry: "It be-comes as obsolete for himself as for anyone else. From this it follows that one of the motives in writing is renewal" (*OP,* 226). Stevens, therefore, pursues a specific agenda of Heideggerian or "religious" estrangement in other pieces in *Transport to Summer,* most notably in the 1947 "A Lot of People Bathing in a Stream." By passing a boundary or limit in the opening line of this poem, one is jettisoned once again into another world of the formless, the contin-gent, and the arbitrary, where yesterday's "yellow" must not remain yellow but must become "refreshed" by yellow green and yellow blue and other "comic colors" (*CP,* 371). The descent into the "flow of space" between the riverbanks is, not unexpectedly, entirely alienating. People who once had "ap-

---

Nietzsche's *Enstehung:* "[Foucault] has found Nietzsche's word *Enstehung* useful to describe the 'pure distance' separating discoveries from one another and permitting their identities to emerge with reference to one another; this field of distance is, he says, an open space of interdiscursive confrontation" (*Beginnings,* 304–305). For a similar reading of "distance," see also Hart, *Trespass of the Sign,* 41–42, and Pierre Macherey, *The Theory of Literary Production,* trans. Geoffrey Wall (London, 1978), 63–64. Barthes offers something slightly different in *A Lover's Discourse: Frag-ments,* trans. Richard Howard (New York, 1978).

37. Giles Gunn, *The Interpretation of Otherness: Literature, Religion, and the American Imagination* (New York, 1979), 178–79.

propriate conceptions" of themselves lose all sense of creaturely decorum and, entering into the grotesque world of nakedness in company with the sun, become bizarrely metamorphosed into "addicts / To blotches," "angular anonymids," and "funny foreigner[s] of meek address" (*CP,* 371). Little wonder, then, that there should be such a relish for the sanctuary of the orderly and familiar at the conclusion:

> How good it was at home again at night
> To prepare for bed, in the frame of the house, and move
> Round the rooms, which do not ever seem to change . . .
>
> (*CP,* 372)

One imagines that John Zeller would mightily approve both of the dispersal of chaos and night in the soothing circular motions established here and of the healthy distance set up between them and the jumble of bathers left off at their periphery. Still, the closing ellipsis, again, reveals that the cycle is not quite complete and provides just enough space to savor a little of the charm of estrangement, like floating without a head past a boundary, for instance, that the need for closure itself can only help to reinforce.

The ultimate estrangement, for which, no doubt, the previous poems were important exercises, would for Stevens inevitably converge on the act of writing itself and on the implications writing might have for belief. Central to this defamiliarization is the whole notion of the romance of imprecision, as well as the belief it fostered in the inscription of irreducible, permanent, and foundational truth, "proposals for universal commensuration," or "premises upon which an authority of the self-givenness of meaning" might be established through the valorization of the text-object. In their place, Stevens would foreground the text-event, not as in-scription but de-scription, writing as a romance of pre-cision, that is, of the force of repetition *before* the incision of the word, which could only be a writing without place, since it expressed only "the relation to the *other* of every book, to that which would be de-scription or un-writing, a writerly exigency outside discourse, outside language." The 1945 "Description without Place," therefore, becomes Stevens' most provocative statement in *Transport to Summer,* evincing the theory of poetry as the life of poetry and, in its analogous relation to the question of belief, the theory of poetry as the theory of life (*OP,* 202).[38]

Canto I reiterates a theme that had traveled rather well with Stevens

38. Rorty, *Philosophy and the Mirror of Nature,* 377; Rapaport, *Heidegger and Derrida,* 34; Derrida, "The 'Retrait' of Metaphor," 33, and *Grammatology,* 46–73; Maurice Blanchot, cited in Taylor, *Altarity,* 247.

since *The Man with the Blue Guitar,* that all truth is perspective. In the very first instance, therefore, since the transcendence of being is impossible, his de-scription is an effect of appearance, just as all knowledge is a manifestation of mere surface: "To seem—it is to be" (*CP,* 339). The sun is an example: "What it seems / It is and in such seeming all things are." The green queen is another. Her existence constituted as a reality in name only, she therefore seems to be only "on the saying of her name." Moreover, this saying opens up in the absence ("golden vacancy" rather than Zeller's "golden solvent") of a former seeming and, in time, will give place to the "reality" of a subsequent seeming, in the perpetual ever-never-changing same of desire's continuum. To this extent, consequently, her truth is what the canto de-scribes as an "illustrious nothing," which certifies only its character of becoming in its changefulness, through time's "week-day coronal" (*CP,* 339).

Canto II establishes the point that in the factitious course of human events we can expect to uncover multiple seemings of any given thing ("the way things look") since there is more than one queen. The most serviceable version, for a time, will be the one that appears more original than most, the "actual" truth we might say, as in the song. However, this version will only be an instance of the blindness of man's "forward" eye (*CP,* 340). Upon re-flection (the eye's "backward"), man realizes that the original is only origi-nary, that it is only given the sense of a *causa sui* and, by implication, that the mind itself is nothing but a great producer of such original seemings. In an aesthetic context, though not exclusively, the seeming is better known as "style"; when made official in any given age or epoch, a "manner"; or in strictly political terms, a "material practice," as Althusser would say.[39] What the canto is thus able to offer as life's "subtlety" is precisely the sense of the multiple perspectivism of *apparent* life—life in the sense of its "moments of enlargement," as Stevens will later refer to it in "Chocorua to Its Neighbor" (*CP,* 298), or in the sense of "the incalculably plural" (*CP,* 340), as here. A "singular man," quite like any of the villagers in the previous "Wild Ducks," however, will be more likely to barricade himself against the plurivalency of red, blue, and argent versions of the queen and, in his flat insistence that "we should be and be," prefer to opt only for the predominating major manner of the green queen as what strikes his eye as most original. Yet such an "iden-tity," like all the others, can only be "a thing that seems" and consequently leaves the hypostatized essentialism of his belief entirely open to question. Ultimately, the foundationalist belief must be accepted in the sense of what

39. Althusser, *Lenin and Philosophy,* 155–59.

is true for *all* beliefs: one "flat appearance" among a host of "delicate clink-ings" (*CP,* 340), that is, a belief more hypothetical than actual and the ex-pression of what we also hear and feel when we come to "know" something, in addition to what we say we see.

The tendency will always be to pick out of a host of potential seemings only one and to declare that one as the truth of Being. Canto III describes this as a process of shrinking the world to the clarity of an "immediate whole" of self-presence (*CP,* 341). Examples are legion: a single page of the "youngest poet," a dark musician's "contriving chords," a commonplace soldier's "ut-most will," and spiritual apotheosis in a "breath emerging out of death" (*CP,* 340–41). All of Stevens' metaphors are especially eloquent, but the more important point the canto insists on is that they are all just that, the "potential seemings" of a poet's metaphors. Yet the tendency is usually to overlook the fact of their optionality here and consciously (or, more likely, subconsciously) seek out in the most appealing of these one "in which being would / Come true": "A point in the fire of music where / Dazzle yields to a clarity and we observe, / And observing is completing and we are content" (*CP,* 341).[40] In so dispensing with the multiplicity of the mind's metaphorical "secret ar-rangements," therefore, we bring our perspectival observation of the world through to a definitive, truthful end—an end that goes without saying, as we (ironically) say—and thereby collapse an immenser change into the self-congratulation of a singular and static "content." Translated to the theologi-cal context, such complacency becomes the rather fallacious attempt to focus on some unitive, spiritual proposition out of perhaps a host of such and to make that the tacit universalization of the world's Supreme Being, whose intentions, the "spirit of one dwelling in a seed, / . . . [of] unpredictable fruit" (*CP,* 341), can forever remain only unknown. Hence, Stevens' wonderfully restive image of "a purple-leaping element that forth / Would froth the whole heaven with its seeming-so" (*CP,* 341). For surely the point of the image is that life is not a condensation but rather a composite of world views (Anne in England, Pablo Neruda in Ceylon, Nietzsche in Basel, and so on), that is, an immense "*Museo Olimpico,*" to recur to the image from "Blue Guitar" (*CP,* 342, 182). Taken together, these "integrations" make our interaction with life an "affair / Of the possible," make our interaction, in other words, condi-tional upon the very "seemings" that make it possible "to be" (*CP,* 342).

The contrast between Nietzsche and Lenin, in Canto IV, is a highly

40. See Rorty, *Philosophy and the Mirror of Nature,* 158, and Derrida's "White Mythology," in *Margins of Philosophy,* 270–71.

instructive illustration of one person who is sensitive to the multiplicity of life's interpretations and of another who is not, who trains his attention instead on the single, univocal prospect. For Lenin, in contrast to Nietzsche, is a totalizing thinker. He stakes everything on a lone, future prospect, symbolized by a Yeatsian ring of bright swans that are scattered in the present, sacrificed to a unitive integration in some far-off moment yet to come, where they will bring the "distances of space and time" together as "one," in the utopia of tomorrow. Clearly not a man of possibility like Nietzsche, Lenin can only be overtaken by "decadence" in the present, dissipating all the potentialities or "suavest keeping" of the moment to future outcomes. No doubt, there is a certain price to be paid when the egocentric eye/I of the revolutionary and his "raised up" mind can so overwhelmingly consecrate themselves to the tunnel vision of "one thinking of apocalyptic legions." Hence, today's "down-drowned" chariots, reaches, and beaches are all woefully bartered for "tomorrow's regions" (*CP*, 343).

Specifically, Lenin is a thinker who fails precisely on two counts. First, he opts for a description that is visionary and thus determinate. Canto V, however, makes it clear that authentic description is emphatically not an ocular project at all:

> Description is
> Composed of a sight indifferent to the eye.
>
> It is an expectation, a desire,
> A palm that rises up beyond the sea,
>
> A little different from reality:
> The difference that we make in what we see
>
> And our memorials of that difference,
> Sprinklings of bright particulars from the sky.
>   (*CP*, 343–44)

Wallace Stevens' pun in "beyond the sea" in this pregnant passage throws emphasis onto de-scriptive writing as process or text-event rather than as a product or object. The composing of that nameless process, motored by the disseminating dynamic of desire we have studied in several of Stevens' previous poems, perhaps issues into a "reality" like political revolution, which closes a certain strategy of political thinking as a palm completes a seascape. Revolution should never be confused with that reality itself, though. Undoubtedly, we *do* make a difference every time we see, yet it is the memorials that mark the presence of making, whereas the difference (or description) it-self marks the absence simultaneously preluding and eluding that very mean-ing. Description, therefore, will not be futural in the sense of capping a pro-gression from past to present, which is the second way in which Lenin's thinking may be faulty. In its most genuine sense, a description of the future is elliptical, a categorical rather than a cyclical predicate, which will be shaped, if it must have an "attentive" form, like an open-ended arc, suggest-ing perhaps that a categorical "Being that is announced within the illegible is beyond . . . categories, beyond, as it writes itself, its own name."[41] If it must have a specific time, the time will be that of Stevens' Metaphysician in the Dark, that is, the dawn as the interval in between "wizened starlight" and the "new day, / Before it comes," which is neither morning nor night, but the de-scription of "just anticipation" (*CP,* 344) that resists definitive naming of this very sort.

"How do we know," Richard Rorty asks, "whether what the Eye of the Mind sees is a mirror (even a distorted mirror—an enchanted glass) or a veil?" If we have been at all attentive to the de-scriptive critique of the essen-tializing vision of the egocentric eye/I, chances are we see *both.* For as the next canto opens, "Description is revelation" (*CP,* 344). Description, that is, is an unveiling that is also a reveiling at the same time, as we noted previ-ously: a dis-covering that is a re-covering, and vice-versa. Nor is description to be confounded with the "thing." Rather it connects only with the thing in its (de)construction, as we saw earlier in "Man Carrying Thing," that is, the thing that proves to be a "false facsimile" if it cannot be artificial in a factitious or seeming sense, one of those "*fac-similes* without an authentic and indivis-ible letter," as Derrida describes them in "The Purveyor of Truth." In Stevens' shift to the romance of the precise, thus, description is not representation but repetition. Where then does the matter of revelation leave us in Stevens' com-parison of description to "the thesis of the plentifullest John" (*CP,* 345)? The clue to the answer lies perhaps in the previous qualification: "Intenser than any actual life could be" (*CP,* 344). Northrop Frye's ascription of "intensity" in the biblical context, as a re-creation of the past in the present, takes us only halfway. One is likely to move further ahead with Derrida's "conceptualiza-tion of intensity or force" or with Charles Altieri's notion of a plentifullest

---

41. Derrida, *Writing and Difference,* 77. Ironically, it would appear that the "ultimate test of the power of art" stemming from a belief in transcendence "grounded in primitive universals," in Cary Nelson's words (*Regression and Recovery,* 124), is rather more what a vulgar Marxist like Lenin, rather than a poet of difference like Wallace Stevens, might be prone to.

intensity as "participation [more] with the forces of process than in the results," which is perhaps something of what Stevens has in mind in the image of "rubies reddened by rubies reddening" in the final line of the poem
(*CP*, 346).[42]

Thus, a revelation that is "the double of our lives" would not be the
Book of John in any mimetic or referential sense. It would be just as Stevens
identifies it, a "text" (*CP*, 344), a word that foregrounds the productive rather
than the reductive character of its operations. Description, as "the book of
reconciliation," is conciliatory in the nature of its productive, conceptual possibility and will have reference *only*, merely, to this hypothetical nature: a
"canon central *in itself*," undeniably (*CP*, 345, emphasis added). A summary
of these ideas opens the last canto of the poem:

> Thus the theory of description matters most.
> It is the theory of the word for those
>
> For whom the word is the making of the world,
> The buzzing world and lisping firmament.
>
> It is a world of words to the end of it,
> In which nothing solid is its solid self.
>
> (*CP*, 345)

Life, in its most significant sense, is now found to be a text without place—a
place, that is, that would imply the closure of the presence of meaning. It is
an absent space, in other words, opened up to an infinite signification: "The
word [as] the making of the world" and "a world of words to the end of it,"
including the subtitle to this chapter. "The limits of my language are the
limits of my world," as Ludwig Wittgenstein would say. *In principio erat
verbum*. The force of endless signification turns out, once again, to be
"no[-]thing," solid only in its insolidity and, moreover, a nothing very close

---

42. Rorty, *Philosophy and the Mirror of Nature*, 46; Derrida, "The Purveyor of Truth," in
The Purloined Poe, ed. Muller and Richardson, 204; Frye, *The Great Code*, 227; Derrida, *Writing
and Difference*, 23; Charles Altieri, "From Symbolist Thought to Immanence: The Ground of
Postmodern American Poetics," *Boundary 2*, I (Spring, 1973), 613. *Cf.* also the conceptualization
of intensity in Deleuze and Guattari as a force of "positive multiplicities where everything is
possible, without exclusiveness or negation, syntheses operating without a plan, where the con-
nections are transverse, the disjunctions included, the conjunctions polyvocal" (*Anti-Oedipus*,
309). In Deleuze and Parnet, intensity (or *Hecceity*, "thisness") is linked to the *event* of desire
(*Dialogues*, 92, 151*n.*) and in Maurice Blanchot, in *The Writing of the Disaster*, trans. Ann Smock
(Lincoln, 1986), to "the extreme of difference, in excess of the being that ontology takes for
granted" (56).

to what we find in the discourse of the later Heidegger: "In the clear night of the Nothing of anxiety the original manifestness of the being as such first arises: that it is a being—and not nothing. . . . That which never and nowhere is a being reveals itself as that which differentiates itself from all beings, which we call Being."[43]

For the Metaphysician in the Dark, the question of belief all comes back to the perspectivism of seeming truth, constituted by the *force* of the individual manner or style. Whether the hidalgo is writ hugely in the mountainous character of his speech or Spain is writ diminutively in the character of a hat, both are effects of the wor(l)d's making: the "invention of a nation in a phrase" (*CP*, 345). "The whole race is a poet," Wallace Stevens will later say in "Men Made Out of Words" from 1946, "that writes down / The eccentric propositions of its fate" (*CP*, 356). Whether a seeming of words or of worlds, though, the making can never be universal and intrinsic, only particular and relative, as in the case of the concluding rubies, the reality of whose intense color is strictly an event of relation *to the other*. "In the absence of center and logos," as Mark Taylor observes, "there is no special time or special place." We should conclude, therefore, that there is only description without place and, like the question of belief, description without end, since "in a description hollowed out of hollow-bright, / The artificer of subjects [is] still half night" (*CP*, 345).[44]

"Description without Place" is without doubt Wallace Stevens' most important theoretical advance on the question of belief in *Transport to Summer*. We turn, finally, to a brief examination of three of the remaining longer poems in the volume, composed a year or two before "Description," in order to have a better understanding of how that poem evolved in Stevens' long meditation on faith. "Credences of Summer," which came a year later in 1946, we reserve for a more extended discussion in the analysis of the "companion poems," in Chapter 6. For now, it is the description of the word that is Stevens' most penetrating insight. And if the making of the word constitutes the making of the world, then no less can be said for the making of belief. Belief in the word is one thing; but belief in the word as an effect of intensity, of style, of *difference*—belief, in a *manner* of speaking—is quite another. "Where *difference* continuously emerges, " as Barbara Herrnstein Smith has remarked, "it must

43. Ludwig Wittgenstein, cited in Christopher Norris, *The Deconstructive Turn: Essays in the Rhetoric of Philosophy* (London, 1983), 144; Heidegger, *Existence and Being*, 339, 353.

44. Taylor, *Erring*, 169.

be either continuously negotiated or continuously suppressed."[45] To get past the suppression of difference and to be able to characterize faith more as the question of the open-endedness of a textual event, Stevens would have to deal with certain repressive and exclusionary tendencies within the human psyche itself—tendencies that become particularly aggravated in the presence of experiences we attribute to pain and, on an even more abstract level, to evil. In "A Word with José Rodríguez-Feo," composed in 1945, pain and evil have become the "relaxations of the known," which a bold entry into "the nature of man's interior world" is required to authenticate, since "[the spirit] has, long since, grown tired, of such ideas" (*CP,* 333–34). "Esthétique du Mal" from 1944 is an extended attempt on Stevens' part to break apart our sedimented representations of these ideas, the nostalgia of "sleek ensolac-ings," as he would come to describe them (*CP,* 322), in order to shift his theological discourse to the repetitions of a more precise romance.

From an egocentric and, by implication, a thoroughly logocentric point of view, the opening section of "Esthétique du Mal" indicates the conven-tional attitude taken toward our sense of fallenness, symbolized by Mount Vesuvius and marked more immediately by the daily reminder of "pain killing pain on the very point of pain" (*CP,* 314). Customary wisdom in such matters dictates a course of distancing and sublimation of our malady, hence the "esthétique," doubled by the French of the title. "Description," in the ac-cepted sense of the term, mitigates the "sultriest fulgurations" of the volcano, an enormous defect of nature that is thus made to tremble in "another ether," a phrase to which we shall return later. Theories of the sublime help to sublime-ate pain, cast it into categories and formulas that accommodate it to our thought, make sure of its place in our lives, and so "correct the catastro-phe" of which our lives are so intrinsically a part. That our distancing of pain makes it a perpetual accompaniment in life, however, is one of the contradic-tory aspects of our narcotic theorizing about the sublime that we are happy to ignore, at the cost of maintaining a more reassuring sense of a necessary self-possession. Consequently, what may be most painful of all for Stevens is manifest in the normative approaches to evil and in the fact that they do not come fully to terms with it but instead succeed only in prolonging and ex-tending it: "How that which rejects it saves it in the end" (*CP,* 315). This paradox perhaps accounts in Section II for the "intelligence of [the artist's] despair" or the dark warblings of afflicted sleep that interrupt his letter writ-

45. Barbara Herrnstein Smith, *Contingencies of Value,* 94.

ing from time to time back in Section I. Clearly, his meditation is divided, but his missives, much like the passive moon by which they are lit, evade this discord and give voice only to "a supremacy always / Above" (*CP*, 314), a desperate, subliminal elision of difference that Stevens characterizes two years later as the tired romance of imprecision (*CP*, 353). Expanded in Section IX of "Esthétique," this romance becomes a "phosphored sleep" that ignores "comic ugliness," the distaff of comedy that is itself a kind of "folly of the moon" (*CP*, 320). The poet must therefore lose this sublime sensibility and make a more strenuous effort to see and, what is more, hear the "destitute" and "haggardie," as against the halcyon, of "Truth's favors sonorously exhibited" (*CP*, 321). He does this by constructing a countersublime or, at any rate, indulging a "sublime sentiment" coincident with what Lyotard would describe as "the unpresentable in presentation itself."[46]

In Section III, Stevens enlarges his critique of pain and the aesthetic evasion of pain, linking them to hell and heaven, respectively. In laboring to be as rigorous as possible concerning these issues, his meditation must conclude only that "*both* heaven and hell / Are *one*" (*CP*, 315, emphasis added). As in "Notes Toward a Supreme Fiction," Stevens wants to clear away all the calcified myths that allow belief to ignore both aspects of the problem of pain. The Christ myth, the narrative of "an over-human god" and "reddest lord," therefore, is perhaps to his way of thinking a wish-fulfillment dream that we have constructed with such deliberate sympathy in order to cover over imaginatively with a "peer / Of the populace" what we are *given* to suffer and to elide the real experience of our "terra infidel" (*CP*, 315). It is the truthful, that is, ontological, projection of mythological belief wherein lies the "fault" of any overhuman god, wherein one might even suspect the real "mal," or evil, of the poem's title lies, picking up on Stevens' pun. Mythological belief is a malady because such a construction fails to acknowledge what must be accepted as our fate: the veritable absence at the core of being human—"too, too human," as Stevens puts it, in a reminiscence of Nietzsche—that is, the "woe both great / And small" we must accept as our destiny. Imaginative projection of this sort, therefore, becomes an "uncourageous genesis"; and the painful world only becomes healthy, once again, when we clear it of all our mythological attitudinizing and "satanic mimicry" and seek instead to find sustenance itself in all the pain that possibly can "be borne." Only then might we subsequently hope "to find our way" (*CP*, 316). Seeing reality for

46. Lyotard, *The Postmodern Condition*, 81.

the first time cleared of the mythic "mortal no," as in Section VIII, curiously turns life's tragedy into something positive, the "yes of the realist" (*CP*, 320) that must be spoken in Nietzschean fashion, since "a passion for yes" is the contract underwriting imagination's negotiation with reality—"a passion for yes that [can] never [be] broken" (*CP*, 320).[47]

The crux of Stevens' meditation, therefore, occurs in Section XI, where we learn the importance of accepting life as a "bitter aspic," fully recognizing that experience rendered in nonmythological terms is quite eccentric, since "we are not / At the centre of a diamond" (*CP*, 322). This insight, however, comes about in evolving a reality that is neither ontological nor epistemological, in a word, "discoverable," but is rather, as we might say in current critical discourse, "grammatological," a reality *constructed* by language and hence "recoverable": "Natives of poverty, children of malheur, / The gaiety of language is our seigneur" (*CP*, 322). This formulation becomes Stevens' "thesis scrivened in delight" at the end of the poem (*CP*, 326) and very likely the inspiration for the "thesis of the plentifullest John" later on in "Description." In this section, though, it becomes the cue for the verbal estrangements of the down-falling paratroopers mowing lawns and the up-springing violets crowding out parishes and parishioners alike, long since drowned in their own sanctimoniousness. Their targets are similar to several of the human arrangements of that decidedly transcendent cast we have seen Stevens' particular style of defamiliarization at work on previously:

> A man of bitter appetite despises
> A well-made scene in which paratroopers
> Select adieux; and he despises this:
> A ship that rolls on a confected ocean,
> The weather pink, the wind in motion; and this:
> A steeple that tip-tops the classic sun's
> Arrangements; and the violets' exhumo.
>
> (*CP*, 322)

The overall tip-topping here repeats the "uptopping top and tip" of Old Zeller, we may recall, whose own oneiric wish fulfillments must also exacerbate the man of bitter appetite, who knows that life's "essential savor" is hunger and not the false mythologies of the ontic "epicure" (*CP*, 323). Translated to the final section of the poem, therefore, the gaiety of language be-

---

47. *Cf.* Bloom, *Poems of Our Climate*, 229; Taylor, *Erring*, 145.

comes Stevens' deconstructive "dark italics" (*CP,* 326), whose writing constitutes what we abundantly see and hear but, more important, picking up on Edward Said's notion of a constitutive "unknown absence, felt by the mind," "what one *feels*" through the force engendering the profusion of life's multiple possibilities: "So many selves, so many sensuous worlds . . . swarming / With the metaphysical changes," yet without the slightest hint of ontotheological transport, "living *as* and *where* we live" (*CP,* 326, emphases added).[48]

The epicure of transport, or, better, the epi-*cure* of catastrophe, in his further development in Section XII, is entirely logocentric in his classical disposal of the world into categories: peopled/unpeopled, world-knowledge/self-knowledge, and so on, all incident with the desperate will for truth. The gaiety of language as a force of differentiation, however, reveals genuine knowledge to be a/categorical, demystified by the interiority of exteriority ("himself in [others]") and the exteriority of interiority ("they in him") and showing how "both worlds" are impossible without the Other (*CP,* 323). Diacritical knowledge thus "destroys both worlds" or at least allows man to escape his exclusionary repressiveness and to create an a/theological "third world without knowledge" (*CP,* 323), always already anticipated back in the first section with the volcano's "trembling in another ether" (*CP,* 314). This third world, moreover, is not a place of rejection but one of acceptance, and in its acceptance specifically of the givenness of pain, this third thing becomes, paradoxically, a world where "there is no pain." Pain, that is, remains a problem only for the epicure because he rejects it. A third world that "accepts whatever is as true" makes no demands on belief save that of love, its only *point d'appui* lying "at the centre of the heart" (*CP,* 323). In this (non)concept of the third world, a (non)place that inevitably issues into Stevens' later "Description," one may detect an astonishing parallel with the *entre deux* in the philosophical discourse of Maurice Blanchot and with *das ganz Andere* in Levinas. Hence, the *Dialogues* of Deleuze and Parnet indicate that "it is certainly no longer a matter of synthesis . . . of 1 and 2, but of a third which always comes from elsewhere and disturbs the binarity of the two, not so much inserting itself in their opposition as in their complementarity."[49]

The epicure, therefore, who reappears, in Section XIII, in the "Medi-

---

48. Said, *Beginnings,* 74.

49. Taylor, *Altarity,* 232–33, 194; Deleuze and Parnet, *Dialogues,* 131. See also the discussion of Stevens' "possibility of a third idea" in the analysis of the epilogue to "Notes Toward a Supreme Fiction" in Chapter 4.

terranean cloister" of the poem's opening is rife for decreation (*NA*, 174).
"Eased of desire" (*CP*, 324), a ghastly prospect in view of "The Motive for
Metaphor," he thinks he has established the "ultimate good" in some maximum meditation on the sublime, making him "sure of reality." However, it
is this state of "unalterable necessity," precisely as the term is used earlier in
this chapter, against which language, described by Stevens here as the "force
of nature in action" (*CP*, 324), must work its effect. Ultimately, this effect—an effect discussed in "The Effects of Analogy," Stevens' important
1948 essay, reserved for study in the next chapter—is to demythologize any
pat formulations of original causes and lasting ends, imaged in father-son
master narratives for example, revealing actually the third world's originary
construction of life's "secondary characters," the secondary expositors we may
recall from "The Creation of Sound." What is unalterable, then, is the tragedy
of life precisely in this secondary sense, a point on which both father and son
(and epicure) "equally are spent" (*CP*, 324). Consequently, if the force of
nature in action can reveal to them that "evil in evil is / Comparative" (*CP*,
324), that it is precisely the force within the maximum that proves the fallacy
of all maximums, then this force that destroys is, truly, the "happiest enemy."
For it reveals that life, in broadest terms, is not so much a "punishment" to
be endured as an "adventure" to be savored: "One feels its action moving in
the blood" (*CP*, 324). A sense of helplessness is incident with the effect of
otherness, yet it must needs be thought only an "assassin's scene" if we continue, like the adults of Stevens' "Epigram," to *fear* the ever-never-changing
same of its movements as an alternative to accepting them.

Why are we unable psychically to accept this fact of force and this force
of fact? Section V of Stevens' poem meditates in some detail on this question,
specifically on our preference for what it calls attention to as the "familiar"
and on our corresponding strict avoidance of a kind of Heideggerian traffic
in the mysterious, that is, the "ai-ai / Of parades in the obscurer selvages"
(*i.e.*, borders, margins, edges) that we forfeit so willingly (*CP*, 317). If there
is to be "sob" and "sorrow" in the actual world, what we can permit of it is
only "the warm, [and] the near," its "unity" in other words, or as much as
we can find of "being's deepest darling." Further, Stevens expands the familiar into the familial, reviving an old argument from "The Comedian"; and by
exploiting that "facade of gloomy, irrational nihilism linked to a dynastic ideology" (the image of a brother handed down from father's eye and mother's
throat), Stevens reveals the fairly typical expressive strategy by which contexts
of obscurer pain and evil are domesticated and darker "things," which appear

threatening in their disclosure, are displaced onto a dynastic narrative of "regalia" and "nebulous brilliancies" (*CP*, 317).[50] All this domestication of interiority to the exclusion of the "ai-ai" later in this section becomes the "dear relation" of a "central [*i.e.*, common] sense," what Stevens images as the permission of the "in-bar." The in-bar, moreover, drives an epistemological wedge between self and the other of "poverty," namely, the "ex-bar" of clouds, distant heads, suns, and so forth. Taken together, though, in-bar and ex-bar repeat Stevens' previous argument of the opposition between the classical and romantic rhetorical paradigms of representation, studied earlier in "Notes Toward a Supreme Fiction," which an alternative, third paradigm of semiotic repetition would aim to deconstruct by way of the violent abyss. This third paradigm has an obvious connection to the spacing of Stevens' "third world" and picks up on the pun in the trembling ether/either back in Section I. "The mind cannot always live in a 'divine ether,'" as one of Stevens' earliest journal entries would have it (*L*, 27).[51]

If we step back to the previous section, Section IV, we perhaps may be better able to understand the view taken toward nature with this idea of barred knowledge in mind. What ought to be a hypothetical openness to every variety of experience in nature's pleasure-pain repertoire becomes a closed book: "Livre de Toutes Sortes de Fleurs d'après Nature." If we follow Stevens' punning, musical analogy, this gathering of all sorts of notes becomes an egregiously sentimentalized Johnny One-Note, the "transparence" of whose "single sound" (*CP*, 316) conspires only to efface difference and to become the "last" word on man's purported "one[-ness]." Another of Stevens' comparisons recalls his use of the rose image at the outset of "Extracts from Addresses to the Academy of Fine Ideas," analyzed back in Chapter 3. For the Spaniard who overlooks the untoward features of the rose endeavors merely to rescue it from nature's more indelicate side and then to jam it into his own sentimental version of experience so as to suit "his own especial eye" (*CP*, 316). In this distorted "paradigm of recovery," all activity is rescue just of this sort, and barefoot philandering among nature's "several maids," the most abhorrent passion.[52] The point of Stevens' critique is also the point of

---

50. Said, *Beginnings*, 66.

51. *Cf.* "the middle voice," which deconstructs "the ether of metaphysics," in Derrida's "Différance" (*Speech and Phenomena*, 130, 147) and Stevens' own "middle witch"/which of "difficult difference" in "The Pure Good of Theory" (*CP*, 333).

52. Michael Davidson, "Ekphrasis and the Postmodern Painter Poem," *Journal of Aesthetics and Art Criticism*, XLII (Fall, 1983), 77b.

Nietzsche's: "The genius of misfortune / Is not a sentimentalist" (*CP*, 316). Still, the unblinkered perception that "fault / Falls out on everything" in the natural course of things and, more especially, that "the genius of . . . our being [is] wrong and wrong" on the analogy of the "genius of the body, which is our world," this more honest perception is so subversive a prospect to the guarded purity of the proprietary mind that it must ignore that so-called evil and dissipate itself, instead, in the sentimental extravagance of mythic "false engagements." Stevens announces in his "Adagia" that "sentimentality is a failure of feeling" (*OP*, 189). A perfect example is the sentimentalist's treatment of the soldier in wartime, which expands the view of nature, later, in Section VII: "How red the rose that is the soldier's wound" (*CP*, 318). This description pushes recuperation in the direction of the myths of the funeral parlor, toward human mortality as "ease" and "deathless rest." The epilogue to Stevens' "Notes" would belie this view, so that only an "indifference to deeper death" could possibly brook such patent falsehoods in real life, imaged here as "a mountain in which no ease is ever found" (*CP*, 319). Only a Metaphysician "in the dark" (Stevens here repeats his favorite phrase) would question such belief.

The final implications both of a totally stable and universally transportable theory of knowledge and of the "universality, unconditionality, impersonality, [and] objectivity" of the value by which such a theory elicits belief Stevens plays out in the final two sections of his text.[53] In Section XIV, he anticipates his excoriating characterization of Lenin a year later in "Description" with the equally vitriolic portrait here of Konstantinov, the "logical lunatic" whose constancy fills Victor Serge with such "blank uneasiness" (*CP*, 324). The basis of the critique is Konstantinov's total preoccupation with rational thought and with the single idea its logic revolves (revolution, quite understandably) to the exclusion of all others "in a world of ideas." This logical search for primal origins and ultimate ends, and its attendant sublimation of all genuine human emotion in meretricious "intellectual structure[s]," is utter lunacy. The reminiscence of Stevens' satire of the gloomy grammarians in "On the Manner of Addressing Clouds" (*CP*, 55) from *Harmonium* is unmistakable even twenty years later:

> One wants to be able to walk
> By the lake at Geneva and consider logic:
> To think of the logicians in their graves

53. Barbara Herrnstein Smith, *Contingencies of Value*, 97.

And of the worlds of logic in their great tombs.
Lakes are more reasonable than oceans. Hence,
A promenade amid the grandeurs of the mind,
By a lake, with clouds like lights among great tombs,
Gives one a blank uneasiness, as if
One might meet Konstantinov, who would interrupt
With his lunacy.

(*CP*, 325)

The equation here between a grave logic and death is the price of a logocentric belief, nicely picked up in the image of the circling of Lake Geneva, particularly in view of what it backgrounds and elides: oceans, clouds, the lake itself, but more especially *all* the people who *must* be made to "live, work, suffer and die" for one, single, solitary, sublime idea in a wilderness of ideas, because "the martyrs of logic" can look only around, not beyond. However, Stevens' "scrivened thesis" in the final section, which makes such belief questionable, would argue that "the greatest poverty is not to live / In a physical world" (*CP*, 325). Moreover, a physical world of acceptable difference has only something of desire to recommend it and nothing of despair. Its gleaming green corn may be a minor experience by comparison, but at least it is a felt one—felt by "the adventurer / *In* humanity" (*CP*, 325, emphasis added). To him, the world is neither exclusively physical nor exclusively nonphysical because, for an adventurer, humanity is not "conceived." He has only his "rotund emotions" to go by and is quite happy to let "the metaphysicals" go sprawling in the August heat and to leave "paradise unknown" (*CP*, 325). This is a poor man's aesthetic of malady, to be sure. Nonetheless, its gaiety of language makes thinking about belief a continuous and ever-renewable possibility, living, as it does, "as and where we live" (*CP*, 326).

The two remaining longer poems in *Transport to Summer* continue Stevens' examination of the hero in a time of war where the theme leaves off in "Esthétique du Mal." In both "Chocorua to Its Neighbor" and "Repetitions of a Young Captain," written in 1943 and 1944, respectively, however, he is concerned to explore as rigorously as possible what expressive permissions are granted the notion of heroism, and humanity in general, in terms of the gaiety of language, the dark italics subtending the romance of the precise. Eugenio Donato, in a landmark essay on this question, has observed that "Romantic poetry is constantly preoccupied with the problems of how to pass from the fragmentation of perception to a totality, and how to arrive at the nature of the 'Object' without losing the privilege of the immediacy of perception." If language, as Stevens seems especially to be arguing in the previous two texts, is "essentially responsible for the impossibility of a relationship that would maintain the object as transcendental presence," that is to say, if "the 'Natural Object' is only an absence inscribed in an image or a representation," then a romance of the precise, from an expressive and interpretive point of view, is going to be a semantically fugitive enterprise, to say the least. Donato goes on to sketch perhaps what Stevens himself may have envisioned the "form" of such a romance would be:

> Beginning with the Romantics, and throughout the nineteenth century, altitude is the spatial emblem of difference and distance from an absolute origin. Hence, for example, a privileged original nature or 'Natural Object' is often placed at an unreachable height in relationship to the representationally temporalized nature in the valleys. Immediacy and epiphany are often postulated in mountains. Height becomes a commonplace metaphor for difference from an origin. . . . Inasmuch as Mont Blanc stands for the highest elevation, it also defines the possibility of the greatest representational difference. It is not surprising then that Mont Blanc should remain beyond the reach of language and, in a way, not even bestow a full perception . . . [since it] is not an origin that can ground perception or representation but instead dispels any hope that the poet might have had to reach an origin through perception or reception.[54]

As early as 1942 in "Notes Toward a Supreme Fiction," Stevens had already begun working with altitude and unreachable height as a problematic of identity in difference and difference in identity, in connection with his formulation of the Promethean constructs of MacCullough and Major Man, and beyond them, the Blanc Mythology of the First Idea postulated in the natural object of the sun. A year later, in 1943, he offers us "Gigantomachia," an attempt to reconceptualize the violence of war, not in the sense of negation or "fatal unity," as we had examined it in Chapter 3, but in the sense of the demystifying force in the motive for metaphor, on the way to the expansion of human possibility and potential. In this particular poem, the shift is made from man's being "in the mass," connected to "ever-present seductions" and "complacent trifles," to "the being that was an abstraction," by way of changes, magnifications, and enlargements, which become scripted through the force of life's "lack-tragic" (*CP*, 289). As a result, "each man himself became a giant / Tipped out with largeness, bearing the heavy / And the high," and the difference this enlargement makes cannot be comprehended in any ordinary, conceptual, or humanistic terms. In "Late Hymn from the Myrrh-Mountain" three years later in 1946, Stevens continues to develop this shift from the knowledge of being, "sense without sense of time," to "the shadow of an external world," approached through what he calls the "tips of artifice" (*CP*, 350), but artifice emptied of every sense of transcendent objectivity (snoods of the madonna, green birds of summer, intimations of constellations, diamonds in the hair, and so forth). From the same year comes the wonderful parody of Marx and Freud in "Mountains Covered with Cats," whose endless master narratives can only repeat the larger fact of life's absence, re-covered in the mountains of Stevens' title. In Stevens' "The Noble Rider and the Sound of Words," Freud is one among many important writers in the history of Western thought who have "cut poetry's throat" (*NA*, 14). Michael Beehler responds to this remark by noting that "since the irrational is, according to Stevens, that which can never be properly named . . . it is clear that its determination in any discourse must be a delusion akin to what Kant, using a similar logic with respect to the sublime, calls fanaticism." Fortunately, Kant, Marx, and Freud all look much different in a postmodern academy from how they looked in Stevens' day. For here, as Steve McCaffery notes, "the intention among contemporary writing must always be towards an utter dismantling of the notion of TRUTH as anything exterior to the signifying practice . . . not as the destination of a referential function in language, but as a writing production, a writing effect *per se*."[55] Hence, the "ruinous storm" (*CP*, 336) of signification in "Sketch of the Ultimate Politician" from 1947, "the total dream . . . where we have yet to live" (*CP*, 335–36).

"Chocorua to Its Neighbor," Stevens' major mountain poem, comes between all of these shorter efforts attempting to problematize privileged, theoretical representations of knowledge. All converge in the demystifying agenda of "Esthétique" and its own foregrounding of a forestructure of unrepresentable origins in Heideggerian terms, suggested particularly by the

---

55. Beehler, "Stevens' Boundaries," 101; Steve McCaffery, *North of Intention: Critical Writings, 1973–1986* (Toronto, 1986), 125. For a further expansion of this argument, see also Beehler, *Discourses of Difference*, 45–46.

"mountain in which no ease is ever found" in Section VII and "the blank uneasiness[es]" in Section XIV.[56] Despite its length, though, "Chocorua" is a tendentious and somewhat unfocused performance and pales in comparison to the overall precision of thought and the sweeping power of expression in Stevens' previous longer poems. We therefore dwell on it only briefly to establish certain continuities in the radicalization of belief already touched on in this chapter. The most important of these, perhaps, is given in the opening stanza and in its stated purpose to establish a perception of man outside his conventional "form," that is, in nonreferential terms. The Rortyean conversational method by which to proceed is in keeping with the open-endness of the project's "large[ness] in space" (*CP*, 296), and the aural privileging of the absent interlocutor (whether Chocorua's shadow or another mountain is never made quite plain) sustains its decentering impetus as well.[57]

In stanza IV, again, thinking about human potential in terms of difference rather than identity requires a defamiliarization of "the body's form" (*CP*, 297), yet an indeterminate process of thought guided more by the prolongations of desire (hence, the recollection of Liadoff) and the feelings indissociable from what Roland Barthes would call "obtuse" or third meaning or here "the feel of a day . . . as yet unseen" (*CP*, 297).[58] Stevens' discourse never gets more obtuse than stanza V, as many commentators have agreed:

> He was a shell of dark blue glass, or ice,
> Or air collected in a deep essay,
> Or light embodied, or almost, a flash
> On more than muscular shoulders, arms and chest,
> Blue's last transparence as it turned to black.
>
> (*CP*, 297)

---

56. See esp. Heidegger, *Being and Time*, §32, and "The Anaximander Fragment," in Martin Heidegger, *Early Greek Thinking*, trans. David Farrell Krell and Frank A. Capuzzi (San Francisco, 1975), 13–58. See William V. Spanos on "fore-having," "fore-sight," and "fore-conception," in "Heidegger, Kierkegaard, and the Hermeneutic Circle: Towards a Postmodern Theory of Interpretation as Dis-closure," *Boundary 2*, IV (Winter, 1976), 457–62. In regard to Stevens' construction of his text, there is also a very suggestive citation from Hölderlin in *Existence and Being*, where Heidegger takes up the whole relation between poetry and philosophy in terms of a dialogue rather similar to the one in "Chocorua." The incomplete excerpt reads, "dwell near to one another on mountains farthest apart" (392). Paul de Man finds the dramatization of landscape in Proust performing a similar function, in *Allegories of Reading: Figural Language in Rousseau, Nietzsche, Rilke, and Proust* (New Haven, 1979), 13.

57. Rorty, *Philosophy and the Mirror of Nature*, 378.

58. Barthes, *Image-Music-Text*, 59.

The strain of antiformalism in these early verses comes to a head in verse XV. There signifieds, repeatedly undercut by signifiers ("image, / But not the person" [*CP,* 299]), problematize the basic representative structure of predication and instead privilege what the text calls the "power" of thought, that is, the force "beyond / [Men's] form." Yet as we have seen many times before, this is a power that is integral to form by "default," valorizing, therefore, the necessity or boundary man must continuously be negotiating in order to test the limits of belief in this life and his "largeness" in the life beyond. Stanza XIX reiterates the point. Potentiality's greatness lies within humanity itself, as the adventurer of "Esthétique" would argue, not in its transcendence in "more than human things" or in the expression of such things "with more / Than human voice" (*CP,* 300). "To speak humanly" and to carry on speaking humanly without the inducement to ground the process in "things" themselves are the marks of man's "acutest speech," articulation as "a discursive practice," in the current critical formulation.[59]

Chocorua's neighbor as an absent other thus becomes the guarantor for the continuation of the entire signifying, discursive process, not its metaphysical and recuperative pretermission. That continuation translates into the "moments of enlargement" in stanza X, often at the point at which simple soldiers drop in battle. The mortality of man makes successive additions to his larger Being ("Of what I am, / The cry is part" [*CP,* 298]) in an attempt to reverse the exclusionary logic of logocentric thought. As an extended figuration of First Ideas in "Notes," mortality's shadow thus continues to play out life's complicate, amassing harmony in war as well as in peace. Should a moment come, as in the concluding stanza, XXVI, when that shadowy Nothing might be secured in man's presence, it is one that cannot last. For "the companion of presences" is a "singular" largess. In the continuing conversation, he speaks a much *greater* part than any "human realizings" (*CP,* 302), from a head, in the last image, that men, once past the poem's impossible closing ellipsis, shall finally dare to put words to yet still fail ultimately to embody.

The failure to ground art and, by extension, belief in any ontologically or epistemologically privileged representation opens Stevens' discourse up, for a final time, to the semiological refiguration of the appropriately titled "Repetitions of a Young Captain." The shift from reception and perception

---

59. *E.g.,* Ernesto Laclau and Chantal Mouffe, *Hegemony and Socialist Strategy: Towards a Radical Democratic Politics* (New York, 1985), 109, 113.

(Donato's terms) to rhetorical conception, perhaps X-ception, is inaugurated in the first canto with the destruction, or at least the opening out, of a theater in an obvious allusion to Stevens' earlier "Of Modern Poetry," in which the mind, in the act of finding what will suffice, discovers "the theatre was changed / To something else" (*CP,* 239). Here, the narrator of the poem, standing in the ruins of memory and what he thought "had been real" from a writerly perspective, suddenly finds himself, under the impress of the rip of wind and war, caught "in the spectacle of a new reality" (*CP,* 306). From the readerly perspective, that is to say, from the point of view of the spectators in the theater, the change in paradigms is a gradual one. In Canto II, they sit in the theater, "in the ruin" (*CP,* 306), as if nothing had happened and are quite content to see reenacted old and familiar representations, "embracings," as they are called, from "the depths of the heart," much like an actor "gapering" the encrusted tissue of the moon, again in Stevens' imagery a sign of the totally passive imagination. It is clear, with the narrator-poet's insistent iteration of former remembrances, however, that change *has* taken place and that the continuing operation of the theater along the figurally representative lines of former times, from his viewpoint, simply will not do: "like a machine left running, and running down" (*CP,* 306). Specifically, the kind of change of which the narrator has only intimations begins to take a kind of shape in the making of several giants in Canto III. Fabricated out of a Nietzschean "calculated chaos" by millions of major men, presumably writers like the narrator, these giants come together in a being whose accoutred form is larger than the others, but it is actually the force of his ultragigantic presence, rather than any "giant sense," that accounts for his importance at this time. Translated into the representational difference of Stevens' romance of the precise, gigantic presentation more accurately becomes the force of absence, noted especially in its connection to the giant red sun and to the generative potentiality that that more active image of an unnameable First Idea (in contrast to the passively reflective moon) by now suggests in Stevens. This force of absence is consequently reworked, here, as "the make-matter, matter-nothing mind" (*CP,* 307). Its very close analogy to the nothingness of Chocorua's shadow makes clear Stevens' aims to foreground in the new theater of expression the nonoriginary "strength" of rhetorical figuration itself, whose chief value in terms of the question of belief resides in the production of truth rather than its final achievement.[60]

60. Said, *Beginnings,* 261. See also McCaffery, *North of Intention,* 14, 33, 61, 78, 111, and 148.

> This being in a reality beyond
> The finikin spectres in the memory,
>
> This elevation, in which he seems to be tall,
> Makes him rise above the houses, looking down.
> His route lies through an image in his mind:
>
> My route lies through an image in my mind,
> It is the route that milky millions find,
> An image that leaves nothing much behind.
>
> (*CP,* 307)

The vacancy of image here, which marks the differentiation of being's "elevation" as absent origin, is an uncanny truth indeed. Yet it would appear to be an insight that language always already had arranged for major men, with the mention of words in Canto IV, "desperate with a know-and-know" (*CP,* 307). Further, this insight is one that keeps being replicated generation after generation down through the ages, which accounts for the power of its repetition in "indifferent sounds." It continues, nonetheless, to draw a blank with regard to the exact source of that power, suggested by Stevens' heraldic *mise en abyme,* transplanted from *Blue Guitar,* whose "presence" ("the clear sovereign that is reality" and "the clearest reality that is sovereign") the writer will still attest to. Thus, though its forms change throughout history, the larger (non)sense of being does not. "The gigantic has a reality of its own," an "adobe of the angels" (*CP,* 308), whose ever-never-changing same is almost a power to be feared. The fear, however, is groundless. A soldier at a railway station, stepping away to investigate a vaguely familiar building that is nothing of his apparent time and place, will himself return changed in his original "form," even though the perceptions of time and place have not altered for him to any significant degree. So, too, does sovereign reality alter in ways other than the purely physical, a "giant without a body" (*CP,* 308), though its perennial rhetoricity remains a perdurable constant.

Section V explores precisely the extent to which the repetitions of sovereignty can be more clearly understood and believed, if at all, establishing what the poem describes as a "glistening reference" to what is "real," as the universe, in Stevens' hypercritical formulation, "supplements the manqué" (*CP,* 309). First, though major men can find few words within which to articulate sovereignty's meaning in comparison to the old "ensigns" of the self (roseate parent and jingling bride are the kind of representations for which the old Theater of Trope was destroyed), still, there does seem to be something grand, perhaps even cathartic, about cobbling together some kind of voluble "memorandum" of "giant sense," even if it might serve only to reveal how paltry and mundane the present world's business must appear by comparison. For Stevens' intention, in the second place, is to clarify the means by which the writer's creative empowerment, in relation to the "expanses" of sovereignty, is produced each time. It is the argument with which we began this study of *Transport to Summer,* rehearsing once again, as it does, the freedom of sovereignty's "society of the spirit" as a function of the constraining necessity of the ordinary universe, in and through which sovereignty must presence itself. Hence, Stevens' doubling of the image of the arc, glanced at earlier in "Description," whose "mid-air" version composes itself in "appropriate" relation to "a half-arc in mid-earth" (*CP,* 309). The third and final point, therefore, establishes a local and relative identity for mankind within the diacritical interval opened up between his larger and entirely unknown self-potential, unpacked in more detail in "Chocorua," and the "millions of instances" (*CP,* 309), of which the narrator-poet is one, revealed to him thus far as a matter of historical and experiential account. "The soldier seeking his point between the two" (*CP,* 309) is thus, for Stevens, a type of the Metaphysician in the Dark and, with the emphasis entirely on "seeking," a type of the eternal quester after belief as well.

In summing up this latest performance in his new Theater of Trope, Stevens recurs to his "Motive for Metaphor" composed the previous year, once again, that is, to "the exactest force" (*CP,* 310) in order to reaffirm the double dynamic of desire that continues to keep the question of belief itself in play. In the amassing co(i)mplication of "steel against intimation," or "theatre for theatre" (*CP,* 309), the continuum of presence and absence appears endless:

> The powdered personals against the giants' rage,
> Blue and its deep inversions in the moon

> Against gold whipped reddened in big-shadowed black,
> Her vague "Secrete me from reality,"
> His "That reality secrete itself,"

> The choice is made.

> > (*CP,* 309)

The wrong choice would be to opt for one side of the tension to the exclusion of the other and so to withdraw the possibility of there continuing to be the future availability of choice altogether. The more far-sighted course is to follow Canon Aspirin's lead in the last chapter and to view the choice as one "of" rather than "between." Once past the binary imperative of dualism, one must allow the present secretions to stand as they are, as the old theater is left standing, and undertake the search for new ones: "Let the rainy arcs / And pathetic magnificences dry in the sky" (*CP,* 310), as the giant orator might be overheard to say. If we are exhorted to be vigilant in the final section of the poem at all, it is surely a chariness we need to exercise concerning the making of choices themselves rather than the willingness to rule with, or be ruled by, any one of them. Moreover, in Stevens' most telling phrase, it is the "precisions of fate" that will make the difference for us—the precisions of a new romance of the precise that will fob nothing off but instead avail us of the multipliticities of Again, the bloodless repetitions of a young captain, for instance, through its foregrounding the "civil nakedness" (*CP,* 310), the blank otherness, signal to the estrangements of "a beau language" given in the final line.

By the end of *Transport to Summer,* therefore, the choices concerning the question of belief become the ones we are empowered to make through the inscription of words. Like Stevens, "we must henceforth ask ourselves what language must be in order to structure . . . what is nevertheless not in itself either word or discourse, and in order to articulate itself on [*sic*] the pure forms of knowledge."[61] In the next chapter, our study of Stevens' two great companion poems will carry us further along in understanding what language, particularly in its imbrication with belief, must be. For now, we are given to reflect on the sheer transport of language itself and in the many occasions of its enlargement reflect on the belief in the possibility that its ever-never-changefulness can be interpreted "as enjoyment of [both] productive and destructive force," in Nietzsche's words, and hence as a "*continual creation*" (*WP,* 1049).

61. Foucault, *The Order of Things,* 382.

CHAPTER 6

VELOCITIES OF CHANGE
Nothing Exceeds like Excess

Solidarity has to be constructed out of little pieces, rather than found already waiting, in the form of an ur-language which all of us recognize when we hear it.
—Richard Rorty, *Contingency, Irony, and Solidarity*

It seems to me an interesting idea: that is to say, the idea that we live in the description of a place and not in the place itself, and in every vital sense we do.
—*The Letters of Wallace Stevens*

[One] does not believe in the disaster. One cannot believe in it, whether one lives or dies. Commensurate with it there is no faith, and at the same time a sort of disinterest, detached from the disaster. Night; white, sleepless night— such is the disaster: the night lacking darkness, but brightened by no light.
—Maurice Blanchot, *The Writing of the Disaster*

ONE of the most curious aspects of Wallace Stevens' longer "Credences of Summer" is the way the poet has chosen to position the text in the fifth book of his *Collected Poems*. Titularly the poem is a rousing invocation to belief celebrated in credences' plural, but upon closer inspection its affirmations become slightly unhinged when we notice that "Notes Toward a Supreme Fiction" is the poem Stevens elected to close out that book. By installing a gaping whole (notes *toward* some nontruth) where we might have expected a sum of the parts to have been lodged, Stevens not only problematizes severely the transcendence promised in the volume's title, *Transport to Summer,* but undercuts even further the orthodox season naturally subtending those credences, turning belief itself into somewhat of a paradox. What is at stake in the whole process of ironization in this and in Stevens' final work, as the present chapter will only begin to suggest, is a radical reconceptualization of language in the transport of belief, a reformulation subsumed under the "gaiety of language" in Stevens' Nietzschean version of it from 1944, as we

224

examined it in the last chapter. One consequently is inclined to think that the work of Stevens' *Transport,* singularly foregrounded by "Credences of Summer," is intended to be honored more in the breach than the observance, in Shakespeare's phrase, which helps to explain the poem's position as anticlimax, two brief lyrics shy of the supremely ironic "Notes." Thus, Helen Vendler's ascriptions of "detachment" and lost "serenity" and Harold Bloom's of "irony or discontinuous allegorical movement" quite accurately portray a much darker text than its light-hearted pastoralism in the season of summer might initially tend to warrant.[1] Moreover, explaining the "Credences of Summer" in a volume strenuously championing "Description *without* Place" (*CP,* 339, emphasis added) would perhaps be most ironic, if it were not for the placement of the companion text, "The Auroras of Autumn," which Stevens chose to open and title his final single volume of verse, published in 1950. Some important critical leverage might in the end be gained on the poet's later work, and on the role he conceives the gaiety of language to be enacting within it, by our pursuing here the curious relation between Stevens' companion poems, which were actually composed within a year of each other, in 1946 and 1947, and specifically by our addressing the thematization of an excessively ironical argument in play between them.

That Stevens' later poetry should more and more privilege an ironic enunciation rather than any of the other rhetorical wagers established in Kenneth Burke's famous tetrad of master tropes, including (additionally) metaphor, metonymy, and synecdoche, ought not to surprise us in the later phases of the poet's work past *Parts of a World.* After all, as Donna Haraway has recently observed, "irony is about contradictions that do not resolve into larger wholes, even dialectically, about the tension of holding incompatible things together because both or all are necessary and true." As we recall Stevens' argument from 1938, "In the sum of the parts, there are only the parts" (*CP,* 204). Now the specific rhetorical negotiation between parts and wholes, the Aristotelian *epiphora* of transport that Paul Ricoeur refers to as the "transaction between contexts," we can readily see fading into the background in Stevens' writing prior to *Parts.* Perhaps we see this even more readily following Hayden White in the *Tropics of Discourse,* since metaphor, which establishes meaning in terms of "equivalence or identity," and the secondary forms of metonymy (whole to part) and of synecdoche (part to whole) are, respectively, the rhetorics of immanence and of transcendence in *Harmonium* and *Ideas of Order.* Viewed diachronically, rather than synchronically, metaphori-

---

1. Vendler, *On Extended Wings,* 235–36; Bloom, *Poems of Our Climate,* 245.

cal identity leaves us, similarly, with the rhetorical closure of a "cycle" of conventional romance, as Stevens saw it early on (*e.g., CP,* 120), when the two books are fitted structurally together.

Gradually, however, as a new romance of the precise, outlined by Stevens in 1946 (*CP,* 353), begins to overtake the elisions of the tired structural one, starting with *The Man with the Blue Guitar* and working its way slowly toward a more riddling authentication in Stevens' "Notes Toward a Supreme Fiction" by way of much of the verbal experimentation in *Parts of a World,* nothing less than the problematic rhetorical strategy of irony will suit Stevens' project. For once the thematization of romance, the enigmatic "ever-never-changing same" (*CP,* 353), shifts from a literal quest to a rhetorical quest(ion) past the "Notes," what is signal to the deregulation of former expressive protocols, in White's words once again, is "a kind of attitude towards knowledge itself which is implicitly critical of all *forms* of metaphorical identification, reduction, or integration of phenomena . . . underlying and sanctioning skepticism as an explanatory tactic . . . and either agnosticism or cynicism as a moral posture."[2] Scepticism, agnosticism, and cynicism, in this decidedly new poststructural context in which we may finally be invited to take up Stevens' last work, all suggest a further ironization for his "Credences of Summer." As the quest for faith, like Stevens' new romance, itself becomes the question of belief, "belief, beyond belief" as Stevens puts it in "Flyer's Fall" (*CP,* 336), we perhaps also begin to see his new discourse forming a significant intersection with the postdoctrinal agenda of contemporary a/the-

---

2. Kenneth Burke, *A Grammar of Motives* (Berkeley, 1969); Donna Haraway, "A Manifesto for Cyborgs: Science, Technology, and Socialist Feminism in the 1980s," in *Coming to Terms: Feminism, Theory, Politics,* ed. Elizabeth Weed (New York, 1989), 173; Paul Ricoeur, *The Rule of Metaphor: Multi-Disciplinary Studies of the Creation of Meaning in Language,* trans. Robert Czerny, Kathleen McLaughlin, and John Costello (Toronto, 1977), 80, 17–18; Hayden White, *Tropics of Discourse: Essays in Cultural Criticism* (Baltimore, 1978), 72–73, 73–74. White's analysis of the rhetorical direction of his models of similarity and difference followed here would appear to square with Ricoeur's assessment of the "movement 'from . . . to'" or "deviation" of metaphor as a global "trope of resemblance" referred to previously. See also Ricoeur, *The Rule of Metaphor,* 12, 24. The whole problem of metaphorical identification foregrounded here is likewise the focus of Peter Carafiol's extraordinary new reading of Transcendentalism in the context of American literary scholarship, in his *The American Ideal: Literary History as a Worldly Activity* (New York, 1991), esp. Chap. 3, "Between Metaphor and Metaphysics: Reading Emerson as 'Onward Thinking.'" As with the trials of belief of Wallace Stevens remapped in this study, "Emerson first takes part in and then transcends the debate between realism and idealism that has dominated American literary scholarship . . . [so that] we can see his prose as participating in the composition of an alternative philosophy, or better perhaps, an alternative *to* metaphysical philosophy with important implications for literary history" (100–101). See also 139, 142, 145, 151, 167, 190n13, 191n16, 196n42, and *passim.*

ology. For it is the program of current a/theological discourse to question all determinate or theocentric *forms* of faith, a point to which we shall return later on in this chapter.

We might first want to begin to understand that "Credences of Summer," as the honorific text of Stevens' fifth book of collected verse, ironizes its conclusion in the way that all metaphorical transport more generally is inclined to be ironized, by the modality of speech that turns every form of belief into its own self-criticism. Hence, the poem devolves to "Auroras" hard by in the *Collected Poems,* expressing a relationship between the two texts in terms of a "suspensive irony." The term is Alan Wilde's and describes a relation that invites the "willingness to live with uncertainty, to tolerate and, in some cases, to welcome a world seen as random and multiple, even, at times, absurd."[3] Such a relation is accurate, as far as it goes, from the point of view of irony's tropological wager. In its privileging of irony alone, however, it significantly misrepresents the role of metaphor that Stevens is insistent on reformulating in his later work and about which the poet would continue to theorize nearly to his last composition.

In the important essay "Three Academic Pieces," for instance, completed in 1947 at the time he was at work on the companion poems, Stevens is quite in accord with Burke on "a gradus ad Metaphoram" of tropological expressiveness; his terms are White's modal radicals of "emplotment": comic, tragic, tragic-comic (ironic?), etc. Stevens also agrees with Burke that metaphor, in its conventional and restricted economic sense, tends toward some ultimate form of meaning expressive of equivalence or "identity" (*NA,* 81, 71– 72). Recognizing the contradiction at the very heart of what Ricoeur would term the substitution theory of metaphor, by which the successive interchanges within the ever-increasing transport of verbal meaning to some terminus of totalizing identity would find metaphor doing away with itself entirely, Stevens would prefer not to suspend the operation of metaphor altogether but to refigure it, to open it out to a more general economy.[4] He calls this more elliptical economy "resemblance," and divorcing it from a process of mere mechanical imitation integral with the repetitions of figural iden-

3. Alan Wilde, *Horizons of Assent: Modernism, Postmodernism, and the Ironic Imagination* (Philadelphia, 1987), 44–48.

4. Ricoeur, *The Rule of Metaphor,* 66. Thus, Steve McCaffery is led to conclude: "[The] reduction of difference to identity is never an absolute moment in metaphor; there is always another constitution that threatens presence, an operation of metaphor not as trope but as locus for the contestation of difference. In effect, there is always the threat of substitution going astray in the substitutional passage, of the movement elsewhere towards the appropriation of the otherness[,] collapsing and actually engendering a heterogeneity" (*North of Intention,* 205).

tification ("We are not dealing with identity . . . [for] identity is the vanishing-point of resemblance," he states emphatically [*NA*, 72]), Stevens connects resemblance to the activity of incessant creation to be found in nature, whose own prodigies of "metamorphosis" serve as an analogue to the "activity of the imagination . . . the imagination [that] is life" (*NA*, 73). Resemblance, therefore, gives us a take on metaphor in its productive rather than its reductive sense. Stevens, recurring to a central term we may also recall from "Description without Place," refers to this resemblance as "intensification," that is, "a sense of reality keen enough to be in excess of the normal sense of reality," just as the intermediacy of metamorphosis could be said to exceed the immediacy of identity.

From a strictly interpretive point of view, moreover, an interactive and genetic intermediacy theory of metaphor, in contrast to a substitutive and nominal immediacy theory, represents a boon to the reader. As Ricoeur again notes, it "lays the foundation for the possibility of paraphrasing a metaphor by means of other words," in just the way that Stevens' own conception of resemblance, as opposed to identity, might prescribe. Ricoeur writes:

> The difference between trivial metaphor and poetic metaphor is not that one can be paraphrased and the other not, but that the paraphrase of the latter is without end. It is endless precisely because it can always spring back to life. . . . [Furthermore] this role cannot come to light unless one turns away from the alliance between resemblance and substitution . . . towards a functioning that is inseparable from the instance of discourse constitutive of the sentence . . . [for] if it serves some purpose in metaphor, resemblance must be a characteristic of the attribution of predicates and not of the substitution of names.

Later in *The Rule of the Metaphor*, Ricoeur makes his case for the "properly predicative or attributive" as opposed to the "substitutive essence" of metaphor thoroughly poststructural by using resemblance exactly as Stevens describes it, to break apart the bipolar metaphoric/metonymic symmetry in the linguistic analysis of Roman Jakobson: "Metaphor—unusual attribution—is a semantic process, in the sense of Emile Benveniste, perhaps even the *genetic* phenomenon *par excellence* in the realm of the instance of discourse."[5] In much the same way, Stevens' earlier metaphoric/metonymic romance cycle is transcended. "It is not too extravagant," therefore, Stevens concludes the

5. Ricoeur, *The Rule of Metaphor*, 188, 194, 198.

prose portion of "Three Academic Pieces," "to think of resemblances and of the repetitions of resemblances as *a source* of the ideal" (*NA*, 81, emphasis added).

It follows that this notion of resemblance, particularly in its ascription as a generative source of repetition, becomes another of Stevens' motives for metaphor from his middle and late periods and thus takes its place right alongside terms such as *intensity,* just mentioned, and others like *intimation* and *style* (*CP*, 288, 345) in several of metaphor's "moments of enlargement" (*CP*, 298). Even further, resemblance, in the fecundating sense of attributive predication, also compels us to revise the sense of irony supervening the relations between Stevens' later texts, helping us to break it out of its own somewhat restrictive economy of suspensive qualification and a skeptical, or perhaps even cynical, engagement in the theories of Wilde and White, rehearsed earlier. Correspondingly, resemblance of an interactive and intermediating kind sensitizes us to a more boldly self-assertive form of ironism, which Rorty has lately been pleased to find, in a rather Stevensian mood, resulting from "awareness of the power of redescription." This redescription, in the constant search for a better and better vocabulary with which to articulate "existing webs of belief and desire," comes more and more to be "dominated by metaphors of making rather than finding, of diversification and novelty rather than convergence to the antecedently present" or, in Stevens' own terms, dominated by the repetitions of resemblance rather than by the representations of identity. Thus, the relation of "Credences of Summer" to the larger text of *Transport to Summer,* and beyond that to *The Auroras of Autumn,* which comes to take their place, boils down once again to an act of choice between competing vocabularies that resemblance, "simply by playing the new off against the old," empowers the poet, as the ironical Metaphysician in the Dark (*CP*, 240), *to make,* according to Rorty: "I call people of this sort 'ironists' because their realization that anything can be made to look good or bad by being redescribed, and their renunciation of the attempt to formulate criteria of choice between final vocabularies, puts them in the position which Sartre called 'meta-stable': never quite able to take themselves seriously because always aware that the terms in which they describe themselves are subject to change, always aware of the contingency and fragility of their final vocabularies, and thus of their selves."[6] In a phrase later to be unpacked in "The Auroras of Autumn," Stevens might refer to the contin-

6. Richard Rorty, *Contingency, Irony, and Solidarity* (New York, 1989), 89, 84, 77, 73, 73–74. Carafiol, *The American Ideal,* elaborates a similar Rortyean argument for Transcendentalism (120, 135, 137, and 146).

gency of the ironist's descriptions here as the "velocities of change" (*CP,* 414), for only "the incredible" that underwrites such contingency in a final ironization of credence ("the truth . . . not the respect of one, / But always of many things") gives the Metaphysician in the Dark "a purpose to believe" (*NA,* 85).

Although "Credences of Summer" is open to an ironic interpretation only by this late stage in Wallace Stevens' linguistic project, assuredly the force of the ironic articulation rather than its rhetorical form is what is of real interest to us. Only irony conceived in this doubly ironic way can explain its own tolerance for "metaphors of making rather than finding," that is, for a differentiating resemblance in contrast to an identifying substitution. In contrast to form as well, there is no universal, generalizable truth against which to measure the experience of this articulation. There is available to us only the force of yet another articulation, such as we shall later encounter in the text of "The Auroras of Autumn," composed soon after "Credences," and then a subsequent articulation after that, and so forth, so that "we should never think that the regress of interpretation can be stopped once and for all, but rather realize that there may always be a vocabulary, a set of descriptions, around the corner which will throw everything into question once again."[7] Thus, when credence is opened out from the objects of belief to the questions of event in this way, "one poem proves another and the whole," as Stevens will later remark in "A Primitive like an Orb" (*CP,* 441).

Long before he reaches "The Auroras of Autumn," however, Stevens as master ironist is already testing the articulative limits of "Credences" by playing its new vocabulary off against a very much older one in the precedent mythos of the *locus amoenus*. In this regard, he is rather remarkably like Roland Barthes in Barthes' own later writing, "tracing paths from received opinion to what he calls *utopias of language,* whose description shows both what it is desirable to change within the status quo and what reconceptions are possible." What precisely, in Stevens' own "utopia of language," is the relation between the status quo and the requirement for redescription of the ironist bent on the velocity for change? David Evett, following closely the landmark studies of Ernst R. Curtius, Stanley Stewart, and A. Bartlett Giamatti among others, summarizes the chief features of the *topos* as it is handled in the classical texts of Theocritus, Virgil, and the Song of Songs

7. Richard Rorty, *Consequences of Pragmatism: Essays, 1972–1980* (Minneapolis, 1982), xlvii*n*52.

and, later, by writers such as Edmund Spenser and Andrew Marvell. Evett writes:

> The *locus amoenus* is comprised of three essential elements: trees, grass, and water. It is a landscape of the mind, an aid to conceptualization, imitated from books, not life, and if it is based on a real place, that place assumes an extraordinary dimension. The *topos* as such has a structural function, which is synchronous, not diachronous; it operates as a single homogeneous rhetorical member. But in the course of historical development it comes to have certain traditional expressive capabilities as well, to connote any or all of the categories of refection, numinous creativity or generation, and eroticism. . . . [Most important] Within the *locus* the lover loves but does not kiss; the weary shepherd rests; the pastoral melancholiac is enabled to reflect on the mutability of all things precisely because the *topos* is, both intrinsically and rhetorically, a refuge from time, a node in a line.[8]

On the most superficial interpretive level, Stevens' "Credences" plays out most of the archetypal features of the *locus amoenus* presented in Evett's model. In the opening canto, time has reached the apogee of midsummer, the high point between the infuriations of spring and the first, brisk inhalations of autumn. Accordingly, the initial thematics of the text fall heavily on growth and fecundity (soft grass, heavy roses, young broods), on peace and leisure as "the mind lays by its trouble," and, most important of all, on the translation of the *locus* to the changeless and perdurable: "The last day of a certain year / Beyond which there is nothing left of time" (*CP,* 372). Within this scope of timeless transport, imagination is totalized and self-presence realized in the image of the hieratic family circle:

> There is nothing more inscribed nor thought nor felt
> And this must comfort the heart's core against
> Its false disasters—these fathers standing round,
> These mothers touching, speaking, being near,
> These lovers waiting in the soft dry grass.
>
> (*CP,* 372)

8. Mary Bittner Wiseman, "Rewriting the Self: Barthes and the Utopias of Language," in *Literature and the Question of Philosophy,* ed. Cascardi, 295; David Evett, "'Paradice's Only

In Canto III the complete refuge from time is figured as "green's green apogee" and symbolized by a natural tower reminiscent of the tree (identified with the cross) in the Song of Songs, and Virgil's tall tower constructed in a marsh, according to his *Eclogues*. As a total point of survey ("Axis of everything") the tower, located itself atop a final mountain, contracts all sense experience into that which can be seen. Even the visionary eye seems supererogatory in this pastoral retreat, though, for the old man standing atop the tower "reads no book" (*CP*, 374). Such "things certain sustaining us in certainty" (*CP*, 375)—an absolute certainty the pursuit of which Vincent Descombes characterizes as the inaugural of modern philosophy—Stevens heralds as the end to all thought, with the achievement of the "huge decorum" in the "completed scene" of the *locus amoenus* at the final canto (*CP*, 378).[9]

Or does he? With this scenic insinuation of the Theater of Trope brought forward from the "Notes" (*CP*, 397) and further elaborated in Canto X by the personae of summer as "characters" playing roles and speaking parts in the *locus*, Stevens subtly begins to alter the entire nature of the *topos*, calling attention more to the factitious, as opposed to the factual, provenance of its structural design. With this alteration in the final canto, for instance, we notice a radical shift in the time sense of the poem; one becomes free only "for a moment," instead of being removed eternally from "malice and sudden cry" (*CP*, 378). With this elongation of the poem's temporal sense, there also occurs a broadening and more textured presentation of narrative materials: the pastoral's characters are mottled, "half pales of red, / Half pales of green." "Knotted, sashed, and seamed" in this way, they fit into summer's own "mottled mood" rather as parts than as continuous and completed wholes. They thus come to challenge the synchronous and homogeneous rhetoricity of the transcendent function of the *locus*, tending to side more with their "inhuman author," who is somewhat absurdly given to meditate their speeches "late at night" even though he cannot hear them, much less see them. Hence, the green's green apogee earlier marking a final recognition and universalization of the real, in the end, curiously becomes transformed into "the apogee of non-meaning," in Descombes' strikingly similar phrase: "For there is nothing left to be done (therefore all action is absurd), nor anything left to be said

Map': The 'Topos' of the 'Locus Amoenus' and the Structure of Marvell's 'Upon Appleton House,'" *PMLA*, LXXXV (May, 1970), 507a, 511b.

9. Vincent Descombes, *Modern French Philosophy*, trans. L. Scott-Fox and J. M. Harding (New York, 1980), 1.

(therefore all speech is insignificant)." That we do require a text like "Credences" to say all of this merely goes to prove, ironically, as Jacques Derrida writes, that "there is no assured destination precisely because of the mark and the proper name: in other words, because of this insignificance."[10] At such a pass, with the pastoral *topos* underwriting "Credences," like so many of the preceding texts sub-scribing to the transport of summer ("Red Fern," "Holiday in Reality," "Late Hymn from the Myrrh-Mountain"), pastoralism itself, then, would appear also to have entered into the ironization of belief.

Suddenly, other questions begin to creep out from the darkened corners of the present poem's disarticulations. Can the female presence, in Canto V, for example, who makes all her compeers in this pastoral retreat "look down," can she possibly sustain, to borrow Evett's terminology once again, the "intrinsic propriety" of the *topos* as an "emblem of rest, relaxation, [and] retirement" and "a vessel for essentially religious feelings"? Is the queen, the canto asks, as "humble as she seems to be?" (*CP*, 374). And if her charitable majesty seems questionable, can the "bristling soldier" who acts as consort actually come to represent the race of men through the sheer strength of "heroic power" alone in such a leisured setting? As such questions as these begin to mount, however, the reader is invited to consider, at a more complex level of interpretation, whether the sources of creativity and generation of the *locus amoenus* itself are at all as numinous as they are given out to be or whether they too might not also have their apparently seamless provenance in more contingent acts of will and spontaneous displays of expression. How does any object or so-called real thing, "fully made, fully apparent, fully found," as Canto VII describes it (*CP*, 376), come to be formed or represented in an act of human perception *except* through the articulation of a will to power? As the canto goes on to reveal, in desiring to presence any object in order to close the gap between ego and other and to eliminate the prolongations of desire entirely in the "capture" of meaning, the "concentered self" time and again reenacts a triple gesture of power over the object (captivation, subjugation, and proclamation) in order that it may be brought within the purview of the mind's "savage scrutiny" (*CP*, 376). Stevens' point here is precisely the point Barthes makes: "To speak, and, with even greater reason, to utter a discourse is not, as is too often repeated, to communicate; it is to *subjugate*: the whole language is a generalized *rection*." Or, as Foucault would say,

10. *Ibid.*, 112; Jacques Derrida, "My Chances/Mes Chances: A Rendezvous with Some Epicurean Stereophonies," in *Taking Chances: Derrida, Psychoanalysis, and Literature*, ed. William Kerrigan and Joseph H. Smith (Baltimore, 1984), 39.

"knowledge follows the advances of power."[11] Every language game, consequently, is a verbal power play. Either selves avert objects or are themselves
averted in the ancient cycle of desire. In either case, meaning is never an ideal
of equivalence but instead an effect of resemblance, what Stevens had alluded
to in "Esthétique du Mal" as the in-bar and ex-bar of transparent representation (*CP*, 317). So no matter how far into the woods we choose to sing our
songs in order to feel secure in face of their objects, according to the present
text, the songs must always remain "unreal" (*CP*, 376) or, at any rate, must
compel us to problematize "the entire notion of reference . . . [and its] traditional realist transparency," what Iain Chambers calls "the horrifying void
of the ultimate referent."[12]

In Canto VIII, therefore, when the trumpet of morning blows through
the sky, it heralds a quite different apocalypse than the one scanned back in
Canto VI. Proclaiming neither the visible's "sharp, illustrious scene" nor the
"more than visible," by which logic even the *locus amoenus* itself should be
done away with, the trumpet signals what has made *both* possible, as the
canto states (*CP*, 376). It proclaims both through the sheer might of its "re-
sounding cry," making plain in sight and memory the powers at stake as the
different "stratagems / Of the spirit," what Derrida perhaps might call the
"protocols of reading," compete for expressive dominance.[13] The trumpet
also supposes, though, that there exists a similar "di[-]vision" of expressive
protocols in the human mind, for this, after all, is "*diction's way*" (*CP*, 377,
emphasis added). Aware of its inherent power of resemblance in this fashion,
the mind's own "cry as clarion" is less likely now to fixate on the credence of
the singular personage: the queen or her consort in Canto V, the encircled
king in Canto VI, or even the "thrice concentred self" in Canto VII. Hearing
in that re-sounding cry the din of "ten thousand tumblers tumbling down"
in Canto VIII (*CP*, 376), the mind is more prone to conceive of the personage
"in a multitude," persuaded now by the generative difference that allows it to
grow "venerable in the unreal" (*CP*, 377), rather than atrophy metaphysically
in the real (or I/deal).

This generative power, so the argument continues in Canto IX, is what

11. Evett, "'Paradice's Only Map,'" 511b, 506a; Roland Barthes, "Inaugural Lecture, Col-
lège de France," in *A Barthes Reader*, ed. Sontag, 460, emphasis on "subjugate" added; Michel
Foucault, *Discipline and Punish: The Birth of the Prison*, trans. Alan Sheridan (New York, 1977),
204. See also Sam Weber, *Institution and Interpretation* (Minneapolis, 1987), 9, 17.

12. Hutcheon, *A Poetics of Postmodernism*, 229; Iain Chambers, *Border Dialogues: Journeys
in Postmodernity* (New York, 1990), 10.

13. Derrida, *Margins of Philosophy*, 246, but see also Derrida, *Writing and Difference*, 276,
along with Weber, *Institution and Interpretation*, 45.

has made it possible for a "complex of emotions" (*CP,* 377) such as the soft and civil *locus amoenus* to come into being. But the power will also cause this complex to fall apart, as another "complex of other emotions" that may not be quite "so soft, so civil" ("The Auroras of Autumn," as we shall see momentarily) comes to take its place. Already, "the gardener's cat is dead, the gardener gone / And last year's garden grows salacious weeds" (*CP,* 377), so that even as suave bush and polished beast continue to be regnant, the velocities of change have always already contrived for a new stratagem of the spirit to take their place and hence open the instrumentality of the pastoral form to question. This speed of a becoming, what the canto refers to as "the spirit of the arranged" and "the fund of life and death" (*CP,* 377), is imaged aurally, once again, in the sound made by a cock robin. It is likely the bird's song "is not part of the listener's own sense" mainly because the credences of summer, conventionally visioned in the pastoral *topos,* are still hung up on metaphysical being. However, just as the civil bird's bean pole comes to replace the natural tower and final mountain previously, so even the *mythos* of summer, as "a hindrance, a stumbling-block, a point of resistance and a starting point for an *opposing strategy*" in Foucault's words, must yield both to what Rorty aptly terms "the ironist's ability to exploit the possibilities of massive description" and to the "requests for concrete alternatives and programs," to poetical asseveration held open to a "historically conditioned vocabulary," in other words.[14]

Stevens' distribution rather than substitution of emotional complexes or verbal assemblages in this canto (*"douceurs, / Tristesses"* [*CP,* 377] in an especially telling phrase) makes the point precisely. Distribution of discursive forces is the sense given by Foucault. In Stevens' discourse, we might say that distribution is to resemblance as substitution is to representation, the difference lying between the velocity of becoming and the stability of being. On the notion of velocity, Deleuze and Parnet observe: "This question of speed is important and also very complex. It doesn't mean the first in the race: you can be late through speed. It doesn't mean changing either: you can be invariable and constant through speed. Speed is to be caught in a becoming—which is not a development or an evolution. . . . What you misnamed style just now—charm or style—is speed." Accordingly, the present interpretation privileges the velocity in change, rather than the thematization of change itself as a demonstrable effect, what Stevens himself had intended by the

---

14. Michel Foucault, *The History of Sexuality, Volume I: An Introduction,* trans. Robert Hurley (New York, 1980), 101; Rorty, *Contingency, Irony, and Solidarity,* 78, 87, 88.

words *manner* and *style* already alluded to in "Description without Place" (*CP,* 340, 345). His distributed emotional complexes in "Credences of Summer," then, become the plurivalent credences of the poem's title, whose availability angles less for the sanctioning of single options than for our freedom to choose among those options themselves, as time, place, and circumstance warrant. The freedom to choose becomes a fully realized possibility only once we are past its repression in the poem's early cantos; most especially it is a possibility at the poem's close, when their manner and mood finally turn mottled, and summer finally turns (w)hole (*CP,* 378). Thus, in the same vein, Roland Barthes writes in his "Inaugural Lecture" that "the forces of freedom which are in literature depend not on the writer's civil person, nor on his political commitment—for he is, after all, only a man among others—nor do they even depend on the doctrinal content of his work, but rather on the labor of displacement he brings to bear upon the language," a view echoed in Stevens' exhortation to his own "civil bird" concerning diction's way.[15]

Perhaps the greatest repression of discursive options occurs in Canto II:

> Postpone the anatomy of summer, as
> The physical pine, the metaphysical pine.
> Let's see the very thing and nothing else.
> Let's see it with the hottest fire of sight.
> Burn everything not part of it to ash.
>
> Trace the gold sun about the whitened sky
> Without evasion by a single metaphor.
> Look at it in its essential barrenness
> And say this, this is the centre that I seek.
>
> (*CP,* 373)

The poem's quite militant intention to do away with the annoying evasions of metaphor in order to get at the essential meaning represented by the *locus,* to fix it, as the canto goes on to say, in "an eternal foliage," and an "arrested peace," ought to strike the reader as extraordinarily contradictory in a poem about the *douceurs* of summer. Such an excessively violent reaction given out by all the imperatives (postpone, burn, trace, look, and so forth) might seem to be antithetical to the pastoral ethos until we realize that Stevens' text is not really about the pastoral at all. It is about the reality of pastoral, "the very

---

15. Foucault, *The History of Sexuality,* 100–101; Deleuze and Parnet, *Dialogues,* 32; Barthes, *A Barthes Reader,* 462.

thing" in the above passage, and how such verbal orders, as expressions of human desire, come to be constructed.[16] From this perspective, such a severe reaction would be quite in order since reality, as Bruno Latour has pointed out in a related context, is cognate with the Latin word *res:* that which resists. What does it resist? Latour answers: "*Trials of strength.* If in a given situation, no dissenter is able to modify the shape of a new object, then that's it, it *is* reality, at least for as long as the trials of strength are not modified."[17] What is interesting (dare I say ironic?) about the trials of strength in the above citation is that the barrenness demanded for the fertile thing, in a place of permanence that would exile desire completely, can itself turn out only to be *another* reality, either physical or metaphysical, that is, *another* evasion by metaphor in a whole movable host of metaphors, to recur to Nietzsche's well-traveled phrase. The real barrenness, then, turns out perhaps to be the "right ignorance" (*CP*, 373) that thinks such permanence can be essentialized. If there is any right ignorance to be believed, however, it is more likely to be one that might unknowingly give credence to the perennial fertility of the thing and to how variously the meaning of the thing might be constructed, a Heideggerian argument that Stevens pursues more rigorously in "Man Carrying Thing" from the same year (*CP*, 350). For it is that kind of right ignorance that can continue to imagine that a "change [were] still possible" (*CP*, 373).

The hope, nonetheless, is exceedingly precarious. For once persuaded of uncertain origins, a foundationalist predisposition is just as likely to balk at indeterminate ends, "the distant" in Canto IV of "Credences of Summer," for whose enigmas the clairvoyant eye evinces such a low tolerance (*CP*, 374). This was Marvell's breaking point in his own ironization of the pastoral *locus*. Having allowed himself in "Upon Appleton House" to indulge the *topos* with the "intellectual analysis," as Evett observes, "of mind celebrating its own power, of domination and distance, of art" (all of Stevens' own privileged terms we should note), Marvell capitulates to an attitude "of stasis, of acquiescence, of awe, of worship" appropriate to the ultimate truth to which he thinks his wrestling with a burdensome convention has led him when "the *topos* finally succeeds in reasserting its rhetorical and mythic totality."[18] Stevens' argument for metaphorical resemblance would push his discourse

16. See esp. Louis Montrose, "'Eliza, Queen of Shepheardes,' and the Pastoral of Power," *ELR,* X (1980), 153–82.

17. Bruno Latour, *Science in Action: How to Follow Scientists and Engineers Through Society* (Cambridge, Mass., 1987), 93.

18. Evett, "'Paradice's Only Map,'" 512a, 513a.

further, acknowledging that such mythic totalization is but "one of the limits of reality" (*CP,* 374). Still, the leap from the clairvoyant eye to the "mingling of colors at a festival" in a language without words is likely to leave the expectant reader rather dumbfounded by all those pastoral vistas piled in the mows and hived in the trees of Oley as the poem concludes. At such a point it must have struck Stevens that even his credences might stop ("The utmost must be good and is . . . our fortune" [*CP,* 374]) unless there could be something doubly ironic in his later work, like "The Auroras of Autumn," say, to set them going again.

"*Form* fascinates when one no longer has the force to understand force from within itself," the force, "that is, to create," Derrida has written.[19] There is not likely a better insight into the opening and closing of the structuralist phases of Stevens' early writing, recycling as it does the conventional tropologies of the high modernist era. With the onset of *The Man with the Blue Guitar* and *Parts of a World* especially, one tends more and more to sense in his work certain counterformalist tendencies: the need to focus more and more of his attention on the power or the force of poetic expression in the arguably poststructural phases of his middle and late period, the revolving of which, in the context of belief in particular, could continue to nourish the wellsprings of creativity obviously denied him along more foundationalist channels. The relation between "Credences of Summer" and "The Auroras of Autumn" is of more than passing interest to us in the latter phase of Wallace Stevens' career perhaps because it recapitulates an impossible tension that the poet would never quite be able to leave behind him. From the perspective of belief in particular, one has to appreciate the considerable gamble Stevens has taken in devoting such inordinate attention in "Credences" to a literary form so antithetical to what today, by postmodern standards, are fairly routine a/theological considerations having to do with the contextualizing, relativizing, and localizing of faith, which, given his sense of irony, were undeniably of far greater interest to him.

Early and late readings of "Credences" that tend to honor it in terms of Stevens' "shift inward to the full activity of a contemplative life," as in Joseph Riddel, and his celebration of some form of "the Romantic sublime," as in Joseph Carroll, perhaps best attest to the risks he took and, for this reason, ought not to be gainsaid. They loom enticingly in the background of any ironist project, as the example of Marvell earlier has shown. For the ironist,

19. Derrida, *Writing and Difference,* 4–5.

as Rorty remarks, "is continually tempted to try for sublimity, not just beauty." He explains further: "That is why he is continually tempted to relapse into metaphysics, to try for one big hidden reality rather than for a pattern among appearances. . . . To try for the sublime is to try to make a pattern out of the entire realm of *possibility*, not just of some little, contingent, actualities. . . . Whereas Plato and Kant had prudently taken this sublimity outside of time altogether, Nietzsche and Heidegger cannot use this dodge. They have to stay in time, but to view themselves as separated from all the rest of time by a decisive event." In Stevens' case, one is given to more than a little speculation concerning whether the writing of yet another longer poem in the seasons of belief so shortly after "Credences" ("The Auroras of Autumn" was first published in the winter, 1948, number of the *Kenyon Review*) may not represent just such a decisive event in the poet's own efforts to counter, to a degree, some of the subliminal seductiveness of an argument not carried far enough. To a significant extent, certain features of the pastoralism of "Credences" represent a metaphysical tradition that had obliterated any hope for the renewal of faith laid to rest by Stevens more than thirty years earlier in a poem like "Sunday Morning." In a postmetaphysical age, therefore, one does not angle for the larger reality and the permanent possibility, it is true. Neither does one merely "manipulate outworn things," however, as Emmanuel Levinas has remarked in a related, Heideggerian context. Rather, "one brings back the unthought to thought and saying." From Stevens' perspective, and certainly from the point of view of what passes for received opinion as well, "Credences" may not have been weighted enough by what is *unthought* in the tradition to keep the question of belief in play. If the earlier poem had spoken from the height of human things, then "The Auroras of Autumn" would respond dialectically with acutest speech but this time "from the depth" (*CP*, 300).[20]

We begin, therefore, not at the beginning of "Auroras" but in Canto III, where Stevens expresses most strenuously the desire to give thought over to the unthought and to speak from the depths of credence. As in much of his early work, particularly *Harmonium*, conventional belief in this section is sequestered in a Jamesean house of fiction, partly visible in the evening light. One of Derrida's citations from Hegel in "White Mythology" captures Stevens' mood and imagery precisely here: "By the close of day, man has erected a building constructed from his own inner Sun; and when in the evening he

20. Riddel, *The Clairvoyant Eye*, 222; Joseph Carroll, *A New Romanticism*, 197; Rorty, *Contingency, Irony, and Solidarity*, 105–106; Levinas, *Ethics and Infinity*, 44.

contemplates this, he esteems it more highly than the original external Sun. For now he stands in a *conscious relation* to his Spirit, and therefore a *free* relation. If we hold this image fast in mind, we shall find it symbolizing the course of History, the great Day's work of Spirit." Stevens chooses the image of a mother's face to particularize the relation to transcendence, the traditional "purpose of the poem" in the house of Being (*CP*, 413). Thus, in conventionally Freudian terms, complete possession of the mother's gaze yields the relation to self-presence, to "transparence" and "present peace" as the canto states (*CP*, 413). Maternal meaning fills the room, as the idea of the house gathered up in the fullness of time fills the mind. Just as Stevens' "Auroras" comes to replace his earlier "Credences" in the process of discursive production, however, so alternates come to replace present forms of belief. Hence, "the prescience of oncoming dreams," initially repressed in the canto, becomes more and more the presentiment that presence is *not* total and that the house "half dissolved" by evening is at least half about a relation to otherness, that is, "the half [its inhabitants] can never possess" (*CP*, 413). Stevens links his "night of secret difference," in Derrida's phrase, to a force that destroys the mother yet does so in such a way that her nature is revealed as factitious (her "necklace is a carving not a kiss") and consequently as susceptible to change.[21] Near the end of the canto, darkness modulates into the poet's favorite wind, whose "grandeurs" announce the passing away of fictional presence with the knock of a rifle-butt, thereby assaulting the "ease" and "shelter of mind" imaged previously in the sleep of the mother. But it is as the boreal night that the power of darkness works its most unsettling effects, signaling an interiority that is exterior and an exteriority that is interior, by lighting Being's rooms, darkened now by dissolution, with a reflected light *from the outside*. Awed by the mystery of such generative power, humankind becomes resigned, and their "good-night, good-night" (*CP*, 413) shows promise, perhaps, of a shift to new fictions, no doubt the realization of the oncoming dreams previously.

Later, in Canto IX, Stevens rehearses once again the ruination of another house of totalized belief, "This drama that we live" (*CP*, 419), but from a slightly altered perspective. In this section, humankind is portrayed a further time huddled within an interiority of Being, or "innocent earth," thinking each other's thoughts, and reenacting a rendezvous with yet another maternal presence.

---

21. Derrida, *Margins of Philosophy*, 269, and *Writing and Difference*, 266.

> This drama that we live—We lay sticky with sleep.
> This sense of the activity of fate—

> The rendezvous, when she came alone,
> By her coming became a freedom of the two,
> An isolation which only the two could share.
>
> (*CP,* 419)

It is clear that this maternal figure's arrival only postpones the absence of dissolution and the dissolution of absence, hence the references to "the guilty dream" at the opening and to "the imminence" of disaster later. For the present, men engorge themselves on a complacency of self-satisfied knowledge, the "decorous honeycomb" (*CP,* 419) reminiscent of the huge decorum of "Credences," then lie stuporous in their sticky dreams of self-relation, like "brothers . . . in a home," which is their fate. The specific drama he has in mind here is Shakespeare's *Hamlet:* "We were as Danes in Denmark all day long . . . hale-hearted landsmen" (*CP,* 419). In particular, Stevens is thinking of the tragic hero's disastrous postponement of time, as Hamlet fattens himself on lethe wharf (I.v.), we may recall, in a similar self-indulgent preoccupation with the potential loss of presence in his "To be, or not to be" (III.i). The "out[-]landish," however, taking Stevens' pun on "landsmen," in the form of another day "queerer than Sunday," cannot be delayed. Time and change inevitably arrive to dissipate the dream of innocence and advance its tragic isolation to a fatal disaster, with the image of corpses "hanging in the trees next spring." Nothing exceeds like excess, apparently, so that the operations of force, as a wind "sharp as salt" (*CP,* 419), contrive to shift the scene, which is innocence's greatest fear.

The "scholar of one candle" in Canto VI, therefore, who can see the multifarious shifts of force, the "Arctic effulgence" of the auroras, flaring on the frame of everything he imagines Being to be, is naturally filled with panic over such inconstant dubbing. The scholar of one candle is Stevens' counterpart to the Metaphysician in the Dark, and experiencing precisely in this way what Bloom terms "the anxiety of the infinite," or an anxiety over what a more writerly Derrida calls "an infinite course of entropy," he naturally feels afraid (*CP,* 417). Derrida's (non)concept for such infinite power is *différance,* and he describes the natural reaction to such an incomprehensible presentiment in terms quite similar to Stevens': "Not only is there no realm of differance, but differance is even the subversion of every realm. This is obviously what makes it threatening and necessarily dreaded by everything in us that desires a realm, the past or future presence of a realm."[22] From the mono-logical perspective of such "a single man contained," life ought *not* to be so impacted with the transformative potential he espies in the auroras:

> the lavishing of itself in change,
> As light changes yellow into gold and gold
> To its opal elements and fire's delight,
>
> Splashed wide-wise because it likes magnificence
> And the solemn pleasures of magnificent space.
>
> (*CP*, 416)

Stevens' point, so playfully worked out in the previous "Credences of Sum-mer," however, is frankly that life is not reducible to the single form or frame. Change makes it a veritable drama of alterity, as the canto's memorable open-ing image of "a theatre floating through the clouds, / Itself a cloud . . . of cloud transformed / To cloud transformed again, idly, the way / A season changes color *to no end*" shows (*CP*, 416, emphasis added). There is, conse-quently, no fixed or determinable teleology at back of change, save for the "misted rock" of change itself. One senses in Stevens' own discourse a vast metaphorical accumulation of "half-thought-of forms," of flying birds, waves of light, cloud drifts, running water, and so forth, all almost bursting to the breaking point, waiting to be played out in the rather more plenipotential than plenitudinous Theater of Trope. It seems only inevitable, then, that such changeful force and forceful change, a nameless "nothing" that eludes all de-termination, *must* be destroyed and so remain forever a "thing nameless" (*CP*, 416). For such is the intractable standoff between one scholar's unific grasp of form and the differentiating pleasures of magnificent, textual space.

We perhaps now begin to sense "The Auroras of Autumn" as just such a textual space and, consequently, a further elaboration of Stevens' theory of metaphorical resemblance, so central to the question of belief taken up in "Credences." In his essay "The Effects of Analogy," written in the same year as "Auroras," Stevens expands the notion of resemblance (*i.e.*, analogy as "resemblance between parallels" [*NA*, 110]) in discussing two theories of the imagination with which the poet is constantly concerned:

22. Bloom, *Poems of Our Climate*, 262; Derrida, *Writing and Difference*, 275; Derrida, *Speech and Phenomena*, 153. *Cf.* also the role of dangerous "metaphor" in philosophic discourse: "Dangerous and foreign as concerns *intuition* (vision or contact), *concept* (the grasping or proper presence of the signified), and *consciousness* (proximity or self-presence)" (Derrida, *Margins of Philosophy*, 270). For a quite different view of the scholar, see Bates, *A Mythology of Self*, 276.

One relates to the imagination as a power within him not so much to destroy reality at will as to put it to his own uses. He comes to feel that his imagination is not wholly his own but that it may be part of *a much larger, much more potent imagination,* which it is his affair to try to get at . . . on the verge of consciousness. . . . The second theory relates to the imagination as a power within him to have such insights into reality as will make it possible for him to be sufficient as a poet *in the very center of consciousness.* . . . The proponents of the first theory believe that it will be a part of their achievement to have created the poetry of the future. . . . The proponents of the second theory believe that to create the poetry of the present is an incalculable difficulty. (*NA*, 115, emphasis added).

Of the two theories, it is clear that the second, with its attachment to a self-sufficient representation, or "reality," located at the very center of consciousness, hence its "incalculable difficulty," that this theory cannot be of much use to Stevens in probing the future course of belief. But the first *can* be, for it connects with Stevens' whole notion of abstraction back in the opening section of "Notes Toward a Supreme Fiction" and, more specifically, with that power through which the poet "gives to life the supreme fictions without which we are unable to conceive of it" (*NA*, 31), thus yielding "The Ultimate Poem Is Abstract" from the same year as "Auroras" (*CP*, 429). Later, in the 1951 essay "The Relations Between Poetry and Painting," this abstract power will become "the operative force within us [that] does not, in fact, seem to be the sensibility, that is to say, the feelings [but] seems to be a constructive faculty, that derives its energy more from the imagination than from the sensibility" and, citing Paul Klee, from "the secret places where original law fosters all evolution" (*NA*, 164, 174). In full pursuit of imaginative energy's "secret places" in this crucial passage, Stevens' discourse, once again, strikes us as quintessentially postmodern insofar as Jean-François Lyotard conceives of that vexed term: "That which, in the modern, puts forward the unpresentable in presentation itself; that which denies itself the solace of good forms . . . that which searches for new presentations, not in order to enjoy them but in order to impart a stronger sense of the unrepresentable."[23]

In Stevens' making a clear separation between imagination and sensibility, which we may correspondingly align with the first and second theories

23. Lyotard, *The Postmodern Condition*, 81.

outlined previously, B. J. Leggett has noted an important "externalizing tendency" in Stevens' thinking and writing in his late period. Typified by "The Auroras of Autumn," he points out, there is a significant shift, by way of "a phenomenon of rupture," from "the personal sensibility, the individuality of the artist" to "the possibility of an imaginative and creative order external to the artist's private sensibility" and to the "play of a cosmic imagination." Leggett goes on to establish a further, rather convincing case for Stevens' attraction to a certain force of otherness, characteristic of his first theory of the imagination, as the result of a fairly close reading of Henri Focillon's *Life of Forms in Art,* published in 1943, though an attraction on Stevens' part to a "force as a movement external to the house of the mind" and to "imaginative laws not supplied by the poems' speakers" conceivably occurs much earlier in the decade, if Stevens' "Notes" is also rigorously taken into account. Leggett seems also to want to define the otherness to which Stevens was drawn in terms of Focillon's forms themselves, when it is clear in poems such as "A Primitive like an Orb" and "Chocorua to Its Neighbor," where the poet speaks of "the power of . . . form" and wanting to get "beyond / [Men's] form, beyond their life" (*CP,* 443, 299), that Stevens was much more fascinated by the *life* at back of the dissemination of these forms, what in "Credences" he refers to as "the spirit of the arranged" and "the fund of life and death," noted earlier (*CP,* 377). Not preoccupied with the *question* of belief, Leggett chooses to view this power of expression in terms of a "transcendent human form," an "unseen essence," and, what is most alarming, "an external intelligence that is *of the same order* as [the scholar's] one candle," though overwhelming "in its magnitude." Consequently, his reading of an undeniably important influence in the poet's later work can only offer to Stevens' arguable ironization of credences "the manifestations of an enthroned god-imagination": an "external presence free from his own spirit," it is true, but in the form of a great symbol like the aurora borealis, "*everywhere present*" in Stevens' longer poem nonetheless and hence the source of a new "reality outside the mind."[24]

Returning to the text, therefore, what we really want to begin to consider is both how Stevens endeavors to ironize his second theory of the imagination, worked through, as a matter of faith in the so-called high modernist mode, various forms of presence in the early work before "Notes," and how he champions instead his first theory, contextualized as a question of belief

24. Leggett, *Poetic Theory,* 148, 159–60, 179, 178, 169, 183, 184 (emphasis added), 189, 196, 173, and 198 (emphasis added).

more and more in terms of the force of absence in the work following. The nameless "nothing" that we left off in Canto VI would appear to return us to the ironization according to the first theory, subtended by metaphorical resemblance, or the effects of analogy. Jacques Derrida, who describes the influence of Focillon on another writer in quite different ways than those charted above, offers the following interpretation of "nothing" that is perhaps more in tune with Stevens' a/theological discourse at this point:

> This universe [a nonplace in Focillon and repeated in Jean Rousset] articulates only that which is in excess of everything, the essential nothing on whose basis everything can appear and be produced within language. . . . This excess is the very possibility of writing and of literary *inspiration* in general. Only *pure absence*— not the absence of this or that, but the absence of everything in which all presence is announced—can *inspire*, in other words, can *work*, and then make one work . . . since nothing is not an object—is the way in which this nothing *itself* is determined by disappearing. . . . The consciousness of having something to say [is] the consciousness of nothing.[25]

If the scholar of one candle fails us in his desire to presence the productive absence of "nothing" in Canto VI, then the figure of the father in Canto IV gives us better reason to hope, immersed as he is in a constantly iterated "space," no doubt "the spacing between desire and fulfillment," that is the essential "nothing" through which the credences of summer might more forcefully be revitalized.[26] Seated by the fire and thus making himself entirely open to the differing and deferring work of the auroras ("motionless and yet / Of motion the ever-brightening origin" [*CP*, 414]), he loses his patriarchal aspect of "bleak regard" and thus finds himself able to repeat the Nietzschean sacred "yes" that says, "Farewell to an idea . . ." (*CP*, 414), and makes him "Master O master" of no-thing, hence a king profound in the last stanza. Here, moved by an excess of force, the Master of Nothing joins Stevens' Necessary Angel from the final section of "Notes" (*CP*, 404) and "leaps from

25. Derrida, *Writing and Difference*, 8. *Cf.* further Derrida, *Margins of Philosophy*, 172n16, and also *Speech and Phenomena*, 127–28n14. Martin Heidegger theorizes about "nothing" in similar ways in "What Is Metaphysics?," in *Basic Writings*, ed. David Farrell Krell (New York, 1977), 100–101, and it is possible to speculate about Stevens' coming under the influence of such a notion via this source in his later years.

26. Derrida, *Dissemination*, 212. *Cf.* also Trinh T. Minh-ha's notion of "the interval" as a "space in which meaning remains fascinated by what escapes and exceeds it," in her "Documentary Is/Not a Name," *October*, LII (Spring, 1990), 96.

heaven to heaven more rapidly" in the proper pursuit of transformative resemblance than "bad angels," perhaps the essentializing epicures from "Esthétique" (*CP,* 316, 323), "leap from heaven to hell in flames" (*CP,* 414). He thus becomes as hard-pressed as the company of actors to register the multiplicities of "the naked wind," the only essential nothing, Derrida observes above, according to which possibility *anything* might be produced.

Anything, of course, includes both the positive and negative sides of human experience, as noted in Canto VII: the grim right alongside the benevolent, the just and the unjust, night and day, summer and winter, and, to be sure, "Credences" and "Auroras." If there is a nameless nothing "that sits enthroned" (*CP,* 417) in our spiritual life (Stevens almost hesitates to call it "an imagination"), then it must equally be thought to be "the white creator of black," as it is the reverse. Although this view leaves the earlier "Credences," as merely a shivering residue foreclosed in the present text, Stevens' point is the same for each poem, that the force of imagination is not unconstrained but works within articulable limits: analogy as a "resemblance *between* parallels" (emphasis added), which is the Original Law fostering all evolution. Thus, "it dare not leap by chance in its own dark"; rather, it must "change from destiny" (*CP,* 417). So it is this infinite calculus of freedom begotten within fate that becomes the most compelling reason for bringing the companion poems together in the present chapter, as Stevens knew only too well himself when he wrote in the present canto that form, or "shape," is a "mournful making" and, as a condition of force, "move[s] to find / What must unmake it" (*CP,* 418). "Stevens's existential project," Mutlu Blasing remarks, is thus "to show that our freedom is our fate, our discourse is our nature, our imagination our destruction." And Paul Ricoeur's general observation that the effects of analogy beget as they transgress is therefore well taken here, which is perhaps what Stevens also has in mind when he characterizes the whole process, in the last line of the present canto, as a "flippant communication."[27]

The utter indeterminacy of imagination's fateful freedom would thus appear ironically to be the "point" of Stevens' opening meditation on the serpent, linked to the northern lights from the point of view of both form

27. Blasing, *American Poetry,* 89; Ricoeur, *The Rule of Metaphor,* 24. Peter Carafiol's reading of Henry David Thoreau's model for producing meaning as a "fronting" of facts is similarly instructive: "It is a process of *making* frontiers, not of discovering them, one that makes facts new by going beyond their customary, or surface meanings as a result of long and intimate relationship. It is not experience of the new but making experience anew, original descriptions of familiar objects that re-create the past" (*The American Ideal,* 135). See also 138, 145–46.

and force: "This is where the serpent lives" (*CP,* 411). Geoffrey Hartman makes the quite relevant suggestion that "the serpent is the first deconstructor of the logos [by proving] that the Word may have more than one sense or a sense other than intended." Harold Bloom notes that "the ultimate meaning of the serpent of the *Auroras* [is] death," *i.e.,* "the necessity of change," but it is perhaps better to think of "death" in this context as Maurice Blanchot describes it in *The Writing of the Disaster,* a text especially relevant to the study of "The Auroras of Autumn": "Not as death itself, but as a death that is always other, with which we do not communicate, but for which we bear the unbearable responsibility. No relation, then (in death), to violence and aggression . . . the disaster would be beyond what we understand by death or abyss. . . . in the disaster I disappear without dying (or die without disappearing)."[28] In Stevens' text, the duplicity is extended in the direction of the serpent's infinite capacity for metamorphosis. A decade earlier, Stevens had dealt with this image in the opening stanza of "Farewell to Florida" (*CP,* 117) as a problematic of transformative change. Now, he perhaps sees a positive power in the image, as it foregrounds a crisis in the whole issue of truth and apparent truth. For, as a disembodied entity in the present canto, the serpent is neither determinate ("body's slough") at the end of a whole tradition of Platonic and Kantean metaphysics nor indeterminate exactly ("another bodiless"), since its Ouroborotic ring of pure and endless light, in the tag from Thomas Traherne, is a head of air and a tail in every sky (*CP,* 411). Like force, whose absent presence is manifested in a present absence, the errant and ambiguous serpent is body and nonbody at once, since, as Charles Winquist observes, "we cannot know the realm of force as force but only as it is implied or represented in the realm of meaning." Stevens would prefer to reverse the perspective and have "form gulping after formlessness" (*CP,* 411), that is, a serpent body flashing without its skin, because the mediacy of skin subverts a whole postmetaphysical chain of "wished-for disappearances" and because one can only invoke meaning by revoking it in one and the same gesture. Our being master of this enigmatic maze, therefore, provokes a double gesture of belief: on the one hand, seeing the auroras as they fix an emblazoned "pole" in the found image of the serpent, and on the other hand, in the unfound image of "another nest," *not* seeing "body and air and forms and images" as

28. Hartman, *Saving the Text,* 8; Bloom, *Poems of Our Climate,* 256; Blanchot, *The Writing of Disaster,* 118–19. Both Bloom (278) and Vendler observe Stevens' sensitivity to the ambiguity of the etymology of dis-aster in the massing of the stars throughout the poem, in Vendler's words, "these flaring lights, and the apprehensive *questions* they raise" (*On Extended Wings,* 268, emphasis added).

ultimately certain signs, what Stevens refers to as the "possession[s] of happiness" (*CP*, 411). In the end, our belief must be "that we should disbelieve" if possible, in other words, that we should take the beliefs so essential to metaphysics, in Rorty's words, "as just another text, just another set of little human things."[29]

At this point, it seems only appropriate for Stevens to deploy a bit of his own White Mythology, as he does with the white cabin, white flowers, and white afternoon in the following canto, in order to bid "farewell to an idea" once again and to install the "consequence / Of an infinite [dis]course," predictably linked to a blowing wind, in its place:

> The season changes. A cold wind chills the beach.
> The long lines of it grow longer, emptier,
> A darkness gathers though it does not fall
>
> And the whiteness grows less vivid on the wall.
> The man who is walking turns blankly on the sand.
> He observes how the north is always enlarging the change.
>
> (*CP*, 412)

In most acute dialogue with "Credences" here (whose north we remember would have all things stop in that one direction), the north that is always enlarging change in the above passage makes sure only that the Metaphysician in the Dark, the incredible ironist who returns Crispin's inland cabin to the margins of "the ructive sea" (*CP*, 41), himself turns, and turns "blankly on the sand." We ourselves re-turn to the season of beliefs from before and think of them now more as the velocities of change, curiously finding assurance in the gathering darkness of force that continually threatens to dissipate form: "The whiteness grows less vivid on the wall." In Derrida's own White Mythology, "metaphysics has erased within itself the fabulous scene that has produced it, the scene that nevertheless remains active and stirring, inscribed in white ink, an invisible design covered over in the palimpsest." Hence, irony for Derrida becomes synonymous with Stevens' own Metaphysician in the Dark, "a trope which cannot stop turning and turning and turning around, since we can only speak of a (rhetorical) turn by way of *another* trope . . . the irony of irony."[30] Thus, chilling the beach and emptying it of all determinate

---

29. Winquist, *Epiphanies of Darkness*, 23; Rorty, *Contingency, Irony, and Solidarity*, 93.

30. Derrida, *Margins of Philosophy*, 213, and *Memoires for Paul de Man*, 152n8, emphasis added. *Cf.* also Derrida's association of "a power of pure equivocality" with the Hebraic *ruah*, or wind, in *Writing and Difference*, 9.

content in this way, velocities of change act as the provocation to further *douceurs / tristesses,* long lines that will grow even longer, as the text itself will eventually bear out.

Mark Taylor is one of several contemporary a/theologians who attach a definite religious reverence to the kind of writing Stevens puns on in the preceding lines as the highly contextualized and variable power of articulatory expression. "Scripture *is* the divine milieu," he writes, and the divine milieu *is* writing." Taylor explains:

> The milieu embodied in word and inscribed in/by writing is divine insofar as it is the creative/destructive medium of everything that is and all that is not. . . . This play of differences or differential web of interrelation is universally constitutive. . . . Though the divine milieu is never simply present or absent, it is the *medium* of all presence and absence. In this complex mean, opposites, that do not remain themselves, cross over into each other and thus dissolve all original identity.[31]

In Canto VIII of "The Auroras of Autumn," Stevens comes very close to this sense of reverence by attaching to the serpentine auroras a type of innocence, "an innocence of the earth and no false sign / Or symbol of malice" (*CP,* 418). He attributes to them a "holiness" that we enter into as innocent children "in the dark," in a favorite phrase from the late work, and that significantly keeps us awake in the midst of "the quiet of sleep," a reference once again to our more usual humanistic dream of transcending the mere innocence of earth and engaging completed presence in a world elsewhere. The dream's time and place continue to be sung for us by the mother within a darkened room back in Canto III, but by this late stage in the poem, we now know it can only be a song half-heard, since the full drama must also include the role the power of the divine milieu *plays* in constituting that place and that time. Moreover, one can speak about the generality of time in this operation, as in "a time of innocence" in stanza one, but "there is never a place" (*CP,* 418)— de-scription without place, as it were—that can be only a matter of historical and contingent determination.

31. Taylor, *Erring,* 116. The problematizing of "original identity" is once more significant here and again foregrounds Stevens' posture as ironist. *Cf.* Deleuze and Parnet: "An ironist is someone who discusses principles; he is seeking a first principle, a principle which comes even before the one that was thought to be first, [and] he finds a course which is even more primary than the others" (*Dialogues,* 68). Hence Blanchot's pregnant suggestion that "the 'possibility' of writing is linked to the 'possibility' of irony" (*The Writing of the Disaster,* 35; *cf.* also 47, 61, and 63).

Even making the auroras "a thing of time" is perhaps risking not a little, threatening to turn them into something too much like an idea that is not at all like the First Idea of "Notes" (*CP*, 418) and thereby finding in force another dreaded credence, which could only *mean* the end of force. "There is an almost irresistible temptation," J. Hillis Miller has recently pointed out, "to think of the thing, matter, law, or force latent in the text as some kind of religious or metaphysical entity, the 'Absolute' as transcendent spirit." He has further suggested (following Walter Benjamin) that foregrounding the "unreadability" of the textual other might be a way of getting around collapsing a linguistic protocol into its transcendental counterpart.[32] Stevens will not go this far. He wants his "calamity," it is true, to exist hypothetically in the idea of it alone, as "pure principle," and to allow its nature to be its own end (*CP*, 418). Still, he desires it to have some availability as a *real* thing as well so that "it should be, and yet not be, a thing." His preference, therefore, is for a de-scription of the auroras that is unreadable and readable *together:* "Like a book at evening beautiful but untrue, / Like a book on rising beautiful and true" (*CP*, 418). In just this way, his own divine milieu will thus resist the intelligence *almost* successfully (*OP*, 197). As he queries in another place in *Opus Posthumous,* "I wonder, have I lived a skeleton's life, / As a questioner about reality" ("First Warmth," *OP*, 117), and again, with more insistent emphasis, "I wonder, have I lived a skeleton's life, / As a disbeliever in reality" ("As You Leave the Room," *OP*, 117).

About the auroras of autumn, which appear in Book IX about halfway through his 1852 novel *Pierre; Or, The Ambiguities,* Herman Melville writes: "We learn that it is not for man to follow the trail of truth too far, since by so doing he entirely loses the directing compass of his mind; for arrived at the Pole, to whose barrenness only it points, there, the needle indifferently respects all points of the horizon alike." By the tenth and final canto of his own text, Wallace Stevens has pushed truth beyond the compass of individual consciousness to the point at which his northern lights can respect all manner of propositional predication: unhappy people in a happy world, unhappy people in an unhappy world, happy people in an unhappy world, and so forth. For we are not left, at the conclusion, with merely the forms of truth, which by themselves would be "too many mirrors for misery" and, so, the full of fate (*CP*, 420). We are also given the full of fortune as the "contrivance" of our fate, thus removing the sense of truth as assertion and inviting

32. Miller, *The Ethics of Reading,* 122.

us to think about truth more in terms of expression—in terms, as Charles Altieri puts it, of "some form of the maker's presence as a constitutive force of meaning," such as the rabbi that Stevens mentions and "the phases of [his] difference" (*CP,* 420) that demystify facile generalization.[33] With this linguistic apperception of belief, mediated by the power of expression as "the vital, the never-failing genius" (*CP,* 420), the Metaphysician in the Dark senses the potential of mankind to live out "all lives" that it might be possible to know without getting hung up on any one of them. Accordingly, in fulfilling meditations both great and small, this genius, which is the fullness both of fortune *and* of fate, contrives a kind of balance or wholeness in men's lives. It can do this, however, only by breaking open our too theologically enclosed and centered selves, mewed up in the "nick of winter," and by converting hushful paradise into something more "harridan" through the action and energy of a haggling wind. How evanescent the credences of summer straw are next to the awful "blaze" of such boreal power, we are led to surmise in Stevens' last line. Michel Foucault once saw the death of God in such a blaze and the nothingness in a world "made and unmade by that excess which transgresses it." Is the truth of *that* nothing the answer of "Auroras" to the direction, back in "Credences," where all things stop? Having taken us just this far along his Milky Way, Stevens' companion poems, in that final conflagration, would leave their ultimate truth exceedingly open to question. For it is in the light of an "incinerating blaze where nothingness appears," as Derrida reminds us, that "we remain in disbelief itself."[34]

33. Herman Melville, *Pierre; Or, The Ambiguities,* ed. Harrison Hayford (New York, 1984), 196; Altieri, "From Expressivist Aesthetics to Expressivist Ethics," in *Literature and the Question of Philosophy,* ed. Cascardi, 149. For a further elaboration of Stevens' characterization of rabbinic thought, which additionally provides "room for difference, conflict, and contradiction" as well as "multiple predication," see Handelman, *The Slayers of Moses,* 56, 160, and further, Derrida, "Shibboleth," 345–46.

34. Foucault, *Language, Counter-Memory, Practice,* 32; Derrida, *Memoires for Paul de Man,* 21.

CHAPTER 7

MIRACULOUS MULTIPLEX
Last Things

The central feature of the change [to "modern" religion] is the collapse of the dualism that was so crucial to all the historic religions. . . . It is not that a single world has replaced a double one but that an infinitely multiplex one has replaced the simple duplex structure. It is not that life has become again a "one possibility thing" but that it has become an infinite possibility thing.
  —Robert Bellah, *Beyond Belief: Essays on Religion in a Post-Traditional World*

I wonder, have I lived a skeleton's life,
As a disbeliever in reality.
                          —Wallace Stevens, "As You Leave the Room"

This real world having reached the apex of its development can be destroyed, in the sense that it can be reduced to intimacy. . . . It will regain intimacy only in darkness. In so doing, it will have reached the highest degree of distinct clarity, but it will so fully realize the possibility of man, or of being, that it will rediscover the night of the animal intimate with the world—*into which it will enter.*

                          —Georges Bataille, *Theory of Religion*

BOTH "Credences of Summer" and "The Auroras of Autumn" were composed by a poet close to seventy years of age. Not surprising, the two volumes of poetry that followed, and that we come finally to take up in this chapter, namely, *The Auroras of Autumn* and *The Rock,* the latter published simultaneously with the *Collected Poems* in 1954, together seem almost to constitute an intense meditation on last things, as a glance at several of the titles in the books indicates: "*The Westwardness of Everything*" (*CP,* 455), "Things of August" (*CP,* 489), "The Plain Sense of Things" (*CP,* 502), "Not Ideas about the Thing but the Thing Itself" (*CP,* 534), and so on. But if the argument advanced in the previous chapter for the relation between the companion

252

poems holds, then even speculation about last things in the last chapter on the last poems of Stevens must be taken with considerable irony. Several of Stevens' observations in the final prose, as we shall see more clearly later, have to be viewed the same way as well. For instance, Stevens observes in the last section of the essay "The Relations Between Poetry and Painting" from 1951 that "in an age in which disbelief is so profoundly prevalent or, if not disbelief, indifference to questions of belief, poetry and painting, and the arts in general, are, in their measure, a compensation for what has been lost" (*NA*, 171). Poetry, or art, we query, as modernism's new article of faith? Imagination as "the reigning prince" and "the next greatest power to faith" (*NA*, 171)? These identifications might be the expected inference, but only until we recall, in the previous "Imagination as Value," written in 1948, that "poetry does not address itself to beliefs" (*NA*, 144). This sentence ought to give us pause. How can the question of belief, in Stevens' late work, at last reconcile these apparently antithetical statements?

The clue, here, lies with the two figures for the reader in the texts taken up in the last chapter. Both the old man on the tower in "Credences" and the scholar of one candle in "Auroras" give us apophantic images of the true believer, which, by this stage in the evolution of Stevens' discourse, we must treat with some degree of suspicion. As far as they are essentializing hypostatizations of ontological outlook and of epistemological insight, respectively, their ironic presentation as mirror images of each other may be suggested in a related context by Thomas Sheehan, who describes both "those who hope to read their way through to some eventual full presence—*Sein* in the sky by and by—but also those who, without sharing that chiliastic expectation, nonetheless hope to read to the end of the text, to the point where reading ends and reverence begins, even if there is nothing to revere but absence." Stevens thus agrees with both Heidegger and Derrida, who themselves are agreed, as Richard Rorty has recently observed, "that inverted logocentrism is still logocentrism, and that some movement more complex and powerful than inversion is needed."[1] It is at precisely this moment, therefore, that we may recall a third figure in the poems, the beachcomber turning and turning and turning *blankly* on the sand, on the margin between land and sea, like the "fat girl terrestrial" at the end of "Notes." At this point, we perhaps see

1. Thomas Sheehan, "Derrida and Heidegger," in *Hermeneutics and Deconstruction*, ed. Silverman and Ihde, 218; Richard Rorty, "Two Meanings of 'Logocentrism': A Reply to Norris," in *Redrawing the Lines: Analytic Philosophy, Deconstruction, and Literary Theory*, ed. Reed Way Dasenbrock (Minneapolis, 1989), 212.

how a vertical and exclusionary discourse of substitution and compensation turns horizontal and becomes less a poetry addressing itself to articles of faith than one (re)enacting or (re)empowering the very conditions for faith itself. Rorty makes a clear separation between a vertical and a horizontal truth precisely along the lines that Stevens would tend to separate matters of faith, "as eternal objects which we try to locate and reveal, and . . . as artifacts whose fundamental design we often have to alter."[2]

It would be a mistake to view "The Auroras of Autumn," tempting as all the serpent and darkness and fall-like imagery is, as merely a "negative theology," a parody of true faith come to replace the aestivations of belief in the preceding "Credences." Such a view would only serve to perpetuate what Louis Althusser and Étienne Balibar have aptly described as the "recognition structure" of ideology, the closed circle of the Lacanian "dual mirror relation," which stands to repeat, either inside or outside, that from which the representation of outworn doctrine is in flight. The serial horizontality of the new discourse, which makes no teleological prejudgments about the outcomes of belief as the cyclical verticality of the old does, opens belief up to the radical foundation of a new space and, on a different site, in Althusser's and Balibar's words, to "a new problematic which allows the real *problem* [*i.e.*, the question of belief] to be posed, the problem misrecognized in the recognition structure in which it is ideologically posed [*e.g.*, poetry, art, imagination *addressed* to belief.]"[3]

The misrecognition of belief continued within the structure of representation was a problem Stevens had recognized back in *Parts of a World*, as we saw in Chapter 3, in his wrestling with the contrapuntal characterizations of Mrs. Uruguay and Lady Lowzen. His subsequent theorizing of alternative conceptualizations of romance (Chapter 5) and of imagination (Chapter 6) in terms of a poststructural text- or belief-event, as we have termed it, is pre-

2. Richard Rorty, *Consequences of Pragmatism (Essays: 1972–1980)* (Minneapolis, 1982), 92. See also Cook, *Poetry, Word-Play, and Word-War*, 273–74. Compare further the "Rhizome" of Gilles Deleuze and Félix Guattari in *On the Line*, trans. John Johnston (New York, 1983), whose "assemblage" offers a precise discursive analogue to Rorty's truthful "artifact" and Stevens' faithful "text-event." As Kathryne Lindberg summarizes, "Trees grow vertically; rhizomatic plants grow horizontally" (*Reading Pound Reading*, 221).

3. Althusser and Balibar, *Reading Capital*, 53. On the issue of "negative theology," see also Derrida, *Speech and Phenomena*, 134, and *Writing and Difference*, 260; *cf.* also Jacques Derrida, "How to Avoid Speaking: Denials," in *Languages of the Unsayable: The Play of Negativity in Literature and Literary Theory*, ed. Sanford Budick and Wolfgang Iser (New York, 1989), for "the supposed movements of negative theology" (12), previously.

cisely the stratagem of the spirit intended to allow the *real* problematic of faith to be posed rather than addressed. It is just here where concepts fail Stevens, however. Martin Heidegger, we should not be too startled to find, runs into the same difficulty of attempting to articulate that which lies just the other side of articulation in dealing with Being (*Ereignis*) as it is to be brought forth in a moment of disclosure, or revelation, within and as man's own essential nature or being: "To think Being without regard to a foundation of Being in terms of beings." Similarly, Jacques Derrida, whose notion of text many are inclined to read as the thoroughly postmetaphysical answer to Heidegger's history of Being, others are inclined to think runs into the same problem with his notion of *différance*: "Neither a *word* nor a *concept*."[4] There can be no doubt that Wallace Stevens, too, in the final years of his life, experienced not a little anxiety over formulating his own last things on the question of belief, which he also hoped might be carried on outside the present metaphysical tradition, beyond the westwardness of everything mentioned previously.

Although we might appear to be metaphysically prejudgmental here, there nonetheless were a few things about which Stevens could have no doubt concerning an a/theological act of faith, quite independent of its realization in actual practice. These "conditions" we might gather together retrospectively from the last few chapters and set to the right in the following table, in contrast to those on the left, the universalizing features of the corresponding transcendental object of faith, definitively cast aside by the later reason foregrounded in all of Stevens' work following "Notes Toward a Supreme Fiction":

literal	figural
propositional	hypothetical
reductive	productive
substitutive	distributive
mimetic	semiotic
proscriptive	descriptive

4. Martin Heidegger, *On Time and Being*, trans. Joan Stambaugh (New York, 1972), 33; Heidegger, *Existence and Being*, 356; Derrida, *Speech and Phenomena*, 130. For exemplary critiques of the contradictions manifest in their apparently aconceptual projects, see esp., for Heidegger, Gasché, *The Tain of the Mirror*, 307ff.; and, for Derrida, Richard Rorty, "Deconstruction and Circumvention," *Critical Inquiry*, XI (September, 1984), and, more recently, Robert Scholes, "Deconstruction and Communication," *Critical Inquiry*, XIV (Winter, 1988), rev. as Chapter 2 in *Protocols of Reading* (New Haven, 1989).

generic	generative
representative	repetitive
exclusionary	inclusionary
orthodox	paradox
assertive	expressive
spatial	temporal

Earlier in this study, I noted how seeing is believing was becoming less and less a truism for Stevens and how he was more frequently beginning to think of seeing and believing together as matters of interpretation. Pairing this insight with the more horizontally processual character of the belief-event in terms of the above conditions, we sense in it a kind of broadening and expanding quality, as opposed to the deepening and delimiting aspect of a more vertical metaphysics, which Alexander Nehamas is inclined, following Nietzsche, to attach to the highly contextualized reading of any given action: "The more extensive process of which an action can be seen as a part can in turn generate a different interpretation of at least part of the original action. This, again, can indicate that a new, more extensive process, perhaps containing at least part of the original one as its own part, must now be invoked. Such a process of continual adjustment has no end. Interpretation ends when interest wanes, not when certainty is reached." Nehamas later observes that "to interpret a text on this model is not to go underneath it, into a meaning covert within it, but to connect it to other texts and to their authors, to see what texts have made it possible and what texts it, in turn, has made possible itself." [5] As Wallace Stevens would say, "Every poem is a poem within a poem" (*OP*, 199).

The sense of an open-ended and unlimited possibility of meaning for the event here is precisely the kind that Stevens envisions for belief as an act of the imagination, but an imagination, he reminds us in "Imagination as Value," not integral to any romantic sensibility, *i.e.*, "imagination as metaphysics" (*NA*, 138). Rather, it is one that exercises "the power of the mind" over things. Moreover, if the believer's imaginative will to power is construed as "a certain single characteristic," he tells us, "it is the source not of a certain single value but of as many values as reside in the possibilities of things" (*NA*, 136, 138). Within just such a plurivalent source we consequently might expect to find the question of belief opening itself up to that new site and

5. Alexander Nehamas, "Writer, Text, Work, Author," in *Literature and the Question of Philosophy*, ed. Cascardi, 278, 287.

that new space *different* from the up/down, inside/outside, real/apparent metaphysical foundationalism of duplex thought.[6] In "A Primitive like an Orb," Stevens tags this new site a "miraculous multiplex," as we shall see later (*CP,* 442), suggesting that faith, like the imagination from which it springs, in the words of our opening epigraph, has at last become "an infinite possibility thing."[7]

Perhaps on this last point, we find a place where Heidegger and Derrida and any other Metaphysician in the Dark in this postanalytical, postmetaphysical, postmodern age, can finally agree. Any effect of language, whether it be reading in the case of Heidegger, writing in Derrida, or believing in Stevens, abjuring as it must single origins and certain ends to favor instead that continual process of adjustment to contingent circumstance—such an effect can know only movement, progression, alteration, the ever-never-changing advance to one more word, one more fact, one more truth: "The, the" (*CP,* 203). In Sheehan's words, again, "we can speak only of a relative priority of open-endedness over closure in an on-going movement" and hence nothing fixed or made stable by the aversions, say, to in-bar or ex-bar but only "an unending semiosis" and, ultimately, "the ineluctability of undecidability." Joseph Riddel's phrasing for this processual movement is equally apt here: "Language unlanguaging itself in the scene of poetic revelation."[8] One thinks once again of form gulping after formlessness in the opening canto of "Auroras" or perhaps of Stevens' own description of the imagination as "the irrepressible revolutionist," elaborated in the same year (*NA,* 154). Its trajectory, however, is never "a complete revolution," Sheehan would scruple to point out, since, like Stevens' old romance, that would be too decidable. It would have to be "more like an earthquake fault that 'sollicits' [*sic*], that is, shakes all forms of certitude and keeps them in constant uncertainty." A

6. "This dichotomized view of the character of the poet and the function of poetry," John Timberman Newcomb records, "has permeated Stevens criticism for the past four decades" and furnishes a painstaking account of its provenance contextualized within a "stubborn two-world dichotomy" that Newcomb relates to "the notorious New Critical ghetto of 'allegory,'" in his recent *Wallace Stevens and Literary Canons* (Jackson, 1992), 160–71, esp. 160, 167, and 168.

7. Robert N. Bellah, *Beyond Belief: Essays on Religion in a Post-Traditional World* (New York, 1976), 40. See further Heidegger, *Discourse on Thinking,* 71, and Jacques Derrida, "An Interview with Derrida (from *Le Nouvel Observateur*)," trans. David Allison, in *Derrida and Difference,* ed. Robert Bernasconi and David Wood (Evanston, 1988), 81. *Cf.* also Cornel West, *The American Evasion of Philosophy: A Genealogy of Pragmatism* (Madison, 1989), 5, 25, 91, 98, 115, 191, and 200.

8. Sheehan, "Derrida and Heidegger," in *Hermeneutics and Deconstruction,* ed. Silverman and Ihde, 214; Riddel, "The Climate of Our Poems," 59.

dozen years ago Stevens had opted for the metaphor of the volcano rather than the earthquake, but to the end of his writing career, the implications of both for the question of belief were identical.[9]

We begin, then, an overview of the last things in Wallace Stevens' poetic oeuvre with a group of poems that aims specifically to problematize cognitive certainty in all its forms and, in particular, the certainty usually taken on faith of a supposed transparent relation between perception and conception in a poem like "What We See Is What We Think." In a way, this text is a continuation of Stevens' earlier "Motive for Metaphor," since once the weight of primary noon, or absolute knowledge, is thought to be venerable and articulate and complete (at the stroke of "twelve" here), the powers of mind, continually on the move, are cued to indulge their further potential for alternative constructions and integrations of experience. Driving a wedge between thinking and seeing in this way, in "the first grey second" past twelve (*CP,* 459), they usher into the mind's cognitive repertoire a whole phantasmatic "disintegration of afternoon," which, up until that point, had all been the other way: "Normal time, / Straight up, an élan without harrowing, / The imprescriptible zenith, free of harangue" (*CP,* 459). In "Imagination as Value," once again Stevens describes the whole process in terms of the Heideggerian defamiliarization I scanned two chapters earlier, by which operation "the typical function of the imagination . . . always makes use of the familiar to produce the unfamiliar" or otherwise "import[s] the unreal into what is real," thereby converting the normal into the abnormal (*NA,* 165, 150, 145–46). What must be scandalous to the "instinctive integrations" of human reason as the "methodizer" or normalizer of the imagination (*NA,* 154–55) is the spectral weavings and scrawlings of text cut into the tried and the true, folded back on sedimented conception like "a pyramid with one side," hence def(r)amed (*CP,* 460). More formative perceptual powers nonetheless prevail. These converge ultimately in the ironic caricaturing of the title framing the poem itself, for by the last line reason's familiar "paramount ado" is completely riven: "What we think is never what we see" (*CP,* 460).

The child caricatures the adult in a similar way in "Questions Are Remarks" from the same year, 1949. The child in this instance is Stevens' grandson Peter, "the expert aetat. 2" (*CP,* 462), and the authenticity of his spiritual

---

9. Sheehan, "Derrida and Heidegger," in *Hermeneutics and Deconstruction,* ed. Silverman and Ihde, 216, 217; but see also Bornstein, *Transformations of Romanticism,* 203ff., Doggett, *The Making of the Poem,* 54ff, and Beehler, *Discourses of Difference,* 150ff. The final quotation comes from Derrida, *Speech and Phenomena,* 153.

innocence (and maturity) lies precisely in his refusing any certainty of meaning or knowledge for the sun's red fire like that meaning imposed by "drowsy, infant, old men" in the hardened form of "antique acceptances." By now a consistent image of absence in Stevens' discourse ("nothingness" in the poem's last stanza), the sun ought to bespeak only doubts, uncertainties, denials, as suggested by the child's name, and not the affirmations of a presencing "rhetoric" (*CP,* 462) as the elongation of "our own projected vanity." [10] Stevens takes a more direct swipe at such self-reflective representations within the sectarianism of institutionalized religion in the 1952 "Song of Fixed Accord" but more especially in "The Old Lutheran Bells at Home," from 1949, specifically in the last two stanzas:

> These are the voices of the pastors calling
> And calling like the long echoes in long sleep,
> Generations of shepherds to generations of sheep.
>
> Each truth is a sect though no bells ring for it.
> And the bells belong to the sextons, after all,
> As they jangle and dangle and kick their feet.
>
> (*CP,* 461–62)

The irremediable separations between pastors and sextons—shepherds and sheep—in these lines inevitably issue into institutional closure and ultimately into spiritual indifference, so nicely captured by the image of the elders' kicking feet. But the child is father to the man, to go back to "Questions Are Remarks" once again, principally because he dares to open himself up to the Nothing that is not there from the very start: "He will never ride the red horse [his mother] describes." Moreover, it is the very open-endedness of his questions themselves that makes him the figure of "capable" imagination (*CP,* 462) after which Stevens has been in search since *Parts of a World* and, in a manner of speaking, the rock upon which to found an a/theological faith. For only the indeterminate structure of the question can leave belief mobile enough to accommodate and adjust itself to the array of infinite possibilities in life's moving "pageant and procession and display" (*CP,* 462). "Always the beautiful answer who asks a more beautiful question," as e. e. cummings once observed. [11] Like the repetitive structure of Stevens' posttheological act of faith, the question itself constitutes its own re-mark.

---

10. John Dominic Crossan, *Raid on the Articulate: Comic Eschatology in Jesus and Borges* (New York, 1976), 174.

11. e. e. cummings, *Complete Poems: 1913–1962* (New York, 1972), 462.

The position the diminutive child occupies in this last poem perhaps suggests the irony that ought to greet us in Stevens' frequently misunderstood "Large Red Man Reading," composed a year earlier, in 1948. It may be that in revolving the question of belief in terms of an Other quite antithetical to any sublime or transcendent construction in texts like "Esthétique du Mal," "Description without Place," and "Credences of Summer," Stevens was finally becoming disenchanted with the enthrallments he might initially have intended with his frequent image of the giant man. For the red giant presented here has very little to do with a defamiliarizing abnormality. On the contrary, for those too fearful "to step barefoot into reality" (*CP*, 423) to reassess what they take so much on faith, like the adult *enfantillage* previously, the large red man depicts "the poem of life" thoroughly familiar to them from tradition. As such, he serves only to buttress the all-too-conventional arrangements of their exceedingly ordinary lives ("the pans above the stove, the pots on the table") and to solidify the motions of their minds and hearts by reading from out the "purple tabulae" and by feeling *for* them (*CP*, 424). Ultimately, the poem aims to mock any rendition of reality suggestive of a self-indulgent "poesis" [*sic*] (*CP*, 424), Stevens' familiar dig at the romantic's passive vision of reality, which unfolds only the merest "outlines of being" under the tabulae's expressive law. The "thought-like Monadnocks" and the longing for "the azury centre of time" in the neighboring "This Solitude of Cataracts," also from 1948, capture this passive vision of reality precisely:

> There was so much that was real that was not real at all.
> He wanted to feel the same way over and over.
>
> He wanted the river to go on flowing the same way,
> To keep on flowing. He wanted to walk beside it,
>
> Under the buttonwoods, beneath a moon nailed fast.
> He wanted his heart to stop beating and his mind to rest
>
> In a permanent realization.
>
> (*CP*, 425)

A mind perhaps even more fearful of change in this passage than the scholar of one candle back in "Auroras" is eventually self-destructive if the heart should, in fact, stop beating. Yet such is its insistence on arresting permanently the river's flow in the poem's opening, unspoken apostrophe and on being completely blind to its changefulness, picked up in Stevens' droll pun on "cataracts." The irony here is that such a longing only isolates the mind even further from life's process, hence the "solitude" of the poem's title. We therefore want to take the mind's relation to another of Stevens' gigantic interpolations in "In the Element of Antagonisms" from 1947 ("On his gold horse striding, like a conjured beast" [*CP,* 426]) with a certain amount of irony also. "It is a relation not to a miscellaneous collection of contingent actualities," as Rorty shrewdly notes in parallel cases, "but to the realm of possibility, a realm through which the larger-than-life hero runs his course, gradually *exhausting* possibilities as he goes," perhaps because he is "not content to arrange little things."[12] "Credences of Summer," from the previous year, had attempted to point out a similar contradiction in the image of the old man piled on a tower piled on a mountain.[13] It should not surprise us to find a similar tower linked to "the chevalier of chevaliers" here (*CP,* 426), the implication of whose golden rescue of mankind from existential temporality would do away with the human race altogether. Again, it is Stevens' important title that alerts us to the ambiguity: "Antagonisms."

All of the poems in this opening group would appear to come together in another important aperçu from "Adagia," namely, that "the fundamental difficulty in any art is the problem of the normal" (*OP,* 195). The imagination makes use of the normal to produce the abnormal in the process of defamiliarization noted earlier, but only because literature is abnormal to begin with and all men are murderers (*OP,* 202, 194). In Stevens' important meditation "Imagination as Value," already alluded to, he puts the matter in more detail:

> Normal people do not accept something abnormal because it has its origin in an abnormal force like the imagination nor at all until they have somehow normalized it as by familiarity. Costume is an instance of imaginative life as social form. At the same time it is an instance of the acceptance of something incessantly abnormal by reducing it to the normal. It cannot be said that life as we live it from day to day wears an imaginative aspect. On the other hand, it can be said that the aspect of life as we live it from day to day conceals the imagination as social form. (*NA,* 145–46)

The relation between an originating force domesticated and covered over by quiescent form is utterly fundamental to the kind of a/theological belief Stevens was attempting to promote after "Notes" and particularly in *Trans-*

---

12. Rorty, *Contingency, Irony, and Solidarity,* 101, 100, emphasis added. See also Gunn, *Thinking Across the American Grain,* 74, 102, 108, 115, and 136.

13. See also Bates, *A Mythology of Self,* 268.

port to Summer, where the relation is worked out in exhaustive detail as we have seen. In his final two books, it is possible to detect a noticeable shift in Stevens' attention from force to form in a great many of the poems, while he nonetheless continues to advance the question of belief in all the poststructural senses outlined earlier. The last things Stevens will have to say about metaphorization are a part of this shift as well. But form carefully studied from the point of view of force in his later work, rather than form privileged for its own sake as in the earlier, is what initially draws us into these last two volumes.

"Page from a Tale," composed in 1948, is another example of this alteration and for this reason deserves to be read far more than it usually is. For no other poem of Stevens' late period better illustrates normal form's refusal of abnormal force than the men aboard the great ship *Balayne* (*CP,* 421). Because these men evince an enormous reluctance, even at the end of the poem, to leave their ship stuck permanently in an ice floe, they become figuratively merely another version of a carefully guarded, self-complacent belief in old and conventional ways, frozen solid within "the wild limits of its habitation" (*CP,* 421). The seaman Hans, by contrast, is removed to safer ground and the warming comfort of a drift fire because, one suspects, he desires to be sensitive and receptive to the forces of change in the images of "loud water and loud wind" (*CP,* 421). Even though he may not understand them entirely, he hears "the difference" nonetheless. Thus, the snippets from Yeats's "Lake Isle of Innisfree" that the men presumably sing aboard ship become perfect extensions of their own lives, words fixed in total comprehension and solidified within a canonical tradition, which A. Walton Litz is quite correct to view as ironic. The stars, however, particularly in their connection to the mind, which in "Adagia" Stevens refers to as the voice of the Other (*OP,* 194), suggest something quite different: "Not tepid stars of torpid places / But bravest at midnight and in lonely spaces . . . with savage faces" (*CP,* 421). Their link to "Auroras" and to the death of normal belief is unmistakable. Abnormal belief, what motions to make a complete break with everything that is known, up to and including the present, therefore, is given later in the poem in the much larger and much more impenetrable image, once again, of the sun:

> No more that which most of all brings back the known,
> But that which destroys it completely by this light
> For that, or a motion not in the astronomies,

> Beyond the habit of sense, anarchic shape
> Afire—it might and it might not in that
> Gothic blue, speed home its portents to their ends.
>
> (*CP*, 422)

The incipient chaos of thought to which this "anarchic shape" exposes mankind, whose meaning is only potentially latent in the "finned flutterings and gaspings of the ice," naturally makes men afraid of the sun. Unlike the wide-awake Hans, whose errant separation already reveals a tolerance for such absence, the rest are more inclined to cultivate the knowledge of presence in sleep and dreams and in further importunings of Yeats's "bee-loud glade" (*CP*, 422).

As in the previous "Notes," however, nothing short of the fullest contemplation of the sun's weltering illuminations might lead men, enervated by habit and outworn faith, to tear apart their present images of "thin potencies" and with eyes held in hands, recollecting "Arcades of Philadelphia the Past" (*CP*, 225), to join yet another of Stevens' Metaphysicians in the Dark on the drift-fire shore. Such importation of abnormal difference into normal identity, what Stevens only by analogy can suggest might be the projection of the idea of God into the idea of man (*NA*, 150), is "incapably evil" (*CP*, 423). This claim is true, though, only from the point of view of the normal, which has never cared very much for difference anyway. As John Caputo shows, "subversiveness is structurally necessary to normalcy, that is, whatever has been normalized is only a certain contingent arrangement of signs whose efficaciousness is responsible for its success but which is so marked by contingency that it is always vulnerable to subversion." Put yet a further way, Roland Barthes remarks that "a tyrant who promulgated preposterous laws would all in all be less violent than the masses which were content to utter *what is self-evident, what follows of itself:* The 'natural' is, in short, *the ultimate outrage.*"[14] What Stevens, accordingly, at the end of the poem, is suggesting might be even *more* evil (*i.e.,* normal, natural), is perhaps the shipmen's continuing to resist entering fully into a completely new mental and spiritual transformation. They do not climb down the side of their habit-forming ship but only make promise of doing so, "soon" (*CP*, 423). A cautious disembarkation, "single file, with electric lamps," to the safety and security of a weak

---

14. Caputo, *Radical Hermeneutics*, 220. Roland Barthes, *Roland Barthes by Roland Barthes,* trans. Richard Howard (New York, 1977), 85; see also 130–31. For Litz previously, see *Introspective Voyager,* 152.

fire on shore is a poor thing in comparison to the "tidal undulation" held in check beneath their icy pathways. At least, though, it is a step away, *ein Schritt zurück,* as Heidegger might say, from the normalcy of the passively reflective mind. Once again, however, the irony of Stevens' title would appear to indicate that the full story of spiritual renovation awaits mankind at another historical juncture: this can only be a page from a much longer tale.

By far, the greater number of poems in Stevens' final volumes are concerned with the formal properties of metaphor. In the last chapter, we examined quite closely the degree to which Stevens' poststructural theorizing about the metaphorical imagination is integral to the question of belief. We turn now to a group of poems endeavoring to sharpen and refine a few last things that were never quite said in the transfer from theory to practice, or at least never said in any great detail about the metaphorical process and its important relation to belief. Stevens' more recent analysis of the imagination in terms of the normal and abnormal and the familiar and unfamiliar helps greatly to focus this new work, since these distinctions merely serve to broaden in more social and functional ways what he already had in mind in his previous differentiation between a poetical expressiveness divided between imitation and identity in the more familiar metaphysical context, on the one hand, and metamorphosis and resemblance in the less familiar postmetaphysical context, on the other. In art as well as in faith, the fundamental difficulty in any metaphor could be "the problem of the normal," too, or what "Adagia" more carefully refers to as the "question of identity" (*OP*, 194). "Metaphor as Degeneration" states the case precisely. Undoubtedly, by "degeneration" in this text Stevens has in mind something very close to what Heidegger intends in his observation that "only within metaphysics is there the metaphorical," that is, "the fusion of differences *into* identity," in Ricoeur's phrase.[15] In order to sustain belief as an open question, Stevens requires a less conventional rhetorical conception of metaphor than one that might merely degenerate into fixed presence in the familiar gesture of metaphysical transcendence. He needs a metaphoricity that is *generative,* a "nonphenomenologizable *quasi-transcendental*" formulation, as Rodolphe Gasché describes it, that "yields a

15. Bruns, *Heidegger's Estrangements,* 126; Ricoeur, *The Rule of Metaphor,* 198. Further, "Heidegger insists," Rapaport writes, "that to read metaphorically is itself not adequate, since metaphor is still a metaphysical or presencing agency which attaches the correspondence to a reified comparison" (*Heidegger and Derrida,* 187). Caputo presents a similar argument with respect to Heidegger's view on theology's stressing the symbolic character of language (*The Mystical Element,* 171). "The word must be the thing it represents; otherwise, it is a symbol" (*OP*, 194) is Stevens' crystallization of this line of thinking.

structure that accounts for the difference between the figural and the proper, and which comprises properties that are by right 'older' than those traditionally attributed to the transcendental and the empirical." He continues: "As that which opens the play between the proper and the metaphoric, and which metaphysics can only name as that which it makes possible, metaphoricity is not endowed with those qualities traditionally attributed to metaphor but rather with attributes which in traditional philosophy would be called constituting or transcendental. Metaphoricity is a transcendental concept of sorts."[16]

Clearly, to return to Stevens' poem, there can be no opening of play in a text whose images, "these reverberations" in the third stanza (*CP*, 444), are specifically intended to make Being "certain," as it states, and thereby to confound "death and the imagination" and to efface metaphoricity before the greater truth. Stevens uses the Swatara River to chart the process of degeneration by collapsing its "flock-flecked" differences into the identity with "air" first, to form some extravagantly aesthetic entity flowing "round the earth and through the skies, / Twisting among the universal spaces," and then by collapsing this universal further into an even more extravagant "landless, waterless ocean." In this final approximation of otherworldly transcendence ("[It] is not Swatara. It is being" [*CP*, 444]), metaphor meets its end, as suggested by the death imagery of "black violets" and "memorial mosses" descendant in the terminal stanza. Moreover, it would not seem to matter much whether one's metaphorical project was directed toward realism or toward idealism, the white wood-man and the black space-man in the first and second stanzas, respectively. If one's overriding purpose were to make no allowance for the changeful reverberations in poetic expressiveness, that is, for the "analogical displacement of Being" in Derrida's terms, fuelled by a distributive otherness rather than a substitutive sameness, then realism and idealism pretty much amount to the same thing: the loss of creativity and the death of belief in any appreciable sense.[17]

"The question of truth," Charles Winquist has observed, "is lodged in the *adequacy* of our metaphorical thought," and a poem such as "Metaphor as Degeneration" is obviously written to problematize that adequacy severely.[18] A much longer and more searching disquisition on the adequacy of metaphor is "The Bouquet," written two years later in 1950, another very much neglected poem from Stevens' late period:

16. Gasché, *The Tain of the Mirror*, 295.
17. Derrida, *Writing and Difference*, 27.
18. Winquist, *Epiphanies of Darkness*, 35, emphasis added.

> The bouquet stands in a jar, as metaphor,
> As lightning itself is, likewise, metaphor
> Crowded with apparitions suddenly gone
>
> And no less suddenly here again, a growth
> Of the reality of the eye, an artifice,
> Nothing much, a flitter that reflects itself.
>
> (*CP,* 448)

In these opening stanzas from the poem's first section, we are invited to reflect on a bouquet of roses as a metaphor for what the poet *makes* of existential experience, the "medium [of] nature" in the first line, as that experience
changes moment to moment like lightning and registers itself on human consciousness. As highly mediated by the crowding apparitions of metaphor as
that experience is, we wonder why the poet chooses to construct with his eye
of artifice one version of the bouquet's "reality" rather than another. We pass
over the actuality of the experience in this construction, since the "world
which remain[s] over, tossing blackly like the sea, chaotic[,] relative to our
distinctions and perhaps to all distinctions, *but there nevertheless,*" in Arthur
Danto's Nietzschean formulation—that world of nature can never be determined to any certain degree, as Barthes had previously intimated. The bouquet is "nothing much" for this reason; hence in the first line, again, it is a
"farouche extreme," that is, sullen, shy, repellent in manner.[19] In the third
section of the poem, Stevens therefore refers to the bouquet as "a realization," especially acute because the "unreal" from which it is drawn is unknowable. But it is acute also because in its present version, made possible by a
temporary quickness of sight, the bouquet stands as one possible "doubling"
of the unreal among a whole voluble repertoire of potential "interpretations,"
or "second things," as they are called (*CP,* 451). Furthermore, any single interpretation is conditioned not so much by any previous ones as by a sheer,
Nietzschean "will to see" and to make sense of that particular moment of
experience. Consequently, Stevens' "meta-men" in this section, figures for the

19. Arthur C. Danto, *Nietzsche as Philosopher* (New York, 1965), 96, emphasis added. "We
can say nothing of [nature] and think nothing of it without producing a myth," according to
F. H. Bradley, a passage that Stevens marked in his copy of Richards' *Coleridge on Imagination*
(Leggett, *Poetic Theory,* 31–32), hence the importance of the second epigraph to this chapter. As
I argued earlier in Chapters 2 and 3, Nietzsche must also have been a tremendous inducement to
the view that "we never see reality immediately but [that] always the moment after is a poetic
idea" and that "we live in mental representations of the past" (*L,* 722). In this letter, written to
Barbara Church, Stevens is also minded of the work of Jean Wahl in connection with the idea.

definitive determiners of truth, merely repeat his earlier observation that their imaginative will to power enables them to perceive the normal in the abnormal, the real in the unreal. Confronting the "infinite of the actual," in Stevens' exacting phrase, they forge one sovereign of a whole host of possible symbols and familiarize it as "a souvenir, a sign, / Of today," an "appanage" in their otherwise "migratory daze" (*CP*, 451). Why one version of the bouquet's reality rather than another comes down to the exercise of free choice in one's verbal options, as Rorty might say. The particular view one ultimately settles on as "normal," then, has nothing inherently truthful or identifiably transcendent about it at all. If the truth be known, nobody (or no thing) is normal (*OP*, 193).

We are perhaps better able to understand the choice involved in the poem's second section by noting how our freedom to make familiar what we will is also conditioned by what we may happen to feel at any given time, "the movement of emotion through the air" that prevents metaphors from dissolving completely into normality and instead keeps normality more at the level of "para-things" (*CP*, 449, 448). If there is any underlying substratum authorizing the (e)motive for metaphor here, it is perennially unknown, a "true nothing" (*CP*, 449) that stands in relation to this ungrounded "paralogy," in Thomas Kent's term, as a white duck stands in relation to the ripples of imagery it sends out behind itself as idea.[20] There is always the ever-present danger, however, that the meta-men as seekers after perfect truth will want to make a *strict* equation between idea and image or at least, in their mania to have "things transfixed, transpierced and well / Perceived," that they will "behold the idea as part / Of the image, behold it with exactness" (*CP*, 449). Clearly, Stevens chooses to vilify the approach to reality with this "other eye" (*CP*, 448), the other eye of "transparent magistrates" who would have the world "turned to the several speeds of glass" in their potent mania to understand it absolutely, a sign, really, of their impotence:

> Bearded with chains of blue-green glitterings
> And wearing hats of angular flick and fleck,
> Cold with an under impotency that they know,
>
> Now that they know, because they know.
>
> (*CP*, 449)

20. Thomas Kent, "Beyond System: The Rhetoric of Paralogy," *College English*, LI (September, 1989), 502. *Cf.* also Jacques Derrida, *The Post Card: From Socrates to Freud and Beyond*, trans. Alan Bass (Chicago, 1987), 120.

The sense that para-things are open to multitudinous interpretation ("choses of Provence, growing / In glue" [*CP*, 449]) without any need for metaphysical closure is a notion entirely lost on these rationalists, so reminiscent of the square-hatted ones from "Six Significant Landscapes" back in *Harmonium* (*CP*, 75). Morever, they do violence to the bouquet by detaching it from its function as a "recognizable medium" of experience and attaching it instead to rigid formulas for truth like romance, for example, "the bitterest vulgar do / And die" (*CP*, 450).[21] In so doing, they render it a "skeleton of repose" and "so much forlorn debris," all because the eye/I of the classic metaphysician must fasten intently to the lines of the bouquet's "eccentric twistings" and distill from them the consciousness of a "thing intact" (*CP*, 450). Such a spurious entry into the house of Being throughout this long section of the poem turns it into a dwelling made of cards that therefore comes crashing to the floor as a fit end to the quest for eternal form.

This very same point is repeated in the poem's concluding fifth section with the arrival of the military officer. Raising once again the specter of the fatal unity of war from *Parts of a World*, the soldier enters the room in search of someone, perhaps the woman of memory referred to in the final line of section two, and, failing to find her, accidentally overturns the floral arrangement in his leave-taking: "The bouquet has slopped over the edge and lies on the floor" (*CP*, 453). This final flourish is intensely ironic. By the end of the poem, the bouquet has become for the reader a highly significant commentary both on all those meta-men who go in search of presence with such a high degree of predetermination, as this soldier obviously has, and on the irreducible absence that threatens to diminish their inviolable certainty every time. The absence, linked to a female in this context, which Stevens exploits further in several other texts from the same period (the "dissociated abundance of being" in "The Woman in Sunshine" [*CP*, 445], the "Ab-abba" of "images, disembodied" in "A Golden Woman in a Silver Mirror" [*CP*, 460–61], the "nothing . . . [of] language" in "Madame La Fleurie" [*CP*, 507], the "meaning in nothingness" in "Celle Qui Fût Héaulmiette" [*CP*, 438])—this absence is underscored by the parallel military occlusion of it in the epilogue to "Notes," we may recall. As such, it doubly reenforces "the otherness within the experiential self—the defamiliarization of the familiar," as Sandra Gilbert and Susan Gubar recently describe it, which conforms precisely to the imagi-

---

21. For "the Romantic dissolution of contradiction" aimed ultimately at "the telos of metaphysics," see Gasché, *The Tain of the Mirror*, 141.

nation as value in Stevens' more regenerate notion of metaphoricity discussed earlier.[22]

A final, important text in Stevens' late work that continues the negative thematization of belief through the degeneration of metaphor is "Prologues to What Is Possible," composed in 1952. Using the "one-ness" of a transparent boat's motion on its way to some sure destination, Stevens in this piece seems almost overly pedantic in the way he sets up the critique of conventional metaphoricity's familiar equivalence between vehicle and tenor, its proceeding to semantic closure, and the "ease of mind" that is expected to result:

> The boat was built of stones that had lost their weight and being
>   no longer heavy
> Had left in them only a brilliance, of unaccustomed origin,
> So that he that stood up in the boat leaning and looking before
>   him
> Did not pass like someone voyaging out of and beyond the
>   familiar.
> . . . .
>   . . . he felt, with an appointed sureness,
> That it contained the meaning into which he wanted to enter,
> A meaning which, as he entered it, would shatter the boat and
>   leave the oarsmen quiet
> As at a point of central arrival, an instant moment, much or little,
> Removed from any shore, from any man or woman, and needing
>   none.
>
> (*CP,* 515–516)

The little allegory of metaphor's commonly conceived operation set up in this passage assures that by not moving out "beyond the familiar," the signifier will always give place to the signified and that the ship of meaning will always comes to its port of "appointed sureness" in the end.

In the second part of the poem, however, such predestined self-assur-

---

22. Sandra M. Gilbert and Susan Gubar, "The Mirror and the Vamp: Reflections on Feminist Criticism," in *The Future of Literary Theory,* ed. Ralph Cohen (New York, 1989), 159. Craig Owens' assessment of the work of Sherri Levine, Cindy Sherman, and Barbara Kruger establishes a similar point. See "The Discourse of Others: Feminists and Postmodernism," in *The Anti-Aesthetic: Essays on Postmodern Culture,* ed. Hal Foster (Port Townsend, Wash., 1983), 57–82, esp. 70–77.

ance can also be the source of a certain "fear." Because this model of rhetorical effacement can only confirm what the user already knows, it can say nothing about how he comes to know it, that is, about how the signifying process allows meaning to declare itself. Thus, "the object with which he was compared / Was beyond his recognizing" (*CP*, 516). "Likeness," therefore, what the text refers to as "the enclosures of hypotheses," is a subtractive, or exclusionary, proposition that can illuminate the products of self-present knowledge but cannot get at all those additional things "beyond resemblance" not appointed for re-cognition in the half-sleep of metaphor's traditional conceptualization. Consequently, it carries the believer "only a little way, and not beyond" the normal "this and that" of summertime self-relation (*CP*, 516). Because recognition is what is centrally problematic in the conventional communication model, in "Study of Images I," written in 1949, we find that "it does no good to speak . . . [of] the study of his images / [As] the study of man," if "in images we awake, / Within the very object that we seek, / Participants of its being": "It does no good" (*CP*, 463). Consequently, if there is to be a "centre of images" for "right joining" or "final relation," as in "Study of Images II," from the same year, it must be "a betrothal known / To none" (*CP*, 464–65). The "Beings of other beings"—women with "other lives," in Stevens' reprise of a female Other—become "manifold" in this companion text when the principle of metaphorical self-affection is rhetorically decentered, yielding a more multiplex "As if, as if, as if" (*CP*, 464).

Emmanuel Levinas observes: "To communicate is indeed to open oneself, but the openness is not complete if it is on the watch for *recognition*. . . . Communication is an adventure of subjectivity different from that which is dominated by the concern to recover itself, different from that of coinciding in consciousness; it will involve uncertainty."[23] Wallace Stevens, too, envisions an adventure of subjectivity for the user of language, but only after he gets past his fear of its potentially abnormal operation:

> What self, for example, did he contain that had not yet been
>   loosed,
> Snarling in him for discovery as his attentions spread,
> As if all his hereditary lights were suddenly increased
> By an access of color, a new and unobserved, slight dithering,

23. Taylor, *Altarity*, 202, but see also Elizabeth W. Bruss, *Beautiful Theories: The Spectacle of Discourse in Contemporary Criticism* (Baltimore, 1982), 81.

The smallest lamp, which added its puissant flick, to which he
  gave
A name and privilege over the ordinary of his commonplace.

(*CP,* 516–17)

The emphasis here on the sudden increase in expressiveness, on its spreading and expanding horizontal quality emphasized in the "dithering" of presence brought forward from "The Bouquet" (*CP,* 452) and "A Collect of Philosophy" (*OP,* 273), all of this clearly reveals Stevens' insistence on an additive and inclusionary model for metaphoricity in the question of belief rather than on a more familiar subtractive and exclusionary one. Yet this whole expansionary project can get underway only when the economy of metaphorical transcendence is dismantled and an economy more attuned to difference, the "unexpected magnitudes" in the poem's final line, is installed as the prologue to what is (im)possible, what Derrida has called "a new transcendental aesthetic," that is, "the possibility of inscriptions in general."[24]

We can perhaps pinpoint metaphoricity's transition from identity to difference most distinctly in a poem like the 1948 "Saint John and the Back-Ache," where the presence of things—"the world [as] presence," according to Saint John—gives place to absence, that is, to the power of expression: "The mind [as] the terriblest force" in that world, which is the position of the Back-Ache, who can suffer Saint John's metaphysics no longer (*CP,* 436). The shift from world back to mind, however, is not an argument for epistemology over ontology. In carefully describing the mind's defending *against* itself, the Back-Ache makes it clear that his position is not merely a metaphysical opposition to the position of Saint John. His argument is simply that unless words are actually the things they represent, according to "Adagia," then they must be symbols, and all identity, including self-identity, must therefore be questionable (*OP,* 194). All presence, in other words, is absence, strictly speaking, and "contrary to what our desire cannot fail to be tempted into *believing,*" as Derrida remarks, "the thing itself always escapes." Because the effect of the object is always "beyond the mind's / Extremest pinch" (*CP,* 436–37), what becomes privileged is the force of the mind's metaphorical repetition rather than the form of its representation, the metaphysics of presence that the Revelation of Saint John continues to labor under. If there must be an "external cause" for revelation's Word, and Stevens' discourse

24. Derrida, *Grammatology,* 290.

must be very guarded on this point, John must seek it, as in "Notes," within "the dumbfoundering abyss / Between us and the object" (*CP,* 437). Nietzsche has asked, "Is not seeing always—seeing abysses?" (*Z,* 157). The sooner Saint John accustoms himself to this "little ignorance *that is everything*" (*CP,* 437, emphasis added), that is to say, to what lies below the tension of expression's punning "lyre," linked once again to a female Other ("Presence is not the woman"), the sooner will the Back-Ache gain relief from the continuous bowing and scraping of transcendent self-abasement through what Roland Barthes might describe as "a liberation of symbolic energy." The movement of energy or force, however, must never be confused with what results from the motility of metaphor itself, the distinction the text scruples to make between the "play of strings" in the poet's lyre and its angelic evocations: "Brilliant blows" (*CP,* 437). Withstanding the absence of presence in this way ("*Kinder-Scenen*" early in life and perhaps the "possible nest in the invisible tree" later), we come finally to understand what Foucault describes as the absence in language itself, that is to say, the paralogy of metaphor, as its most compelling instance. Its association with an "unknown" serpent in the poem's concluding reminiscence of "Auroras"—a serpent that is both "venom" and "wisdom" at once—is therefore Stevens' final Wordsworthian insight into a "presence [that] lies far too deep" for terminal articulation.[25]

To round out this second group of poems in Stevens' final work, we might look at a poem that many would agree does lie far too deep, at least for critical articulation. B. J. Leggett has described "The Owl in the Sarcophagus," written in 1947, a year before the previous text, as "certainly [Stevens'] most opaque poem," whereas Harold Bloom has called it "uninterpretable." But if we are at last sensitive in Stevens' discourse to the evolution of entirely new theories of romance, of imagination, and now, finally, of metaphor in the genealogy of the question of belief, we must, as Winquist observes, "choose to go into the night of our experience to be hearers of the unsaid word . . . [and] take the residue of the daylight world into the night if we are to work in the authentic ambiguity of mixed discourse."[26] As with so many of the commentaries in the last chapters of this study, it is perhaps disastrous to attempt to work sequentially through any of Stevens' longer texts. Years of reading him patiently and carefully can often reveal the most

25. Derrida, *Speech and Phenomena,* 104, emphasis added; Barthes, *Image-Music-Text,* 158; Foucault, *Language, Counter-Memory, Practice,* 57.

26. Leggett, *Poetic Theory,* 170; Bloom, *Poems of Our Climate,* 292; Winquist, *Epiphanies of Darkness,* 41.

fruitful entry points to be those located in places quite far removed from his introductions. In the present case, we must go to the very end of this obscure poem to understand that Stevens is writing a "mythology of modern death" (*CP*, 435) consisting of three figures ("monsters of elegy") who are Death's supreme images: the two male figures of Sleep and Peace and the third female figure of Knowledge, identified in earlier sections. Whether these figures are all children of the mind or the mind itself is their offspring (*CP*, 436), Stevens' fudging here, the "mufflings" (*CP*, 435), is obviously part of his attempt to resist making any *absolute* determinations in this allegory of the creative process. By now we should understand certainty to be death in all his later poetry, which is why the three "people" so formed are creatures by which the mind, either as parent or child, lives *and* dies in the last line. Their final truth would be fatal to know for sure; it would be a truth, therefore, enclosed by Death as a belly encloses a dove in Stevens' previous work or as a coffin encloses Hegel's dusk-flying owl in the poem's title here.

Like his Metaphysician in the Dark, Wallace Stevens can be only speculative in matters of a/theological belief. In the poem's opening section, therefore, "the thought of those dark three" is described as "the forms of dark desire" (*CP*, 432). To an extent, the two brothers, high Sleep and high Peace, along with their less defined female counterpart, "she that says / Good-by in the darkness" (*CP*, 431), all have a certain determination. This specificity, however, is only because in the history of Western thought these forms must be made "visible to the eye that needs, / Needs out of the whole necessity of sight" (*CP*, 432). Stevens, whom we have seen many times attempting to resist the blandishments of such logocentrism, would much prefer to remove them from the overdetermination of this metaphysical narrative entirely:

> They move
>
> About the night. They live without our light,
> In an element not the heaviness of time,
> In which reality is prodigy.
>
> (*CP*, 432)

Still, Sleep and Peace would appear to give some degree of sanction to the dead that make up this tradition, for Sleep's "highness" quiets its believers, while Peace provides the shoulders upon which "even the heavens rest." The female form, however, not unexpectedly, disrupts the twin brothers' mythology of Being, resisting its totalization by inventing forms of farewell in all that darkness, directed particularly at those who "cannot say good-by themselves" (*CP*, 431). Her speaking quietly thus displaces the earlier metaphysics of sight with "the ear [that] repeats," but repeats "without a voice," we are told, likely in order to avoid another kind of Derridean metaphysics of speech. The confrontation between male and female forms over the disruption of presence intensifies, as brother Sleep modulates into a father and brother Peace into a cousin, a close relation "by a hundred names" (*CP*, 432). We consequently have a whole tradition threatening to solidify itself into "abortive figures," rocklike and motionless "impenetrable symbols," unless "between life / And death," in Stevens' instrumental typography, some force ("a flash of voice," so reminiscent of the motive for metaphor) might keep all of them mobile by re-figuring and re-creating them. As a result, we find the female Other becoming transformed into an "earthly mother," but one who is present in memory only. In this impossible trope for regeneration, "the Alpha and Omega of both the life of letters and the letters of life," she will offer new belief to mankind as "the mother of / The dead," yet only if recollected as the absent originary of mankind's Sleep and Peace: "Keep you, keep you, I am gone, oh keep you as / My memory, is the mother of us all" (*CP*, 432). Mark Halliday's recent extraordinary argument for the "consistent failure by Stevens to describe the female other . . . as a separate subjectivity, an independent actor and perceiver outside his own mind," therefore, hardly seems supportable in view of the presentation of the female here and those others previously examined.[27]

Sections three and four of the poem proceed to take up the specific roles of Sleep and Peace in the regenerate operation of metaphor within the question of belief. As the "wild-ringed eye," the poet is first allowed to breathe deeply the atmosphere of Sleep. Section three makes it the archē of the articulatory process, attributing to Sleep the qualities of pure intelligence from which all his ideas must be derived:

> Sleep realized
> Was the whiteness that is the ultimate intellect,
> A diamond jubilance beyond the fire,
>
> That gives its power to the wild-ringed eye.
>   (*CP*, 433)

27. Sandra M. Gilbert and Susan Gubar, *The War of the Words* (New Haven, 1988), 267, Vol. I of Gilbert and Gubar, *No Man's Land: The Place of the Woman Writer in the Twentieth Century*, 3 vols. projected; Mark Halliday, *Stevens and the Interpersonal* (Princeton, 1991), 54. Even more repulsive is Halliday's claim that "Stevens loved the idea that there is a level at which difference between persons becomes irrelevant while true and important things can still be said about us" (119–20); see also 166, 178–79n36.

As in Stevens' earlier "From the Packet of Anacharsis," the ever-changing unity of that intelligence is totally incomprehensible until it becomes extended into particular meanings that Stevens images as foldings or robings (the "weaving and the crinkling and the vex" [*CP*, 433]) that surround the intellect, imaged further in the familiar comparisons to a giant's body and a moving mountain. Thus, violet streakings are to the neutral white what rufflings on water are to a vexing breeze. They are the *telos*, or ending, to poetic inspiration, when thinking, in the form of Peace in section four, finally surfaces as "that figure stationed at our end, / Always, in brilliance, fatal, final, formed" (*CP*, 434). Together, then, Sleep and Peace spell out a kind of *abecedarium poeticae*, through a rigorous declension of the metaphoric process: After *A*, the archē of absent intellect, comes *B*, the present "alphabet / By which to spell out holy doom and end, / A bee for the remembering of happiness" (*CP*, 434). And for *C*? This is perhaps the Cyclops in section four's final stanza, a figure for the generations of poets, the wild-ringed eyes, once again, who throughout time have fashioned countless forms of apparel for man's giant intellect and have doomed him to what Mutlu Blasing, pursuing a similar line of argument, calls "the deadly identification of poetry and truth," in the rhetoric of a giant intellect like Emerson, for instance.[28] By an even further extrapolation, we perhaps arrive at the canon itself and the whole cloth out of which this further declension of Peace is cut:

> The whole spirit sparkling in its cloth,
> Generations of the imagination piled
> In the manner of its stitchings, of its thread,
> In the weaving round the wonder of its need,
>
> And the first flowers upon it.
>
> (*CP*, 434)

Going with Stevens' droll pun, we best understand Peace as the newest piece added to the tradition, the "robe that is our glory," and as the latest inspiration offered to our believing minds. Inserted between Sleep and the poet, this "godolphin" fellow must nonetheless continue to appear infinitely mysterious to us: infinite ("brilliant height") because the tradition shows no sign of abating and mysterious ("shither-shade," "nothingness") because no poet can possibly predict any future turnings the course of belief might take that

28. Blasing, *American Poetry*, 88.

he has not, up to the present, already charted. Much the likeness of his brother, then, he is "estranged, estranged," but to the Metaphysician in the Dark, he is a sign of "good solace" for all that (*CP,* 434).

Just what sends the poet from his immaculate beginning in Sleep's ever-early candor to his immaculate end in Peace's late plural, paraphrasing the line from "Notes" (*CP,* 382), is the last thing concerning metaphoricity's transformative declensions, which Stevens reserves for section five. There, he refers to it as "invisible change," an "inner thing" under the aspect of the female Other earlier:

> It was not her look but a knowledge that she had.
> She was a self that knew, an inner thing,
> Subtler than look's declaiming, although she moved
>
> With a sad splendor, beyond artifice,
> Impassioned by the knowledge that she had,
> There on the edges of oblivion.
>
> (*CP,* 435)

Located in the self as "knowledge," this last "thing" nonetheless resists being known or determined by that self, rather like Derrida's location of a deconstructive force that refuses all cognitive appropriation *within* rather than outside a text or discourse itself.[29] Hence, Stevens opens with this description: "She that says good-by losing in self / The sense of self . . . stood tall in self not symbol, quick / And potent, an influence felt instead of seen" (*CP,* 435). As a totally absent presence, Stevens denies her any kind of ontological status, perhaps making her most discoverable at the very point at which she is least so, the way invisible change realizes change itself when all change has ceased to be. Stevens' later "Angel Surrounded by Paysans" from 1949 provides the best gloss for this difficult thought: the necessary angel of earth whose "repetitions of half-meanings" are understood, like the half-figure itself, only in the moment when it has turned all too quickly and has vanished (*CP,* 496–97).[30] The backward gestures of her hand are quite central to Knowledge's non-appearance here. Analyzed in some detail as one of Stevens' important meta-

29. See Gasché, *The Tain of the Mirror,* 163.

30. On Stevens' necessary angel, *cf.* Jacques Derrida's description of the "completely angelic structure," which is "the structure of every scene of writing in general," in "Of an Apocalyptic Tone Recently Adopted in Philosophy," *Semeia,* XXIII (1982), 87. *Cf.* also Luce Irigaray, "Sexual Difference," in *French Feminist Thought: A Reader,* ed. Toril Moi (New York, 1989), 126; Gasché, "Joining the Text," 157, 159; and Jacqueline Vaught Brogan, "'Sister of the Minotaur': Sexism and Stevens," *Wallace Stevens Journal,* XII (Fall, 1988), 115.

phors for metaphysical appropriation in Chapter 3, the hand now is deployed to signify the unspecifiable: to hold men closely in discovery by, paradoxically, with-holding metaphoricity's own discoverability, allowing itself to be manifested in the speed or movement, the velocities of change formerly, in the very act of discovery itself. It is better in the end that she be enfolded "in the silence that follows her last word—" (*CP*, 435), in this section's final line, for whereof one cannot speak, as Wittgenstein reminds us in closing out his *Tractatus*, thereof one must be silent.[31]

Wallace Stevens had written "The Owl in the Sarcophagus" in 1947 partly to commemorate the death of his dear friend Henry Church (*L*, 566). This was the friend to whom, in life five years previously, he had dedicated his more expansive "Notes." The preponderance of death imagery in the later text strikingly registers the alteration in mood, no doubt reflective of the experience of mortality at such close range and intensified by the poet's own physical decline as both acromegalic and diabetic in his final years. From what we can learn, both in the poetry and prose, concerning a more defamiliarized and defamiliarizing version of the imagination in relation to belief, however, it would seem rather untoward to conclude that mortality, in whichever physical presentiment from this period, could trigger "a loss of faith at a level more profound than [Stevens] had ever prepared himself to expect."[32] On the contrary, it is precisely a meditation on mortality's last things that could spark faith's renewal. For as I suggested in the last section, the last thing Stevens could possibly envision for faith that would signal its loss was its termination in some form of the normal or the same that, from the imagination's point of view, was strictly continuous with death. Any such sign of "an aversion to the abnormal," in other words, was a "disposition toward a point of view derogatory to the imagination" (*NA*, 153). Since death itself was about as normative a condition as human existence was ever likely to reach, invariably it becomes for Stevens in several of his later poems almost the *sine qua non* through which "to extend [imagination's] abnormality" and, by extension, belief's as well (*NA*, 153).

In a purely theological context, we may be prone to think of the terminus of faith in the spiritually deadening sense of an egregiously normative fundamentalism. Since all of Stevens' contexts are rhetorical, though, the in-

---

31. Ludwig Wittgenstein, *Tractatus Logico-Philosophicus*, trans. C. K. Ogden (1922; rpr. Great Britain, 1981), 189.

32. Joan Richardson, *Wallace Stevens: The Later Years, 1923–1955* (New York, 1988), 290.

tersection of the question of belief manifests itself in the parallel context of literalism, or what we might choose to refer to in this next group of poems as "The Plain Sense of Things," from the 1952 poem by that name. In his hammering away at the distinction between the literal and the metaphorical, which brings forward his thematization of the real and unreal previously, Stevens' point is repeatedly the one Richard Rorty has made of late, that is, to mark a differentiation "not as a distinction between two sorts of meaning, nor as a distinction between two sorts of interpretation, but as a distinction between familiar and unfamiliar uses [of language]." Thus, in *The Necessary Angel,* Stevens insists "the typical function of the imagination . . . always makes use of the familiar to produce the unfamiliar" (165). That the potential for such a declension exists in language, as we have seen, marks the prologue to what is possible as far as belief is concerned. However, words carried to the furthest point of such a declension, that is, to their furthest point of familiarity, deliver us up to spirituality's "inert savoir," depicted quite memorably in the opening stanzas of "The Plain Sense of Things":

> After the leaves have fallen, we return
> To a plain sense of things. It is as if
> We had come to an end of the imagination,
> Inanimate in an inert savoir.
>
> It is difficult even to choose the adjective
> For this blank cold, this sadness without cause.
> The great structure has become a minor house.
> No turban walks across the lessened floors.
>
> (*CP,* 502)

The plain sense in this passage might indeed mark the end of the imagination if it were literally possible for words to become coincident with things, real things—"Really!," as we like to say. But we live in the mind, for the most part Stevens would say, and such an identifiable familiarity is one of degree only and, as such, a question of the extent to which artifice has proceeded within us (*NA,* 140–41) or, put the other way—the way Derrida puts it—of the extent to which the "so-called 'thing itself' is always already a *representamen* shielded from the simplicity of intuitive evidence."[33] Either way, as

33. Rorty, *Contingency, Irony, and Solidarity,* 17; Derrida, *Grammatology,* 49. See also Bernd Magnus, "The End of 'The End of Philosophy,'" 7, along with John D. Caputo, "From

Frank Kermode observes, "any linguistic act, including a page of literary explication, is from some points of view as complicated as anything in *Finnegans Wake*," and "people who talk about putting things in plain language should be aware of that: There is no plain language."[34] It is for this reason, and for this reason alone, that Stevens can declare later on in the poem, "Yet the absence of the imagination had / Itself to be imagined" (*CP*, 503). At some point, in other words, even the normal that might appear to represent imagination at its most deprived was once an extension of the abnormal, that is, as I quoted Nietzsche back in Chapter 3, truth that has forgotten it once was metaphorical and has become here "an inevitable knowledge, / Required, as a necessity requires" (*CP*, 503). What is more, the absence of the imagination, as "The Owl in the Sarcophagus" alerts us, is a riddling truth. In its inert savoir, it doubles as the metaleptic condition for the continuance of the very metaphoricity that, in the end, must imagine or explain itself, hence the "sense" in the present poem's title that must be made plain. It is in this ironic "sense"—the sense in which there is no plain sense—that a tremendous hope for the future of belief lies, despite the reduction above of the great structure of Being to "a minor house." The failure of this "fantastic effort" is a reflection only on the passing of the representation of human consciousness at the center of metaphysical faith, symbolized by the "turban" walking across the mind's lessened floors. Now, in the "blank cold" of imaginative absence, repetition reinforces the plain sense of belief "without reflections" (*CP*, 503). Despite all the fetid ruin at the end of the poem, therefore, in the waste of mud and lilies and rats, there is nonetheless a kind of optimism, "a sort of silence" as at the end of "Sarcophagus," that the textuality of the written word itself will continue to revolve the question of belief much beyond all of the fallen "leaves" expended in so many of its trial annunciations.

The postmetaphysical prospect of a differing and deferred presence or plain sense, therefore, becomes that "snatch of belief" that marks yet another metonymic chain of repetition in the endless sequence of "Long and Sluggish Lines," also from 1952:

---

the Primordiality of Absence to the Absence of Primordiality," 195, both in *Hermeneutics and Deconstruction,* ed. Silverman and Ihde.

34. Kermode quoted in Herbert N. Schneidau. "The Word Against the Word: Derrida on Textuality," *Semeia,* XXIII (1982), 18 (de Man, *Allegories of Reading,* 10, is related). Elsewhere, Kermode argues that texts do not exist plainly in themselves at a level of imaginary zero but are constantly mediated by contexts: custom, authority, tradition, and so forth. "There is no 'inert savoir'; to speak as if there were is already to speak 'as if'" ("The Plain Sense of Things," 191–92).

The trees have a look as if they bore sad names
And kept saying over and over one same, same thing,

In a kind of uproar, because an opposite, a contradiction,
Has enraged them and made them want to talk it down.

               (*CP,* 522)

As part of textuality's more general "metaleptic issue of the 'deviations' of metaphor," in Joseph Riddel's phrase, the repetition of the "thing" here attaches itself to that wakefulness inside the sleep of metaphysics so prominent in "Auroras" and, in the opening of this poem, promises to make so little difference to a poet at more than seventy, yet a difference nonetheless.[35] In "An Old Man Asleep," from 1952, this difference accordingly takes the shape of a "whole peculiar plot" quite outside the classic epistemes of representation in "self and earth" that have underwritten faith up to the present ("Your beliefs and disbeliefs" [*CP,* 501]) but whose "dumb [*i.e.,* plain] sense" must give place to para-things beyond the somnolence of these two worlds mentioned in the opening line. Stevens labors, however, to point out that this precession of simulacra in a discourse so reminiscent of Baudrillard is not merely another argument for transcendence. In another 1952 poem, "One of the Inhabitants of the West," for instance, he satirizes the notion of prophetic revelation whose single vision, anticipated by one-ness in the title, a thoroughgoing textualizing belief must adamantly oppose. The eschatology being mocked is the divination of one of certain "mechanisms of angelic thought"— a mechanism that is outmoded because it locks meaning into rigid, epiphanic moments ("the establishments / Of wind and light and cloud," for example [*CP,* 503]) awaiting some kind of apocalyptic fulfillment that never seems to arrive. The prophet of such a vision ("the archangel of evening") invariably reads the world one way and one way only, as the corruption of a pastoral text through some tragic Fall: "So much guilt lies buried / Beneath the innocence / Of autumn days" (*CP,* 504). His formulaic approach to experience, to the very last European Alp and the very last drop of the sheeted Atlantic, thus joins him to all those other "figures of Medusa," men of stone whose invariable work of explication makes them impervious to completely optional readings of text: the alterity of "a well-rosed two-light," for instance, in contrast to the inevitable evening's one, lone star (*CP,* 504).

35. Riddel, "The Climate of Our Poems," 173.

Stevens, however, refuses to be weighed down by such vast numbers of stony interpreters. In fact, their imperviousness to the question of belief challenges him to a greater hope. "Doubtless this majority has let itself be *reduced to the order of things*," as Georges Bataille explains the case in his *Theory of Religion*:

> But this generalized reduction, this perfect fulfillment of the thing, is the necessary condition for the conscious and fully developed posing of the problem of man's reduction to thinghood. Only in a world where the thing has reduced everything, where what was once opposed to it reveals the poverty of equivocal positions—and inevitable shifts—can intimacy [*i.e.,* a more productive order] affirm itself without any more compromises than the thing. Only the gigantic development of the means of production is capable of fully revealing the meaning of production . . . the fulfillment of *self-consciousness* in the free outbursts of the intimate [divine] order.

If only in the textual playfulness buried at the center of its bizarre title, "Lebensweisheitspielerei," also written in 1952, attempts to make a promising shift in the direction of the more intimate order inspired by the freedom of equivocation as described by Bataille. But this text still has a good distance to go to get past the doomsayers who continue to insist on the metaphorical equivalence between the fall of sunlight of an afternoon and "the poverty / Of autumnal space" and then "the stale grandeur of annihilation" that they feel necessarily has to follow from this declension (*CP,* 505). To break free of the real source of annihilation in this dwindled sphere, the generalized reduction of "what he is and as he is" of the genuinely unaccomplished (*CP,* 505), the true Metaphysician in the Dark must jettison the plain-sense "myth of transparency," with its "air of unconstructed neutrality" at the very heart of metaphysical belief. He must begin working instead from "The Hermitage at the Centre" or "Vacancy in the Park," both written in 1952, that is, from the Absence at the center of imagination's metaphoricity previously. In the former text, Stevens makes "the vacant place that remains when all metaphysical thinking is destroyed," in Rorty's words, the subject of "unintelligible thought" (*CP,* 505) in an effort to reverse the logocentric inevitability in the poems just mentioned or in implicated pieces such as "Our Stars Come from Ireland" and "The Irish Cliffs of Moher," from 1948 and 1952 respectively, both dealing with childhood loss as another of those "somnambulations" of poetry (*CP*, 502).[36] In "The Hermitage," therefore, Stevens offers quite other ways of reading the fallen "leaves on the macadam," in the favorite pun, when the textuality is kept open in the way a secret hermitage might suggest. This image could imply that an apparent end to interpretation might just be the beginning, as remarked in the last stanza, that autumn elsewhere in the poem, for example, might be an access to more desirable grass in the recline of temperate heaven or that the tottering of a great wind might be the call for birds of more wit, "intelligible twittering" in exchange for "unintelligible thought" in more repetitively discursive terms (*CP*, 505). The exchange here thus becomes the "unexplained completion" in "The Poem That Took the Place of a Mountain" from 1952 as well, where the "exact rock" of the textual space must be filled with "inexactnesses," since the view of total presence is one that imagination's program of regeneration ("word for word") can only edge toward, never entirely approximate, as the original site of metaphor's "unique and solitary home" (*CP*, 512).[37] Thus, "one last look at the ducks" in the concluding image of "The Hermitage" is not some visionary *fait accompli*. Recollecting its use in "The Bouquet" earlier, we find that the image becomes productive of a possible look at lucent children gathered round some un-named female in a ring. Removing the fixed determination of textualizing belief in this way, Stevens opens up a space for tales that are as likely to get told the day before yesterday as they are the day after tomorrow and, just as suddenly, to be "all dissolved and gone" (*CP*, 505).

By the time Stevens comes round to composing "Not Ideas about the Thing but the Thing Itself" in 1954, the last poem to appear in *The Rock* and in *Collected Poems,* he can deal with the thing itself, after Nietzsche and after Heidegger and the whole *Nouvelle Nouvelle Revue Française* group, only in the most circumlocutionary and ironical way possible. After all, a poem about the thing itself could be nothing but a presentation of ideas, proving once again that the "new knowledge of reality" in Stevens' very last collected line is wholly unintelligible from an analytical standpoint, as in the previous poem; it is a presentiment of some ultimately unknowable and unnameable

36. Georges Bataille, *Theory of Religion,* trans. Robert Hurley (New York, 1989), 94; Bruss, *Beautiful Theories,* 22; Rorty, *Consequences,* 49.

37. The link to the previous "Vacancy in the Park" and "The Hermitage at the Centre" via Stevens' unintelligible thought more generally is found at the end of Shelley's own mountain poem, "Mont Blanc": "And what were thou, and earth, and stars, and sea, / If to the human mind's imaginings / Silence and solitude were vacancy?" (142–44). See Percy Bysshe Shelley, *Shelley: Poetical Works,* ed. Thomas Hutchinson (New York, 1967), 535.

anteriority, originary to ideas, that the believing poet circles to fix and frame through the abecedarium of language but ultimately hazards to target only at his peril:

> That scrawny cry—it was
> A chorister whose c preceded the choir.
> It was part of the colossal sun,
>
> Surrounded by its choral rings,
> Still far away. It was like
> A new knowledge of reality.
>
> (*CP,* 534)

The colossal sun can be deployed for a final time here in connection with the unreachable *Ding an Sich* for all of the reasons set out in the opening section of "Notes" yet also because, as we learn in one of Stevens' late letters, "we see it too infrequently to know it [even] when we see it" (*L,* 602). Consequently, the "vast ventriloquism" (*CP,* 534), set in motion by an essentially unrepresentable no-thing, one fated to become "faded papier-mâché" in the somnambulism of hoped-for presence, continues to prolong the question of belief. For it is the resistance of the thing itself to the finality of ideas in the will to believe that is all the Metaphysician in the Dark is ever likely to know for sure and that as a result keeps his hope for new faith alive.[38] Yet we ought never to be really sure, just as before we ought never really to know which side of the preposition Stevens' absence of imagination would land us. We have to go to a somewhat longer and earlier text to fathom much more clearly the shift Stevens intends generally in his last work—a shift from a belief in last things to a questioning of belief that a great deal of his impenetrable textuality would over and over continue to provoke.

"Things of August," written in 1949, promises to chart this shift in the

---

38. Bringing Stevens' notion of the thing itself forward into more politically and culturally resonant contexts, we are again given to note how the impenetrability of certain objects or things nonetheless secures enormous hope for keeping alive much of the quite varied discourse firmly trained on them. As examples, I am thinking particularly of Naomi Schor's work on the detail in the feminist context (*Reading in Detail: Aesthetics and the Feminine* [New York, 1987], esp, 86, 91, 96–97); Thomas Yingling's on AIDS in gender studies more generally ("AIDS in America: Postmodern Governance, Identity, and Experience," in *inside/out: Lesbian Theories, Gay Theories,* ed. Diana Fuss [New York, 1991], 291–310, esp. 306–307); and Mary Ann Doane's work on televisual catastrophe in the media ("Information, Crisis, Catastrophe," in *Logics of Television: Essays in Cultural Criticism,* ed. Patricia Mellencamp [Bloomington, 1990], 222–39, esp. 234, 236, 238), among others.

very first verse of the opening canto in the choice it presents the reader between "an old and disused ambit of the soul" and "a new aspect, bright in
discovery—" (*CP,* 489). Turning to Canto VIII, we discover that the old
ambit is the by-now familiar formulation of belief in terms of the classic epistemological rhetoric of self-knowledge, *i.e.,* "the presence of a solitude of the
self," or "whole man," that dissolves multiplicity and plurality into "the voice
of union" (*CP,* 494). Thus, "tempers and beliefs" become *one* temper and *one*
belief such that "differences lost / Difference and were one." Along with these
exclusions goes the loss of any sense of a forward movement of time, or in
terms more typical of modernist (as opposed to postmodernist) rhetoric as
Steven Connor sees it, "to view history and human life as an endless series of
cycles [in order] to attempt to defeat transience, by bending it into pattern."[39] Thus, the old ambit here is pure nostalgia, privileging instead the
sense of archaic form ("a movement of the outlines of similarity"), which,
under the aspect of a rising moon as the familiar sign of passive intelligence,
becomes projected further into the "archaic forms" of giants and, beyond
these, into a single "archaic space" that takes on the totalizing form of a lone,
impersonal, supergigantic patriarch: "The father, the ancestor, the bearded
peer, / The total of human shadows bright as glass" (*CP,* 494). In the abstraction of such an expanse, theoretically, we all come to resemble one another
"at [or in] the sight." How intolerable the idea of exclusion always is in such
an abstract model is made clear, however, in Canto VII, where the view from
its tower that puts us in mind of a similar site back in "Credences" is described as "high and deadly" (*CP,* 493). It thus would seem that there is rather
too high a price to be paid for understanding "things" in an at-home sort of
way, for always being predeterminedly certain about what one sees as the
necessary condition for self-knowledge:

> That, in the shadowless atmosphere,
> The knowledge of things lay round but unperceived:
> The height was not quite proper;
> The position was wrong.
>
>   (*CP,* 493)

The Yeatsian descent from the tower to the house as this section closes, from
"the spun sky" to the mundanity of novels on tables and geraniums on sills,
is therefore an endeavor to open more widely the doors of perception and to
feel more responsively "the satisfactions / Of that transparent air" (*CP,* 493).

39. Steven Connor, *Postmodernist Culture: An Introduction to Theories of the Contemporary*
(Oxford, 1989), 117.

Unlike Yeats, however, whose descent has the very determined point of arrival in the "foul rag-and-bone shop of the heart," thus setting up yet another model of presence in things, Stevens descends to lay hold of the farther-reaching insight, in Canto IX, that "the meanings are [all] our own" (*CP,* 495).[40] By his angling for belief not so much in terms of the correspondence to things themselves as in terms of the meanings that we *make* of things, that is, the "text of intelligent men" that argues more for the distance separating words from things, belief becomes less a question of knowing or not knowing. Things are because "we wanted it so" (*CP,* 495) or, to recur to Rorty's insight dealt with in the last chapter, because our metaphors are for making rather than for matching or, even more radically, for doing rather than meaning, as Connor would perhaps argue.[41] Hence Stevens writes "Two Illustrations That the World Is What You *Make* of It" (emphasis added) in 1952, and we note especially Part Two, "*The World Is Larger in Summer,*" whose desuetude reveals what the effort of matching must come to (*CP,* 514–15). In making, though, we are always given "a sense of the distance of the sun," as in Part One, "*The Constant Disquisition of the Wind*" (*CP,* 513). Herman Rapaport's further clarification is useful here: "In Derrida's context, the thing is in a state of announcing its arrival into the world as thing only insofar as its discloses itself as distanced (dis-stanced) from other things. The thing, therefore, comes into being only to the extent that it has never quite fully arrived into the world as a thing-in-itself."[42] The implications as far as belief is concerned are that it has no center or that if it has one, its center is completely indecipherable, "unintelligible, / As in a hermitage" (*CP,* 495), in Stevens' anticipation of several of the poems (already discussed) that were to follow. Even to *make* this unintelligibility known, however, requires belief to become entirely pendant on "rigid inscription," imbricated, that is, with the reading and writing that proceeds only from desire—the desire apparently that made Yeats so sick. Consequently, the new knowledge of reality scanned previously becomes here Stevens' "new text of the world, / A scribble of fret and fear and fate" (*CP,* 494), one whose acknowledgment requires mental bravura and visionary courage since, right from the footing of noon to the very pillar of midnight, everything is constituted by textuality. So for matters of faith as well: "It is a text that we shall be needing" (*CP,* 495).

With another hermitage inscribed in the question of belief, therefore,

---

40. See esp. Frye, *The Stubborn Structure,* 271, 274–75.

41. Rorty, *Contingency, Irony, and Solidarity,* 77; Connor, *Postmodernist Culture,* 10, 129.

42. Rapaport, *Heidegger and Derrida,* 146. See also Heidegger, *Poetry, Language, Thought,* 167–68, 173–74, 181, and Caputo, *The Mystical Element,* 242, 171, 188.

Stevens comes back once more in Canto VI of the present poem, with which we may conclude his lengthy meditation on last things in this section, to the White Mythology he left off in "Auroras." By Stevens' denying in Canto VII the synchronization of consciousness projected in Canto VIII above—denying "a recover-ability," as Herman Rapaport aptly describes it, "of a historical time wherein the subject can be present to itself as itself in its past and future moments"—Canto VI need only repeat for a further time the trade-off between the blank Other of the sun's "rex Impolitor" and the self-referential "tricorn" of moon bid adieu in the poem's conclusion (*CP*, 495).[43] Over and over, the Metaphysician in the Dark is compelled to make sense of this absence of imagination beyond the self yet, again and again, is never quite able to satisfy his knowledge of it, much as we feel the burden of Stevens' own repetition of his themes in a great deal of this late work, so far beyond the trials of self-affirmation in the earlier poetry. It is selfhood now that has been entirely co-opted by the unfathomable things of this world external to it and for which the writer/believer becomes enlisted as merely a kind of blank spokesman:

> The world images for the beholder.
> He is born the blank mechanic of the mountains,
>
> The blank frere of fields, their matin laborer.
> He is the possessed of sense not the possessor.
>
> (*CP*, 492)

In this manner, the things of August become an "invisible" Other, a faculty almost of "ellipses and deviations," which entirely dislodges man from theologocentric faith, since the world as a human "inhuman" is that within which man exists, it is true, "but never as himself" (*CP*, 493). Stevens' female Other makes a return appearance here, as before, to disarticulate the degeneration of internal and external alike and in the very same way as the world's last things: "chosen," as by some faithful necessity, but, bafflingly and riddlingly, not by the believer himself. Resisting the degeneration of metaphor in this way—that is, resisting the reduction to the things of conventional orthodoxy—can Stevens' a/theology now be the very breakthrough toward which his need for faith has been aimed all along? Do we find in the parturient image that greets us a little closer to the beginning of the poem, something much braver and freer, demanded by a new ambit of the soul, hot for discovery?

43. Rapaport, *Heidegger and Derrida*, 141.

Spread outward. Crack the round dome. Break through.
Have liberty not as the air within a grave

Or down a well. Breathe freedom, oh, my native,
In the space of horizons that neither love nor hate.

(*CP*, 490)

As we noted in the previous section, and in a poem particularly like "Things of August," not a little of Stevens' late work, when viewed from the standpoint of the question of belief, takes on a certain character of repetitiveness. Given what we have been careful to understand about the imagination as value in such a posttheological discourse, however, and especially about the quasi-phenomenological role that metaphoricity plays within it, we can hardly think repetition is at all a defect in these last things. In the a/theology of belief's text-event, we are given in Stevens' final volumes a highly volatile discourse, one full of assertions and reversals, feints and low blows, tackings and doublings and tracings, and, always, qualifications, intensifications, supplementations, and multiplications. One tends to feel in Stevens' case, more than in most, that "only because something has already been said," as Stanley Fish has remarked in the broader interpretive context, can Stevens "now say something different," despite how similar that new thing might be to other things articulated much earlier. Perhaps Sam Weber helps to refine even further the point that needs to be made about Stevens' repetitions by ascribing a highly suspensive motility to interpretation that could just as easily apply to the question of belief itself: "As a movement of *Entstellung*, [it] must be conceived not as the more or less faithful reproduction or representation of an antecedent, self-identical object, meaning, or 'presence,' but as a process of repetition and dislocation, the limits of which must always remain more or less problematic and unstable." As John Caputo notes, therefore, "Genuine repetition repeats forward and bears the responsibility to produce what it would become." Much of this problematic and unstable forward quality Stevens had attached to the proleptic notion of "abstraction," as we saw in "Notes"—a notion that terms like *abnormal* and *unfamiliar* in his later theorizing go a long way to help clarify.

In "The Ultimate Poem Is Abstract," we have a statement that would aim to dislocate a whole ontotheological tradition by making a virtue of such mercurial iteration. As a frontal attack on the classical metaphysician's categorical hypostatization of "This Beautiful World Of Ours," hemming and hawing a frankly enigmatic planet "red, and right" (*CP*, 429), Stevens' text would answer such smug determination with repeated questions, as in the very first line: "This day writhes with what?" Neither is the strategy of the contrary Metaphysician in the Dark one that angles for a particular answer to a particular question. One goes on asking questions, redistributing the "placid space" of metaphysical certainty and privileging instead the a/categorical "windings" and a/theological "dodges" of a postanalytical belief, which Mark Taylor has lately been pleased to characterize as "mazing grace." For the human intellect is not "fleet" but is rather a complex of writ(h)ings ("obliques and distances," as they are called [*CP*, 430]), thus causing the axiological tower and apogee of transparent worship of "Credences" to become darkened now as the "cloud-pole / Of communication," thereby perpetuating the conversation of mankind within an interminable continuum. Stevens' initiative here is one begun as long ago as the second edition of *Ideas of Order,* that is, to remove his discourse from the fixed middle of some impossible beautiful world of "enormous sense" and to set it "helplessly at the edge." Dislocated from any possible conception of designated presence, "enough to be" (*CP*, 430), he frees it up sufficiently to repeat his postcards from the volcano of "Notes" almost a decade later: the ultimate poem *is* abstract.[44]

In addition to the principled repetitive rhetoricity of Stevens' late discourse, made wholly functional to the question of belief, we might also tend to notice the recurrence of a certain type of characterization that Stevens has in mind to target as a possible model for the Metaphysician in the Dark, indentured to his a/theological project. "The Countryman," composed in 1950, is one example. In this text, the highly mobile Swatara River requires a countryman rather than a homebody to follow its highly erratic and serpentine course; thus it needs a being who, like its own restless waters, is the nameless likeness "as of a character everywhere" (*CP*, 429). Perhaps this explains why his attention is fixed on neither origin nor end (*CP*, 428), why indeed he seems to be more interested in the in-between of the Swatara's "swarthy motion," where any medium located between two terms "*both* sows confusion *between* opposites *and* stands *between* the opposites 'at once,'" as the countryman himself appears to be standing.[45] More especially, he appears to be fascinated by the manner in which the swarthy Swatara vexes all transparent understanding, moving "blackly and without crystal" in its headlong

---

44. Stanley Fish, *Is There a Text in This Class? The Authority of Interpretative Communities* (Cambridge, Mass., 1980), 350; Weber, *Institution and Interpretation,* 80; Caputo, *Radical Hermeneutics,* 59; Taylor, *Erring,* 160.

45. Derrida, *Dissemination,* 212.

descent, exercising its force in closest parallel to the energies of language, almost breathing its name repetitively as it churns along.

In a comment that brings the work of river, countryman, and, more broadly, the language of belief all together in this last text, Emmanuel Levinas writes that "a work conceived radically is a movement of the same toward the Other which never returns to the same." He adds further that "to the myth of Ulysses returning to Ithaca, we wish to oppose the story of Abraham who leaves his fatherland forever for a yet unknown land, and forbids his servant even to bring back his son to the point of departure."[46] The comment is useful not only for providing us with a further insight into the protean nature of faith's repetitive milieu in Stevens' discourse but also for the significant intersection it forms with two further characterizations of the Metaphysician in the Dark in his later work. For the parody of the Ulysses myth that Levinas' words appear to invite, we turn to Stevens' "The World as Meditation," written in 1952:

> Is it Ulysses that approaches from the east,
> The interminable adventurer? The trees are mended.
> That winter is washed away. Someone is moving
>
> On the horizon and lifting himself up above it.
> A form of fire approaches the cretonnes of Penelope,
> Whose mere savage presence awakens the world in which
>   she dwells.
>
>   (*CP,* 520)

When the "savage presence" of Ulysses as a "form of fire" will eventually return to complete Penelope's being, "the final fortune of desire" coming full circle in the images of necklace and belt, then, hypothetically, This Beautiful World Of Ours will once more be set to right: the trees will all be mended, the winter will be washed away, and the dogs will give up their watch. Yet Stevens in this text insists on holding Penelope's faith in Ulysses' return open to question, in another of his interrogatory opening lines and later: "It was Ulysses and it was not" (*CP,* 521). By countering the re-presentation of the Other suggested only by the "planet's encouragement" in this mock-narrative, Stevens would extend the "essential exercise" of belief indefinitely, as yet another effect of metalepsis. Penelope, a type of the Metaphysician in the Dark

---

46. Emmanuel Levinas, "The Trace of the Other," in *Deconstruction in Context: Literature and Philosophy,* ed. Mark C. Taylor (Chicago, 1986), 348.

so reminiscent of the former countryman, would thus use her barbarous strength to persevere in "repeating [Ulysses'] name with its patient syllables" as the most appropriate response to the absence of presence that keeps "coming constantly so near" throughout the length of the poem but which never quite arrives, not even by its end. Hence, Stevens employs the Georges Enesco epigraph to open the poem: the perpetual dream that continues both night and day, for which the *exercice essentiel*, in fiction as well as in faith, is the codependent and correspondent imagination through which, as in the case of Penelope, the self comes to be "composed" rather than reposed or even disposed (*CP*, 521). There may even be a further intersection with Heidegger in the poem's title. When Heidegger speaks of "meditative" (*besinnlich*) thinking, Caputo once again helps us to see what he means: "To 'think' means to have cleared away all concepts and representations and every trace of willing in order to be open to what is truly thought-worthy. And in each case this 'thinking' is attained only by a 'leap' from rational to meditative [*i.e.*, imaginative] thought."[47]

As a parallel to Levinas' nomadic Abraham, who departs the fatherland for places unknown, in Stevens' late work we are offered the figure of George Santayana in the magnificent 1952 "To An Old Philosopher in Rome." We have to be careful not to confuse the characterization in the poem with the poet's old professor from his Harvard youth, about whom Stevens' feelings in real life were ambiguous, to say the least.[48] Santayana, quite simply, is one of Stevens' models of the abnormal imagination (*NA*, 147–48), and his decampment from America to dedicate his life entirely to writing, and his much later removal to a convent in Rome to wait out his final days, would probably have struck the poet as a rather intriguing case of life imitating art. In the specific context of the poem itself, however, we best understand the value Santayana holds for Stevens in terms of his problematic characterization as a force for logocentric dislocation. If this character is a figure in full pursuit of the question of belief, we should hardly expect him to find it totally fulfilled within the convent's festival "sphere" or in some "hovering excellence" completely "beyond the eye" (*CP*, 508–509). Not that Stevens would reject the possibility that such transcendence might be *one* of faith's hypothetical forms, a "celestial possible" to which the light, tearing at the candle's wick, could metaphorically be laboring to attach itself. Santayana's own value to the poet,

47. Caputo, *The Mystical Element*, 213–14. For the ironic contrast, *cf.* Mr. Homburg in "Looking Across the Fields and Watching the Birds Fly," also from 1952.

48. See Joan Richardson, *Stevens: The Later Years*, 354, and *L*, 637.

though, goes beyond conventional apologetics, the "total grandeur of a total edifice" in the last stanza, and lies entirely in his stature as a master, a com-miserable man, and "an inquisitor" of such structures (*CP,* 510). He merits praise because he stops *on* the threshold of "as if" rather than *within* the certainty of design, form, frame, or any other putative realization within the closure of metaphysical thought—the threshold, that is to say, between "the extreme of the known in the presence of the extreme / Of the unknown" (*CP,* 508). It is the absence of the known, "the distances of space" in which men grow small, that drives what it might be possible to know into presence: "It is poverty's speech that seeks us out the most" (*CP,* 510).[49]

As a type of the Metaphysician in the Dark, then, Santayana is heroic in the autumn of his life because he continues to question that which eludes the ascertainable structures of faith, that is, the "more merciful Rome" that lies just outside the Rome of the here and now, in all its "naked majesty" of bird-nest arches and rain-stained vaults and newsboys muttering in the streets (*CP,* 510, 508). Like Canon Aspirin, then, back in "Notes," he chooses to include the things that are included in each other: Rome as a determinable shape within "the ancient circles of shapes," on the one hand, and Rome as an absent prospect, "beneath the shadow of a shape," on the other (*CP,* 508–509). To Stevens, the old philosopher's greatness lies precisely in the fact that he acknowledges *both,* so that belief might have simultaneously an "unintel-ligible absolution *and* an end," that is, "the human end in the spirit's great-est [*i.e.,* unreachable] reach" (*CP,* 508, emphasis added). And it is in such con-fusion that Santayana can speak with the orator's at once accurate and riddling eloquence:

> Your dozing in the depths of wakefulness,
> In the warmth of your bed, at the edge of your chair, alive
> Yet living in two worlds, impenitent

49. Thus in Macherey, "Lost in the pursuit of an absence, distracted from its own pres-ence . . . in this space where language confronts itself . . . is constructed *that true distance* which is the condition of any real progression—the discourse of the book" (*Theory of Literary Produc-tion,* 63–64, emphasis added). Stevens' threshold of "as if" may also invite us to update Santa-yana's interrogation of "structures" within the more recent cultural studies movement, which, according to Tony Bennet's reading of Stuart Hall, "commit[s] itself to the production of or-ganic intellectuals in the mode of the 'as if,'" in his "Putting Policy into Cultural Studies," in *Cultural Studies,* ed. Lawrence Grossberg, Cary Nelson, and Paula A. Treichler (New York, 1992), 23–37, esp. 34*n*14. See also in the same volume, Stuart Hall, "Cultural Studies and Its Theoretical Legacies," where in true Stevensian form, the "organic intellectual" recognizes that "metaphors are serious things [since] they affect one's practice" (277–94, esp. 281–82).

As to one, and, as to one, most penitent,
Impatient for the grandeur that you need

In so much misery; and yet finding it
Only in misery, the afflatus of ruin,
Profound poetry of the poor and of the dead,
As in the last drop of the deepest blood,
As it falls from the heart and lies there to be seen,

Even as the blood of an empire, it might be,
For a citizen of heaven though still of Rome.

(*CP*, 509–10)

Unlike the crude captains of conventional orthodoxy, Santayana works his quiet miracle by maintaining the majesty of "loftiest things" in speech's poverty (*CP*, 510), hence "the afflatus of ruin" in the above passage. For him, the life of the city never lets go, nor would he have it any other way. Abjuring, therefore, faith's usual transcendent afflatus by denying "mercy should be a mystery," or any "solitude of sense" for that matter, he does not go gentle into that good night. Instead, he continues to affirm the question of belief as a complicate and amassing harmony, imaged perhaps in the convent bells' repetition of solemn names, the reverberation of whose "peculiar chords" continues, in Stevens' riddling phrase, "clinging to whisper still" (*CP*, 510). *Still* as both adjective and adverb in this final tribute becomes Stevens' rather ingenious way of keeping the question of faith open, at the edge of a/theology's own "wakefulness," not at the end of any total grandeur but merely in the theatrical enlargement of Santayana's humble, amber room: "On the threshold [merely] of heaven" (*CP*, 510, 508).

One of the most curious things about Stevens' tribute to Santayana, noticeable in the lines cited previously, is that his homage to the old man is of the kind due to a poet rather than to a philosopher. If this does appear odd, it is only because Santayana is not a philosopher in any normal conception of the term, analogous to the way, for instance, Derrida seems to strike Richard Rorty now as less a philosopher than a novelist such as Marcel Proust, and Proust less a novelist than a philosopher like Derrida. They have achieved normative "autonomy," Rorty would argue, and none of the conventionally unimaginative standards previously used to pass judgment on their kind generically, or in any other way, would appear to apply.[50] Until the

50. Rorty, *Contingency, Irony, and Solidarity*, 136–37, 152; but see also Gasché, *The Tain of the Mirror*, 255ff.

freshness wears off, a new interpretation of "science" or "communism" be-comes less than a momentous exhibition of metaphor and both become the stock and trade of common sense's quite literal and transparent language, in the same way each of these projects, like those of Proust and Derrida, can strike Stevens' deregulating imagination as particularly innovative as well, at least for a time (*NA,* 139, 142). What is perhaps more to the point, from the perspective of imagination's will to belief, is the inadequacy of philosophy's traditional logic in helping to advance spirituality to the innovative level of the Metaphysician in the Dark, characterized by a figure like Santayana. Two trios of stanzas from Stevens' "A Primitive like an Orb" are especially ger-mane to this issue. In the poem's three opening verses, for instance, Stevens right away proposes to disabuse the reader that an "essential" form of poetic expression can be conceptualized through philosophic logic—a conceptual-izing process that he disparages in everyday experience as the "cast-iron of our lives" and in the "spiritual fiddlings" of aesthetics as "this essential gold" (*CP,* 440). The logic disposed at "the centre of things" ("this gorging good") must therefore be "re-disposed" in a more difficult "apperception." As in the case of Santayana, it is a "space grown wide" that shifts oppositional logic to the "separate sense" of a more difficult diacritical relationing *away* from a centered expressiveness and that therefore misorders the usual common sense applied to fiction: "It is and it / Is not and, therefore, is" (*CP,* 440).

Totalizing logical conceptions for the central poem like "inherent or-der" and "composition of the whole" in the text's middle stanzas thus give place to the *activities* engaged in their formulation. Consequently, modern-ism's graphic foregrounding of a "final ring" to circumscribe the question of belief yields, in a more postmodern formulation, to the "roundness that pulls [it] tight," in other words, to the force at back of the poet's or philosopher's form, in Stevens' powerful image of "the muscles of a magnet" (*CP,* 442). What logic might once have located as the "familiar fire" of faith's ultimate source ("trumpeting seraphs in the eye," and "pleasant outbursts on the ear") a postlogical or even prelogical apperception would less certainly invoke as "unfamiliar escapades: whirroos / And scintillant sizzlings such as children like" (*CP,* 442), in "a space 'logically' anterior and alien," as Gasché describes it, "to that of the regulated contradictions of metaphysics." Derrida (follow-ing Levinas) undoubtedly would characterize the dissymmetry in this shift as the "curvature of intersubjective space signif[ying] the divine *intention* of all truth," in place of traditional theology's more conventional "circuit of adequation." For his part, Stevens would suggest a "miraculous multiplex" (*CP,* 442), likewise choosing to re-pose the orthodox "O, Altitudo" within

the contributions made to it by its sequent parts. With this a/logical privileging of the "essential compact" of lesser poems rather than the eschatalogical
whole as soaring altitude or principle or "vis," he endeavors to make his more
active order of belief at the same time a more accessible one, a beneficence
that restores "a nature to its natives" (*CP,* 442). The reason children like it so
much is quite likely because, as in the case of Santayana, it lessens exceedingly
the "serious folds" of dogma's otherwise solemn and entirely outmoded "majesty" (*CP,* 442). We should perhaps also notice the reappearance of Stevens'
giant in this section of the poem, but in a less prominently featured way
and in the resumption of the prone-position, "on the horizon, glistening"
(*CP,* 442), that he had assumed in his inaugural presentation back in "Notes"
(*CP,* 387). At that level of textual deregulation, which Bloom quite correctly
equates with poetic language itself, "we plunge into the horizontality of a
pure surface," as Derrida would say, the point with which we began this
chapter.[51]

In all of Stevens' hypothetical characterizations for his Metaphysician in the
Dark, repeated very much in the spirit of that Otherness discussed by Levinas
that I ascribed to them in the previous section, we notice in particular how
important is the idea of location, or, perhaps more exactly, the space of their
dislocation. In my earlier treatment of this issue in the purely formalist phase
of Stevens' concern with faith, both Stevens' allegorical withdrawal into some
kind of house of fiction as in *Ideas of Order* and, more specifically, his retreat
into a comfortable and secure room in *Harmonium* give us the natural conditions of a spirit homing in on itself and affording itself a presence of immediate relation "in here" with which to mitigate the forces of disruption
and division stemming from an incursion in the world of experience "out
there." One last group of poems from Stevens' final work on the question of
belief, however, labors with great care to dismantle the earlier womb/room
motif and thus returns us once again to the intense degree of irony continuous with the postformalist a/theology that Stevens indulged in right up to his
death in 1955. In "Final Soliloquy of the Interior Paramour," from 1950, for
instance, the lighting of the first light of evening "as in a room" that is "here,"
gives place in the very last stanza of the poem to "being there" (*CP,* 524).
Clearly, the disjunction aims to preserve the sense of alienation that the Metaphysician in the Dark must continue to feel every time he sets about to con-

---

51. Gasché, *The Tain of the Mirror,* 149; Derrida, *Writing and Difference,* 108, emphasis
added; Derrida, "The Purveyor of Truth," in *The Purloined Poe,* ed. Muller and Richardson, 193;
Bloom, *Poems of Our Climate,* 295; Derrida, *Writing and Difference,* 298.

struct his dwelling in the evening air out of "this same light"—the light of the central mind, that is—in which *we say,* and Stevens' qualification is highly cautionary here, that "God and the imagination are one" (*CP,* 524).[52] Most readings of this poem, including the latest by James Merrill in the *Voices and Visions* television segment devoted to Stevens, tend to be attracted to the primary outcomes of the imagination, to the "first light" that we, in a quite familiar way, enlarge into the sequestration of an "intensest rendezvous," a world in which we can collect ourselves by thinking "one thing" beyond all other things ("Out of all the indifferences") in order, ultimately, to grant ourselves lasting peace:

> Within a single thing, a single shawl
> Wrapped tightly round us, since we are poor, a warmth,
> A light, a power, the miraculous influence.

> (*CP,* 524)

Yet it is so important to notice how Stevens, again, tries to distance us from accepting that final soliloquy of interiority as the ultimate, the last word and thing in the question of belief. It is "for small reason," according to the first stanza, that we do so. So intent are we on arriving at some final "order" or "knowledge" (the "here, now" [*CP,* 524]) that we completely overlook "that which arranged the rendezvous," as the text insists, and "the obscurity" at back of that order, which we might only feel. If "the core of religion is the experience of the Wholly Other," as John Dominic Crossan suggests, it is perhaps not too strained a supposition to think that Stevens locates his own obscurity in the ellipsis in the text that opens behind the oneness of imagination and God.[53] And to suppose further that we take no notice of how such an identification in the immediacy of here is constituted by way of what might chance to be located in that darkness there, since for us "being . . . together is enough." Can the effect of the dislocation that Stevens is actually attempting in this room, then, be to suggest with great irony that the paramour's interior soliloquy is, in fact, an anterior colloquy whose first refusal must be that "highest candle," since it lessens the night serving as provocation and legitimation of her more authentic identity *in dialogue* with the dark?

In another darkened room from the same year, Stevens repeats his cri-

---

52. *Cf.* also Derrida: "YHWH simultaneously demands and forbids, in his deconstructive gesture, that one understand his proper name within language, he mandates and crosses out the translation, he dooms us to impossible and necessary translation" (*The Post Card,* 165).

53. John Dominic Crossan, *In Parables: The Challenge of the Historical Jesus* (San Francisco, 1973), 18.

tique of the pretension to absolute knowledge, so antithetical to postmodern belief, in "The Novel," where the question succumbs with some difficulty to "the fatality of *seeing things* too well" in the final stanza (*CP,* 459, emphasis added). The critique seems a little odd to apply to José, the main character in the poem. For José himself finds it odd that the Argentine, in the inserted parable early in the text, should have taken to a poorly heated room, a "*re-trato*" from the cruel winter outside, since the Argentine was a novel reader, like himself. And novel reading, above all, shows us that no physical things have control over our lives, only mental ones do, since "reality" is nothing but a mediation of existential experience in the mind, or, as Elizabeth Bruss, in a somewhat parallel way notes in the case of the novelist William Gass: "What Gass means by 'the thing itself' is not the opaque printers ink but the projections that we make from it." If anything, we succumb to an overfamiliarity with these mental versions of life, inducing once again the normality or fatality of seeing. Novels, therefore, affect to trace "an unfamiliar in the familiar room" (*CP,* 458), and the effect of their *style* all comes back to the power of the mind's thinking and seeing.[54] Hence, "stillness," any present or "real" view of the world, is attributable to "the stillness of the mind" (*CP,* 458), as I noted previously in the connection of this pun to Santayana.

The opening of the poem in "the foyer of summer," therefore, is an affectation or "credence" that Stevens would impute to linguistic construction (and interpretation) rather than to representation and, as such, is quite easily made interchangeable with "the first red of red winter," which comes to replace summer's "original illusion," if the mind is its own place, as Milton tells us (*CP,* 457). However, devoid of this coming and going of illusions (Nietzsche's mobile army of metaphors once again), our minds and lives are otherwise reduced to an emptiness:

> The sun stands like a Spaniard as he departs,
> Stepping from the foyer of summer into that
> Of the past, the rodomontadean emptiness.
>
> (*CP,* 457)

Mother's fear, consequently, that José will freeze in his hibernal retreat is entirely groundless. "Tranquillity is what one thinks," after all (*CP,* 458), and José's memories of more clement and tranquil days ("vividest Varadero"

---

54. Bruss, *Beautiful Theories,* 161. On the effect of style, see Rorty, *Contingency, Irony, and Solidarity,* 124n6, and also Carafiol, *The American Ideal,* 145.

[*CP,* 457]) are active enough, even for the endless lol-lolling of poetry. So why the fear at the end of the poem, the fear that lies on José's breast and that creeps into his heart? Could it be a fear that he shares with the earlier interior paramour? Could it be the fear at the ease with which *one* reality in the unguarded metaphysical mind becomes *total* reality, the last thing that perhaps had made his Argentinian alter-ego escape to his own inner room to die? Could the fear lying on José's breast, by transference, be the fear of Absence that, in the form of major man previously in "Notes" (*CP,* 388), lies on the breast of mankind in general, in his moments of later reason? And could *that* fear represent the potential loss of the presence of "the Arcadian imagination" (*CP,* 459) that must inevitably give place to a multiplex seasons of belief when the "fatality of seeing things" is understood too well for what it really is and the *sanctum sanctorum* of self-regarding faith has ultimately to be abandoned?

Perhaps the fear, here, though, is a manifestation of anxiety at the pre-sentiment of a new postontological dispensation in the form, once again, of Stevens' female Other. Joined to that is anxiety at the playing out of the mind's defending against itself, noted earlier in "Saint John and the Back-Ache," but also found in the poem "Puella Parvula," composed in 1949 immediately after "Saint John" and positioned in *Collected Poems* just before "The Novel":

> Every thread of summer is at last unwoven.
> By one caterpillar is great Africa devoured
> And Gibraltar is dissolved like spit in the wind.
>
> . . . .
>
> Over all these the mighty imagination triumphs
> Like a trumpet and says, in this season of memory,
> When the leaves fall like things mournful of the past,
>
> Keep quiet in the heart, O wild bitch. O mind
> Gone wild, be what he tells you to be: *Puella.*
> Write *pax* across the window pane. And then
>
> Be still.
>
> (*CP,* 456)

With the elephant roaring on the roof and the lion gnashing in the yard, the room of the misogynistic "dauntless master" in this poem is a beleaguered one indeed. His vicious attack on the force of difference in the above passage,

in the name of a *"summarium in excelsis"* (*CP,* 456), is perhaps so much whistling in the dark, since our regenerate imagination has nothing at all to do
with a "season of memory," as Stevens once remarked in an important letter
written in connection with his "Notes": "We cannot ignore or obliterate
death, yet we do not live in memory. Life is always new; it is always beginning. The fiction is part of this beginning" (*L,* 434).

Thus, in the 1947 poem entitled "The Beginning," if there is to be the
inaugural of a completely renovated faith, it must start, in the very first instance, with the complete abandonment of the imagination's foundational
self-regard. Then it must move to the condition of a blank and unreflective
vacancy, thereby restoring the subject as "an implicate of communicative
praxis":[55]

> The house is empty. But here is where she sat
> To comb her dewy hair, a touchless light,
>
> Perplexed by its darker iridescences.
> This was the glass in which she used to look
>
> At the moment's being, without history,
> The self of summer perfectly perceived,
>
> . . . .
>   . . . cast-off, on the floor.
>
> Now, the first tutoyers of tragedy
> Speak softly, to begin with, in the eaves.
>   (*CP,* 427–28)

The distance spanned between "the highest candle [that] lights the dark" in
the earlier "Interior Paramour" and the Metaphysician in the Dark's "touch-
less light" above is perhaps nothing less than a lifetime spent probing the
articles of one's faith. The only difference between himself in the present and
the dauntless master of "Puella Parvula," who he undeniably was, too, at one
time, is simply that now there no longer is any "fury in transcendent forms"
but only a multiplex of repetitions, very much like the crickets each babbling
"the uniqueness of its sound" in the barely lit setting of "A Quiet Normal
Life" (*CP,* 523).

---

55. Calvin O. Schrag, "Subjectivity and Praxis at the End of Philosophy," in *Hermeneutics and Deconstruction,* ed. Silverman and Ihde, 28.

We therefore end this long meditation on the last things in Stevens' concluding volumes by turning, finally, to a poem that would have done completely with the inner sanctum of a universalizing faith. By abandoning this image of transcendent inwardness, Stevens would also have done with faith's need for a completing self-relation that, ultimately, would arrest and extirpate entirely the question of belief. In the appropriately titled "St. Armorer's Church from the Outside," written in 1952, Stevens' differentiation between a faith fixed and fully formed and another fluid and actively responsive to change is caught between the Church of St. Armorer, connoting an inflexible vigilance, and its inner chapel, "Terre Ensevelie," suggesting a more worldly openness (very loosely, "Terre C'est la Vie"). On the one hand, we are given the institutionalized orthodoxy from the past, an immense success at one time that rose loftily and stood mightily, that "fixed one for good in geranium-colored day" (*CP*, 529), but that has now fallen into disuse, with a sumac growing on its altar, a badly leaking roof, and a stifling air of disuse and decay created by rotting hay and the foreign smell of plaster. On the other hand, the chapel under St. Armorer's walls has an air of newness and freshness about it, a "clearness, greenness, blueness" (*CP*, 530) that suggests the vitality of an inherent changefulness: "That which is always beginning because it is part / Of that which is always beginning, over and over" (*CP*, 530). Gradually, one comes to suspect that for his conception of a chapel inside the larger church, Stevens has in mind something along the lines of a force of difference that originarily is always already infecting and potentially transforming any closely guarded identity, in Gasché's term an "infrastructure" of differential regulation as it were, and turning it into a question of its own reason for being. Hence, Stevens describes the chapel's *vif* as "this dizzle-dazzle of being new / And of becoming, for which the chapel spreads out / Its arches in its vivid element" (*CP*, 530). Clearly, with the suggestion of spacing in the chapel's spreading here, "not befalling an already constituted space," as Derrida might say, "but producing the spatiality of space," Stevens intends as a *possible* ground for a potentially new faith, in place of the former foundational objects of knowledge, a kind of event or metaleptic process, linked to a mysterious Otherness in its association with a "new-colored sun" and the spread hallucinations of its "outward blank" (*CP*, 529).[56] It is this process or motive that sets into motion a whole train of doctrinal forms,

56. Gasché, *The Tain of the Mirror*, 142; Derrida, *Grammatology*, 290.

"time's given perfections," from which mankind is given to choose in order that each generation, in its own individual way, might fulfill the need to live up to its potential, "to be actual and as it is":

> The first car out of a tunnel en voyage
>
> Into lands of ruddy-ruby fruits, achieved
> Not merely desired, for sale, and market things
> That press, strong peasants in a peasant world,
> Their purports to a final seriousness.
>
> (*CP,* 530)

It would seem to be a fairly safe assumption, moreover, that in foregrounding the force rather than the form of faith as a nonsubstantive "chapel of breath" and an "acceptance of . . . prose" Stevens aims to ascribe the question of belief to the power of language as the "new account of everything old" (*CP,* 529), much as Heidegger would ascribe to it the force for ontological difference, as I noted back in Chapter 6. In a difficult image, this power becomes "an ember yes among its cindery noes" (in Stevens' pun on the Greek *nous,* or mind, thought) that would appear to call to us from an Otherness in a Heideggerian "soundless voice of Being," which, up to now, has really only been the concern for "a mystic eye" (*CP,* 529).[57] Neither is this power a "sign" of life but is, rather, the very presence of the (un)intelligible, which creates the sign as power's "symbol," for such Otherness is the very becomingness of "life, / Itself" (*CP,* 529). Framing belief, finally, in linguistic terms ("A sacred syllable rising from sacked speech" [*CP,* 530]), Stevens can thus impart to faith a changefulness as the forms of speech change, while at the same time acknowledging this new belief's imperviousness to the corruptions to which the achievement of meaning is always heir, since it is the very means by which meaning itself becomes produced. Although inhabited by such a process, the larger church's sacked pronouncements are consequently "nothing of this present" (*CP,* 530). Yet curiously, deep within St. Armorer's fractured walls, that chapel of breath, by turning and turning faith *outward and beyond* its

---

57. Heidegger, *Existence and Being,* 358, and also *Poetry, Language, Thought,* 208. *Cf.* also Heidegger's observation that "one might come to the idea that the most extreme sharpness and depth of thought belong to genuine and great mysticism," for which Caputo offers the following: "False mysticism does not give up 'representations' but it prefers confusing and contradictory representations. Genuine and great mysticism does not make use of 'representations' at all, but rather it lets the rose rise up in its simple presence, the way the rose 'is,' prior to the categories of representational thought" (*The Mystical Element,* 141, 142).

guarded yet decrepit insularity, is that very institution's only hope for keeping its truth alive, the "origin and keep," as the final stanza puts it, for a better health. And for the continuing better health, to be sure, of the Metaphysician in the Dark, as well. So that at Stevens' end, though we perhaps might never know for certain, what should it matter whether or not he underwent an orthodox conversion on his deathbed? In Stanley Cavell's words, his "salvation lies in reversing the story, in ending the story of the end . . . in order to reverse the curse of the world laid on it in its Judeo-Christian end."[58] Turning the very last thing in his own life into yet another question of belief, Wallace Stevens walks finally very much in the spirit of his own chapel of breath and, in the last words of one of his last poems, "does as he lives and likes" (*CP,* 530).

58. Stanley Cavell, *Must We Mean What We Say? A Book of Essays* (New York, 1969), 149. The details of the controversy surrounding Stevens' "conversion," referred to rather infelicitously by his biographer as a "final prank," are given in Joan Richardson, *Stevens: The Later Years,* 426–27. Milton J. Bates, as a result of a conversation with Father Arthur P. Hanley, the chaplain of Saint Francis Hospital in Hartford, where Stevens eventually died, documents that according to Father Hanley, "the archbishop of the Archdiocese of Hartford requested that Stevens' baptism not be recorded or made public lest people think that Saint Francis Hospital actively sought to convert non-Catholic patients" (*A Mythology of Self,* 296–97n30). *Cf.* also Brazeau, *Parts of a World,* 290–91, 294–96.

PARADISAL PARLANCE
Postmodernism and the Question of Belief

The end approaches, but the apocalypse is long-lived. The question remains
and comes back: what can be the limits of a demystification?
—Jacques Derrida, *Of an Apocalyptic Tone Recently Adopted in Philosophy*

Ever since the "united three"—Herakles, Dionysos, and Christ—have left the
world, the evening of the world's age has been declining toward its night. The
world's night is spreading its darkness. The era is defined by the god's failure
to arrive, by the "default of God."
—Martin Heidegger, *Poetry, Language, Thought*

I find letters from God dropt in the street, and every one is sign'd by God's
  name,
And I leave them where they are, for I know that whereso'er I go
Others will punctually come for ever and ever.
—Walt Whitman, *Song of Myself*

IN enlisting still one further perspective in the genealogy of belief throughout the *Collected Poems* of Wallace Stevens, let us at last return to "An Ordinary Evening in New Haven," left hanging back in the polemical words of
the introduction to this whole study. We might begin with a meditation on
Stevens' title and turn first to Canto IX to consider how it is implicated in
the poet's spiritual renovation, for which we are offered the pun on "heaven"
in the city's very name. Much of the nostalgia surrounding this word, from a
very rigid old-time-religion point of view, would in a moment of candor
perhaps insist on an "Old Haven" rather than a "New" one. For in this
light—and the light and dark imagery is central to the issue here, if not, as in
the epigraphs, the issue itself—from a conventionally enlightened perspective, an "Old Haven" is embedded in our quest for certain Being, for some
permanent, metaphysical reality, in Stevens' highly ironic use of that word

302

throughout this section, within which to anchor a permanent faith.[1] If we play the pun out far enough back in time, we perhaps find ourselves within the academic discourse of "Havana." No doubt, Stevens is somewhat insistent on that recollection in the opening two lines here, with their mention of a "hotel" to which we "keep coming back and coming back / To the real: to the hotel" (*CP*, 471). Having sent our minds reeling down memory lane in this fashion, Stevens playfully offers the further provocation of a demand for what the popular mentality in these issues might term "straight talk." Straight talk's demand is for an absolute guarantee of a word's mediation of a corresponding thing, the rather naïve "alliance of speech and Being in the unique word," as Derrida might phrase it, or, in Stevens' reconstruction, a "pure reality" that would be left "untouched / By trope or deviation."[2] With this provocation afoot, we should in all likelihood wish even further to get past mediation itself and be led by a certain sight to an exact point of Being where nothing exists but pure faith, without even having to think about it:

> straight to the word,
> Straight to the transfixing object, to the object
>
> At the exactest point at which it is itself,
> Transfixing by being purely what it is,
> A view of New Haven, say, through the certain eye,
>
> The eye made clear of uncertainty, with the sight
> Of simple seeing, without reflection. We seek
> Nothing beyond reality.
>
> (*CP*, 471)

Here we at last might find a "pattern of heaven," as the canto concludes, a totally visible and inclusive epiphanic moment by which, in the nurture of the saints, the spirit and all its "alchemicana" (*CP*, 471) would come into their own at last.

1. Stevens' irony is in keeping with the postmodern discourse throughout this text and throughout all of his later writing more broadly, as argued in Chapter 6, for it is precisely the rhetoric of irony, as Linda Hutcheon contends in "A Postmodern Problematics," in *Ethics/Aesthetics: Postmodern Positions,* ed. Robert Merrill (Washington, D.C., 1988), that "prevent[s] the postmodern from being nostalgic [for] there is no desire to return to the past as a time of simpler or more worthy values." She continues: "The conjunction of the present and the past [in postmodernism] is intended to make us question—that is, analyze and try to understand—both how we make and make sense of our culture" (8).

2. Derrida, *Margins of Philosophy,* 27.

Yet as in so many moments like this one repeated in the previous three chapters, the quest for such a permanence is really only a reflex of the *passive* imagination, which Stevens consistently connects with the image of the moon. Hence, in the following Canto X, what appears is "lunar light," whose moon is haunted by a man of bronze representing death, since, in ontotheological terms, his mind is already "made up" (*CP*, 472). What is "fatal in the moon" and makes it empty of reality's straight-fore-word-ness previously, this new canto observes, is its refusal to admit a *change* that is constant—the constancy of inconstancy earlier in "Notes" (*CP*, 389). It is precisely our faith *in* change, the promises in morning and evening, the arrival and departure of the sun, and so forth, that provides us with the true in-sight into the mode of reality being sought. From this vantage, it is now not a permanence of In-word-ness to recollect the argument from the introduction but more a responsiveness to the external, a hyperlexic Out-word-ness, if you will, by which "coherence, unity, and meaning are generated through the proliferation of surfaces, not through the discovery of a single principle that underlies them." Stevens himself calls this making "gay the hallucinations in surfaces" (*CP*, 472), and his further asseveration that "we do not know what is real and what is not" has a tremendous resonance with the word *real* in Roland Barthes, who similarly contends that it is "not representable" and, further, that "it is because men ceaselessly try to represent it by words that there is a history of literature" in the first place. We should perhaps add, a genealogy of belief as well.[3]

Stevens' inviting us in the previous canto to alter our notions of faith vis-à-vis change also invites us to reconsider the notion that God might be incarnated in some object, as in Canto XIV. In a thoroughly orthodox and doctrinal quest for transcendence, the central form of Christianity, for instance, in which one expects the created humanity of God to be recreated in

---

3. Nehamas, "Writer, Text, Work, Author," in *Literature and the Question of Philosophy*, ed. Cascardi, 280–81; Barthes, *A Barthes Reader*, 465. Stevens' peculiarly postmodern stance is resonantly Foucauldian as well. "The postmodern concern with surfaces rather than with deep explanations," David Couzens Hoy observes in this context, "implies that instead of explaining, postmoderns are interpreting." By this, he means that "instead of taking themselves to be discovering an independently given reality governed by lawlike regularities, they see themselves as doing something more like interpreting texts." See David Couzens Hoy, "Foucault: Modern or Postmodern," in *After Foucault: Humanistic Knowledge, Postmodern Challenges,* ed. Jonathan Arac (New Brunswick, N.J., 1991), 12–41, esp. 28. Along the same line, see also in the same volume, H. D. Harootunian, "Foucault, Genealogy, History: The Pursuit of Otherness," 110–37, esp. 133.

the divinity of risen Man, one tends to sense that objects are in the world mainly to be gotten around or moved beyond. From this perspective, even the dry eucalyptus appears to seek "god in the rainy cloud" (*CP*, 475). Now, however, if there should be no getting around or going beyond, in the constitution of faith by language, say, as in the last chapter's "chapel of breath," the question of belief is a matter very much à la mode noted previously. The answer we give to the question would very much depend on the manner by which we choose to come to terms with the object, in order to render it to our believing eyes and ears. In short, the answer would depend greatly on "a choice of the comodious adjective" (*CP*, 475). Consequently, if there is divinity at all, it is, in one of Stevens' most telling lines in the poem, "the description that makes [the object] divinity," in other words (if that were even possible at this late stage), "paradisal parlance" (*CP*, 475). Divinity, therefore, is not some puritanical grim reality stilled by sight and removed from change. Instead, it is a reality grimly *moved* by that change, a "point of reverberation," in another of Stevens' important puns. Its grimness thus becomes entirely in-different to any appropriating spiritual eye/I desiring, through the object, to withdraw completely outside change. This reasoning would explain why Professor Eucalyptus of the canto abjures making the "tink-tonk" in the water spout a "substitute" (*CP*, 475) for some rain god but prefers, alternatively, to find divinity in the sounds of the water itself, despite how well- or ill-perceived these might appear to be. His sounding out the rain spout in this way is rather like a Heideggerian form of allegory, Gerald Bruns might say, "a taking-off from the text rather than an exegesis that extracts something from the text in order to hold it up to the light," in other words, "a dark text [that] surrenders nothing of itself."[4] For this reason, Professor Eucalyptus, another type of Metaphysician in the Dark, need not look beyond the object in order to shore up his faith: New Heaven *is* New Haven. Or, in the line of Stevens that anticipated this darker, a/theological prospect more than a dozen years ago: "Oxidia *is* Olympia" (*CP*, 182, emphasis added).

With the above de-scription of faith clearly before us, we watch Stevens later in the poem going after former modes of belief that tend to negate the distributive metalepsis of its displacements in language. In Canto XX, for example, the trans-scripts of clouds muttered in twilight (*CP*, 479) present

---

4. Northrop Frye, *Fearful Symmetry: A Study of William Blake* (Princeton, 1947), 120, 384; Bruns, *Heidegger's Estrangements*, 69.

metaphorical substitutions, once again, that threaten to foreclose the whole process. Hence, in Canto XXI, the "two romanzas" are the metaphysical equivalents for those transcriptions that must be viewed in the context of the will to presence the pure sphere (*CP*, 480–81) of the previous canto, surely another resuscitation of the Gorgeous Wheel, dealt with back in Chapter 1. In the twin forms of idealism and realism, which had first made their dialectical appearance, we recall, from "Extracts from Addresses to the Academy of Fine Ideas," that is to say, in the forms of the romance "out of the black shepherd's isle," which isolates Being at a distance ("Cythère," equivalent to see there), and of the "alternate romanza," which locates it in "the near" much closer to the senses ("The clear," equivalent to see here)—these forms, taken together, threaten to solidify yet another semiological "versus myth," in Barthes' phrase, in order to reify belief within the foundationalism paramount to a "celestial mode" (*CP*, 480). What Stevens tirelessly insists on throughout all of his later poetry, and no more emphatically than in the present canto, however, is that both forms must be contextualized and valorized in terms of their constructedness as objects, thus foregrounding the human will in the process of their fabrication. Stevens' question of belief is accordingly "postmodern" in such terms because, as David Couzens Hoy aptly reminds us, "the postmodern paradigm is not profundity but complexity."[5] Revolving the question of belief in the longer view, therefore, one does not seek the sphere's erection in metaphysics' "single voice" but looks rather to language's generalized rection in pragmatism's "will of necessity," the "will of wills" as the canto phrases it (*CP*, 480). Consequently, while the constatives of faith may be manipulated or evaded altogether, the will to power them into articulation may not, for it lies within the very expressive performatives of language experienced everywhere: "The boo-ha of the wind" (*CP*, 481).

   In Canto XVII, Stevens can be even more specific about this ubiquitous "commonplace," as he calls it (*CP*, 478), about language that underwrites either of the structural paradigms rehearsed above. Here, he breaks them down in the cycle of romance into the radicals of comedy (the far of a "blue verdured" and "lofty symbol") and tragedy (the near of night's "wasted figurations"). Stevens' point, however, is that these "fitful sayings" are merely reflections composed by something far more pervasive, a "serious strength" or power, which he hazards to locate in another "point": the verbal center of man himself. As in the earlier "Notes," though, what provokes the perfor-

5. Hoy, "Foucault: Modern or Postmodern," 28.

matives of language at that center is certainly no "pin-idleness" (*CP,* 477). It is a linguistic moment, in J. Hillis Miller's well-traveled phrase, "the moment when a poem, or indeed any text, turns back on itself and puts its own medium in question," a moment of undecidable Absence or uncertain Otherness, therefore, which provokes man's will to decide the certainties of romance, in a final reappearance in this study of Stevens' White Mythology:

> A blank underlies the trials of device,
>
> The dominant blank, the unapproachable.
> This is the mirror of the high serious.
>
> (*CP,* 477)[6]

Empowering belief in this passage is a highly polished, linguistic surface upon which man endlessly chooses to project and inscribe his image in either the ideal-comic or the real-tragic trials of textuality's infinite potential for "reflection" or "device." In another place, Miller, following Kant, would call the enactment of such "trials" the law of textuality—"The law in question is the law as such"—and, undeniably, the previous necessity of Stevens' "will of wills," elaborated further here, attempts to establish very much the same indecipherable point.[7]

Of the thirty-odd cantos in "An Ordinary Evening in New Haven," from which Stevens chose an initial set of eleven to be published the year before *The Auroras of Autumn,* fairly much the last third of the longer poem, in one way or another, aims to exploit the uncertainties of Absence over which the question of belief becomes proliferatingly suspended, as described previously and picked up in this chapter's opening epigraph from Whitman. The general contour of Stevens' argument is hardly original. In Canto XXIII, for instance, we find his image of the sun against which the protocols of semanticization are exfoliated being imported from "Notes" as "half the world" of New Haven, "the bodiless half" (*CP,* 481). Our embodiments of this vacancy, or future "illumination," in a striking reminiscence of Walter

---

6. Miller, *The Linguistic Moment,* 339. On Stevens' location of this moment of blankness beneath "the trials of device," *cf.* Rapaport: "The 'white mythology' concerns the idealistic presupposition that beneath economies of words there exists a pure, unadulterated language which is only approximated by the usurous economies . . . a fantasized scene inscribed in white ink, an invisible design covered over by a palimpsest . . . a place of metaphysical speculation that evades the 'assessments of time,' a phantasm that negates writing as both temporal (historical) and spatial (writerly) . . . [as a] *theology of writing*" (*Heidegger and Derrida,* 37–38, emphasis added).

7. Miller, *The Ethics of Reading,* 23–25.

Benjamin, are cozened and coaxed and eventually constituted in the "late going colors" of the past, perhaps the two romanzas earlier, which form "the other half" of New Haven that we say we see and, no doubt, believe. In keeping with the mirror image of high seriousness in the previous citation, however, textuality is a glass that we see through only darkly, and Stevens positions this other half of New Haven "at evening" and "after dark" to remind us that faith comes to us in the textual versions of our waking lives ("day's separate several selves" [*CP,* 482]) as a prospect only *"lighted by space"* (emphasis added), what a Metaphysician in the Dark undeniably knows more than anyone. "To look through the mirror," as Rodolphe Gasché thus observes, "is to look at its reverse side, at the dull side doubling the mirror's specular play, in short, at the *tain* of the mirror . . . [where] dissemination writes itself."[8] Moreover, because desire continues to prolong life's seminal adventure by creating the disseminations of romance, "forms of farewell" as they are called (*CP,* 482), in response to the dominant blank, the two halves of New Haven, nonetheless, "come together as one." It is in this strange "identity," the sun's present Absence and the night's absent Presence, *i.e.,* "Being part," that we continue to face the future with our past; it is in this strange rift opened up between the two that our "disembodiments" (as well as our embodiments) are kept (in)constantly and (un)certainly occurring (*CP,* 482).

In Canto XXV, this strange identity modulates into a kind of life force and seems fated to dog the poet on his mirrored way, remorselessly, for all time:

> Life fixed him, wandering on the stair of glass,
> With its attentive eyes. And, as he stood,
> On his balcony, outsensing distances,
>
> There were looks that caught him out of empty air.
> *C'est toujours la vie qui me regarde* . . . This was
> Who watched him, always, for unfaithful thought.
>
> > (*CP,* 483)

The "unfaithful thought" in this passage from the point of view of absence ("empty air") is the believing poet's conventional longing for transcendence, as in "outsensing distances." Later in the canto, this longing has the possibility of becoming arrested in the "isolated moments" of perhaps ideal-comic or real-tragic forms, unless the force for change is allowed to continue to

---

8. Gasché, *The Tain of the Mirror,* 238.

revolve them beyond any such spurious permanence: "Isolations / Were false" (*CP,* 484). Stevens thus carries us back to the changefulness of the "common-place" (*CP,* 483) of language, once again, whose boo-ha would continuously ensure that the real would be "turned into something most unreal" all over again (*CP,* 483). For this imperative of constant inconstancy, he once more revives his argument for an answerable style in the image of the hard hidalgo from "Description Without Place" (*CP,* 345). The force of his "permanent, abstract" look positioned nightly by the poet's bed, "without a word," serves as a steady reminder to the poet that despite his lapses into faithless thought, "nothing about him ever stay[s] the same" (*CP,* 484, 483), like the question of belief itself.

Under the impress of change, the abstract hidalgo modulates quickly into the "Ruler of Reality" in Canto XXVII, and it is the "total excellence" of the ruler that Stevens is most insistent on—an excellence manifest in the total book of life rather than the book of death. Stevens is insistent because as the "fore-meaning" (*CP,* 485) of the poet's music, "pre-commitment" as Heidegger would say, the ruler is perpetually to be theorized from a temporal void and in poetic practice thus becomes an endless "allegory," in Paul de Man's conceptualization, "always implying an unreachable anteriority." From ruler of reality, he is speedily transformed into a theorist of life, and in the following canto we are made to recognize that it is the very text of "An Ordinary Evening" itself that has been constituted by his preontological, preepistemological, *i.e.,* his a/theological postulation, as in one of the poem's most celebrated but frequently misunderstood passages:

> This endlessly elaborating poem
> Displays the theory of poetry,
> As the life of poetry. A more severe,
>
> More harassing master would extemporize
> Subtler, more urgent proof that the theory
> Of poetry is the theory of life,
>
> As it is, in the intricate evasions of as,
> In things seen and unseen, created from nothingness,
> The heavens, the hells, the worlds, the longed for lands.
>
> (*CP,* 486)

If belief is the reality that its ruler insistently labors to problematize, this passage would completely defamiliarize our commitment to it as an object of thought and have us think about it more as an ongoing event, as we had explored it back in Chapter 5—an event "created from nothingness" as the abstraction of Absence to be sure but an event no less real for all of that. What gives to belief its eventful momentum, moreover, has less to do with its categorical predication or invasion of meaning than with its rhetorical evasion ("the intricate evasions of as"), thus directing all of our attention toward its questionable status as the product, to borrow Stanley Fish's words, "of contextual or interpretive circumstances and not as the property of an acontextual language or an independent world."[9]

The "interpretive circumstances" that Stevens appears specifically to have in mind in the "as" of intricate evasion, structured into the question of belief, have a striking parallel to the "as-structure" in the famous section thirty-two of Heidegger's *Being and Time:* "The 'as' makes up the structure of the explicitness of something that is understood. It constitutes the interpretation. In dealing with what is environmentally ready-to-hand by interpreting it circumspectively, we 'see' it *as* . . . but what we have thus interpreted [*Ausgelegte*] need not necessarily be also taken apart [*auseinander zu legen*] by making an assertion which definitely characterizes it. Any mere prepredicative seeing of the ready-to-hand is, in itself, something which already understands and interprets." Gasché's gloss on this important statement of "the primary articulation of understanding" in Heidegger's discourse alerts us to a relationship similar to the one between Stevens' "fore-meaning" and interpretive "mode" earlier: "It marks a structural level of articulation anterior by right to all possible linguistic utterance . . . [a discourse that] precedes all predicative and thematic expression and vocalization of understanding and states-of-mind. . . . It represents the very *possibility* of vocalization, of speech, of speech acts, of language as the mundane or worldly mode of the being of the *logos* . . . and thus corresponds to the ontologically fundamental structure of the meaning of Being . . . in terms of the as-structure."[10] This gloss tells us, therefore, that the question of belief as a discursive displacement away from a fundament of expressive possibility, which is itself thoroughly interpretive and hence un- or prepredicative, and in contrast to modernism's hierarchical sedimentations "In-words" is a postmodern movement pointed completely the other way. It is a movement "Out-words," that is, from "heav-

9. John D. Caputo, "The Thought of Being and the Conversation of Mankind: The Case of Heidegger and Rorty," *Review of Metaphysics*, XXXVI (March, 1983), 669; de Man, *Blindness and Insight*, 222; Fish, *Is There a Text in This Class?*, 268.

10. Heidegger, *Being and Time*, 189; Gasché, *The Tain of the Mirror*, 300. Santayana positioned on the "Threshold, / As if," in "To An Old Philosopher in Rome" (*CP*, 511), noted in the last chapter is undoubtedly anticipated by Stevens' "as-structure" here.

ens" and "hells" to "worlds" and "longed-for lands," the "worldly mode of the being of the *logos*" in the citation from Gasché, rather than the "independent" one alluded to by Fish or, in Stevens' own discourse, New Heaven *as* New Haven and (not to put too fine a point on it) New Haven "*as* it is" (*CP,* 486, emphasis added). The theory of poetry "lies" in just such changeful construction, to go with Stevens' Nietzschean pun. This alterable constructedness, after all, is the life of poetry. It is also the theory of life, however, and as such gives us a late insight into Stevens' theory of belief, which comes down, finally, to the endless elaborations of faith in "as": the question of belief, to go with yet another pun, as the X-temporizations (*CP,* 486) of a subtle and "harassing" *i.e.,* rigorous master.[11]

We might now, finally, return to the earlier sections of the poem in order to understand completely Stevens' insistence on dismantling the logocentric models of belief dealt with in the earlier chapters of this study. In Canto VI, for instance, it is "profound absentia" (*CP,* 469) that contours faith's trajectory for its "immaculate interpreters" now, rather than the substitutive theorizations of immanence and transcendence, the "verticals of Adam," as Dylan Thomas once referred to them.[12] Our choice in these matters, as the canto presents them, is between making belief either the reality of a beginning ("Naked Alpha," alpha standing for absentia) or the reality of the end ("hierophant Omega," the circular O, Altitudo of hermeneutic presence). "A" is the child that in Stevens tends to be privileged as the sign of difference, as we might recall for instance in "Questions Are Remarks" (*CP,* 462); "Omega" or "Z" ("twisted, stooping, polymathic") is the emblem of rationalists in square rooms, of Susanna's lustful elders, or of the benighted Sorbonne savants. Each of these patriarchal groups would have process halted in some abasement to "dense investiture" or "luminous vassal[age]," whose forms, by this point, are only too familiar: Sidneyan pallid perceptions of metaphysical "distances," on the one hand, or Shelleyan "prolongations of the human," on the other (*CP,* 469). Even though A appears to have the edge in this schema (in Stevens' reversal, Omega now kneels "on the edge of

---

11. "Since Copernicus," in the "Out-Words" of an equally subtle and harassing master, "man has been rolling from the center toward X." See Friedrich Nietzsche, "Toward an *Out*line" (*WP,* 8). Thus, in "An Ordinary Evening"'s Canto XIII:

> [The ephebe] is neither priest nor proctor at low eve,
> Under the birds, among the perilous owls,
> In the big X of the returning primitive.
>
> (*CP,* 474)

12. Dylan Thomas, "Altarwise by Owl-Light," in *The Poems of Dylan Thomas,* ed. Daniel Jones (New York, 1971), 117.

space"), it, too, becomes like Z without the acknowledgment of absentia at the core of this "scene" of instruction; hence, that "difference," in the canto's final stanza, between "the end" and "*the way* / To the end" (*CP,* 469, emphasis added) underscores the fact that there can be *no* "choice / Custodians of the glory of the scene." A must always already be beginning, just as Z must continue to be refreshed at every end. For belief is always Alpha and Omega, the real and the unreal, embodiment and disembodiment: *two in one.*

For this reason, the Metaphysician in the Dark can never mistake his own texts, "leaves in whirlings in the gutters" in Canto XII, for "the presence of thought" (*CP,* 474). The dense play between "as" and "is" throughout this section—the poem as it is, the windy night as it is, sight and insight as they are, etc.—stresses repeatedly that "these things have their history, their reasons for being the way they are . . . and that [their] starting point is not a (natural) given but a (cultural) construct, usually blind to itself." There is nothing ontologically permanent, in other words, in the poet's productions, so that when "the marble statues / [Become] like newspapers blown by the wind" (*CP,* 473), Stevens' imagery here focuses again on the evasion of meaning in contrast to its invasion or saturation. Within the context of faith itself, then, rather than being grounded in "the life of the world," a poet's beliefs become his "words [for] the world." Only to the degree that the materiality of his words joins in the "res" of that world can his beliefs be said to presence anything.[13] Consequently, the poem as belief is the "cry of its occasion" and *not* the occasion itself: "Part of the res itself and not about it [since] / The poet speaks the poem as it is" (*CP,* 473). The "cry," here, in one of Stevens' most famous lines, registers his flat rejection of transcendence, of the "sight" that proceeds to presence beyond the self or of the "insight" that would fix it in self-presence *tout court.* Since his "Notes Toward a Supreme Fiction," we are quite well aware that both gestures are approximations merely: sight and insight "as they are" (*CP,* 473). *As* such, they situate belief in absentia, once more ("things about" as the text states) or, more specifically, in the in-between-ness of *is* (present absence) and *was* (absent presence):

> The mobile and the immobile flickering
> In the area between is and was are leaves,
> Leaves burnished in autumnal burnished trees.
>
> (*CP,* 474)

---

13. Barbara Johnson, "Translator's Introduction" to Derrida, *Dissemination,* xv; Carafiol, *The American Ideal,* 105, 125, 159, 162; Rapaport, *Heidegger and Derrida,* 187.

If we substitute Stevens' belief for Hillis Miller's law in the following, we come as close as we are ever likely to get in fathoming the intricate evasions of this riddling passage: "The law is always somewhere else or at some other time, back there when the law was first imposed or off to the future when I may at last confront it directly, in unmediated vision. Within that space, *between here and that unattainable there of the law as such,* between now and the beginning or the end, narrative [Stevens' "words of the world"] enters as the relation of the search for a perhaps impossible proximity to the law."[14] The search for an impossible proximity is perhaps another way of negating the question of belief as a plenitudinous object (what it is) to favor its lacunary event: "The poem as it is" (*CP,* 473). "In the end," as the canto concludes, this event becomes the [w]hole psychology of the self, in the further playful paronomasia of the town's weather (whether) and litter (letter). Stevens' endlessly punning text squares well with the question of belief, since "nothing can ever be said purely and simply but is always in excess of itself, spilling over and spreading in every direction . . . [so that] one could not say in what the logic of such a language could consist." Unless, of course, as in Emerson's "onward thinking," in "replacing the standard of fidelity to an external reality with . . . an ongoing experimental improvisation," language presents us with "an internal (il)logic that evades all standards."[15]

We find the finale to our own endlessly elaborating commentary on this endlessly signifying text, curiously, in its beginning. For it is there this study first began, in the intricate elaboration of Stevens' rejection of a post-Romantic formalism caught, as in the opening canto, in the near mythology of a gigantic "festival sphere" and in the far mythology of some giant of transcendent truth itself ("great bosom, beard and being" [*CP,* 466]). This second giant might still come along again to kill the first, unless at last we ourselves come finally to fit both into a much larger rhetorical continuum than either of these templates. For it is their discursive dynamics that are at last to be recognized as the Metaphysician in the Dark's *perpetual* condition of desire: belief opened outward to a/theology and, as the canto succinctly puts it, to "the question that is a giant himself" (*CP,* 465), the demystification of which, as in the opening epigraph, remains still to be undertaken. However, if Stevens' "plain version" of the question is any kind of answer, a naïve

---

14. Miller, *The Ethics of Reading,* 25, emphasis added.

15. Bruns, *Heidegger's Estrangements,* 163; Carafiol, *The American Ideal,* 115. *Cf.* also Jane Gallop, *The Daughter's Seduction: Feminism and Psychoanalysis* (Ithaca, 1982), 55, and Kristeva, *Powers of Horror,* 191.

construction that any extended commentary on the poem chances to risk, we have it on the canto's own authority that such an ex-plain-ation, at the very first level of interpretation, is "a thing apart" (*CP*, 465), perhaps following Heidegger's earlier suggestion. Yet this is only very much like New Haven itself: a rank tangle of inconstancies and incompletions and indeterminacies ("Dark things without a double, after all" [*CP*, 465]), all suggested by its link to the impossible absence of the sun, once again, and by its "dilapidate / Appearances," rather than its "meanings" and "communications" (*CP*, 465). The implication from the very first line of the poem, then, and on into the rest of its thirty-one sections, is that Wallace Stevens writes a text without closure, a vast reticulated web characterized only by "an and yet, and yet, and yet—" that, as his introduction states, must be seen "as part," and only *as* part, of "the never-ending meditation." This study has elected to designate Stevens' never-ending meditation the "question of belief." As such, however, his question, in its broadest sense, enters into a much "larger poem" for a much "larger audience": the theory of life itself. Consequently, "An Ordinary Evening in New Haven" is merely a recent imagining of reality, part of our own "vulgate of experience" since this latest resemblance of the sun, ultimately for Stevens, has no theoretical resemblance—no double or counterpart or dialectical opposite—only an *as* that would appear to constitute the explicit structure of something understood, "As if the crude collops came together as one" (*CP*, 466) but, of course, never *really* can.

We must read all the way to the conclusion of the poem in order to start fully to comprehend reality's absence of solid premise and, more curiously, to discover in Stevens' own finale our true beginning.

> It is not in the premise that reality
> Is a solid. It may be a shade that traverses
> A dust, a force that traverses a shade.
>
> (*CP*, 489)

By Canto XXXI, it should be fairly clear that it has been Stevens' own textual production, in response to the question of belief, that, in words of the *Anti-Oedipus* astonishingly similar to those of the poet here, "calls forth forces that no longer permit themselves to be contained in representation . . . traversing it through and through: 'an immense expanse of shade' extended beneath the level of representation."[16] By demystifying the notion that the reality of belief

---

16. Deleuze and Guattari, *Anti-Oedipus*, 229.

is an articulation of "final form" (*CP,* 488), Stevens reiterates his earlier point in Canto XXVII concerning the asymptotic approximation of the whole question in Segmenta or versions—inversions, reversions, diversions, perversions—and offering his own flickings from finikin to finikin as a case in point:

> These are the edgings and inchings of final form,
> The swarming activities of the formulae
> Of statement, directly and indirectly getting at,
>
> Like an evening evoking the spectrum of violet,
> A philosopher practicing scales on his piano,
> A woman writing a note and tearing it up.
>
> (*CP,* 488)

In place of a final answer to the question, Stevens' textuality ultimately draws a blank, like the photographs of the late president in the canto's third stanza. With no climactic, theological illumination, we are thus left with "dead candles at the window" or perhaps even "fire-foams in the motions of the sea" instead. Like Stevens' ghostly Metaphysician, we take our leave of this searching poem in the dark. Perhaps, however, even darkness is too deliberately enunciative, so that it is the continuous motions of the poet's eventful text that we are ineluctably thrown back on, all those edgings and inchings and practicings and writings and traversings and tearings. For at least there we can be sure that the form of belief will never count for more than the force of its question, and there, too, that the force of the question will never promise less than *another* ordinary evening, in a world without end . . .

BIBLIOGRAPHY

Abrams, Meyer H. *The Mirror and the Lamp: Romantic Theory and the Critical Tradition*. New York, 1953.

——. *Natural Supernaturalism: Tradition and Revolution in Romantic Literature*. New York, 1973.

Adorno, T[heodor] W. *Aesthetic Theory*. Translated by C. Lenhardt. Edited by Gretel Adorno and Rolf Tiedelmann. London, 1982.

——. *Prisms*. Translated by Samuel Weber and Shierry Weber. Cambridge, Mass., 1986.

Allison, David B., ed. *The New Nietzsche: Contemporary Styles of Interpretation*. Cambridge, Mass., 1985.

Althusser, Louis. *Lenin and Philosophy and Other Essays*. Translated by Ben Brewster. New York, 1971.

Althusser, Louis, and Étienne Balibar. *Reading Capital*. Translated by Ben Brewster. London, 1977.

Altieri, Charles. "From Symbolist Thought to Immanence: The Ground of Postmodern American Poetics." *Boundary 2*, I (Spring, 1973), 605–41.

Altizer, Thomas J. J. *The Descent into Hell: A Study of the Radical Reversal of the Christian Consciousness*. New York, 1979.

Ashbery, John. *Three Poems*. New York, 1972.

Auden, W. H. *The Dyer's Hand, and Other Essays*. New York, 1968.

Baird, James. *The Dome and the Rock: Structure in the Poetry of Wallace Stevens*. Baltimore, 1968.

Bakhtin, M. M. *The Dialogic Imagination: Four Essays*. Translated by Michael Holquist and Caryl Emerson. Edited by Michael Holquist. University of Texas Press Slavic Series, I. Austin, 1981.

Barthes, Roland. *A Barthes Reader*. Edited by Susan Sontag. New York, 1982.

——. *Empire of Signs*. Translated by Richard Howard. New York, 1982.

317

———. *Image-Music-Text*. Translated and edited by Stephen Heath. New York, 1977.

———. *A Lover's Discourse: Fragments*. Translated by Richard Howard. New York, 1978.

———. *The Pleasure of the Text*. Translated by Richard Miller. New York, 1975.

———. *Roland Barthes by Roland Barthes*. Translated by Richard Howard. New York, 1977.

Bataille, Georges. *Inner Experience*. Translated by Leslie Anne Boldt. New York, 1988.

———. *Theory of Religion*. Translated by Robert Hurley. New York, 1989.

Bate, Walter Jackson, ed. *Criticism: The Major Texts*. New York, 1952.

Bates, Milton J. "Major Man and Overman: Wallace Stevens' Use of Nietzsche." *Southern Review*, n.s., XV (October, 1979), 811–39.

———. "Stevens' Books at the Huntington: An Annotated Checklist." *Wallace Stevens Journal*, II (Fall, 1978), 45–61.

———. "Stevens' Books at the Huntington: An Annotated Checklist (Concluded)." *Wallace Stevens Journal*, III (Spring, 1979), 15–33.

———. *Wallace Stevens: A Mythology of Self*. Berkeley, 1985.

Baudrillard, Jean. *Selected Writings*. Edited by Mark Poster. Stanford, 1988.

Beehler, Michael. "Stevens' Boundaries." *Wallace Stevens Journal*, VII (Fall, 1983), 99–107.

———. *T. S. Eliot, Wallace Stevens, and the Discourses of Difference*. Baton Rouge, 1987.

Bellah, Robert N. *Beyond Belief: Essays on Religion in a Post-Traditional World*. New York, 1976.

Belsey, Catherine. *Critical Practice*. New York, 1980.

Benamou, Michel. *Wallace Stevens and the Symbolist Imagination*. Princeton, 1972.

Bennet, Tony. "Putting Policy into Cultural Studies." In *Cultural Studies*, edited by Lawrence Grossberg, Cary Nelson, and Paula A. Treichler. New York, 1992.

Berger, Charles. *Forms of Farewell: The Late Poetry of Wallace Stevens*. Madison, 1985.

Bergman, David. *Gaiety Transfigured: Gay Self-Representation in American Literature*. Madison, 1991.

Bernasconi, Robert. *The Question of Language in Heidegger's History of Being*. Atlantic Highlands, N.J., 1985.

Blanchot, Maurice. *The Writing of the Disaster*. Translated by Ann Smock. Lincoln, 1986.

Blasing, Mutlu Konuk. *American Poetry: The Rhetoric of Its Forms*. New Haven, 1987.

Blau, Herbert. *The Eye of Prey: Subversions of the Postmodern*. Bloomington, 1987.

Bloom, Harold. *Wallace Stevens: The Poems of Our Climate*. Ithaca, 1976.

———, ed. *Romanticism and Consciousness: Essays in Criticism*. New York, 1970.

Booker, M. Keith. "A War Between Mind and Sky: Bakhtin and Poetry, Stevens and Politics." *Wallace Stevens Journal*, XIV (Spring, 1990), 71–85.

Bornstein, George. *Transformations of Romanticism in Yeats, Eliot, and Stevens*. Chicago, 1976.

Borroff, Marie, ed. *Wallace Stevens: A Collection of Critical Essays*. Englewood Cliffs, N.J., 1963.

Bové, Paul A. *Destructive Poetics: Heidegger and Modern Poetry*. New York, 1980.

Brazeau, Peter. *Parts of a World: Wallace Stevens Remembered, an Oral Biography*. New York, 1983.

——. "Wallace Stevens at the University of Massachusetts: Check List of an Archive." *Wallace Stevens Journal*, II (Spring, 1978), 50–54.

Brecht, Bertolt. *Brecht on Theatre: The Development of an Aesthetic*. Translated by John Willett. London, 1986.

Brogan, Jacqueline Vaught. "'Sister of the Minotaur': Sexism and Stevens." *Wallace Stevens Journal*, XII (Fall, 1988), 102–18.

Bruns, Gerald L. *Heidegger's Estrangements: Language, Truth, and Poetry in the Later Writings*. New Haven, 1989.

——. *Modern Poetry and the Idea of Language*. New Haven, 1974.

Bruss, Elizabeth W. *Beautiful Theories: The Spectacle of Discourse in Contemporary Criticism*. Baltimore, 1982.

Burke, Kenneth. *A Grammar of Motives*. Berkeley, 1969.

Buttel, Robert. *Wallace Stevens: The Making of "Harmonium."* Princeton, 1967.

Byers, Thomas B. *What I Cannot Say: Self, Word, and World in Whitman, Stevens, and Merwin*. Urbana, 1989.

Cain, William. *The Crisis in Criticism: Theory, Literature, and Reform in English Studies*. Baltimore, 1984.

Caputo, John D. *The Mystical Element in Heidegger's Thought*. New York, 1986.

——. *Radical Hermeneutics: Repetition, Deconstruction, and the Hermeneutic Project*. Bloomington, 1987.

——. "The Thought of Being and the Conversation of Mankind: The Case of Heidegger and Rorty." *Review of Metaphysics*, XXXVI (March, 1983), 661–85.

——. "Three Transgressions: Nietzsche, Heidegger, and Derrida." *Research in Phenomenology*, XV (1985), 61–78.

Carafiol, Peter. *The American Ideal: Literary History as a Worldly Activity*. New York, 1991.

Carroll, David. *Paraesthetics: Foucault, Lyotard, Derrida*. New York, 1987.

Carroll, Joseph. *Wallace Stevens' Supreme Fiction: A New Romanticism*. Baton Rouge, 1987.

Carton, Evan. *The Rhetoric of American Romance: Dialectic and Identity in Emerson, Dickinson, Poe, and Hawthorne*. Baltimore, 1985.

Cascardi, Anthony J., ed. *Literature and the Question of Philosophy*. Baltimore, 1987.

Cavell, Stanley. *Must We Mean What We Say? A Book of Essays*. New York, 1969.

Chambers, Iain. *Border Dialogues: Journeys in Postmodernity*. New York, 1990.

Connor, Steven. *Postmodernist Culture: An Introduction to Theories of the Contemporary*. Oxford, 1989.

Cook, Eleanor. *Poetry, Word-Play, and Word-War in Wallace Stevens.* Princeton, 1988.

Crane, Hart. *The Complete Poems and Selected Letters and Prose of Hart Crane.* Edited by Brom Weber. Garden City, N.Y., 1966.

Crossan, John Dominic. *Raid on the Articulate: Comic Eschatology in Jesus and Borges.* New York, 1976.

———. *In Parables: The Challenge of the Historical Jesus.* San Francisco, 1973.

cummings, e. e. *Complete Poems: 1913–1962.* New York, 1972.

Danto, Arthur C. *Nietzsche as Philosopher.* New York, 1965.

Dasenbrock, Reed Way, ed. *Redrawing the Lines: Analytic Philosophy, Deconstruction, and Literary Theory.* Minneapolis, 1989.

Davidson, Michael. "Archaeologist of Morning: Charles Olson, Edward Dorn and Historical Method." *ELH,* XLVII (1980), 158–79.

———. "Ekphrasis and the Postmodern Painter Poem." *Journal of Aesthetics and Art Criticism,* XLII (Fall, 1983), 69–79.

de Certeau, Michel. *Heterologies: Discourse on the Other.* Translated by Brian Massumi. Theory and History of Literature, XVII. Minneapolis, 1986.

de Lauretis, Teresa. "Eccentric Subjects: Feminist Theory and Historical Consciousness." *Feminist Studies,* XVI, no. 1 (1990), 115–50.

Deleuze, Gilles, and Félix Guattari. *Anti-Oedipus: Capitalism and Schizophrenia.* Translated by Robert Hurley, Mark Seem, and Helen R. Lane. Minneapolis, 1983.

———. *On the Line.* Translated by John Johnston. New York. 1983.

Deleuze, Gilles, and Claire Parnet. *Dialogues.* Translated by Hugh Tomlinson and Barbara Habberjam. New York, 1987.

de Man, Paul. *Allegories of Reading: Figural Language in Rousseau, Nietzsche, Rilke, and Proust.* New York, 1979.

———. *Blindness and Insight: Essays in the Rhetoric of Contemporary Criticism.* Theory and History of Literature, VII. Minneapolis, 1971.

Derrida, Jacques. *The Archeology of the Frivolous: Reading Condillac.* Translated by John P. Leavey, Jr. Lincoln, 1973.

———. *Dissemination.* Translated by Barbara Johnson. Chicago, 1981.

———. "'Fors.'" Translated by Barbara Johnson. *Georgia Review,* XXXI (Spring, 1977), 64–116.

———. "How to Avoid Speaking: Denials." In *Languages of the Unsayable: The Play of Negativity in Literature and Literary Theory,* edited by Sanford Budick and Wolfgang Iser. New York, 1989.

———. "An Interview with Derrida (from *Le Nouvel Observateur*)." Translated by David Allison. In *Derrida and Différance,* edited by Robert Bernasconi and David Wood. Evanston, 1988.

———. "Limited Inc. abc." *Glyph,* II (1977), 162–254.

———. *Margins of Philosophy.* Translated by Alan Bass. Chicago, 1982.

————. *Memoires for Paul de Man*. Translated by Cecile Lindsay *et al*. New York, 1989.

————. "My Chances/Mes Chances: A Rendezvous with Some Epicurean Stereophonies." In *Taking Chances: Derrida, Psychoanalysis, and Literature*, edited by William Kerrigan and Joseph H. Smith. Baltimore, 1984.

————. "Of an Apocalyptic Tone Recently Adopted in Philosophy." *Semeia*, XXIII (1982), 61–97.

————. *Of Grammatology*. Translated by Gayatri Chakravorty Spivak. Baltimore, 1974.

————. *Of Spirit*. Translated by Geoffrey Bennington and Rachel Bowlby. Chicago, 1989.

————. *Positions*. Translated by Alan Bass. Chicago, 1981.

————. *The Post Card: From Socrates to Freud and Beyond*. Translated by Alan Bass. Chicago, 1987.

————. "The 'Retrait' of Metaphor." *Enclitic*, II (1978), 5–33.

————. "Shibboleth." In *Midrash and Literature*, edited by Geoffrey H. Hartman and Sanford Budick. New Haven, 1986.

————. *Signéponge / Signsponge*. Translated by Richard Rand, New York, 1984.

————. *Speech and Phenomena, and Other Essays on Husserl's Theory of Signs*. Translated by David B. Allison. Northwestern University Studies in Phenomenology and Existential Philosophy. Evanston, 1973.

————. *Spurs / Eperons: Nietzsche's Styles*. Translated by Barbara Harlow. Chicago, 1979.

————. *The Truth in Painting*. Translated by Geoff Bennington and Ian McLeod. Chicago, 1987.

————. *Writing and Difference*. Translated by Alan Bass. Chicago, 1978.

Descombes, Vincent. *Modern French Philosophy*. Translated by L. Scott-Fox and J. M. Harding. New York, 1980.

Dickinson, Emily. *The Complete Poems of Emily Dickinson*. Edited by Thomas H. Johnson. Boston, 1960.

Doane, Mary Ann. "Information, Crisis, Catastrophe." In *Logics of Television: Essays in Cultural Criticism*, edited by Patricia Mellencamp. Bloomington, 1990.

Doggett, Frank. *Stevens' Poetry of Thought*. Baltimore, 1966.

————. *Wallace Stevens: The Making of the Poem*. Baltimore, 1980.

Doggett, Frank, and Robert Buttel, eds. *Wallace Stevens: A Celebration*. Princeton, 1980.

Donato, Eugenio. "The Ruins of Memory: Archeological Fragments and Textual Artifacts." *MLN*, XCIII (1978), 575–96.

Edelstein, J. M. *Wallace Stevens: A Descriptive Bibliography*. Pittsburgh, 1973.

Eliot, T. S. *The Complete Poems and Plays: 1909–1950*. New York, 1971.

————. *Four Quartets*. 1944; rpr. Great Britain, 1972.

————. *Selected Prose of T. S. Eliot*. Edited by Frank Kermode. New York, 1975.

Enck, John J. *Wallace Stevens: Images and Judgments*. Carbondale, Ill., 1964.

Evett, David. "'Paradice's Only Map': The 'Topos' of the 'Locus Amoenus' and the Structure of Marvell's 'Upon Appleton House,'" *PMLA*, LXXXV (May, 1970), 504–13.

Fish, Stanley. *Doing What Comes Naturally: Change, Rhetoric, and the Practice of Theory in Literary and Legal Studies*. Durham, 1989.

———. *Is There a Text in This Class? The Authority of Interpretative Communities*. Cambridge, Mass., 1980.

Foucault, Michel. *The Archaeology of Knowledge*. Translated by A. M. Sheridan Smith. London, 1972.

———. *Discipline and Punish: The Birth of the Prison*. Translated by Alan Sheridan. New York, 1977.

———. *The History of Sexuality, Volume I: An Introduction*. Translated by Robert Hurely. New York, 1980.

———. *Language, Counter-Memory, Practice: Selected Essays and Interviews*. Translated by Sherry Simon and Donald F. Bouchard. Edited by Donald F. Bouchard. Ithaca, 1977.

———. *Madness and Civilization: A History of Insanity in the Age of Reason*. Translated by Richard Howard. New York, 1973.

———. *The Order of Things: An Archaeology of the Human Sciences*. New York, 1970.

———. *Politics, Philosophy, Culture: Interviews and Other Writings, 1977–1984*. New York, 1988.

———. *Power / Knowledge: Selected Writings and Other Interviews 1972–1977*. Translated by Colin Gordon *et al.* Edited by Colin Gordon. New York, 1980.

Freud, Sigmund. *The Standard Edition of the Complete Psychological Works of Sigmund Freud*. Translated by James Strachey. 24 vols. London, 1953–74.

Frye, Northrop. *Anatomy of Criticism: Four Essays*. New York, 1957.

———. *Fables of Identity: Studies in Poetic Mythology*. New York, 1963.

———. *Fearful Symmetry: A Study of William Blake*. Princeton, 1947.

———. *The Great Code: The Bible as Narrative*. Toronto, 1982.

———. *The Secular Scripture: A Study of the Structure of Romance*. Cambridge, Mass., 1976.

———. *Spiritus Mundi: Essays on Literature, Myth, and Society*. Bloomington, 1976.

———. *The Stubborn Structure: Essays on Criticism and Society*. Ithaca, 1970.

Fuchs, Daniel. *The Comic Spirit of Wallace Stevens*. Durham, 1963.

Gallop, Jane. *The Daughter's Seduction: Feminism and Psychoanalysis*. Ithaca, 1982.

Gasché, Rodolphe. "Joining the Text: From Heidegger to Derrida." In *The Yale Critics: Deconstruction in America*, edited by Jonathan Arac, Wlad Godzich, and Wallace Martin. Theory and History of Literature, VI. Minneapolis, 1983.

———. "'Like the Rose—Without Why': Postmodern Transcendentalism and Practical Philosophy." *Diacritics*, XIX (Fall/Winter, 1989), 101–13.

————. *The Tain of the Mirror: Derrida and the Philosophy of Reflection.* Cambridge, Mass. 1986.

Gelpi, Albert, ed. *Wallace Stevens: The Poetics of Modernism.* New York, 1985.

Gilbert, Sandra M., and Susan Gubar. "The Mirror and the Vamp: Reflections on Feminist Criticism." In *The Future of Literary Theory,* edited by Ralph Cohen. New York, 1989.

————. *Sexchanges.* New Haven, 1989. Vol. II of Gilbert and Gubar, *No Man's Land: The Place of the Woman Writer in the Twentieth Century,* 3 vols. projected.

————. *The War of the Words.* New Haven, 1988. Vol. I of Gilbert and Gubar, *No Man's Land: The Place of the Woman Writer in the Twentieth Century.* 3 vols. projected.

Giroux, Henry A. *Theory and Resistance in Education: A Pedagogy for the Opposition.* South Hadley, Mass., 1983.

Gombrich, E. H. *Art and Illusion: A Study in the Psychology of Pictorial Representation.* Bollingen Series, XXXV. Princeton, 1961.

Gunn, Giles. *The Interpretation of Otherness: Literature, Religion, and the American Imagination.* New York, 1979.

————. *Thinking Across the American Grain: Ideology, Intellect, and the New Pragmatism.* Chicago, 1992.

Hall, Stuart. "Cultural Studies and Its Theoretical Legacies." In *Cultural Studies,* edited by Lawrence Grossberg, Cary Nelson, and Paula A. Treichler. New York, 1992.

Halliday, Mark. *Stevens and the Interpersonal.* Princeton, 1991.

Handelman, Susan A. *The Slayers of Moses: The Emergence of Rabbinic Interpretation in Modern Literary Theory.* Albany, 1982.

Haraway, Donna. "A Manifesto for Cyborgs: Science, Technology, and Socialist Feminism in the 1980s." In *Coming to Terms: Feminism, Theory, Politics,* edited by Elizabeth Weed. New York, 1989.

Harootunian, H. D. "Foucault, Genealogy, History: The Pursuit of Otherness." In *After Foucault: Humanistic Knowledge, Postmodern Challenges,* edited by Jonathan Arac. New Brunswick, N.J., 1991.

Hart, Kevin. *The Trespass of the Sign: Deconstruction, Theology and Philosophy.* New York, 1989.

Hartley, George. *Textual Politics and the Language Poets.* Bloomington, 1989.

Hartman, Geoffrey H. *Saving the Text: Literature/Derrida/Philosophy.* Baltimore, 1981.

Heidegger, Martin. *Being and Time.* Translated by John Macquarrie and Edward Robinson. New York, 1962.

————. *Discourse on Thinking.* Translated by John M. Anderson and E. Hans Freund. New York, 1966.

————. *Early Greek Thinking.* Translated by David Farrell Krell and Frank A. Capuzzi. San Francisco, 1975.

————. *Existence and Being*. Chicago, 1949.

————. *Identity and Difference*. Translated by Joan Stambaugh. New York, 1969.

————. *An Introduction to Metaphysics*. Translated by Ralph Manheim. Garden City, N.Y., 1959.

————. *Martin Heidegger: Basic Writings, from "Being and Time" (1927) to "The Task of Thinking" (1964)*. Edited by David Farrell Krell. New York, 1977.

————. *On Time and Being*. Translated by Joan Stambaugh. New York, 1972.

————. *On the Way to Language*. Translated by Peter D. Hertz. New York, 1971.

————. *Poetry, Language, Thought*. Translated by Albert Hofstadter. New York, 1975.

————. *The Question Concerning Technology and Other Essays*. Translated by William Lovitt. New York, 1977.

————. *What Is Called Thinking?* Translated by J. Glenn Gray. New York, 1968.

————. "What Is Metaphysics?" In *Basic Writings,* edited by David Farrell Krell. New York, 1977.

————. *The Will to Power as Art*. Translated by David Farrell Krell. San Francisco, 1979. Vol. I of Heidegger, *Nietzsche*. 4 vols.

Herbert, George. *The English Poems of George Herbert*. Edited by C. A. Patrides. London, 1974.

Hines, Thomas J. *The Later Poetry of Wallace Stevens: Phenomenological Parallels with Husserl and Heidegger*. Lewisburg, Pa., 1976.

Hoy, David Couzens. "Foucault: Modern or Postmodern." In *After Foucault: Humanistic Knowledge, Postmodern Challenges,* edited by Jonathan Arac. New Brunswick, N.J., 1991.

Hutcheon, Linda. *A Poetics of Postmodernism: History, Theory, Fiction*. New York, 1988.

————. "The Postmodern Problematizing of History." *English Studies in Canada,* XIV (December, 1988), 365–82.

Irigaray, Luce. "Sexual Difference." In *French Feminist Thought: A Reader,* edited by Toril Moi. New York, 1989.

————. *Speculum of the Other Woman*. Translated by Gillian C. Gill. Ithaca, 1985.

Irwin, John T. *American Hieroglyphics: The Symbol of the Egyptian Hieroglyphics in the American Renaissance*. New Haven, 1980.

Jameson, Fredric. *The Political Unconscious: Narrative as a Socially Symbolic Act*. Ithaca, 1981.

Jardine, Alice. *Gynesis: Configurations of Woman and Modernity*. Ithaca, 1985.

Jarraway, David. "*My Life* Through the 80's: The Exemplary L-A-N-G-U-A-G-E of Lyn Hejinian." *Contemporary Literature,* XXXIII (Summer, 1992).

Joyce, James. *A Portrait of the Artist as a Young Man*. Harmondsworth, Eng., 1966.

Juhasz, Suzanne. *Metaphor and the Poetry of Williams, Pound, and Stevens*. Lewisburg, Pa., 1974.

Kaufmann, Walter. *Nietzsche: Philosopher, Psychologist, Antichrist*. 4th ed. Princeton, 1950.

Kent, Thomas. "Beyond System: The Rhetoric of Paralogy." *College English,* LI (September, 1989), 492–507.

Kermode, Frank. "The Plain Sense of Things." In *Midrash and Literature,* edited by Geoffrey H. Hartman and Sanford Budick. New Haven, 1986.

———. *The Sense of an Ending: Studies in the Theory of Fiction.* Oxford, 1968.

Kessler, Edward. *Images of Wallace Stevens.* New York, 1972.

Krausz, Michael, ed. *Relativism: Interpretation and Confrontation.* Notre Dame, 1989.

Krieger, Murray. *The New Apologists for Poetry.* Minneapolis, 1956.

Kristeva, Julia. *Desire in Language: A Semiotic Approach to Literature and Art.* Translated by Leon S. Roudiez, Thomas Gora, and Alice Jardine. Edited by Leon S. Roudiez. New York, 1980.

———. *The Kristeva Reader.* Edited by Toril Moi. New York, 1986.

———. *Powers of Horror: An Essay on Abjection.* Translated by Leon S. Roudiez. New York, 1982.

———. *Revolution in Poetic Language.* Translated by Margaret Waller. New York, 1984.

Kronick, Joseph G. *American Poetics of History: From Emerson to the Moderns.* Baton Rouge, 1984.

———. "Dr. Heidegger's Experiment." *Boundary 2,* XVII (Fall, 1990), 116–53.

Lacan, Jacques. *Écrits: A Selection.* Translated by Alan Sheridan. New York, 1977.

———. *Feminine Sexuality: Jacques Lacan and the École Freudienne.* Translated by J. Rose. Edited by J. Mitchell and J. Rose. New York, 1982.

Laclau, Ernesto. "Politics and the Limits of Modernity." In *Universal Abandon? The Politics of Postmodernism,* edited by Andrew Ross. Minneapolis, 1988.

Laclau, Ernesto, and Chantal Mouffe. *Hegemony and Socialist Strategy: Towards a Radical Democratic Politics.* New York, 1985.

La Guardia, David M. *Advance on Chaos: The Sanctifying Imagination of Wallace Stevens.* Hanover, N.H. 1983.

Langer, Susanne K. *Philosophy in a New Key: A Study in the Symbolism of Reason, Rite, and Art.* Cambridge, Mass., 1957.

Latour, Bruno. *Science in Action: How to Follow Scientists and Engineers Through Society.* Cambridge, Mass., 1987.

Leggett, B. J. "Apollonian and Dionysian in 'Peter Quince at the Clavier.'" *Wallace Stevens Journal,* XIV (Spring, 1990), 39–61.

———. *Early Stevens: The Nietzschean Intertext.* Durham, 1992.

———. *Wallace Stevens and Poetic Theory: Concerning the Supreme Fiction.* Chapel Hill, 1987.

Lensing, George S. *Wallace Stevens: A Poet's Growth.* Baton Rouge, 1986.

Lentricchia, Frank. *After the New Criticism.* Chicago, 1980.

———. *Ariel and the Police: Michel Foucault, William James, Wallace Stevens.* Madison, 1988.

————. *The Gaiety of Language: An Essay on the Radical Poetics of W. B. Yeats and Wallace Stevens.* Los Angeles, 1968.

Leonard, J. S., and C. E. Wharton. *The Fluent Mundo: Wallace Stevens and the Structure of Reality.* Athens, Ga., 1988.

Levinas, Emmanuel. *Ethics and Infinity: Conversations with Phillippe Nemo.* Translated by Richard A. Cohen. Pittsburgh, 1985.

————. "The Trace of the Other." In *Deconstruction in Context: Literature and Philosophy,* edited by Mark C. Taylor. Chicago, 1986.

Lindberg, Kathryne V. *Reading Pound Reading: Modernism After Nietzsche.* New York, 1987.

Litz, A. Walton. *Introspective Voyager: The Poetic Development of Wallace Stevens.* New York, 1972.

Longenbach, James. *Wallace Stevens: The Plain Sense of Things.* New York, 1991.

Lyotard, Jean-François. *The Postmodern Condition: A Report on Knowledge.* Translated by Geoff Bennington and Brian Massumi. Theory and History of Literature, X. Minneapolis, 1984.

Lyotard, Jean-François, and Jean-Loup Thébaud. *Just Gaming.* Translated by Wlad Godzich. Theory and History of Literature, XX. Minneapolis, 1985.

Macherey, Pierre. *A Theory of Literary Production.* Translated by Geoffrey Wall. London, 1978.

Martin, Biddy, and Chandra Talpade Mohanty. "Feminist Politics: What's Home Got to Do with It?" In *Feminist Studies/Critical Studies,* edited by Teresa de Lauretis. Bloomington, 1986.

Marx, Karl, and Friedrich Engels. *Marx and Engels: Basic Writings on Politics and Philosophy.* Edited by Lewis S. Feuer. New York, 1959.

McCaffery, Steve. *North of Intention: Critical Writings, 1973–1986.* Toronto, 1986.

Megill, Allan. *Prophets of Extremity: Nietzsche, Heidegger, Foucault, Derrida.* Berkeley, 1985.

Melville, Herman. *Pierre; Or, The Ambiguities.* Edited by Harrison Hayford. New York, 1984.

Merrill, Robert, ed. *Ethics/Aesthetics: Postmodern Positions.* Washington, D.C., 1988.

Michaels, Walter Benn. *The Gold Standard and the Logic of Naturalism.* Berkeley, 1987.

Miller, J. Hillis. *The Ethics of Reading: Kant, de Man, Eliot, Trollope, James, and Benjamin.* New York, 1987.

————. *The Linguistic Moment: From Wordsworth to Stevens.* Princeton, 1985.

————. *Poets of Reality: Six Twentieth-Century Writers.* New York, 1965.

————. "Stevens' Rock and Criticism as Cure." *Georgia Review,* XXX (Spring, 1976), 5–31.

————. *Versions of Pygmalion.* Cambridge, Mass., 1990.

Minh-ha, Trinh T. "Documentary Is/Not a Name." *October,* LII (Spring, 1990), 77–97.

Montrose, Louis. "'Eliza, Queen of Shepheardes,' and the Pastoral of Power." *ELR,* X (1980), 153–82.

Morris, Adalaide Kirby. *Wallace Stevens: Imagination and Faith.* Princeton, 1974.

Morse, Samuel French. *Wallace Stevens: Poetry as Life.* New York, 1970.

Muller, John P., and William J. Richardson, eds. *The Purloined Poe: Lacan, Derrida and Psychoanalytic Reading,* Baltimore, 1988.

Nehamas, Alexander. *Nietzsche: Life as Literature.* Cambridge, Mass., 1985.

Nelson, Cary. *Repression and Recovery: Modern American Poetry and the Politics of Cultural Memory, 1910–1945.* Madison, 1989.

Newcomb, John Timberman. *Wallace Stevens and Literary Canons.* Jackson, 1992.

Norris, Christopher. *The Contest of Faculties: Philosophy and Theory After Deconstruction.* London, 1985.

———. *The Deconstructive Turn: Essays in the Rhetoric of Philosophy.* London, 1983.

O'Hara, Daniel, ed. *Why Nietzsche Now?* Bloomington, 1985.

Owens, Craig. "The Discourse of Others: Feminists and Postmodernism." In *The Anti-Aesthetic: Essays on Postmodern Culture,* edited by Hal Foster. Port Townsend, Wash., 1983.

Pack, Robert. *Wallace Stevens: An Approach to His Poetry and Thought.* New York, 1958.

Parker, Patricia A. "The Motive for Metaphor: Stevens and Derrida." *Wallace Stevens Journal,* VII (Fall, 1983), 76–88.

Patke, Rajeev S. *The Long Poems of Wallace Stevens: An Interpretative Study.* Cambridge, Eng., 1985.

Pearce, Roy Harvey. *The Continuity of American Poetry.* Princeton, 1961.

Pearce, Roy Harvey, and J. Hillis Miller, eds. *The Act of the Mind: Essays on the Poetry of Wallace Stevens.* Baltimore, 1965.

Perkins, David, ed. *English Romantic Writers.* New York, 1967.

Perlis, Alan. *Wallace Stevens: A World of Transforming Shapes.* Lewisburg, Pa., 1976.

Peterson, Margaret. *Wallace Stevens and the Idealist Tradition.* Ann Arbor, 1983.

Pound, Ezra. *Literary Essays of Ezra Pound.* Edited by T. S. Eliot. New York, 1968.

———. *The Spirit of Romance.* London, 1952.

Quinones, Ricardo J. *Mapping Literary Modernism: Time and Development.* Princeton, 1985.

Rapaport, Herman. *Heidegger and Derrida: Reflections on Time and Language.* Lincoln, 1989.

Raschke, Carl A. *The Alchemy of the Word: Language and the End of Theology.* Missoula, Mont., 1979.

Regueiro, Helen. *The Limits of Imagination: Wordsworth, Yeats, and Stevens.* Ithaca, 1976.

Rehder, Robert. *The Poetry of Wallace Stevens.* London, 1988.

Reising, Russell. *The Unusable Past: Theory and the Study of American Literature.* New York, 1986.

Richardson, Joan. *Wallace Stevens: The Later Years, 1923–1955*. New York, 1988.

Richardson, William. *Heidegger: From Phenomenology to Thought*. The Hague, 1963.

Ricoeur, Paul. *Freud and Philosophy: An Essay on Interpretation*. Translated by Denis Savage. New Haven, 1970.

————. *The Rule of Metaphor: Multi-Disciplinary Studies of the Creation of Meaning in Language*. Translated by Robert Czerny, Kathleen McLaughlin, and John Costello. Toronto, 1977.

Riddel, Joseph N. *The Clairvoyant Eye: The Poetry and Poetics of Wallace Stevens*. Baton Rouge, 1965.

————. "The Climate of Our Poems." *Wallace Stevens Journal*, VII (Fall, 1983), 59–75.

————. "Interpreting Stevens: An Essay on Poetry and Thinking." *Boundary 2*, I (Fall, 1972), 85–97.

————. *The Inverted Bell: Modernism and the Counter-Poetics of William Carlos Williams*. Baton Rouge, 1974.

Rorty, Richard. *Consequences of Pragmatism (Essays: 1972–1980)*. Minneapolis, 1982.

————. *Contingency, Irony, and Solidarity*. New York, 1989.

————. "Deconstruction and Circumvention." *Critical Inquiry*, XI (September, 1984), 1–23.

————. *Philosophy and the Mirror of Nature*. Princeton, 1979.

Said, Edward. *Beginnings: Intention and Method*. New York, 1985.

————. *Orientalism*. New York, 1979.

Scharlemann, Robert P. "The Being of God When God Is Not Being God: Deconstructing the History of Theism." In *Deconstruction and Theology*, edited by Thomas J. J. Altizer *et al*. New York, 1982.

Schaum, Melita. *Wallace Stevens and the Critical Schools*. Tuscaloosa, 1988.

Schneidau, Herbert N. "The Word Against the Word: Derrida on Textuality." *Semeia*, XXIII (1982), 5–28.

Scholes, Robert. "Deconstruction and Communication." *Critical Inquiry*, XIV (Winter, 1988), 279–95.

————. *Protocols of Reading*. New Haven, 1989.

Schor, Naomi. *Reading in Detail: Aesthetics and the Feminine*. New York, 1987.

Scott, Nathan A., Jr. *The Poetics of Belief: Studies in Coleridge, Arnold, Pater, Santayana, Stevens, and Heidegger*. Chapel Hill, 1985.

Sexson, Michael. *The Quest of Self in the Collected Poems of Wallace Stevens*. Studies in Art and Religious Interpretation, I. Lewiston, N.Y., 1981.

Sheehan, Thomas, ed. *Heidegger: The Man and the Thinker*. Chicago, 1981.

Shelley, Percy Bysshe. *Shelley: Poetical Works*. Edited by Thomas Hutchinson. New York, 1967.

Silverman, Hugh J., and Don Ihde, eds. *Hermeneutics and Deconstruction*. New York, 1985.

Smith, Barbara Herrnstein. *Contingencies of Value: Alternative Perspectives for Critical Theory*. Cambridge, Mass., 1988.

Smith, Paul. *Discerning the Subject*. Minneapolis, 1988.

Spanos, William V. "Heidegger, Kierkegaard, and the Hermeneutic Circle: Towards a Postmodern Theory of Interpretation as Dis-closure." *Boundary 2*, IV (Winter, 1976), 457–62.

———. *Repetitions: The Postmodern Occasion in Literature and Culture*. Baton Rouge, 1987.

———, ed. *Martin Heidegger and the Question of Literature: Toward a Postmodern Literary Hermeneutics*. Bloomington, 1979.

Taylor, Mark C. *Altarity*. Chicago, 1987.

———. *Deconstructing Theology*. New York, n.d.

———. *Erring: A Postmodern A/Theology*. Chicago, 1984.

———. "Foiling Reflection." *Diacritics*, XVIII (Spring, 1988), 54–65.

Thiher, Allen. *Words in Reflection: Modern Language Theory and Postmodern Fiction*. Chicago, 1984.

Thomas, Dylan. *The Poems of Dylan Thomas*. Edited by Daniel Jones. New York, 1971.

Torgovnick, Marianna. *Gone Primitive: Savage Intellects, Modern Lives*. Chicago, 1990.

Tracy, David. *Plurality and Ambiguity: Hermeneutics, Religion, Hope*. San Francisco, 1987.

Tucker, Robert C., ed. *The Marx-Engels Reader*. 2nd ed. New York, 1978.

Vendler, Helen Hennessy. *On Extended Wings: Wallace Stevens' Longer Poems*. Cambridge, Mass., 1969.

Walsh, Thomas F. *Concordance to the Poetry of Wallace Stevens*. University Park, Pa., 1963.

Weber, Sam. *Institution and Interpretation*. Theory and History of Literature, XXXI. Minneapolis, 1987.

West, Cornel. *The American Evasion of Philosophy: A Genealogy of Pragmatism*. Madison, 1989.

Weston, Susan B. *Wallace Stevens: An Introduction to the Poetry*. New York, 1977.

White, Hayden. *Tropics of Discourse: Essays in Cultural Criticism*. Baltimore, 1978.

Whitman, Walt. *Complete Poetry and Collected Prose*. Edited by Justin Kaplan. New York, 1982.

Wilde, Alan. *Horizons of Assent: Modernism, Postmodernism, and the Ironic Imagination*. Philadelphia, 1987.

Williams, William Carlos. *The Embodiment of Knowledge*. Edited by Ron Loewinsohn. New York, 1974.

Willis, Sharon. "Feminism's Interrupted Genealogies." *Diacritics*, XVIII (Spring, 1988), 29–41.

Winquist, Charles. "Body, Text, Imagination." In *Deconstruction and Theology*, edited by Thomas J. J. Altizer *et al.* New York, 1982.

———. *Epiphanies of Darkness: Deconstruction in Theology*. Philadelphia, 1986.

Wittgenstein, Ludwig. *Tractatus Logico-Philosophicus*. Translated by C. K. Ogden. 1922; rpr. Great Britain, 1981.

Woodman, Leonora. *Stanza My Stone: Wallace Stevens and the Hermetic Tradition.* West Lafayette, Ind., 1983.

Yingling, Thomas. "AIDS in America: Postmodern Governance, Identity, and Experience." In *inside/out: Lesbian Theories, Gay Theories,* edited by Diana Fuss. New York, 1991.

INDEX